To Heughie

Ji: Shirley, Nancy
        Helen
        Wesby Jim
            Regina

May 31, 2008

# Life
*Overflowing*

## 6 PILLARS FOR
## ABUNDANT LIVING

# T. D. JAKES

# Life
## *Overflowing*

### 6 PILLARS FOR
### ABUNDANT LIVING

BETHANYHOUSE
Minneapolis, Minnesota

*Life Overflowing*
*6 Pillars for Abundant Living*
Copyright © 2000, 2008
T.D. Jakes
Originally published in six volumes under the titles *Loved by God, Experiencing Jesus, Intimacy With God, Life Overflowing, Celebrating Marriage, Overcoming the Enemy*

Cover design by Josh Madison

Published by Bethany House Publishers
11400 Hampshire Avenue South
Bloomington, Minnesota 55438

Bethany House Publishers is a division of
Baker Publishing Group, Grand Rapids, Michigan.

Printed in the United States of America

ISBN 978-0-7642-0494-4

# CONTENTS

# PART ONE

*Loved by God*

# Introduction

---

The Ephesians understood wealth.

Ephesus was a city with marble streets, mosaic sidewalks, a massive temple that was considered one of the wonders of the Greek world, a busy port, a popular athletic arena, one of the finest libraries in the first century, and villas filled with artwork, tapestries, silks, and exotic birds and animals. Even today, the coliseum at Ephesus is considered one of the finest performing arts centers in the world.

Caravans from the east routinely ended their journeys at Ephesus, and ships from ports throughout the Mediterranean brought the riches of Egypt, Rome, Greece, Spain, and northern Africa.

The apostle Paul came to town and blew their minds by presenting a type of wealth they had never encountered before. Paul presented to them the God of all riches, the God who gave His only begotten Son, His most precious possession.

We discover how precious Jesus was to God when we examine the Greek word translated "only begotten." Jesus was of exceeding value to God because He was extremely rare. God's willingness to share and sacrifice for us this wholly unique treasure, His only begotten Son, was the supreme expression of His love for us.

The wealth the apostle Paul brought to Ephesus is Jesus Christ. In Him is everything a human being could ever dream of, hope for, or desire—and more.

# 1

# THE GOD OF
# ALL RICHES

There has never been a time in history when most people did not believe that possessing great wealth was the key to happiness. Yet time and again we have seen millionaires and billionaires live miserable lives and even end their lives. We have watched their children wander through life aimlessly, self-destructive. Some have even used their wealth to destroy others. Why? Because their wealth consisted of temporal things, not eternal.

Material wealth is not evil in and of itself. Ten dollars in the hands of a criminal or a pastor is still ten dollars! The Bible says it is the *love* of money that is the root of all evil. (See 1 Timothy 6:10.)

Mankind must connect to the God of all riches to truly enjoy—and to avoid being controlled and owned by—material wealth. Thank God, when that divine connection takes place and we are gloriously born again, the Holy Spirit comes to dwell in our hearts and we begin the adventure of the truly privileged: discovering our riches in Christ.

## KNOWING OUR SOURCE

To be convinced that we are about to receive great riches, we must be confident that the person *giving* the riches is capable of doing so. A check is only as good as the check-writer's ability to pay.

As children of God, we must know that our heavenly Father possesses everything we need in life, a promise He makes to us throughout the Bible. Paul opens his letter to the Ephesians by declaring the grace, resources, and power of God, the author of all wealth. It is important to know that the verses at the beginning of Ephesians chapter 1 are speaking primarily of God the Father and His redemptive plan and work. From "Blessed be the God and Father" in verse 3, through verse 14, "unto the praise of his glory," the Holy Spirit is revealing to us the majesty, riches, and power of Almighty God, the Father of our Lord Jesus Christ. Although the revelation of the Father God impacts our lives significantly for all time, this particular passage is not about us. It is about *Him*—His glory and His grace.

**Paul, an apostle of Jesus Christ by the will of God, to the saints which are at Ephesus, and to the faithful in Christ Jesus: Grace be to you, and peace, from God our Father, and from the Lord Jesus Christ. Blessed be the God and Father of our Lord Jesus Christ, who hath blessed us with all spiritual blessings in heavenly places in Christ.**

**—Ephesians 1:1–3**

Paul considers the foundation for all of our blessings in Christ to be this fact: *God* is blessed. He is not frail, impoverished, or impotent. He has every resource at His disposal, both things seen and unseen. Nothing lies beyond His ownership. God only temporarily allows man to use these resources.

God is all-powerful. He is fully capable and able in all situations, at all times, and regardless of circumstances to exert control over His resources. God has authority over all things. He can and will do what He *says* He can and will do when it comes to blessings and the transfer of wealth.

Mining companies don't *own* the gold and silver and other precious stones and metals of this earth.

Oil companies don't *own* the oil and gas resources of the earth.

Man can never truly *own* any of the earth's resources because every resource is *created* by God.

*The One who creates is the one who owns!*

Who owns ideas?

Who owns creativity?

Who owns motivation or enthusiasm?

Who owns ability?

Who owns talents?

Who created these capacities in man?

God did! What God creates, He owns. He imparts these resources to people and allows them to use them, but He never relin-
quishes ownership. Behind every transaction and every transfer of
wealth on this earth are ability, ideas, invention, innovation, and energy. All are owned by God, because all are created by God and imparted by God.

The Devil doesn't own anything.

The gang doesn't own your neighborhood.

The criminal doesn't own what he steals.

God may have *allowed* a transfer of authority over certain resources temporarily, but it is always *God* who allows it. No one can
force the hand of God or lay rightful claim to the things He has created.

God delights in blessing His children. It is His desire to show us
all His kingdom has to offer us. When we are born again, we become God's children; we are His family. And in any family, there is
a difference between what outsiders know about the family and
what family members know. In the same way, being a part of the
family of God automatically brings with it the privilege of knowing
God in an intimate way.

The point I'm making is that when you are a child of God, you
have the awesome honor of gazing upon the riches of your Father's
wealth. And because you know what He has, your expectation
from Him and your confidence in Him are enhanced. My children
expect that when they come to me and ask for money, I will give
it to them. They never question if I have it, how I'm going to get
it, or where it comes from—they just know I'll give it to them.
However, being a good father, I will exercise restraint at times.
Thus, I am not only good *to* them, but I am good *for* them. And
that is how God is to us.

God often withholds blessing and prosperity from us for a season in order to temper our character or to correct flawed behavior.
Then when the blessing comes, we will be mature enough to handle it. If He gave it to us prematurely, it could destroy us. Without
that understanding, it is easy to become discouraged and even turn
from God in anger if, when we exercise our faith with expectancy
and confidence in God, what we have asked for does not come to
us when we think we should have it. However, if our faith in God's
wisdom to direct our lives is greater than our personal agenda, we

will hold on tenaciously to our faith in His promise, grow up, and wait patiently for the blessing to come.

Once we recognize God as the benevolent and wise owner of everything, we want to know just how far our inheritance extends! The truth that must sink into our spirits is *Blessed be God!* Anything that we perceive to be a blessing in heaven or on earth, God *is* that, *has* that, or *does* that to the infinite degree! Any resource that is related to value or wealth belongs to, comes from, and is controlled by God, our Father, who desires to bless *us*.

The perception we have about the grandeur and blessedness of God becomes the reservoir from which we draw the refreshing waters of God's blessings for our lives. And knowing the blessings of God motivates us to worship. Paul is not only telling us that God *is* blessed, *he is blessing God.*

Thanksgiving, praise, and worship are so important because the more we worship God, the more He is *magnified* in our hearts, where we know Him as the Father who loves us; and in our minds, where we know Him as the supplier of all our needs. And when we see Him as the great and awesome God that He is, our problems wither and become microscopic. It is easier to believe God can and will meet our needs and resolve our problems when we grasp the power of His majesty and His compassion.

## FAITH IS THE RECEIVER OF WEALTH

Our faith grows stronger as we perceive God's greatness as both sovereign and loving heavenly Father. Then we become more receptive to His blessings because God always responds to *faith*. In the Scriptures we read that Jesus said to those who came to Him for miracles of healing and deliverance, "As you have believed, it will be done to you" and "Your faith has made you whole."

Then touched he their eyes, saying, According to your faith be it unto you.
—**Matthew 9:29**

And Jesus said unto the centurion, Go thy way; and as thou hast believed, so be it done unto thee. And his servant was healed in the selfsame hour.
—**Matthew 8:13**

14

Faith is the catalyst that accelerates the divine transfer of wealth to us as believers in Christ Jesus. Faith is what motivates God to release His resources on our behalf, and faith conditions us to receive them.

Having faith to believe God *wants* to bless us is another great challenge to receiving His blessings. When we see God as indifferent, our faith is diminished, our prayers are muttered halfheartedly, our tenacity weakens, and we have no ability to receive miracles from God.

We must build ourselves up on our most holy faith by praying in the Spirit (see Jude 20) and continually feeding our spirits and renewing our minds with the Word of God, because faith comes by hearing the Word and strengthens our inner man. (See Romans 10:17.) The Holy Spirit and the Word are the dynamic duo God has given us to become superheroes of faith, to become like Jesus.

## A DONE DEAL

**Blessed be the God and Father of our Lord Jesus Christ, who *hath* blessed us with all spiritual blessings in heavenly places in Christ.**
### —Ephesians 1:3 (emphasis mine)

The blessings God has prepared for us have already been put into place. This is a finished work. It is complete, settled, over, and done with. The blessings of God are not rooted in our expectation or hope, but in a heavenly reality. From God's viewpoint, we possess the land of blessing right now. All of the blessings we can ever receive from God have already been created, established, and are in a "holding pattern," waiting for us to possess them. We tend to look at the blessings of the Lord as "potentially ours," but God sees them as "possessively ours."

We are like Joshua, when he stood on the banks of the Jordan looking over into the Promised Land. The Lord told him that every piece of land where he would put his foot had already been given to him. (See Joshua 1:3.) Joshua hadn't crossed the Jordan River yet. He wasn't living in the land. Enemies were still living there, and there were battles ahead. But the fact was, the land belonged to Joshua and to the Israelites. God had given it to them—past tense, done deal, established work.

Let's suppose that I said to my son, "That car out in the drive-way is yours. Here are the keys. Take it away." Does that car belong to my son? Yes. Because I said so. Has he possessed it yet? Not until he goes out there, gets in it, turns the key in the ignition, and drives away. It's his but he has to take it.

It sounds like a paradox to say, "It's yours" and then to say, "Go, take it," but that's the position God puts us in. The problem many people have is that they don't *know* what is already theirs. And even when they know, they don't believe it or act on it. Before my son would go out and get in that car and drive away, he would have to know and believe the truth of what I said to him: "Son, that car is your car. I have given it to you." He would have to believe the car was owned by me in the first place, believe I had the power to give it to him, and then believe I wanted to give it to him.

Do you believe God owns what you need?

Do you believe God has the power to give you what you need?

Do you believe He wants to meet your needs?

The first step to possessing our inheritance is *knowing* and *believing* God has what we need. The second step is personally taking possession of what has been decreed, bequeathed, or given to us. Most believers seem to spend their entire lives reading the will and shouting over the contract, but never moving out and obtaining what God has given them. We sing about the promises, talk about them, write music about them, teach about them, read about them—yet never *live* in them. Why? Because we aren't willing to fight the spiritual battles that must be fought in order to take possession of what is rightfully ours.

Everything you could possibly need is available to you in the full measure you could ever desire it. Let me assure you today, you are rich beyond measure! But you still have to lay hold of what God has promised to you and what God has already given to you. God said to Joshua, "Be strong and of a good courage; be not afraid, neither be thou dismayed: for the Lord thy God is with thee whithersoever thou goest" (Joshua 1:9).

Joshua had work to do. It was going to take strength and courage to occupy a land infested with enemies. What gave Joshua the strength and courage to go forward was knowing that the Lord was with him and that He had already assured Joshua's victory. It is knowing God that gives us the strength and courage we need to step out in faith and obtain all that He has for us. The degree of our faith is based upon our intimacy with our heavenly Father.

Tremendous life-changing, abundant blessings are waiting for us if we will only pursue them and possess them in faith.

# 2

# ALL SPIRITUAL
# BLESSINGS

---

**Blessed be the God and Father of our Lord Jesus Christ, who
hath blessed us with all spiritual blessings in heavenly places
in Christ.**
## —Ephesians 1:3

We know that God's wealth includes everything in the universe
that He created, but this verse in Ephesians means much more and
goes far beyond anything we can perceive of or imagine. This verse
calls us to reach an understanding that puts our entire life in proper
perspective: The blessings God has provided for us in heavenly
places in Christ are first and foremost *spiritual blessings.*

Paul is not talking about prosperity in terms of dollars and
cents, the clothes we wear, the homes we live in, or the cars we
drive. He is talking about spiritual blessings. Spiritual blessings,
however, are *related* to material, physical, financial, emotional, and
mental blessings. As believers, we are instructed to begin with and
always focus on the spiritual blessings. Then, it is the outworking of
those spiritual blessings that produces an abundant life in the practical and material realm in which we live.

What many believers in Christ Jesus haven't fully recognized is
that all natural and material blessings are the fruit of spiritual blessings. The root of all blessing lies in the spirit realm. A fruit tree cannot bear fruit if it has no root. If the trunk of the tree is cut away
from its roots, that chunk of wood has no potential for bearing fruit,

and neither do its leaves and branches. The life of a tree flows from the hidden, unseen root system that lies beneath the soil. Life flows up into the visible tree out of the invisible depths of the soil, and the branches produce fruit that is good, beneficial, and abundant.

In like manner, our spiritual life is invisible and hidden within. The life that Christ Jesus imparts to us in the invisible recesses of our heart flows up into the visible realm and produces fruit that can be seen. The fruit of the Spirit is love, joy, peace, patience, gentleness, goodness, faith, humility, and self-control. The person who is rich in spirit is the person who is able to produce the fruit that will result in all of the physical and natural blessings necessary for living like Jesus on this earth.

Understanding, moving into, and possessing spiritual blessings increase your capacity to receive all of the natural and physical blessings of this life. Spiritual blessings are the key to achieving fullness of life.

## ETERNAL BLESSINGS

**While we look not at the things which are seen, but at the things which are not seen: for the things which are seen are temporal; but the things which are not seen are eternal.**
**—2 Corinthians 4:18**

In the last chapter, we saw that God has already blessed us with all spiritual blessings. This concept is easy to understand once we see that spiritual blessings are *eternal*. They existed before we did, and when we became God's child, He deposited them into our new, recreated spirit by the Holy Spirit.

Are you aware that all of the spiritual blessings you will ever need or desire are already resident inside you? They have already been imparted to you. You received them the moment you accepted Jesus Christ as your Savior. All spiritual blessings—the full-to-overflowing bounty of all that God is and has for you—are now resident in you because the Holy Spirit lives in you!

Spiritual blessings last forever, because they emanate from the Holy Spirit, who is eternal. But natural blessings are for a season and are temporary, no matter how great or wonderful they may seem to us at the time. Therefore, we must always guard our hearts and minds to maintain godly priorities. Our treasure should be found in God and not in things. The Bible is very clear on this point. Jesus said,

**Lay not up for yourselves treasures upon earth, where moth and rust doth corrupt, and where thieves break through and steal: But lay up for yourselves treasures in heaven, where neither moth nor rust doth corrupt, and where thieves do not break through nor steal: For where your treasure is, there will your heart be also.**
**—Matthew 6:19–21**

No matter what form of physical or material treasure we may possess, the greater treasure is always the spiritual treasures of God. Notice the balance in Jesus' teaching:

**Therefore take no thought, saying, What shall we eat? or, What shall we drink? or, Wherewithal shall we be clothed? (For after all these things do the Gentiles seek:) for your heavenly Father knoweth that ye have need of all these things. But seek ye first the kingdom of God, and his righteousness; and all these things shall be added unto you.**
**—Matthew 6:31–33**

In the time in which we live, to be "anxious" means to be eager or excited about something. We say, for instance, "I am anxious for my guests to arrive." However, in the Greek text, the word *anxious* has another meaning: "to be unduly concerned, to have anxiety, or to worry about something."

Jesus emphatically tells us many times in the Gospels that we are not to be anxious or to worry about anything in life. God knows what we need and it is His delight to supply what we need. If spiritual blessings are our top priority and the kingdom of God is our number-one pursuit, God will take care of all the material things that concern us without any anxiety or frustration on our part.

**Every good gift and every perfect gift is from above, and cometh down from the Father of lights, with whom is no variableness, neither shadow of turning.**
**—James 1:17**

Every blessing begins with God, and for us to obtain His blessings, we must perceive, receive, and possess them first in the spirit realm. We must turn from our personal agendas, concerns, and selfish desires and worship Him in spirit and in truth in everything we think, say, and do. By this we are choosing to connect with the eternal God, not the temporal world. We are literally plugging ourselves in to His eternal thoughts and ways, causing us to conduct ourselves according to His will.

## THREE SPIRITUAL BLESSINGS

Before we go further, I want us to examine three spiritual blessings that are the foundation of our wealth as believers: faith, grace, and strength. A rudimentary understanding of these three powerful principles of the Christian life will allow any believer to walk in God's abundance and blessing.

**Faith.** All the faith we need has already been allocated to us and deposited in us. The Bible tells us that God has dealt to every man the measure of faith: "For I say, through the grace given unto me, to every man that is among you . . . God hath dealt to every man the measure of faith" (Romans 12:3).

We already have all the faith we need! Furthermore, we have the agent of faith working in us—the Holy Spirit. In Jude 20, we are instructed to pray in the Holy Ghost, because this strengthens and builds our faith. In Romans 10:17, we are told that faith rises up and expands in our hearts as we read, hear, and study God's Word. Faith is what moves God. Faith is our key to accessing the full power of God. Like a key in the ignition of a vehicle ignites the engine, our faith ignites the heart of God and releases His love, wisdom, power, and presence into any situation or circumstance.

**Grace.** Grace is the attitude of God that causes His love to transcend our sin and deliver to us the full measure of His support and work. Grace means that we don't have to strive and struggle through this life to prove ourselves and to make it on our own. We no longer have to live in oppression or depression because God has given us His favor. His grace is what enables us to move forward and run the race with confidence—without shame or condemnation—because we know His love for us is unconditional.

But where sin abounded, grace did much more abound.
**—Romans 5:20**

Who hath saved us, and called us with an holy calling, not according to our works, but according to his own purpose and

grace, which was given us in Christ Jesus before the world began.
—**2 Timothy 1:9**

By whom also we have access by faith into this grace wherein we stand, and rejoice in hope of the glory of God.
—**Romans 5:2**

Throughout the epistles we find verse after verse reminding us that God's grace is what transforms us, renews us, and makes us strong in faith. Our part is not to struggle to make things happen but to acknowledge the grace of God and take joy as the Holy Spirit makes things happen in us and through us to others.

Make no mistake, however; grace does not free us from work or effort! When we understand God's grace, we have the confidence and assurance needed to do the work of the kingdom, knowing that God's blessing is upon us.

Grace is also the power that enables us to endure and progress through insufferable challenges. Paul knew this and testified to empowering grace, in 2 Corinthians 12:8–10, concerning his "thorn in the flesh." If you've ever had a splinter in your finger or a cactus needle stuck in your leg, you know it is very painful and incredibly distressing! It won't kill you, but it will make your life miserable until it is removed. Paul's thorn was not going to kill him, but it was a constant source of vexation and frustration to his ministry. However, he found God's grace to be sufficient. The grace of God undergirded his faith, spurring him on to persevere through every battle and gain the victory.

In Acts 20:32, when Paul makes his emotional good-bye to the Ephesian leaders, he commends them to "the word of his grace, which is able to build you up." In verses 28–31, he warns them that after his departure vicious wolves will try to infiltrate their flocks and steal or destroy their sheep. Only "the word of his grace" would keep the Ephesian church strong enough in God to identify the wolves and dispel them from their midst.

The effect of Paul's words on the Ephesian leaders, in Acts 20, proved powerful. We know they took his commendation to heart and immediately acted upon it, and we see that the grace with which Paul greeted them in Ephesians 1:2 was the persevering strength that enabled them to receive Jesus' commendation in Revelation 2:2–3: "I know thy works, and thy labour, and thy patience, and how thou canst not bear them which are evil: and thou hast tried them which say they are apostles, and are not, and hast found them liars: and hast borne, and hast patience, and for my name's sake hast laboured, and hast not fainted."

**Strength.** Our strength comes from the omnipotent Holy Spirit, who resides within us. His strength allows us to stand in times of difficulty, endure heartache and sorrow, resist temptation, and remain steadfast in faith. The Holy Spirit uses difficult times to strengthen us for future and greater blessings. Each of us is in the process of being fashioned into a mighty pillar in the temple of our Lord! "For our light affliction, which is but for a moment, worketh for us a far more exceeding and eternal weight of glory" (2 Corinthians 4:17).

We can never forget that what God has called us to do is beyond our abilities, talents, and strength. Consequently, God infuses us with His divine enablement, the supernatural energy to do superhuman exploits for the kingdom. Paul actually looked forward to trials and testing that challenged his natural strength and ability:

**And he said unto me, My grace is sufficient for thee: for my strength is made perfect in weakness. Most gladly therefore will I rather glory in my infirmities, that the power of Christ may rest upon me. Therefore I take pleasure in infirmities, in reproaches, in necessities, in persecutions, in distresses for Christ's sake: for when I am weak, then am I strong.**
**—2 Corinthians 12:9–10**

When difficult things happen to us, if we will trust in Jesus, He will fill us with His strength to carry on and go to the next level. And after a few experiences of being filled with the strength of God to persevere, the mere thought of doing anything in our own strength again becomes repugnant to us! God's strength is far superior.

Faith. Grace. Strength. These three blessings of God are an unbeatable combination: the ability to believe . . . the confidence to act . . . and the power to persevere. Everything becomes accessible and possible when these spiritual blessings are active in us!

## THE OUTWARD WORKING OF INWARD WEALTH

When we face a problem, the Lord doesn't jump up and cry, "Oh my, I've got to do something. John is in trouble, and Mary has gotten into a terrible mess! I'd better act!" No! The Lord has already done all He is going to do. In fact, He did His work so well that when He rose up into the heavenlies He sat down at the right hand of the Majesty on High. (See Hebrews 1:3.) Our high priest, Jesus Christ, is *sitting* on His throne. He has ceased from His labor. He has already procured our salvation with His blood and He has poured out on all who believe in Him all spiritual blessings that pertain to life and godliness. (See 2 Peter 1:3–4.)

The process of maturing in Christ Jesus is simply learning how to work out what God has already placed in us. Spiritual maturity is living from the spiritual reality resident in us through the Holy Spirit.

A baby in its mother's womb has every gene, every chromosome, every trait already built into it from the moment of conception. Likewise, God has placed the Holy Spirit in us to reveal the spiritual characteristics, capabilities, and possibilities He has put within us for every aspect of our lives.

Furthermore, when we accept Jesus Christ as our Savior, we don't get just a few spiritual blessings. When Christ comes into us and we come into Christ, we are given *all* spiritual blessings. Paul wrote to the Corinthians: "Eye hath not seen, nor ear heard, neither have entered into the heart of man, the things which God hath prepared for them that love him" (1 Corinthians 2:9).

When you are a newborn babe in Christ Jesus, you don't know all you have, who you are, or what lies ahead for you. As a baby in a crib you don't know that you will soon crawl around on the floor and eventually be able to talk and walk. In the same way, as a newborn babe in Christ, you don't yet know all the spiritual blessings God has placed inside you. You don't know all that He has planned for you or all that He desires to do in you, through you, and for you.

Nonetheless, the fullness of spiritual blessings resides in you. Your work is to grow in your understanding of those blessings and then to appropriate them and live from them. Spiritual blessings are like a divine seed that has been planted firmly in the heart of faith. As time goes by, that seed is watered with the Word.

When we go through a crisis time in our walk with the Lord, we don't need to go out and look for faith, grace, strength, or any other spiritual blessing. We have them already residing within us. What we need to learn in our walk with the Lord is how to access and walk in what is already there. We must realize that there isn't another believer on this earth who possesses more of God than we possess right now. *The difference is that some believers have learned how to access and walk in their spiritual blessings more than others.*

I see many Christians today who go from this meeting to that meeting, from this person to that person, hoping that somebody has more of God's power. They are hoping that when that "more powerful" person prays for them, they will receive the miracle they desire. The Lord's plan for us is to get to the point where we don't need to constantly turn to others to do what He desires to do directly within us.

God's desire is that we become aware of all the spiritual blessings He has already imparted to us, and then that we access those blessings and employ them for His glory. We are to use our spiritual blessings not only to see our own needs met but to advance the purposes and plans of God on this earth, in this generation, whenever and wherever we have the opportunity.

If we could see the full harvest God has already imparted to us and planted within us, our minds and hearts could not contain it! Our eyes would be blinded by the glory of it, and our souls would burst with the thought of it. But one word of warning: The Enemy also knows our potential. He is not ignorant of God's plan or God's gifts to us. He knows the harvest we can experience in our lives. He knows the potential of the blessings God has for us.

Therefore, when Satan comes against us, troubling us, oppressing us, we need to recognize that he is not only challenging where we are or what we are doing. The Devil is troubled over what has been deposited in us! He knows what can be released from us. He is intimidated by our destiny and is fighting to keep us from moving into and possessing the blessings that are ours in Christ.

**Eye hath not seen, nor ear heard, neither have entered into the heart of man, the things which God hath prepared for them that love him. But God hath revealed them unto us by his Spirit: for the Spirit searcheth all things, yea, the deep things of God.**
**—1 Corinthians 2:9–10**

The vast potential for wealth that can be released from the church is virtually incomprehensible. Most of us can't even begin to imagine all that God desires to do in us, through us, or for us.

# 3

# CHOSEN

According as he hath chosen us in him before the foundation
of the world, that we should be holy and without blame before him in love.
## —Ephesians 1:4

If not one person on the face of the earth showed any love
toward you or valued you in the slightest way, Ephesians 1:4 shat-
ters and dispels all that rejection and bondage by telling you that
*God chose you.* He chose you to be His child before He created the
heavens and the earth. You are not an accident, a mistake, or an error. You were in God's heart and mind and plan for the universe
long before the earth heard your first cry. Don't let anyone tell you
and don't ever think or say that you are unloved or unwanted!

There is no better way to appreciate the value of being *chosen*
than to explore the definition of the word. Technically it means "to
call out." We can conclude that the Lord called us out of something.
Yes, He did call us out of the kingdom of darkness into the kingdom of His dear Son, but there is more to discover in the word
*chosen.*

The grammar in the Greek language has a function for verbs
called voice. The voice of the verb tells us about the relationship
between the action of the verb and the subject. In this case, the
voice teaches us that not only were we chosen, but we were chosen *for* the Lord *by* the Lord. His choosing us was not simply for an

assignment in the kingdom, but we were chosen *for Him*. We are His treasure. Malachi 3:17 states that when God comes to make up His jewels, we shall be His. We are not only participants in the work of the kingdom, we are the treasure of God and for God.

The timing of this choosing is also very important. God made the decision "from the foundation of the world." We were chosen, called out, before the Lord ever flung the stars in space, set the rivers in motion, or filled the nightingale's mouth with song. We were on God's mind from the very beginning of creation. We are not a last-minute change of mind or a reaction to a problem but an integral part of God's initial design.

We are chosen by God to be His precious child.

We are created and handcrafted by our Creator for a specific purpose.

We are wanted and valued by the Almighty King of the entire universe.

What a wonderful blessing it is—what a great source of emotional and spiritual wealth—to know that we are God's *chosen ones*!

We each know in the natural how special it is to be chosen. When we were children, we knew it was special to be chosen for a particular team, drama part, choir solo, or class project. When we started dating, we felt special when we were "chosen" to date someone we liked and admired. When we married, we were grateful that our spouse "chose" us to be his or her marriage partner and lover. When we gave birth to our children, we were awed that God "chose" us and entrusted us with their precious lives. But there is nothing more awesome than to know that God chose us long before our birth to be in relationship with Him and to fulfill a part of His eternal plan.

God also chose you to be His child and to be a part of the body of Christ on the earth at precisely this time and in precisely the location where you find yourself. God does not randomly snatch some piece of wood that has fallen down through a crack in the wall and say, "Oh, all right, I'll go ahead and add this to the house." No! With great determination, deliberation, and design God has said, "I want *you*. I'm going to use you for this particular job. I want your specific personality and your unique set of talents in this precise position at this significant time."

The Lord has crafted you and formed you and shaped you. He has molded you and made you. He knows your strengths, your weaknesses, and your character, and He has caused you to be a perfect fit and a perfect tool for a very precise and important role in His plan. You have been chosen just as the cedars of Lebanon were selected, one by one, for the building of Solomon's temple. Jesus said to His disciples, "You have not chosen Me, but I have chosen you." (See John 15:16.) The same is true for us today as His disciples on this earth.

What good news! No matter what might be right or wrong with us, or what we might like or dislike about ourselves, we must be all right with God, because He has chosen us for His work. He is going to use us for the fulfillment of His plan. He is going to apply our unique personalities and abilities to a particular place and time in history.

Stop to think about this any time you feel tempted to start trying to be like another person. If you give up being who you are in order to become like somebody else, you are going to be duplicating a piece in the puzzle that God already has! God needs you to be *you*. He made you in a precise way for a precise purpose, and only *you* will do. When He called you, He wanted *you*. When He chose you, He wanted *you*. You are His treasure and His delight!

## HOLY AND BLAMELESS

Remember Ephesians 1:4 at the opening of this chapter: "He hath chosen us in him before the foundation of the world, that we should be holy and without blame before him in love."

The first half of this verse deals with what has already been done, that before God ever created the universe, He chose us to be His precious children. The second half of the verse deals with what *will* be done as a result of our being chosen. You cannot be holy and without blame if you are not chosen!

The word *holy* and the "doctrine of holiness" based upon this word have often been misunderstood. Many theologically oriented rules and regulations have been tied to this word and to this doctrine. There are complete religious organizations that identify themselves by the word *holiness*. To some Christians, *holy* often means a manner of dress, restriction of activities, and pride in the fact that certain sins have no effect on them. Unfortunately for them, *holy* does not mean any of those things!

The word *holy* is translated from the Greek word that means "dedicated to God, sacred, reserved for God and His service." Holiness is not a Christian version of *Robert's Rules of Order*. While the Lord wants us to live in victory and moral integrity, He placed other specific teachings in His Word to cover those areas in our lives.

The word *holy* focuses our attention on our relationship to God. We are chosen or "called out" to be holy or "available for the exclusive use of God." We are dedicated to His purpose. A wonderful picture of this concept is found in the Old Testament tabernacle. When Moses received the charge to build the tabernacle, he was given specific pieces of furniture to construct and utensils to craft for the work that would take place there. Before they were dedicated to the temple, those forks, spoons, basins, and fleshhooks were ordinary tools. But once they were consecrated to the tabernacle, they became holy instruments, set apart for the Lord's work.

In the same way, believers in Jesus Christ are dedicated to and made holy for the service of our Lord. God's plan is that we walk before Him completely consecrated and set apart for Him alone. Many people spend a lifetime wondering, "Why am I here? What purpose does God have for me?" God's purpose is that you be His holy vessel! When a believer goes through life with that truth always on his mind and embedded in his heart, he can never stray far from God's will.

We are also to walk "without blame." In the Greek, the word for blameless means "to be without flaw or without blemish." The word takes us back to the Old Testament sacrifices. When a lamb was offered to God in worship, its condition had to be flawless. A sickly, weak, or blemished lamb was disqualified as an acceptable offering to God.

Jesus Christ was our spotless and perfect sacrificial Lamb. He qualified for the position of our substitute by virtue of His blameless life. In Ephesians 1:4, Paul recognizes the sinless life of Jesus Christ and shows us that we are positionally holy—set apart for the exclusive use of God—and blameless, without flaw or blemish, in Christ.

Our experience, on the other hand, is not always quite as pristine! We are holy in the sense of being available for God's exclusive use. However, being holy takes both a mental commitment to pleasing God and a physical discipline to shun those things that offend Christ. Being blameless or without flaw in our daily experience can only be accomplished by submitting ourselves to the care and management of Jesus Christ. His Word, which continually cleanses us, and His Spirit, who enables us to resist our innate tendencies to fall and fail, are essential components for walking out the reality that we are blameless.

Ephesians 1:4 says we are "holy and without blame *before him.*" The word *before* denotes presenting ourselves to Jesus, constantly aware of His presence in our lives. Jesus told us that He would never leave us nor forsake us (see Hebrews 13:5), and that statement means so much more than just showing up when we get into trouble. In essence, Jesus was saying, "I want you to be aware of something: You cannot go anywhere or do anything that I will not be there with you. You are always *before* me."

The end of Ephesians 1:4 brings us to the capstone of the verse: "in love." I must tell you that there is great disagreement among Bible scholars and commentators about whether "in love" should be linked to verse 4 or verse 5, which begins "Having predestinated . . ." This controversy poses the question, "Are we holy and blameless before Him in love, or are we predestinated in love?" In my view, the exact answer will be known when we stand with Jesus and the apostle Paul in heaven. In the meantime, I see no heresy in enjoying God's love in both verses!

Without a doubt the understanding that we have been chosen as God's treasure and for His purpose, that we are holy and set apart for His exclusive use, that we are found blameless in Christ Jesus, and that we are always in His presence must lead us to experience His incredible love. And certainly without the experience of His grace-filled, life-transforming, unconditional love it would be impossible for us to manifest a holy, blameless walk of love toward others.

## ACCORDING TO LOVE

No believer can live out Ephesians 1:4 in her own strength, ability, or desire. We must go back to the word *according* at the beginning of this verse to find the key to releasing the power of being holy and blameless before Him. *According* is translated from a Greek word that means "even as, in conformity with the fact." I like to say that being in Christ places us "in the same dimension" as Jesus, conforming us to His image and declaring us holy and without blame before God.

In English, the word *according* is likened to a musical term: a chord, a harmonious blending together of notes. Our destiny is to be harmonious with what God has chosen for us. We must align ourselves—get in tune—with what God has planned for us to be and do. Any note that is dissonant or out of harmony with God's plan and purpose is a note that is going to jangle the nerves and cause distress to the body. It is going to create a noise, not a pleasant sound. It is going to disrupt, interfere, and be counterproductive to what God has planned for us and those whose lives we touch.

Our job is to recognize what God has planned for us and what is counter to His purposes, and then to choose only those things that are in harmony with God's plan. Have you ever sung harmony with another person? If you have, you know that the other person hits the first note and then you hit a note that sounds good with their note. Harmony only exists because there is first a melody. In our lives, God is the lead singer! He sings the melody, and our role is to harmonize with Him. We must match His rhythm and His tempo. We must yield the "lead" to Him, saying, *Yes, I'll be your holy vessel, totally submitted to whatever you desire to do in me and through me.*

What we are describing here is nothing more than the act of being before Him in love. Isn't it interesting that the apostle Paul uses this musical analogy to describe love in another great epistle:

**Though I speak with the tongues of men and of angels, and have not charity *[love]*, I am become as sounding brass, or a tinkling cymbal. And though I have the gift of prophecy, and understand all mysteries, and all knowledge; and though I have all faith, so that I could remove mountains, and have not charity *[love]*, I am nothing. And though I bestow all my goods to feed the poor, and though I give my body to be burned, and have not charity *[love]*, it profiteth me nothing.**
**—1 Corinthians 13:1–3 (brackets mine)**

Our destiny can only be discovered and lived out as we walk in harmony with God, "according to" or "in the same dimension as" the powerful understanding that He has chosen us from time eternal. We are His precious vessel of honor. In Christ we are pure and without blemish. We are always conscious of His presence in our lives. In the knowledge of these truths, we will sing in tune with His song of love toward us and through us to reach the world.

# 4

# PREDESTINED

Having predestinated us unto the adoption of children by
Jesus Christ to himself, according to the good pleasure of his
will.

—Ephesians 1:5

One of the greatest experiences a person will ever enjoy in life
is being wanted by another person. To be needed, desired, and
wanted is the supreme antidote for loneliness, depression, and low
self-esteem. But as precious as being wanted by another person is,
it pales in comparison to being chosen by God.

## BEFORE ENCIRCLED

In verse 4, we saw the word that means "to be called out or
chosen." In verse 5, we have another word that details God's sovereign choice: It is a compound word meaning "before" and "encircle." God picked us out, encircled us, before we were born.

God's choice was not a reaction to our overtures toward Him.
He didn't choose us because of our actions, lifestyle, or pleading. He
chose us prior to our life's beginning. He made the decision to be
good to us without provocation, inducement, or cajoling. None of
our weaknesses, failures, or personality flaws had any effect on His
decision. We had no influence on His choice, because we didn't ex-

ist yet, and we had no access to Him. God predestined us, or determined beforehand, that we would be His children.

In simple terms, to predestine or to "before encircle" is to predetermine. It means to have something in mind from the beginning. God is not making up His plan as He goes. His plan is set, established, in place. And He knows precisely what He needs at any given point to fulfill His plan.

I used to think that when movies were made, the director and actors started at the first scene and then worked their way through the movie, scene by scene, until the last scene was shot. That's not how it is done, however. Many times the last scene or a scene in the middle of the movie is shot first. Then the first scenes are filmed so that they work into the latter scenes. In many cases the very beginning of the movie is the last part filmed. The movie can be produced in this way because everyone is working from a script that gives them the whole story, beginning to end.

In a similar manner, the Lord has the full script for all time. He sees the end from the beginning and every scene in between. The destiny of the world is determined. The outcome of history is fixed. That's one of the reasons God doesn't get hysterical about the things that cause us to get hysterical. When we run to Him and say, "I've been hit so hard! Don't you care? Couldn't you stop this fight?" the Lord responds calmly by saying, "The fight is fixed. I know who wins in the end."

The Lord has a master plan and strategy for every scene in your life. He sees how everything will fit together to tell a complete story that will bring glory to Him. What an awesome thought, that we can be part of a scheme that is so grand and marvelous. Hell itself cannot thwart the plans of God. And we are part of God's plan. We were chosen before the beginning of time for the role He has for us to play.

God's plan is fixed. It cannot and will not be edited or changed any more than God will change His own nature. He cannot be forced into a detour or delay. God is constant—the same yesterday, today, and forever. (See Hebrews 13:8.) You may ask, "What about the sin of Adam and Eve in the garden of Eden? Was that God's plan?"

Satan created a dilemma when Adam fell into sin. He took what God loved and seduced him into partaking of what God hated: sin. Satan's purpose was to get God to work against himself and to be in conflict with himself by simultaneously loving man and hating sin. Do you see the problem Satan created for God? For God to kill what He hated (sin), He would also have to kill what He loved (man).

God had a strategy for dealing with this dilemma. In fact, He had a strategy in place before Satan created the dilemma! The Scriptures say that Jesus was the Lamb slain before the foundation of the world. (See Revelation 13:8.) In other words, before God created time or the universe, He devised the plan of redemption. Before man was created, in His omnipotence and foreknowledge, God made provision for His will to be accomplished in every moment of history. That's why Satan has never been able to create a dilemma for God that God has not already out-strategized. There is nothing the Devil can throw at us and no obstacle he can put in our way that will alter the purpose of God for our lives. There is no way Satan can outmaneuver God!

We must get to the place where we recognize that God *acts*— He never *reacts*. He is never on the defensive, but always on the offensive. He never lets the Enemy throw the first punch so that He has no response. God acts sovereignly. Nothing the Enemy does can abort what God has decreed, and no action of the Enemy can thwart His plan.

## ADOPTED CHILDREN ARE WANTED CHILDREN

Remember Ephesians 1:5: He has predestinated us unto adoption. We are His children through Jesus Christ, according to the good pleasure of his will. When God "before encircled" us, He had something very specific in mind. He was adopting us. The Greek word used here represents children who are full-grown. This verse of Scripture is telling us that God adopted us as full-grown adults!

In our culture, adoption generally focuses on small children or babies. The thought is to avoid having personality conflicts and to appear as normal as possible by bringing an infant or very young child into the family. However, in the time in which Paul wrote, adoption was usually restricted to people of means. When a person had great wealth but no heir, he would look for a full-grown man who possessed the qualities he wanted to be remembered for after he was dead. He would adopt, knowing his name would be well represented in the future.

Older children and adults are not easily adopted because they are set in their ways, personality, and character. However, biblical adoption takes advantage of this fact to express the love of God, for God adopted us knowing who we were and how we were. God didn't choose to adopt us because we were qualified. He chose the failing, incompetent, and poorly trained. None of those flaws hindered or deterred Him from choosing us. God's adopting us gave us value and significance.

"For ye see your calling, brethren, how that not many wise men after the flesh, not many mighty, not many noble, are called" (1 Corinthians 1:26). Adoption blesses us because it assures us God wanted us regardless of our faults, failings, and weaknesses. He predestined us, picked us out, and encircled us by himself and for himself to be His child.

Today when a couple is going to have a child, they speculate about what the child will be like and who the child will be. Our modern technology has stolen some of the mystique of child-bearing by allowing us to know the sex of the child before he is born. But not even technology can predict with accuracy what the child will be like. We cannot know for certain whether she will be bright or challenged, articulate or mute, passionate or sedate. The best a couple can hope for is a healthy child who has a teachable spirit.

Adoption, on the other hand, is not such a mystery. In many cases, when a family adopts a child, they know what their child looks like. If the child is older, they will know what his interests are to a degree. They are aware of his personality traits and quirks. Likewise, when a child is adopted, the child will know at some point that his adoptive parents wanted him for who he is.

Nobody ever adopted a child they didn't want. Some people give birth to babies they don't want, but nobody *adopts* a baby they don't want. God has wanted you since before the world was created. The relationship He has desired for you for countless ages past is that you be His adopted child. Through the ages, He arranged the details of His plan in order to bring you to the point where you would accept Jesus Christ as your Savior and be a part of His family.

Many people think they got saved because one morning they awoke and decided they wanted to be saved. Certainly there comes a point where we must say yes to what God has already said yes to, but the greater reality is this: You are saved because it was the good pleasure of His will to save you. God wanted you. He drew you with cords of love.

## HIS GOOD PLEASURE

Nothing defeats the good effects and satisfaction of something done for us like the discovery that it was done with a bad attitude. When we learn that someone did something for us because they were forced to, or they did it grumbling through the whole process, we take no pleasure in what they did.

Paul assures us that God adopted us "according to the pleasure of his will." If God had not taken pleasure in us, our salvation would have become nothing more than a mandatory rescue mission. We would have been delivered, but no intimate relationship with our Deliverer would be possible. There was great potential for God to have taken this mandatory route. We were an undone people who repeatedly rejected His offers of love. Our rebellion had no effect, however, on His commitment to save us. The decision was made in eternity past for one reason only: It *pleased* Him.

The Greek word for *will* used here is "a desire that proceeds from one's heart or emotions." I cannot imagine what it is about us that would cause God to desire us and to derive pleasure from merely thinking about being good to us. He was pleased about our being saved long before He actually saved us! Before we arrived on the scene, God the Director knew exactly who was going to play what part in His extravaganza of life on earth.

An actress might go to audition for a part in a play, and when she gets that part she might think that she got it totally on her own merit and acting skill. What a surprise for her to later learn that the director knew precisely who and what he was looking for. He knew long before the auditions took place what kind of person it would take to play the part. He knew the personality, the look, and the characteristics required. She didn't "win" the part—she was pre-selected for it. She simply pursued and said yes to the part that was already predetermined for her.

God's will for us is intimately born from the joy He takes in us. He has predestined us to be His child, the apple of His eye, and He has done this because it was the desire of His heart and because it gave Him the utmost pleasure.

## THE DIVINE ARCHITECT

A verse of Scripture that always used to blow my mind is Psalm 127:1: "Except the Lord build the house, they labour in vain that build it." I thought, *If God has already built the house, why is anybody laboring to build it and how could it be in vain?* Then one day I began to understand that God is not the carpenter. He's the *architect*. He builds by design, and then we, like carpenters, manifest in time and space what God has designed in eternity. An architect lays out on paper all the specs and weights and dimensions and then stands back and appraises his plan. He can "see" that plan fully realized. He envisions all that He has drawn on paper in three-dimensional reality in his mind, including the landscaping!

The blueprint for a building is in place before construction begins. A building isn't constructed to a certain point and then stopped so the architect can work on the plumbing layout or the electrical plan. All the plans are in place before the first shovelful of dirt is moved.

God's plan has been in place for all time and before time. God's blueprints are exact, precise, and complete. They give all the details necessary for the whole project, start to finish. His master blueprint includes a specific blueprint for each of us individually. God sees the fullness of who we can be right down to the minutest detail. His plan for us is flawless, far better than any plan we could ever conceive for ourselves.

When we try to build a plan for ourselves that is different from God's perfect plan, we labor in vain. Our efforts are futile. They count for nothing. On the other hand, when we yield to God's plan by the power of the Holy Spirit at work in us, we move toward perfection and wholeness.

When we understand and accept our position as believers in Jesus Christ—that God has predestined us to be His children and this gives Him the greatest pleasure—our only obligation is to choose what God has chosen for us. We must say yes to all that He has designed—our purpose, our relationship with Him and other people, our destiny, our ministry.

"Study to show thyself approved unto God, a workman that needeth not to be ashamed, rightly dividing the word of truth" (2 Timothy 2:15). We are to be workmen who have developed all our capabilities, talents, and spiritual assets. When the time comes to employ those talents for God's purposes, we can perform with excellence and the Holy Spirit will empower us, strengthen us, guide us, and help us. Then a most remarkable miracle occurs! Not only is God abundantly pleased with us, but we find ourselves completely overwhelmed by the joy and pleasure of being His child and fulfilling His plan.

# 5

# BELOVED

---

**To the praise of the glory of his grace, wherein he hath made us accepted in the beloved.**
**—Ephesians 1:6**

I used to spend a great deal of time and energy trying to be accepted by other people. I wanted them to like me, respect me, admire me, and desire to have me around. But once I realized and fully understood that I was accepted in the beloved of God, I no longer walked into a room hoping the crowd accepted me. It ceased to be significant to me what others thought about me or whether I was accepted into certain circles. A person who comprehends that they are accepted in the beloved is a person who has all the acceptance he will ever need.

Please do not misunderstand what I am saying here. I did not become indifferent, uncaring, and unmoved by people. This is not what happens when we are set free from the opinions of others by our acceptance in the beloved! On the contrary, I became more concerned, more caring, and deeply moved by other people's needs, *because my own needs were being met by God.*

Once I grasped the depth and breadth of God's acceptance of me, all of my motivation turned to pleasing Him alone. And when your every thought is consumed with pleasing God and carrying out His agenda, you find very quickly that He is interested in touching other people in the same way He touched you. So rather than being desperate for another person's love and good opinion of me, I became desperate for them to know God and to be accepted in the beloved as well.

## GRACE IS THE PLACE

In the original Greek text, the word for *accepted* is derived from the word for grace. This word gives a much broader meaning to acceptance! God does not merely tolerate our presence, He has *graced* us. He has given us something we could not possibly give ourselves. He has graced us with His most cherished and loved possession: Jesus Christ. He has placed us in the beloved, in Christ.

The Greek word for *beloved* is close to a word that most believers are very familiar with: *agape*. Where agape is the love of God expressed, *agapao* is the object of His love, someone who gives Him eternal joy. So God has graced us by placing us in Christ, His beloved, and in Christ we are now the object of His love and give Him eternal joy. We are now free to breathe in and breathe out His unconditional love. He has bestowed His honor upon us and crowns us with His glory.

Notice that Ephesians 1:6 refers to our being accepted—in the past tense, something God decided before time existed. We don't have to hope we're accepted, work to be accepted, or wonder if we'll ever be accepted. We already are accepted! We've got a membership card, a pass, and an ID badge that says, "Accepted in the beloved." Why? Because for eternity God has loved and will always love Jesus, and we are in Him.

It is important for us to recognize that we are accepted not on the basis of who we are, but on the basis of our position in Christ Jesus. We aren't accepted on the basis of the résumé we compile or the track record we achieve. We are accepted because we have received Jesus as our Lord and Savior and are now in Christ.

## TRANSFORMING GRACE

The fact that God has accepted me in the beloved transformed my prayer life. Once I realized that I already had a pass directly into the throne room of God and He wanted me to be there, I no longer tried to talk God into hearing me. I could come boldly before Him at two o'clock in the morning, and I wasn't going to awaken Him, disturb Him, or interrupt Him. I could call on Him and know immediately that I was received with love and heard with concern. God was going to hear me and answer me just as He heard and answered Jesus.

When you grasp the fact that you are accepted in the beloved and that you have the *full* acceptance of God, your low self-esteem is going to be healed. All of your reluctance to come to God with your sins and your needs is going to vanish.

**There is therefore now no condemnation to them which are in Christ Jesus, who walk not after the flesh, but after the Spirit.**
**—Romans 8:1**

We cannot stop or in any way diminish God's flow of love toward us.

Nothing can move us from the position of being loved by God.

Nothing can change the way God feels about us.

Nothing can alter the fact that God will continue to love us no matter what.

Receiving God's love heals us on the inside.

Receiving God's love allows us to feel value, worth, and dignity.

Receiving God's love allows us to respect ourselves.

Receiving God's love motivates us to discipline ourselves.

Receiving God's love enables us to return His love, love ourselves, and love others.

We are not only chosen by God, we are eternally loved by God.

## THE GLORY OF HIS GRACE

**To the praise of the glory of his grace, wherein he hath made us accepted in the beloved.**
**—Ephesians 1:6**

The word *wherein* points us to why we have been accepted in the beloved: the glory of God's grace. We may have made the decision to receive Jesus as Lord and Savior, but the opportunity was there for us not because we were good enough, but because God was good enough to offer it.

And this grace is not a thin, capricious, just-enough grace. God's grace is glorious and beyond human understanding.

We are transformed by our position in Christ Jesus because we come face-to-face with the living reality of God's glorious grace toward us. In this most privileged position, we must never cease to humbly offer our praise of thanksgiving and awe to God, whose very nature made us accepted in the beloved.

# 6

# REDEEMED AND FORGIVEN

**In whom we have redemption through his blood, the forgiveness of sins, according to the riches of his grace.**
**—Ephesians 1:7**

Most people I know, including believers, are more concerned about their "current condition" than their "eternal position." Let me declare today: It's time we quit worrying about our *condition* and started focusing on our *position,* because our condition will never change until we understand our position. Any condition of our life is temporal. Conditions change. They come and go. Our position, on the other hand, is eternal. It never diminishes, it never changes, and it cannot be destroyed. Our position in Christ Jesus is first and foremost that we are redeemed and forgiven.

Redemption literally means "payment of ransom." Now, we're not talking about someone in a black ski mask in your bedroom at two in the morning snatching you and leaving a note for your parents that says he will kill you if they don't give him a million dollars by high noon the next day. Adam was not kidnapped in the garden of Eden. He knowingly and willfully disobeyed God's directive and ate of the tree of the knowledge of good and evil.

Our redemption, or payment of ransom, pictures God as the righteous judge who must hold us in prison, under sentence of eternal death and damnation, because of our sin. But when He sees the blood of Jesus, God is satisfied that the ransom for sin has been paid in full.

**For all have sinned, and come short of the glory of God.**
**—Romans 3:23**

The only way we could be free from our inevitable death sentence was that a ransom be paid. The problem was, no matter how hard we tried, we could not in five lifetimes pay this debt. Only Jesus could satisfy the debt because He was the only one who could offer a life completely free from sin. Jesus offered himself as a substitute for us.

**Forasmuch as ye know that ye were not redeemed with corruptible things, as silver and gold . . . but with the precious blood of Christ, as of a lamb without blemish and without spot.**
**—1 Peter 1:18–19**

When God saw Jesus' precious blood, His wrath upon the sin of man was appeased, our debt was paid, and our release secured. When we receive Jesus as our Lord and Savior, we are free to enjoy the blessings of God and fellowship with Him. In fact, the payment of our debt was what Jesus had in mind at Calvary when He said, "It is finished," but the more accurate translation is "Paid in full." Jesus paid in full forever our debt to God—and God was fully satisfied.

## NEW POSITION MEANS NEW CONDITION

Our incarceration was positional, but it manifested in our condition. Before we believed in Jesus we were slaves to sin. We couldn't help but sin. It was our very nature to sin. Whatever the Devil tempted us to do, we usually did it and didn't think anything about it. Then Jesus took us out of the slave auction and said, "Sin, never again will you have control over him!" He looked at us and said, "You are free! You can choose to walk boldly in the Spirit and to do what is holy, blameless, and loving before God."

It is not enough for an emancipation proclamation of redemption to be issued if the slaves don't know about it! And the master of slaves is the last person in the world who wants to tell them that an emancipation proclamation has been issued. If you don't know you are free, you'll remain in bondage in your mind, and where the mind goes, so goes your life. That's why the Devil's main ministry is to convince you that there is no redemption.

If you don't know that you have redemption through Jesus' blood, you'll continue to do whatever your slave master tells you. You'll be like a bird that remains in a cage even though the door to the cage has been opened by the power of Almighty God.

I'm here to tell you today that you are FREE! You no longer have to sin! You may say, "Are you saying that a believer doesn't sin or that a believer never sins?" No—I'm saying a believer doesn't *have* to sin.

**My little children, these things write I unto you, that ye sin not. And if any man sin, we have an advocate with the Father, Jesus Christ the righteous.**

**—1 John 2:1**

Some believers do sin, but they don't have to. They can choose not to. Sin doesn't have to be part of the believer's life. And if we do sin, 1 John 1:9 tells us we must go quickly to the Father to confess it, and He will erase it and cleanse us from all unrighteousness. We can live free of sin.

What is dominating you right now? Are you aware that you can be free of that domination?

Are you in bondage to sexual sins and desires you can't control?

Are you locked into a way of thinking that leads you into the darkness of depression?

Are you ensnared with hate for certain people and always angry in certain situations?

Hear me! Jesus has *redeemed* you from that. You don't need to be in bondage any longer. You don't need to listen to the old slave master of your soul another second. You have been bought out of the marketplace of sin, and the Devil and your flesh no longer have a right to speak to your life, control you, or dominate you. You have the full right to use the name of Jesus to rebuke every depression, fear, carnal desire, and humanistic thought that attempts to bind you, inhibit you, or keep you from freedom to love and worship God. Jesus holds the papers that say, "Paid in full!"

Any time the Devil says to you, "That's just your nature . . . that's just the way you are . . . that's the way God made you . . . that's normal human behavior"—you can count on two things being true.

First, the behavior the Devil is calling normal, acceptable, or inevitable is anything but normal, acceptable, or inevitable for the believer. It may be normal for the sinner who hasn't received Jesus Christ as Savior, but it isn't normal for the believer.

**Know ye not that the unrighteous shall not inherit the kingdom of God? Be not deceived: neither fornicators, nor idolaters, nor adulterers, nor effeminate, nor abusers of themselves with mankind, nor thieves, nor covetous, nor drunkards, nor revilers, nor extortioners, shall inherit the kingdom of God. And such were some of you: but ye are washed, but ye are sanctified, but ye are justified in the name of the Lord Jesus, and by the Spirit of our God.**

**—1 Corinthians 6:9–11**

Believers are no longer what they once were. We have been washed, sanctified, and justified by the shed blood of Jesus, and now we have the sweet but strong presence of the Holy Spirit in our lives. What was once normal is no longer normal. Only God's will and ways are normal.

Second, the Devil is a liar and he cannot tell the truth about you or about what is true in God's eyes. He is the father of lies. (See John 8:44.)

Jesus says to you, "Here's my nature. It's the nature God has for you. Live in it. You don't need to live the way you lived before. You don't need to do what you did before. You can be free of those old habits, attitudes, and lusts. You can be free of those old fears, doubts, and negative thoughts. I came to give you life and to give it to you fully and abundantly." (See John 10:10.)

To the person who has been a slave, there is nothing more valuable—no mark of wealth that is more meaningful or important—than being set free. Freedom is the prize of all people, everywhere, in all ages. It is one of the greatest and most valuable "possessions" any person can have.

The truly wealthy are those who possess the riches of heaven, and one of those riches is redemption, which frees us from the wrath of God. Because Jesus gave His life and our debt of sin was paid, God is no longer our enemy. When we come into Christ and are born again, the reality of redemption changes our entire perspective on life. We now begin to comprehend the freedoms our new position yields: to be God's child, to know Him, to commune with Him, to worship Him, and to carry out His marvelous and miraculous plan for our lives—free from the shackles of sin.

To be free from sin means that we are able to accept and act upon the reality that we are chosen and loved.

To be free from sin means that we have a potential for spiritual growth and learning.

To be free from sin means that all the bondages of the flesh that have kept us limited and immobile are removed. Our spirits are free to soar, to dream God's dreams, to enter into God's purposes, and to claim God's promises.

## A NEW START

**In whom we have redemption through his blood, the forgiveness of sins, according to the riches of his grace.**
**—Ephesians 1:7**

The ransom for our debt of sin has been paid in full and God is satisfied. In light of this incredible and nearly incomprehensible truth, I declare to you that you no longer need to be a slave to sin. It is because you also have *forgiveness* of sins, which is intimately related to and a product of redemption.

In the original text, the word for *forgiveness* means more than a dismissal of accountability. It is the cancellation of an obligation, punishment, or guilt. The penalty for your sin is gone, washed away by the blood of Jesus! Not only have you been redeemed from slavery to sin, but all of your sins have been completely erased. Your evil past has been obliterated and washed away by Jesus Christ, and every sin you commit after you are born again is also washed away when you repent of it: "As far as the east is from the west, so far hath he removed our transgressions from us" (Psalm 103:12).

When the Lord forgives, He chooses also to forget: "I will forgive their iniquity, and I will remember their sin no more" (Jeremiah 31:34). "I will be merciful to their unrighteousness, and their sins and their iniquities will I remember no more" (Hebrews 8:12).

The Bible doesn't say that God is forgetful or that He can't remember. It says God chooses not to remember. He *wills* to forget. There are many believers today who need to *will* to forget their sins once they have confessed them to God and have been forgiven of them.

The more we recall our sins and rehearse them, the more we reinforce those memories. The more we think about our past sins, the more we keep the knowledge of them alive in our soul. Then when we hold our sin in our thought bank, it is more likely that we will act on that thought.

The memory of sin is a deadly force. When sin is allowed to lie dormant in our minds and hearts, it is still alive. We are allowing it to have power over us. Only by forgiving ourselves and forgetting our sin can we truly kill its influence and impact on us.

Choose to forget what God has forgiven and forgotten!

## THE RICHES OF GOD'S GRACE

The phrase "riches of his grace" expresses the value of God's unmerited favor toward us. In Ephesians 1:7, the word *riches* means "abundant and precious." Abundant and precious aren't always compatible concepts. For example, a diamond is precious because it is not found in abundance. Abundance means a lot of something and precious means rare or unique. What makes God's grace precious is that the purchase price for our redemption is the blood of Jesus shed at Calvary. Jesus' blood and only His blood qualified to purchase our redemption. It wasn't the blood itself but the fact that He was absolutely free from sin and therefore pure and perfect.

However, Paul declares that the grace of God we enjoy is both precious and abundant. Abundant suggests the manner in which those riches are distributed. We do not receive a sampling of His grace! He lavishes His grace on us! The picture is that God indulges himself in the luxury of pouring His grace upon our lives.

Our forgiveness is based solely on the riches of God's grace. God chooses to forgive us because His grace is both exceedingly abundant and precious beyond imagination. He chooses to see us as completely pure, beyond our wildest dreams, because we are in Christ Jesus. Paul wrote to the Ephesians very directly about this matter:

**For by grace are ye saved through faith; and that not of yourselves: it is the gift of God: Not of works, lest any man should boast.**

**—Ephesians 2:8–9**

You can't earn forgiveness.
You can't buy it.
You can't achieve it.
You can't accomplish it.
You can't become so good that you deserve it.

God chooses to grace us with forgiveness not because we are so worthy and wonderful, but because Jesus made us worthy and wonderful by the shedding of His blood. The only thing that is required of us to receive forgiveness is to admit that we need it and to ask Him for it. Again, John wrote, "If we confess our sins, he is faithful and just to forgive us our sins, and to cleanse us from all unrighteousness" (1 John 1:9).

When we confess our sins, which is to admit our sins, God forgives us. He does so for the sake of Jesus. He looks upon the shed blood of Jesus and says, "Because of what my Son did for you on the cross, and because you are accepting what my Son did for you, I forgive you." Forgiveness is never about what we have done but about what Jesus has done!

Forgiveness is a grace gift from God, and there is no genuine forgiveness apart from Him. Many people in the world today are trying to forgive themselves for horrible sins. They are looking into mirrors and saying to themselves, "I'm okay. I'm good. I'm just fine the way I am." Apart from Christ, they are trying to forgive what they have no authority or power to forgive. Jesus said that He had authority to forgive sin, and He proved it by healing the physical body. (See Mark 2:10 and Matthew 9:6.) Then Jesus passed His authority on to us:

**Then said Jesus to them again, Peace be unto you: as my Father hath sent me, even so send I you. And when he had said this, he breathed on them, and saith unto them, Receive ye the Holy Ghost: Whose soever sins ye remit, they are remitted unto them; and whose soever sins ye retain, they are retained.**
**—John 20:21–23**

Out of the unfathomable riches of God's grace, the limitless and precious grace of God, we are swept away in the tide of His ocean of mercy and find ourselves going beyond our own redemption to extend God's grace to others. As God forgives us and we receive His forgiveness, we are able to forgive ourselves and others.

**For thou, Lord, art good, and ready to forgive; and plenteous in mercy unto all them that call upon thee.**
**—Psalm 86:5**

How many people in the world—and the church is no exception—are walking in overwhelming shame and guilt because they cannot forgive themselves, or debilitating anger and frustration because they cannot forgive those who have offended and hurt them? I believe many, and possibly most, of the world's problems and struggles would disappear if the life-transforming truths of redemption and forgiveness were understood by believers and lived before the world. The life of God courses freely through the one who knows and fully comprehends that he is redeemed and forgiven.

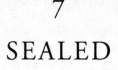

# 7

# SEALED

Wherein he hath abounded toward us in all wisdom and prudence; having made known unto us the mystery of his will, according to his good pleasure which he hath purposed in himself: That in the dispensation of the fulness of times he might gather together in one all things in Christ, both which are in heaven, and which are on earth; even in him.
—Ephesians 1:8–10

These verses of Scripture are interconnected and intimately linked to one another as well as to both the verses that precede and follow them. The apostle Paul probably used the colorful and descriptive term *abounded* because it depicts an excessively extravagant gesture that reflects the incredible riches of God's grace.

We are then moved to the next level of revelation: God's wisdom and prudence are lavished upon us. But we cannot stop there, because wisdom and prudence impact directly and describe in detail the "mystery of his will." Next, we are immediately confronted again with the fact that all this is "according to his good pleasure which he hath purposed in himself" and has nothing at all to do with us, our goodness, or good deeds. This passage speaks solely of the goodness of our God.

Verse 9 brings us to the brink of spiritual overload when we see that God is making known "the mystery of his will . . . that in the dispensation of the fulness of times he might gather together in one all things in Christ, both which are in heaven, and which are on earth." This verse epitomizes the literal theme of chapter 1 of Ephesians: Look what God has done for you and given to you! It is precious. It is gracious. It is awesome and magnificent and beyond description. It was determined in eternity past, based solely on God's grace and goodness, and delivered to you now.

In verse 8, wisdom and prudence show us how God delivered redemption to us. Wisdom not only speaks of skill and discernment but also of infinite goodness and grace. Wisdom is then coupled with prudence, which means "the most effective way to attain the desired end." As glorious as the riches of God's grace are, the method of how God brought all of this into being is equally glorious. With incredible skill and goodness He used the most beneficial and effective path to forge our redemption.

A tremendous illustration of this point can be found in the state of Nevada. There we find a monument to the creative genius of man called the Hoover Dam. It is so big you can see it from an airplane five miles above the ground. When you visit the Hoover Dam, the tour guide first allows you to gaze upon this great marvel that restrains and controls the flow of trillions of tons of water. It is awesome to behold. After you take in all that splendor, the guide takes you to a presentation room, where you view a documentary about the construction of the dam.

People who watch the movie are spellbound as they see and hear how the dam was built. For you see, as majestic as the Hoover Dam is in its final state, the way they built it is just as superb and awe-inspiring. Likewise, in verse 8, Paul says that as precious as our redemption is, God has chosen to reveal not only the fact that we are redeemed but the manner in which we were redeemed. We are incited to worship God not only because of what He did for us but how He did it.

Prudence is applying wisdom to any circumstance or situation. Prudence is the outworking of wisdom. It is wisdom appropriated and applied to the practical situations and circumstances of life. There is no problem God cannot solve, no situation He cannot deal with.

Wisdom and prudence lie at the heart of all of our human capabilities. It is wonderful to possess great physical strength, but we must know when and how to use it to be effective in the kingdom of God. Prudence takes wisdom and employs knowledge as God desires, developing intellectual capacity but also walking in good sense. Wisdom and prudence harvest and develop talent for God's glory and purposes.

## THE MYSTERY OF GOD'S WILL

**Having made known unto us the mystery of his will, according to his good pleasure which he hath purposed in himself: That in the dispensation of the fulness of times he might gather together in one all things in Christ, both which are in heaven, and which are on earth; even in him.**
**—Ephesians 1:9–10**

As we examine this passage, we see that verse 10 describes the mystery of God's will mentioned in verse 9. The mystery referred to here is that Jesus Christ is the reconciler. At the perfect time, as God purposed in himself from before the foundation of the world, all things in heaven and earth will one be in Christ. The mystery that is now being revealed to us is this: Jesus Christ is the place of reconciliation.

Now the word *dispensation* must not be confused with the Christian doctrine that there are specific time periods in which God works in certain ways: the Dispensation of Grace, the Dispensation of Human Government, etc. The word translated *dispensation* here technically means "house rule or law." Its applied meaning is "administration, management, or stewardship."

It pleased God to share with us the mystery, the concealed details of His will, which were before this time unavailable to us. The mystery of His will essentially is Jesus Christ reconciling God to man. The specifics of the "mystery of his will" are how Jesus administrates or dispenses the will of God as the reconciler.

"The fulness of times" refers to the moment in time when the work of Jesus Christ is fully accomplished. In that work, Jesus reconciles the estranged parties, God and sinful man. The reconciliation spoken of here is both comprehensive and powerful. God had a solution to the problem of sin all along, but He didn't reveal His solution—Jesus Christ—until the fullness of times.

The mystery of God's will is not His will concerning our personal lives, but His will for the future of all mankind. His will for us is always embedded in that larger and more comprehensive will.

## GOD'S INHERITANCE

In whom *[Christ Jesus]* also we have obtained an inheritance, be-ing predestinated according to the purpose of him who worketh all things after the counsel of his own will.
**—Ephesians 1:11 (brackets mine)**

A careful study of the phrase "obtained an inheritance" reveals that the Greek language reads quite differently from the King James translation. Literally, as we are in Christ, we have not "obtained an inheritance," but we have been *made* an inheritance, "being predes-tinated [before encircled] according to the purpose of him [God the Father]." At this point, our hands and hearts must rise up to wor-ship the God who has repeatedly told us and revealed to us that we are His precious chosen ones. At the death of His Son, God marked us as His personal inheritance!

Verse 11 then goes on to say that our great God "worketh all things after the counsel of his own will." Every step of the way, every day, and in countless ways, God is working all things in our lives toward the glorious future He has planned for us. He is con-tinually working *all* things—not some things, not a few things, but *all* things—to the point where we will know, receive, and live within the fullness of all He has for us in Christ Jesus.

What does it mean for God to "work" all things? It means He is constantly manipulating, moving, maneuvering, and arranging all things according to His purposes. Things don't happen at random in our lives. They don't happen because of coincidence. God is at work, bringing about His purposes. If we are experiencing tribula-tion, we must glory in it! Tribulation works patience, and patience, experience, and experience, hope, and hope dispels all shame. (See Romans 5:3–5.) God is in the process of taking the worst things imaginable and turning them for great good in our lives. Circum-stances may not seem good at times, but look at the hand that is be-hind those circumstances, "working" those circumstances!

We must hear the Lord speaking to our spirits, "I'm working it out. Don't judge yet. The final conclusion hasn't been revealed yet. I'm not through yet. Just keep looking at the master blueprint of my will."

"That we should be to the praise of his glory, who first trusted in Christ" (Ephesians 1:12). As God is working all things for the highest and greatest good of all, we who have trusted in Christ should live to the praise of His glory. We are incited to continuously praise and worship and glorify Him because we are His inheritance and He has everything in our lives worked out.

## UNDER CONSTRUCTION

**In whom ye also trusted, after that ye heard the word of truth, the gospel of your salvation: in whom also after that ye believed, ye were sealed with that holy Spirit of promise, which is the earnest of our inheritance until the redemption of the purchased possession, unto the praise of his glory.**
**—Ephesians 1:13–14**

We can trust God. Why? Because we have heard the word of truth—the Gospel—and believed. God's Word is absolutely trustworthy and we can be completely secure in Him. But this verse reveals another more authoritative verification that our trust in God is solid: We are sealed with the Holy Spirit. An example of this kind of seal is the stone that covered the tomb in which Jesus was laid. A seal could also be used to keep something secret. When God gave John a glimpse of the future in the book of the Revelation, aspects of what John saw were "sealed" and kept secret.

But in Ephesians 1:13, the word *seal* has a glorious meaning. This seal is a mark of identification. This mark denotes ownership and therefore protection. Even when standing in a crowd of people, the believer carries God the Father's mark of holy distinction.

"Nevertheless the foundation of God standeth sure, having this seal, the Lord knoweth them that are his" (2 Timothy 2:19). God knows those who are His. The seal He has placed on us attests, certifies, and acknowledges that we belong to God. Therefore, we enjoy His full protection. This protection covers the attacks the Enemy launches against our minds and against our lives.

I recently had some legal work done and had a notary public put his seal on the legal document I was signing. That seal authenticated the document. It showed that the document was legitimate and that my identity was verified. The Holy Spirit in us is the *seal of God* on our lives. He is the sign to the Devil that we belong to God and that we are authentically and indisputably God's. God's redemptive work in us is sealed, settled, complete, incontestable, and legitimate. Just as the Holy Spirit authenticated to Peter and the

Jewish believers that the Gentiles in Cornelius's house were legitimately God's in Acts 10:34–35, the Holy Spirit authenticates to the Devil, the world, and mankind that we are legitimately and irrevocably His.

The Devil sees and recognizes the seal of the Holy Spirit on our lives. In Acts 19:11–20, there were some men imitating Paul by using the name of Jesus to try to cast out a demon, but they were not believers. They didn't have the seal of the Holy Spirit. So the demon said to them, "Jesus I know, and Paul I know; but who are you?" and literally tore the clothes off their backs and ran them out of town!

I would strongly suggest to you that if you haven't truly given your life to Jesus Christ, if you have not been sealed by the Holy Ghost, but you have been going to church and playing some religious game, stop it right now and get right with God! Don't mess around with the name of Jesus and the power of God, because even the Devil recognizes what is legitimately and rightfully God's. You must have the powerful presence of the Holy Spirit in your life to be sealed and protected.

The text states that the Holy Spirit is also "the earnest of our inheritance" (Ephesians 1:14). The word *earnest* here means "first installment; deposit; down payment; pledge that pays a part of the purchase price in advance, and so secures a legal claim to the article in question or makes a valid contract."

This seal of the Holy Spirit is God's holy and solemn pledge that He will redeem us completely from everything that torments us and causes us concern—past, present, and future. The Holy Spirit is God's legal claim and His valid contract signifying that He is the author and finisher of our faith and will bring us into glory with Him. The Holy Spirit is God's investment in our future. He is our empowerer, our energizer and encourager, who assures us we are going to make it.

The down payment God gives to us must not be confused with the kind of down payment people place on houses or other property. It would be a perfect analogy if we never violated the spirit of that down payment. The concept is that our down payment should assure the seller that we fully intend to purchase the property in question. However, people routinely forfeit their down payment when they no longer have an interest in the property, or they write so many conditions into the contract that they nullify the power of their earnest money.

But it is not so with God! His down payment is a sure guarantee of more to come. Paul states that the earnest of the Holy Spirit is given to us "until the redemption of the purchased possession," or until our redemption is fully manifested. Our full redemption was purchased with the precious blood of Jesus Christ at Calvary, but the entire manifestation of that transaction will not be seen until we are in our resurrection bodies.

Have you ever been on a construction site? There is a point in the construction of any building when the entire project is in disarray. There's steel and block everywhere, dirt and sand in piles, everyone wearing hard hats and safety glasses, and the site looks like anything but a building. However, it doesn't matter how things look at that stage. The architect is there with his blueprint. He has a vision for what the place is going to look like when it's finished. It's coming together. Although it may be days, months, or years, the building is being built.

So it is with us. We may think we are a mess right now, and we may be! If the church is doing its work correctly, there should be lots of people who have been pulled from the messiest situations of sin imaginable and who are still in the process of being cleaned up. We are under construction! There's a purpose and plan behind all that is going on in our lives. Things are coming together. We are a magnificent temple of the Holy Spirit under construction!

The Holy Spirit is a sign to us that we have been sealed into eternal life and God's family and we belong to God. We are free in Christ Jesus and He is not going to abandon us. We are to stand on the fact that the Holy Spirit is working in us and through us and allow Him to show the love and power of God through us to others.

When the Devil comes against us, we should say, "I am accepted in the Beloved. I have been redeemed by the blood. I know I've been forgiven. I know to whom I belong and why. I'm under contract and I'm under construction. I have the seal of the Holy Spirit on my life and my life is hid in Christ with God. I live by the faith of the Son of God, who loved me and gave himself a ransom for me. It is in Him that I live and move and have my being."

If the Devil comes at me, I hit him with about twenty-five Scriptures and then I start praising God for the Holy Spirit in my life. The Holy Spirit is my seal of authentic ownership by God, and in the presence of that seal, the Devil can't touch me. It doesn't matter what I'm going through. My body might be sick, but my spirit has been sealed. My finances might be lacking, but my spirit has been sealed.

Everything I am and will become, everything I have and will have, and the glorious redemption in which I am sealed by the Holy Spirit are all for one purpose: to praise Him and glorify Him. Hallelujah!

# 8

# HOPE

Wherefore I also, after I heard of your faith in the Lord Jesus, and love unto all the saints, cease not to give thanks for
you, making mention of you in my prayers.
—Ephesians 1:15–16

The first chapter of Ephesians makes a turn in verse 15 when
Paul begins a very lengthy, fervent, and specific prayer for the
Ephesian congregation. Writing from his prison cell in Rome, he
says that from the moment he heard of their conversion, he unceas-
ingly offered thanksgiving to God for them and began praying for
them. The Ephesians are standing strong! They are growing. They
are manifesting faith in Jesus Christ and loving one another. And
this prayer speaks again of His intimate and loving relationship with
them. Then, in verse 17, he begins to tell them exactly what he is
praying for them and the church at large to receive.

## THE KNOWLEDGE OF HIM

That the God of our Lord Jesus Christ, the Father of glory, may
give unto you the spirit of wisdom and revelation in the knowledge of him.
—Ephesians 1:17

After introducing our masterful God, Paul makes the request to
the Father of glory to give His children "the spirit of wisdom and

revelation." Paul wants us to know our magnificent God in all His wisdom, which is gained by "knowledge of him." When we *know* the God of all wisdom, His wisdom becomes ours.

Many believers are quick to seek more of God's power and love, but few are quick to seek diligently for more wisdom, discernment, and understanding. The wisdom and revelation of God contain the wealth of the believer, because wisdom and revelation reveal God's will and His heart in any situation. If we know God, we will know His will and His heart.

**If any of you lack wisdom, let him ask of God, that giveth to all men liberally, and upbraideth not; and it shall be given him.**
**—James 1:5**

Liberally, abundantly, without reproach or recrimination, God desires to impart wisdom to us.

*Liberally* is freely and generously.

*Abundantly* is sufficiently and excessively.

*Without reproach or recrimination* is willingly and eagerly.

The Bible tells us plainly and repeatedly how valuable wisdom is to the believer.

**Wisdom is better than rubies; and all the things that may be desired are not to be compared to it. By *[wisdom]* kings reign, and princes decree justice. Riches and honour are with *[wisdom]*; yea, durable riches and righteousness. *[The fruit of wisdom]* is better than gold, yea, than fine gold; and *[the]* revenue *[of wisdom]* than choice silver. Blessed are they that keep *[the ways of wisdom]*. For whoso findeth *[wisdom]* findeth life, and shall obtain favour of the Lord.**
**—Proverbs 8:11, 15, 18–19, 32, 35, (brackets mine)**

God wants us to know Him because He knows that wisdom and revelation come with the knowledge of Him. And believers cannot fulfill their call and possess the joy of their salvation without wisdom and revelation. The key is knowing God.

Nothing is more wonderful than knowing God! I did not say knowing *about* God. Many people know about God, even those who don't believe in Jesus Christ. *Knowing* God is something entirely different! It is having an intimate, daily, walking-and-talking relationship with Him. Knowing God is experiencing His presence in us and moving through us at all times.

At one point in his life, Paul knew about God. He knew about Jesus of Nazareth, but he didn't believe in Jesus. He held the coats of those who stoned Stephen, one of the first deacons of the church. He zealously persecuted the first Christians and was openly out for their blood. But then, as he was on his way to Damascus to persecute the Christians there, he was blinded by a bright light that literally knocked him to the ground. He heard a voice saying to him, "Saul, Saul, why persecutest thou me?" And he answered, "Who art thou, Lord?" The Lord spoke back, "I am Jesus whom thou persecutest" (Acts 9:4–5). Later Paul would write:

**Yea doubtless, and I count all things but loss for the excellency of the knowledge of Christ Jesus my Lord.**
**—Philippians 3:8**

Nothing mattered to Paul. Nothing was of any worth or value or significance. All things were considered a loss to Him except knowing Jesus.

Paul was not an ignorant man. He spoke several languages, was affluent, intellectual, articulate, and a profound, prolific writer. He spoke clearly and zealously about what he believed. He was a man who could bring great order and structure to ideas. Of the tribe of Benjamin, the tribe from which kings had come, he was part of the Sanhedrin, the ruling body of Judaism. He was a man to be respected, but when he *knew* Jesus, nothing else mattered.

Paul's prayer was that the Ephesians would *know* God as He really is. He knew that if they came to the knowledge of Him, nothing else would matter to them. Their love for God would multiply. When we love someone, we can never know them enough. We are always wanting to grow in the knowledge of them. Although we can never know God fully, it is nevertheless our lifelong pursuit. He always has more wisdom to impart, more of His presence to bestow, more of His power to grant, and more of His love to pour into our hearts.

I have met people who know Greek and Hebrew. They know church history, church protocol, doctrine, and theology. The question is, "Do they know God?" If they know Him, all of the rest falls into line and is of less importance. Knowing God is the greatest "knowing" of all, and the good news to every Christian is that we can know Him. He desires to reveal himself to us!

Do you *know* Jesus today?

Do you desire to know Him even more?

## ENLIGHTENMENT

**The eyes of your understanding being enlightened; that ye may know what is the hope of his calling, and what the riches of the glory of his inheritance in the saints.**
**—Ephesians 1:18**

Imagine you are in a totally dark room when someone turns on a flashlight. The picture of that flashlight dispelling the darkness by its light describes the word *enlightened*. The tense of the verb suggests that we have been enlightened and continue to be so in the present. It is a continual process of being exposed to the illumination of God's work and will.

In every area of darkness in our lives, whether the darkness of memories in the past or darkness about things with which our minds continue to struggle, the Lord's light can shine and give us understanding. Paul prays that even in the darkest cellar of the souls of the Ephesians, in the nooks and crevices of their minds and emotions, the light of God's truth will shine.

Where the truth of God's light shines, He manifests His power. When God's light shines, His presence is felt, His power begins to flow, and change occurs. So whatever our understanding may be of a situation, a relationship, or an experience, if we pray for God's truth to illuminate our understanding, we will know all we need to know.

The work of the Holy Spirit is a work of renewal. We have to change our old habits, whether physical, emotional, or mental, into new habits that line up with the Word of God. This renewal process begins with God's light of truth shining on our understanding. It is a process in which we come into greater revelation and knowledge about what it means to be in Christ and to have the Holy Spirit dwelling in us.

Please note that *renewing* is not the same as revising or making something better. Renewing is actually causing something to become new and different, with the implication of its being superior to what was there before. The concept is analogous to being a new creature in Christ Jesus. Our spirit is not improved or cleaned up when we are born again. Our spirit is made completely new by the power of the Holy Spirit.

Having our minds renewed or made completely new by God's Word and the illumination of the Holy Spirit is extremely important to us because the transition from being in the world to being in the kingdom of God is a drastic one. The principles and procedures of the kingdom are very different from those we were accustomed to in the world. And when we have been used to doing something a certain way and are instructed to change that habit, we need assurance and direction.

We need to know that the new methods and procedures will work for us, and God gave us that assurance by displaying His great power when He saved us. If He was loving and gracious enough to save us out of Satan's grasp and the kingdom of darkness, how much more will He do for us now that we are His children? At this revelation, our eyes seek to be enlightened and we are exposed to more and more of the glorious work of Jesus Christ. Our faith is strengthened and expanded. We discover that the more we know God, the more we trust Him in situations we have not experienced before and circumstances that have intimidated us in the past. Our faith soars and our confidence in Him becomes steadfast and immovable.

Do you know your purpose in life today? Ask the Lord to enlighten your understanding.

Do you know why certain things are happening to you today? Ask the Lord to enlighten your understanding.

Do you know the source of turmoil behind certain circumstances or situations? Ask the Lord to enlighten your understanding.

Are you depressed, troubled, or worried today? Ask the Lord to enlighten your understanding.

God wants you to know Him so that you can know how to deal with any given situation in life. He has chosen to reveal to you what unbelievers cannot know and what the prophets of old were not allowed to know. (See 1 Peter 1:12.) What is even more fascinating is that the phrase "that ye may know" is not meant to suggest an academic knowing or a self-help knowing. The word in the original Greek text does not mean "to possess information about," but rather "to be intimately acquainted with, to stand in a close relation to something." God wants you to be intimately acquainted with "the hope of his calling, and what [are] the riches of the glory of his inheritance in the saints."

## LIFE WITHOUT END

To hope is to believe God has prepared a future for us. Not only have we been chosen for a purpose in the here and now, not only are we loved, redeemed, forgiven, and given access to unlimited wisdom and revelation, but we have been given the great gift of eternity! As believers in Christ Jesus, our future stretches into forever. Our life has no end.

**For I know the thoughts that I think toward you, saith the Lord, thoughts of peace, and not of evil, to give you an expected end.**
**—Jeremiah 29:11**

In the New King James Version, this verse concludes, "to give you a future and a hope."

God's plan for us doesn't end in this lifetime.

God's purposes for us are not bound to this earth.

God has an eternal plan and purpose for our lives.

The more we see Jesus, and the more our understanding is enlightened by Him, the greater our hope for the future. Why? Because we realize that Jesus is in our future as much as He is in our present. The more we know Jesus, the more we are going to recognize that we cannot fail in this life, because God has destined us for eternal life with Him.

The great comfort we receive from hope lies in the fact that we are never going to be alone or without purpose, provision, or life. We are in Christ now and forever. And once that understanding comes to us, we are going to be more and more willing to perform great exploits for the kingdom of God.

We are going to dare to be who God created us to be.

We are going to dare to speak the name of Jesus in every situation and in every circumstance of our lives.

We are going to dare to manifest the Holy Spirit to a greater extent as we carry out our daily responsibilities.

The more we walk in the hope of our calling in Christ Jesus the more we will be bold to use the power God gives us. Hope allows us to take the risks necessary to accomplish great things, receive His blessings, and have great influence in bringing others to Jesus Christ.

# 9

# POWER

Wherefore I also, after I heard of your faith in the Lord Jesus, and love unto all the saints, cease not to give thanks for you, making mention of you in my prayers; that the God of our Lord Jesus Christ, the Father of glory, may give unto you the spirit of wisdom and revelation in the knowledge of him: The eyes of your understanding being enlightened; that ye may know what is the hope of his calling, and what the riches of the glory of his inheritance in the saints.
—Ephesians 1:15–18

Paul is praying for us to receive all wisdom and revelation as we grow in the knowledge of God, for the light to expand in our hearts and minds so we might grasp the reality of our hope in God's eternal plan and purpose for our lives. Then when we think our souls will burst with the vastness of all God has provided for us, we are bombarded with powerful words.

## FIVE WORDS TO PACK A PUNCH

And what is the exceeding greatness of his power to us-ward who believe, according to the working of his mighty power.
—Ephesians 1:19

In verse 19 alone, Paul uses five different words to describe the vast power of God that is placed at our disposal as His children. The word translated *exceeding* depicts something that is far beyond our wildest expectations. It is the greatness of God's power. The first *power* mentioned refers to "inherent power"—power that it is in our possession but dependent on our releasing it or activating it.

The Hoover Dam is a wall of concrete that controls the flow of trillions of tons of water. When all of the outlets are closed, the dam continues to have the potential to unleash a massive body of water into the Colorado River. It is an inherent power waiting to be released. Paul says the inherent power of God is beyond our imagining!

Immediately after Paul gives us a glimpse of the vast potential power we possess in Christ Jesus he mentions "the working of his mighty power." Here the word *working* is the word from which we derive the word *energy*. It speaks of energy—His mighty power—that is being expended, exercised, and put into full operation.

Mighty power here means raw strength, literally an endowment of physical prowess. His power is made available toward us "who believe." All of those who come through the door of faith have access to the full and exceeding greatness and limitlessness of God's power!

God has unlimited resources, enduring that we can do all that He has called us to do. He has unlimited capacity for taking us from where we are to where He desires us to be.

## RESURRECTION POWER

**And what is the exceeding greatness of his power to us-ward who believe, according to the working of his mighty power, which he wrought in Christ, when he raised him from the dead, and set him at his own right hand in the heavenly places.**
**—Ephesians 1:19–20**

In the Old Testament, the "exceeding greatness" of God's power was manifested when He parted the Red Sea and the Israelites were saved from the armies of Pharaoh. Even today in the Passover celebration, God reminds the Jews of His power by saying, "Am I not the God who brought you across the Red Sea?" It was in crossing the Red Sea that they were supernaturally delivered from their enemy.

For the believer, the "exceeding greatness" of God's power is displayed in the resurrection of Jesus Christ from the dead. These verses say that God wrought His power in Christ at the resurrection. *Wrought* here means "to actively prove oneself strong." God not only proved himself strong at the resurrection of Jesus, He proved himself stronger than any force or being in the universe! It is because of the resurrection that we are delivered from Satan, the power of death, and evil. When Jesus rose from the dead, taking the sting from death and victory from the grave, He proved forever that He is the Lord of *all* things.

As the Jews refer again and again to their deliverance from Egypt at the parting of the Red Sea, Christians must never tire of recalling the resurrection of Jesus Christ.

It is the resurrection that assures us of our salvation.

It is in the resurrection that we have our greatest hope—eternal life.

It is the resurrection that reveals the fullness of the power of God toward us.

It is in recalling the resurrection that our faith in God is made secure.

Is there any power greater than the power to restore life to something that is dead?

Resurrection power is made available to us!

Let this truth about God's power sink deep into your spirit. What seems dead to you today that God desires to be alive and whole? Your marriage? Your professional life? Your credit rating? Your creativity? Your witness for God?

God brings dead things to life as surely as He brought Jesus back to life. He restores them to wholeness and endows them with eternal purpose. God not only gives life, but He also gives new meaning to life. He gives us eternal purpose.

## ULTIMATE AUTHORITY

Which he wrought in Christ, when he raised him from the dead, and set him at his own right hand in the heavenly places, far above all principality, and power, and might, and dominion, and every name that is named, not only in this world, but also in that which is to come: and hath put all things under his feet, and gave him to be the head over all things to the church, which is his body, the fulness of him that filleth all in all.
**—Ephesians 1:20–23**

When God resurrected Jesus from the dead, He sat Him at His right hand, in the place of all authority. It is one thing to understand and know about the power of God, but it is quite another to have the authority to use it and operate in His power. God seated Jesus at His right hand to symbolize that all power was now subject to the authority of Jesus, His Son.

Paul lists the specific powers and authorities over which Jesus has rule:

**Principalities:** Spirit beings, either angelic or demonic, who have rulership.

**Powers:** The powers that principalities or spiritual leaders wield.

**Might:** Inherent power.

**Dominion:** Rule over territories.

**Every name:** "Every name that is named . . . in this world [and] in that which is to come."

The bully down the street may have a reputation for being tough in your neighborhood, but he is still subject to the name of Jesus!

The celebrities of this world may think they have it all under their control, but they are still subject to the authority of Jesus!

The angelic host of heaven (one angel alone slew the entire army of Sennacherib, the enemy of Israel, in one night—2 Kings 19:35) are subject to the authority of Jesus!

Even the named angels in the Bible—Gabriel and Michael—are subject to the name of Jesus!

No matter how famous or infamous someone is, all are subject to the authority and power of Jesus Christ. Name any form of power or might in the natural realm or in the spirit realm—satanic forces, angelic beings, military might, terrorists, assassins, diseases, plagues, explosive devices, weather patterns, geological formations—and God's power is greater. Not only every form of influence, power, or authority; but every human being and every material object in creation is subject to God's resurrection power.

**And hath put all things under his feet, and gave him to be the head over all things to the church, which is his body, the fulness of him that filleth all in all.**
**—Ephesians 1:22–23**

Paul uses a very forceful word for "hath put." It literally means "to set things in order." God has not only made every person and every thing subject to the authority of Jesus Christ; He has set us in order by His authority. Everyone and everything in the created world is under the authority of, and is set in order by, Jesus Christ.

The problems you may be having with your family are under His feet.

The problems in your career are under His feet.

The corruption all around you is under His feet.

Paul also reminded the Ephesians that God "gave him to be the head over all things to the church." He is the sum total of the whole equation of life and all things related to the church. When everything is added up, the answer is "Jesus." God has given Jesus as a gift to the church. We are the most privileged class of people ever assembled in the history of mankind because we have as our leader and head the Lord Jesus Christ.

In Jesus Christ, no weapon formed against us shall prosper!

In Jesus Christ, we have authority over all the power of the Enemy!

In Jesus Christ, we are locked into the limitless, universe-shaking power of God!

# 10

# CONCLUSION:
# ALL IN ALL

---

**And hath put all things under his feet, and gave him to be the head over all things to the church, which is his body, the fulness of him that filleth all in all.**
**—Ephesians 1:22–23**

Ephesians 1:23 is a revelation of the relationship between Jesus as the Head of the church and the church as His body. This Scripture sums up all the wealth we have in Christ Jesus. In the natural human being, the head always commands the body, but in the spiritual reality of the body of Christ, Jesus is much more than our commander. He is our life! His life literally flows through us as He guides and directs us and we submit to His will. In every sense, we are one.

"The fulness of him that filleth all in all" means that the fullness of Jesus fills the church. He is continually being to us all that we need. He completes us with His love, moves us by His compassion, directs us with His wisdom, and empowers us with authority.

Jesus is everything a human being could ever dream of, hope for, or desire.

He is God's grace and glory expressed toward us and through us.

Through Him all spiritual blessings are poured into our lives.

In Him we are chosen, predestined, made holy, without blame, accepted, redeemed, forgiven.

In Him the mystery of God's eternal will and purpose is made known.

In Him we are God's personal treasure and inheritance, sealed by the Holy Spirit.

In Him we grow in the knowledge of God to possess His wisdom and revelation.

In Him the eyes of our understanding are enlightened, our eternal hope and calling made sure.

In Him we have authority over every evil force that opposes God and His children.

Jesus is the one who fills all in all. Jesus uses all the resources of heaven and earth to fill us to overflowing: spiritually, mentally, emotionally, socially, and physically. There is nothing He cannot and will not do to see His body succeed.

After studying Ephesians, chapter 1, we cannot doubt we are wealthy beyond any earthly concept. There is no amount of money equal to our redemption, eternal life, and all our spiritual blessings. God placed a value upon all this wealth: He deemed it worthy of the blood of Jesus. And so the Lamb was slain from the foundations of the world. He was given for us because for some incredible, unfathomable reason, God wanted you and me.

# PART TWO

*Experiencing Jesus*

# Introduction

From the moment we are conceived, we have a built-in desire to run the world around us so that it benefits us and serves us. Let's face it: We are all born with a self-centered, me-first identity. We emerge from the womb a crybaby, our sole purpose being to see that every whim, desire, and need is fulfilled by those who have obviously been placed in our lives to accomplish this. In our eyes, the world revolves around *us*.

The description I have just given is the essence of the sin nature. There is not one sin we can name that cannot be labeled selfish and self-centered. Furthermore, original sin is addressed in the first commandment, which contains the antidote to the sin nature:

**Thou shalt have no other gods before me.**
**—Exodus 20:3**

God's purpose for our lives is that instead of a me-first identity, we have a God-first identity. We are to step off the throne of our hearts and give God full rule and reign in our lives. We are to raise our hands in complete surrender to the truth that our well-being, fulfillment, and happiness are totally dependent upon our relationship with Him

Pride says, "I am the ruler of my own life. I make myself."

Humility says, "God is the ruler of my life. He makes me."

God's Word says:

**We are his workmanship, created in Christ Jesus unto good works.**
**—Ephesians 2:10**

*The issue of God's workmanship in our lives is that it goes against our pride!*

Imagine a carpenter looking at the architect's blueprints for a large building project and saying, "Well, that's all good and fine, but I think I'll add a wall over here and remove a wall over there and build a wing onto the building over there. Nobody will know. I'll just add the plumbing and wiring and air-conditioning and heating ducts as I go along. Forget what the architect designed. It's what I want to do."

That carpenter would be removed from the project immediately, and anything he had built according to his own design would be torn down and put in the trash pile. The same principle applies to God's workmanship in our lives. He has the best plan. He sees the end from the beginning and all the battles and obstacles in between. All of our efforts must be in line with His plan for our lives to achieve the maximum joy, purpose, and function.

One of the most important lessons any believer or any body of believers can learn is this: We do not make ourselves. *God makes us.* And when God makes us, He does the full deal! There is no detail too minuscule or crisis too big that He does not provide for our complete redemption from everything that is evil in this life.

Consider Abraham, who had a close encounter of the God kind.

**Now the Lord had said unto Abram, Get thee out of thy country, and from thy kindred, and from thy father's house, unto a land that I will show thee: And I will make of thee a great nation, and I will bless thee, and make thy name great; and thou shalt be a blessing: And I will bless them that bless thee, and curse him that curseth thee: and in thee shall all families of the earth be blessed.**

**—Genesis 12:1–3**

There were seven things God promised Abraham in this passage of Scripture, and one of those was greatness. God said, "I will make your name great." When we first consider that promise, we leap with glee, as most of us desire to be great. However, God's idea of greatness and our idea of greatness may be completely different. For instance, we often think of great men as being wealthy men. But what made Abraham a great man was not necessarily his extensive wealth, although God gave him great wealth. We also think of men who have accomplished supernatural feats as being great. But it might not have been Abraham's ability to sire sons past his productive years, although God gave him that ability, which made him great. Perhaps it wasn't even the fact that he controlled masses of wealth and land, was the guest of noblemen, and was the personal friend to kings in various countries that made Abraham great.

No, if we were to attempt to locate Abraham's greatness, it would probably be more aptly placed in his great faith in God. Called from the Gentile, moon-worshiping country of Ur, Abraham heard God's voice in the wind and had the sensitivity and ability to see the invisible and do the impossible. In any case, whatever the measuring device God uses to determine greatness, the issue for us today is: *Who* made Abraham great?

Why is this such an important question? Because it hits at the heart of the Gospel: God's workmanship, not our workmanship, in our lives. We did not call our names out from before the foundation of the world, create ourselves, and when we fell, provide ourselves with the way of salvation. Neither did we provide the blueprint for our lives. What causes most of us to err and build monuments to our own vanity is that we have a low tolerance for delayed gratification. We do not want to wait on God to make us great. Like Satan, who said his five "I wills" to God in a rebellious declaration of eternal independence (see Isaiah 14:13–14), we say to God, "You don't have to make me great, I will." For some reason, we really believe we can do it faster and better than God. Oh, the illogical pride of man!

It is that self-imposed, egotistical inclination to exalt oneself that causes us to build walls, churches, companies, and countless other self-designed projects that are not on God's original blueprints or His divine specification sheet. And it is because of this that many believers today are experiencing the painful results of being a public success and a private failure. Without faith or patience, they have forsaken God's plan and promise for their lives and turned to their own thinking, when God's plan for them is far beyond their wildest dreams and creativity.

If we have any doubt of the veracity of God's love and faithfulness toward us, our study of Ephesians, chapter 1—"Loved by God"—will dispel it. Now, in Ephesians 2, the apostle Paul launches into a rich and vivid description of the direct impact Ephesians 1—

# 1

# WE WERE DEAD

How long has it been since you heard a saint of God glowingly and passionately express their gratitude that God saved them and delivered them from eternal darkness and damnation? If that is all God ever did for us, we have reason to shout and rejoice for the rest of our lives! To comprehend the incredible miracle we have experienced through our new life in Jesus Christ, the apostle Paul begins the second chapter of Ephesians reminding us how despicable and ugly and dark our lives were before the light of Christ made us new and clean and free. We must never forget how our Lord and Savior delivered us from the terrible abyss of spiritual death!

## DEATH IS SEPARATION

**And you hath he quickened, who were dead in trespasses and sins; wherein in time past ye walked according to the course of this world, according to the prince of the power of the air, the spirit that now worketh in the children of disobedience: Among whom also we all had our conversation in times past in the lusts of our flesh, fulfilling the desires of the flesh and of the mind; and were by nature the children of wrath, even as others.**
**—Ephesians 2:1–3**

We were *dead* in our trespasses and sins. Obviously, because we were still walking around on this earth, *dead* is referring to spiritual death, not physical death.

The Greek word for *dead* here can mean either the death of the body or the death of the spirit. The word lends itself to the graphic picture of a lifeless, colorless body on a slab in the morgue with the stench of decay surrounding it.

Generally in the church today we are taught that before we were born again, we were spiritually dead. But for the Ephesians and for many of us who did not grow up in church, it is startling to hear that before we accepted Jesus as Lord and Savior, we were dead. When the Bible talks about death, however, it is not talking about the cessation of life, but separation.

In the case of physical death, the Bible means the separation of the spirit from the body. Death is not the cessation of life in the sense of existence, but the move from one state of being to another. When a person dies and their spirit separates from their body, their spirit will continue to live somewhere, either in heaven or in hell. We thank God that as Christians, to be separated from the body is to be present with the Lord! (See 2 Corinthians 5:8.) When we die and our spirits separate from our bodies, we go to heaven.

To take this a step further, at the point of death, when the spirit separates from the physical body, that body can no longer relate to or function on earth. In like manner, the spirit that is dead is separated from God and cannot relate to or function in the kingdom of God. This state of being spiritually dead is due to our being in trespasses and sins. Sin separates us from God spiritually and silences our soul.

Moreover, Paul tells us that *we were dead* in our trespasses and sins. All of us! We were walking around, thinking, talking, and breathing in trespasses and sins. When we were spiritually dead, we may have acknowledged God, but we had no intimate knowledge of Him. We were dead to Him and separated from Him because of our trespasses and sins. This is because God cannot have association with sin. He cannot coexist with something He hates, something utterly opposed to His nature, character, and vision. It is impossible for a holy and righteous God to coexist with unholy, unrighteous man in the same way it is impossible for light to allow darkness in a room. He loves the sinner and wants us to come to a state of holiness and wholeness in Him.

It was God's love for all of us sinners that provided the remedy for our sin: Jesus, who was without sin, *became* sin on the cross, gave His life and spilt His blood to pay our debt of sin and make a way for us to become right with God. (See Romans 5:17.) But before we accepted this gracious gift of salvation, God could not have intimate fellowship with us, as we were dead and walked in the darkness of our own thoughts and ways.

## TWO EVIL FACILITATORS

Paul purposely causes us to look back to the time before we were saved, before we were quickened and made alive by the Holy Spirit. He says, "Do you recognize that we were dead—walking around dead, buying property dead, going to school dead, getting married dead, and having children dead?" We were really not living at all. That's why we were driven to so many different things to try to make us feel alive. We tried to buy life in a bottle or capture it in a drug. We gave all our efforts to a career in hopes that fortune and fame would fill our inner cravings for fulfillment. We tried to find life in a relationship or a series of relationships, or having sex with anyone who would have us.

**Wherein in time past ye walked according to the course of this world, according to the prince of the power of the air, the spirit that now worketh in the children of disobedience.**
**—Ephesians 2:2**

In this verse of Scripture, "according to" can also have the connotation of moving downward, of being caught in a downward spiral. Paul is reminding us emphatically that when we were dead in trespasses and sins, everything opposed to God continually worked upon us to pull us down, force us under, make us sink lower and lower, and drive us farther and farther away from God.

When I think of the English word *according,* I think of the musical term *chord.* A chord is a group of notes that are combined because of their ability to resonate a harmonious sound. Each note is harmonious with the others, and the sound is pleasant to the ear. When we were in harmony with a fallen world, going in the same direction and producing a tone that flowed with the world system, Paul says we walked according to the course of this world. His statement implies that we were in complete harmony with Satan's thinking, nature, and deeds.

Salvation and the very name of Jesus Christ is a dissonant sound to the world system and destroys the continuity of the satanic chord. When we are born again, we begin to sing and love and live in harmony with God's kingdom. The plan for our life becomes His plan and we hook up with His eternal purposes. Therefore, we become a strange, irritating noise to those who are still in concert with the world.

To keep us in harmony with them, the world and satanic forces had one objective from the time we were born: to keep us from receiving Jesus Christ as Lord and Savior. And each second we were dead in trespasses and sins, they drove us to become more and more depraved.

First, we walked according to or were being dominated by the course of this world. In whatever course, whatever lane, or whatever channel the world was going, that's where we were going. You see, just as God's kingdom has ways and rules and principles by which it operates, so does the evil world that opposes Him. A simple example is that while God's kingdom runs on faith, the world system runs on fear. If you read the Bible, you will be filled with faith, but turn on the television or talk to your unsaved neighbors for a while and you will probably be filled with dread and discouragement. The world system floods the earth with negativity, hopelessness, and intimidation.

Another clear distinction is that God's kingdom runs on purity and holiness, but the world system runs on lust and uncleanness (sexual perversion). If you read the Bible, you will be made clean and whole, but go to the movies or a magazine stand in an airport and you will probably be bombarded by filth. The exclusive one-flesh, for-marriage-only, between-a-man-and-a-woman-only sexual relationship according to the Bible is rarely modeled and displayed in the world. According to the world, everybody who's anybody can have sex with anyone they desire because the world encourages an animalistic view of mankind.

Then there is a very subtle and often more evil flip side to this immoral, amoral, and depraved worldly lifestyle. The world system can also keep people away from the saving grace of Jesus Christ by convincing them they are doing "good" and are inherently "good," which is worse!

**But we are all as an unclean thing, and all our righteousnesses are as filthy rags; and we all do fade as a leaf; and our iniquities, like the wind, have taken us away.**
**—Isaiah 64:6**

When you are in the gutter of sin and depravity you have some idea that you need to be saved! But when you think you're "all that," in church every Sunday, leading the Boy Scouts on Tuesday, and feeding the homeless on Saturday, you are clueless! You have been thoroughly deceived by your good works to believe you are so good that God would never deny you admission into heaven.

It is in this evil flip side that we find the "religious folk." You know who I'm talking about! They look the look and talk the talk and may even seem to walk the walk, but they don't *know* God. Inside they are as dead as the prostitute on the street or the junkie in the alley. The problem is, they don't see it because they are "good folk." Thinking we are good in ourselves is the greatest deception of all, because we do not see our desperate need for God and salvation.

Whether the manifestation of spiritual death is in "good" or evil, the world system is opposed to God's kingdom. We also walked according to the prince of the power of the air, under the dominion of Satan and his demonic forces. The Greek word translated *prince* refers to a person or being who is the first one in order of authority, or the leader. Satan's territory is "the air," which most commentators agree is the atmosphere where human beings live. Satan's power is limited and he operates only as the god of this world, but we should never underestimate his power!

While we were dead in trespasses and sins, Satan was our spiritual master. His demons were in the air around us, programming us to oppose God, resist Jesus, and walk according to the course of this world. They drove us to waste our lives thinking we were "good," or destroy ourselves and take others with us in evil. The Bible tells us that demons operate primarily through our thoughts. That's what I meant when I said that they program us from the time we are born. Many times what we think is our own thinking is really demonic. Consider the following three examples of "good" and "evil" thought patterns:

"I can get anything I want" or "I'll never get what I want."

"I'm the best-lookin' thing this world has seen in a long time, and I can have anyone I want" or "I'm so ugly, no one will ever love me."

"I've got what it takes to do anything, and I know I can climb any ladder to success" or "I'm just stupid, and I'll be lucky to get any kind of job."

There are two extremes of satanic thought: For those who Satan knows are prone to be easily discouraged and put down, he repeatedly introduces thoughts of being slighted, ugly, and stupid. For those who he knows are inclined to be very independent and self-assured, he encourages pride and independence from God by telling them they are the best, brightest, and most beautiful.

The Devil and his demons enforce the values and principles of the world system in the lives of spiritually dead individuals—and such were we all! If it meant making us happy and successful and feeling good about ourselves to keep us from God, that's how the Devil tried to program our thinking. If it meant keeping us in the ghetto—angry, bitter, and blaming everybody but ourselves for our misery—that's what the Devil ordered for us. Anything to keep us from Jesus!

## CHILDREN OF DISOBEDIENCE

**Wherein in time past ye walked according to the course of this world, according to the prince of the power of the air, the spirit that now worketh in the children of disobedience: Among whom also we all had our conversation in times past in the lusts of our flesh, fulfilling the desires of the flesh and of the mind; and were by nature the children of wrath, even as others.**
**—Ephesians 2:2–3**

There was a spirit working in us before we were made new by the blood of Jesus Christ, and that spirit epitomized all that the world system and the Devil were about. We were children of disobedience, and *disobedience* is the principle word here. It means to be totally incompliant and unpersuadable. An illustration of this from the Old Testament is when the children of Israel were called *stiff-necked*. They turned their backs on God, worshiped idols, did their own thing, and the Word of God fell on deaf ears. They could not be persuaded to listen and were not willing to submit to God's Word.

Writing to the Romans, Paul gives another clear description of "children of disobedience" when he describes sinners as being consumed with "uncleanness through the lusts of their own hearts," filled with "vile affections," having a "reprobate mind," and existing in "all unrighteousness." (See Romans 1:24–31.)

Before we were born again, among the children of disobedience in times past, we had our conversation, or lived a lifestyle, by the "lusts of our flesh, fulfilling the desires of the flesh and of the mind." We tried to bring ourselves to life in our flesh! We purchased all kinds of things in hopes that they would make us happy and fulfilled. We drank this, injected that, smoked this, took that pill—just to feel alive. Or we exercised, worked out, took our vitamins, ate healthy, and drank bottled water to feel whole and good about ourselves.

In Romans, chapter 1, Paul talks about the final, most terrible state a human being can be in—one of the worst judgments to be decreed upon us—when God gives us over to our own passions and lusts! We become prisoners of our insatiable cravings, striving to fulfill whatever the mind conjures up to satisfy our flesh. That's a bottomless pit called human depravity. If there were no devil, and the world were a godly place, we would still cry, "O God, save me from myself! Don't leave me to merely fulfill the desires of my flesh!"

**For as by one man's disobedience many were made sinners, so by the obedience of one shall many be made righteous.**
**—Romans 5:19**

The Bible tells us that as sons and daughters of Adam, we were born with a nature to sin. Nobody had to teach little Johnny how to lie. He has not been listening to lying tapes. There have been no classes in preschool that teach how to lie. Inherent in his nature, under pressure, Johnny lies because it is in him. He is selfish, self-centered, and self-preserving in the very core of his being because he has a sin nature!

At first it sounds pretty good to fulfill the desires of our flesh. Hmmm. It seems to be a good thing that the mind responds to the mandates of the flesh, striving to fulfill our every whim and wish. But at the end of all the superficial intimacy, promiscuity, running from place to place, and sinking in the abyss of depravity, there's still that hollowness. We are somewhere down in the basement of our secret lusts and drives and cravings, and after each party's over, there's that little nagging, aching emptiness—not coming from the flesh or the mind, because the flesh is having a party and the mind is conjuring up new things! It's the spirit that's whispering, "But you're still empty."

## CHILDREN OF WRATH

Some of us engaged in all kinds of activities to feel more alive. We clamored for more possessions, more power, more experiences, more thrills, and more "highs." Others of us were driven to good works, running all over the place trying to help people and make ourselves feel useful and important. We involved ourselves in all kinds of relationships in the hope that being in love or having sex or having a baby would make us feel more alive. But in the end none of it ever worked. None of it lasted. None of it satisfied. Because none of it ever produced spiritual life!

When all the self-made efforts were over, there was still something missing in our innermost being; there was still a hollow feeling; something was "dead" inside. We were children of wrath. We were warring and seething against all that is holy and pure and self-less by serving the god of self, fulfilling every carnal desire and carrying out every natural inclination—good or evil.

In these three verses of Scripture, Ephesians 2:1–3, Paul has painted the darkest and ugliest picture of who we were and how we operated before Christ Jesus entered our lives. I believe the Holy Spirit wants us to grasp with intensity and passion the more-than-imaginable miracle we have experienced in the new birth, when we were liberated from the world system, satanic power, and the eternally dark abyss of our sin nature.

We cannot possibly appreciate the full weight and significance of God's first act of workmanship in our lives—redemption—without understanding what we have been redeemed from. We must never forget the terrible existence, the state of being dead in trespasses and sins, from which God redeemed us through the blood of Jesus Christ!

# 2

# HE QUICKENED US

Consider this phenomenon for a moment: We were dead in our trespasses and sins, controlled by the evil system of this world, under the influence and direction of Satan and demonic forces, driven by our carnal lusts and cravings—and yet we are saved today! How could this be? Satan was supernaturally powerful and much smarter than we were, the world system surrounded us from birth, and we were imprisoned in our carnal, sin nature—yet we somehow managed to escape its deathly grasp. How could this miracle have happened? We were not bright enough, strong enough, or good enough to figure this thing out. But God!

**But God, who is rich in mercy, for his great love wherewith he loved us, even when we were dead in sins, hath quickened us together with Christ, (by grace ye are saved).**
**—Ephesians 2:4–5**

But God! Here is a masterful manifestation of God's workmanship in our lives: the new birth, our glorious salvation. We had gone all the way down to the bottom. We had fallen off the bridge with the first man, Adam, had sunk all the way to the gates of hell with condemnation, and the gates of hell opened up their thirsty jaws to engulf us—but God! Paul is talking about the turning point away from human depravity. There is no other turning point away from human depravity but God.

There is nothing else to fill the emptiness of the human spirit *but God*.

There is no other solution for racial prejudice and injustice *but God*.

There is no other satisfaction for the craving of the flesh and lust *but God*.

There is no healing for the brokenhearted, lonely, and desperate *but God*.

There is no healing for the angry and frustrated *but God*.

There is no way to escape being just like your mother, your father, and your grandparents, and being subject to all of their curses, *but God*.

God's workmanship also brought us to the moment when we would accept Christ Jesus as our Savior and Lord. He didn't allow us to be aborted or miscarried! He didn't allow us to be stillborn, to die of crib death, or to be killed by any number of childhood accidents or diseases. He never took His hand off our lives. Even if we were abused or rejected as a child, God brought us through that experience alive and kept us from losing our sanity. He brought us to an understanding of Jesus Christ as our Savior and raised us up so that we could fulfill His purpose and reflect His glory in spite of every effort of the Devil to destroy us, diminish us, defame us, or discourage us.

The "but God" element in Ephesians is the breaking of the first and original generational curse. It is proof positive that God can break the downward spiral of a family of sin. Adam's sin caused the greatest and perhaps the only generational curse that matters. Had he produced a son before he fell into sin, he would have started the "chosen generation" that Jesus Christ ultimately established. But alas, it was in his fallen, degenerate state that his first two sons, Cain and Abel, were born. When Cain slew Abel, we saw the fruit of the already-operating downward spiral of sin, and you and I are members of the fallen family. We were born like all of Adam's sons—contaminated with the sin nature.

We were born dead, but God quickened us. The quickening Spirit of God fell upon us like a paramedic rushes to the scene of a crime, finding a world asphyxiated by its overindulgence and lacking the breath of God. From that moment, quickened and made alive forever, all the curses from our natural father, Adam, were broken. When Jesus went to the cross, He forever altered what had been the tragic saga of a fallen family. God had an unlimited over-abundance of mercy and chose to lavish it on us.

**For ye know the grace of our Lord Jesus Christ, that, though he was rich, yet for your sakes he became poor, that ye through his poverty might be rich.**
**—2 Corinthians 8:9**

## ALIVE TO GOD

There was that magnificent moment in time when everything came together and we recognized two truths simultaneously: We could not possibly fill the eternal cavern of emptiness within ourselves, but God could. At that point, which was for many of us a time of deepest despair or futility, we turned to receive the richness of His mercy and the greatness of His love. We surrendered our lives to Jesus Christ and God "quickened us together with Christ." Literally, God made our dead spirit alive with the same power with which He resurrected Jesus from the dead! Revelation 1:5 declares that Jesus was the *firstborn from the dead,* the first to be "quickened," or made alive.

When we were born again, the Spirit of God took up residence in us and quickened, or breathed His eternal life into, our dead spirit. Without God's Spirit, my spirit was dead, but when the Holy Spirit moved into my spirit, I became alive in the innermost parts of my being! My spirit became alive with the life of God! His Spirit and my spirit are now living in covenant relationship together. In Him I live and move and have my being, awareness, and consciousness.

The Spirit of God came into your heart, quickened you, and like a sleeping giant emerging out of a cave, you woke up and became aware of a God who was there all the time. When Jacob discovered God, he said, "God is present and I knew it not." (See Genesis 28:16.) Remember if you can, or consider right now, that moment when you first *felt* the presence of God in your life, when the Spirit of God bore witness with your spirit that you were His child and your heart cried, "Abba, Father!" Is there anything more exciting and fulfilling in life than being alive to God? If that was all there was to the new birth, it would be worth it! But God doesn't stop there.

At the same moment we are quickened by the Holy Spirit and made alive to God, we receive all the wealth and spiritual blessings Paul describes in Ephesians, chapter 1. Now, being alive to God, His Word comes alive and leaps off the pages into our hearts, and the Holy Spirit begins to whisper all the glorious realities of our new life in Christ. We are alive to the fullness of God:

- He chose us from before the foundation of the world to be holy and blameless before Him.
- He predestined us to be His precious adopted children because it pleased Him to do so.
- In His grace toward us, He made us accepted in the Beloved; no longer rejected.
- He gloriously redeemed us from being dead in our trespasses and sins; forgave us.
- He lavished upon us His abundance of wisdom and prudence so we could operate effectively.
- Because it was His pleasure to do so, He revealed to us the mystery of His will.
- He declared that we are His inheritance; we will bring Him nothing but praise and glory.
- He sealed us with the Holy Spirit, setting His mark upon us for all to see.

Is your heart not leaping out of your chest at the revelation of all you have been given as a child of God? You were quickened "together with Christ." In God's eyes, all those who are in Christ—past, present, future—are the body of Christ resurrected. When God resurrected Jesus from the grave, He resurrected all of us with Him. When we were quickened, all the wealth and spiritual blessings of Christ became ours. Hallelujah!

Now, wouldn't it be sad to work to give everything you have to your children and they not use what you gave them? It must be frustrating to God to go through what He did to empower us and enrich us and then watch us murmur and complain as if we didn't have anything. It must be hard for God to hear us pray for Him to do what He has already done, to see us wallow in problems that He's already given us power to overcome. We act as if our hands are tied, saying, "God, you've got to do something," when He already did it all two thousand years ago! This is the great love wherewith He has loved us. He didn't wait for us to cry for help. He anticipated our need and delivered us.

Federal Express brought a package to my house the other day and I wasn't home, so they left a note on the door that said, "We could not deliver." That doesn't mean they didn't have the package or that the person didn't send the package in the first place. It simply means that deliverance was not completed because I did not receive the package. Deliverance is when our wealthy God delivers a package to us and we receive what He has given. When we reach out and take hold of what God has done for us in the new birth, we surrender to His workmanship in our lives and our deliverance is complete.

Many times when people become Christians, one of the hardest things to do is to retrain them not to continue to operate according to the world system, the prince of the power of the air, and their old sin nature now that they're quickened in their spirit and alive to God. Like Israel, God delivered them out of Egypt, but it took years to get Egypt out of them. Often we come out of our past lives (see Ephesians 2:3) and find a new battle is taking place between the old man and the new man. Thank God, this is a battle He has given us the equipment and strength and wisdom to win!

That's why we need teaching like what we find in Ephesians. We must continually be challenged, awakened by God's Word and His Spirit that we are not dead anymore! God's very life has entered our inner man and quickened us. We don't have to operate in bondage to sin anymore. We don't have to respond to anger in a self-destructive manner. It's no longer necessary for us to get others "straightened out" and going our way. No more do we have to flip out on people and operate in our flesh. We can be free of our mother's temper and our father's rage and all of the things that operated in us because our spirit was dead. Because God has breathed into us the breath of life, we are no longer controlled by generational curses, the systems of this world, or our depraved flesh. We must *know and continually be aware* of the fact that we are miraculously and supernaturally changed by God on the inside!

## UNDER NEW MANAGEMENT

One of the most amazing things to me is when I hear Christians lobbying and fighting and arguing, trying to get Christian principles into the world system. It just blows my mind that we somehow think we can get sinners to live like saints. We're having a great enough challenge getting the saints to live like saints! How have we managed to confuse morality with regeneration?

Regeneration will produce morality, but any attempt at morality without regeneration only produces hypocrisy and arrogance, which are still the fruits of a dead spirit. We Christians often confuse the work of the Holy Spirit in us, thinking it is something we did. The reality is that without God, we can do nothing! If someone is not quickened by the Holy Spirit and alive to God, they are caught in the wind of the world system, tossed to and fro by a myriad of demonic lies, and lost in the sea of their lusts and prejudices.

So what happens when the brothers and sisters come pointing their fingers at them, yelling at them, and telling them to live a different way? They don't even understand what we're talking about! Rhetoric and debate cannot correct a heart problem. We cannot pass a bill that makes people love one another. Only when the church steps out of the political arena, goes back into the pulpit, and hits the streets to preach the glorious Gospel of Jesus Christ will the hearts of men be changed and our world transformed.

If we could fix men from the outside in, then Buddha or Confucius or Aristotle would have been effective. All of the great thinkers of the ages would have been able to approach people through thinking and mind power, challenging them with principles and concepts to change their behavior. But our message is, "Verily, verily I say unto you, ye must be born again, recreated in your spirit by Christ Jesus."

We must live in the reality that we have moved to a different kingdom and are under different management. We have changed residences and have been given a brand-new identity on the inside of us. Then we must allow God to work out from within us our salvation, and that takes some "fear and trembling"! Under the new management of God, we are continuously standing on the edge of eternity until Jesus returns. Our perspective has gone beyond the here and now to how the here and now fits into God's plan for all the ages.

When we become like Jesus, the world will take notice! They will come to our door and ask us to pray for them. They will want to be around us because they sense in their dead spirit that our spirit is alive to God. The greatest impact we can have on the world is to fully submit to God's workmanship in our lives.

## UNIQUENESS WITHIN

When you received Jesus as your personal Lord and Savior, God breathed His Spirit into you, making you a new creature. God is your Creator, and you are a designer original! God made you a one-of-a-kind creation who is so unique and precious, you are priceless. He made you brand-new on the inside, and the greatest adventure for eternity is discovering who you are in Him.

Nobody else has been placed by God in your family, in your neighborhood, with your friends, in your church, and in your city. Nobody else like you has been put on the earth with exactly the same set of talents, personality quirks, strengths, weaknesses, abilities, and disabilities that you have. He knows the length of your days and the outer limits of your potential.

You have been made a minister of reconciliation, as have we all. (See 2 Corinthians 5:18.) You may never stand in the pulpit of a church, but you are called to preach and teach the Gospel, to heal the sick, to cast out demons, and to make disciples in whatever walk of life God has called you. All of this was deposited into you at the moment of your new birth!

So many people I meet are not happy with the workmanship of God in their lives because they are forever comparing themselves to others, wanting to be like someone else. It is a slap in God's face to look at another person and say, "I want to be like him." God tenderly and uniquely designed you to be just the way He wanted you to be. He made you for himself and He made you in a way that can never be duplicated.

When you compare yourself to another person, you are saying to God, "You made a mistake. You could have done a better job." No one has the right to criticize God in that way. He is the Creator, who looks at each of His created beings and says, "It is good."

Why is it so important that we understand our uniqueness in Christ? Because we are the body of Christ, and God's desire is to empower us to reach a lost and dying world *together*. He wants to *quicken* the church! But He cannot empower and quicken a body where the foot wants to be the hand and the eyes want to be the ears and the elbow wants to be the knee. We must rest in His workmanship in us as individuals so that He can move us forward corporately. Then we can be His glorious church, showing forth to the world how they too can be quickened and made alive to God.

God's workmanship was evident when we were dead in trespasses and sins in that He brought us to salvation despite the pressures and influences of the world, our flesh, and the Devil. His workmanship is revealed in a majestic and awesome fashion, as He is the Creator of our born-again spirit, making us alive to Him. Now that we are quickened and under His management, He is bringing us and will continue to bring us through a specific set of situations and circumstances to complete His purpose, reflect His glory, and give Him delight. For this He built into us the capacity to grow, develop, change, and adapt—to become like Jesus.

# 3

# HE RAISED US
# AND SEATED US

G od's present workmanship in our lives is conforming us to the
image of Christ Jesus. Now, we don't have to get all freaked
out and feel like we are losing our uniqueness and identity as individuals, because that is not what being conformed to the image of
Jesus means!

**For whom he did foreknow, he also did predestinate to be con-
formed to the image of his Son, that he might be the firstborn
among many brethren.**
### —Romans 8:29

*Conformed* means more than just to be fashioned in the likeness
or image of someone. It actually goes beyond the superficial outward appearance and denotes an inward conformity. In practical
terms, what this is saying is that we are not being made into an exact clone or replica of Jesus, but we are to express ourselves from
the innermost parts of our being as He does. We are to love as He
loves, be moved with compassion as He is moved with compassion,
abide in God's Word as He abides in God's Word, and follow the
leading of the Holy Spirit as He follows the leading of the Holy
Spirit.

The concept of being conformed to the image of Jesus Christ
is made real to us in Ephesians 2:4–7. After God quickens us, He
places us in a spiritual position for all eternity that enables us to be
conformed to the image of Jesus while we are on this earth.

## WHO ARE "US"?

But God, who is rich in mercy, for his great love wherewith he loved us, even when we were dead in sins, hath quickened us together with Christ, (by grace ye are saved;) and hath raised us up together, and made us sit together in heavenly places in Christ Jesus: That in the ages to come he might show the exceeding riches of his grace in his kindness toward us through Christ Jesus.

**—Ephesians 2:4–7**

One of the benefits of our position in Christ is that we are being conformed into His image! Literally, our outlook on life, our demeanor, and the way we react to situations are starting to look like what Jesus would do in the same circumstances. Even more important, God is dealing with us to emulate the relationship He has with His Son, Jesus Christ. God wants us to come into oneness not only with Him, but with each other. Our position demands that we become like God. While that is impossible for us to accomplish on our own, our position in Christ brings with it the power and ability to be who we are in Him.

As we consider the term *us* in these verses of Scripture, the question arises, "Who are 'us'?" It causes us to reflect on the phrase "quickened us together," in the fifth verse. If He has quickened us together, we must know who we are quickened together with. We are no longer considering the *individual* being made alive through faith in Jesus Christ. Now Paul is talking about our being quickened *together*. He is speaking of joining more than one in this quickening.

If we miss this important truth, we will walk away from the second chapter completely ignorant of Paul's heart for reconciliation in the body of Christ. He is building a case that will show that the church is the only entity on earth and in heaven that not only tears down the wall of partition between Jew and Gentile but also quickens the two together in Christ. Do you see that there is a dynamic, supernatural union being described here?

Paul's heart is to show that the church is not Jew or Gentile, but the joining together of the two as one body in Christ Jesus. This is a theme he later illustrates by describing the mystery of the marriage union. Just as the man and the woman become one in holy matrimony, the once idolatrous Gentiles are joined with the chosen people of the old covenant. As children with hearts open to their Savior and hands clasped with one another and raised in praise to their God, they are quickened together by grace into this marvelous new dimension we call the church.

God gives a graphic picture of His grace exhibited in opulent style as it is painted on the canvas of the Gentile heart. Gentiles whose immorality and perversion polluted the streets with debauchery and degradation are permitted to be joined with a people who have walked devoutly with Jehovah in the Old Testament. Gentiles who were separated from the commonwealth of Israel and the covenant of God are now not only connected to it, but are quickened into a new institution of grace, the church.

We will see as the chapter progresses that Paul will close it with the theme of people being joined together, for it is this divine union that forms a habitation of God through the spirit. The God who quickens "us" together in the early parts of chapter 2 now dwells in that corporate gathering by verse 22. The two become one. They become "us." Without developing an "us" mentality, the church will be forever divided by race, denomination, and creed—unable to be that holy habitation of God.

It was Paul's intent both in Ephesians as well as in Romans to explain that this is where the Enemy builds the strongest breach in the body of Christ. It is an attempt to divide us so that God's presence and power can never be manifested in our individual and corporate lives. This breach is between brothers. It is not Cain against Adam. It is Cain against Abel. It is not Jacob against Isaac. It is Jacob against Esau. Our struggle is not merely reconciliation with God, but reconciling with our brothers and sisters. This principle is so vital, Jesus told us:

**Therefore if thou bring thy gift to the altar, and there rememberest that thy brother hath ought against thee; leave there thy gift before the altar, and go thy way; first be reconciled to thy brother, and then come and offer thy gift.**
**—Matthew 5:23–24**

Do not try to be quickened with God when you will not be reconciled with your brother! While I realize Paul's focus in Ephesians 2 is on Gentiles and Jews, I also know that God's workmanship in the church will always require that two become one. When we come to grips with the fact that God is not interested in selfish individual agendas but moves in a corporate vision, then and only then will we know the mystery and dynamics of the "us."

In essence, God is calling us to love one another as He has loved us.

## POSITION IS EVERYTHING

There is an element of God's workmanship that is one of the biggest challenges and deepest mysteries in the Christian life, and that is understanding His awesome love for us. His love for us has a bigger impact on us as individuals and on the body of Christ as a whole than any other aspect of our relationship with Him. Ephesians 2:4–7 gives us a dramatic illustration of His love, that even when we were dead in our trespasses and sins, God quickened us. He loved us when we were dead! He loved us and breathed His life into us. He brought us out of death and darkness into eternal life and light.

God's love for us goes far beyond human understanding, and that is why Paul says it twice in one verse: "For his great love wherewith he loved us." When you read something twice in a row in the Bible, you can be certain the Holy Spirit is emphasizing something extremely important.

Then the apostle Paul makes the statement every believer knows so well: "For by grace ye are saved." The Greek construction here indicates that God saved us completely at a point in time in our past, yet our salvation continues in the present. The way Paul has worded this is both dramatic and emphatic. He is telling us that every breath of our salvation breathed in the present is due to the grace by which we were saved in the past. No matter what takes place, there is no one to receive the glory but Jesus.

The workmanship of God in our lives through grace is inestimable. We will discuss the grace of God in more depth in the next chapter, but for now I must interject this. Anywhere and everywhere that Paul could mention the fact that we are saved by grace and kept by grace, he does so!

Now, in verse 6, Paul describes our new position as a child of God. In one motion He raises us, and in the next motion He makes us sit. Those are two different things. First, to be raised up from that lower state of being dead in trespasses and sins is to be placed over the world system, the prince of the power of the air, and our old sin nature. We have come to a place of authority and power over the very things that once held us captive and kept us in bondage. That is good news!

Then we are seated with Jesus in the heavenlies. God raised us up and never said anything about going down again! It was not His intention that we go down and then be raised up and go down and then be raised up again. He raised us up and then made us sit, *period*. That's because He has placed us in a stable position. Remember, the wolf is coming! But when he comes, he will find us *sitting* in heavenly places—not shaken, not moved, not disturbed, but stable.

Sitting is a position, not a transition. If we are in transition, we are not sitting! When we sit, that means we are here for as long as God wants us here. We have entered into a position in God that we refuse to forfeit for anybody or anything because we have arrived at the place where we are going to abide and stay and not be moved.

This is our position in Christ right now and in every circumstance of life. I often say that most Christians today are preoccupied with their *condition* when they should be consumed by their *position*. They rejoice when they get a check in the mail: "Ooooh, He blessed me today!" They get up and testify: "The lump is gone!" Those are conditions. They are temporal things. And I have news for any person who gets healed: You're going to have to fight for your health again! And to those who have received an unexpected gift: You may have received a check today, but you're going to need some more money tomorrow.

When we celebrate our condition, we are majoring in the minor and ignoring the major, which is our position. When we start focusing on our position, we will be standing on a foundation the Devil can't shake. Our condition changes from moment to moment, and it is wonderful and grand when we pray and the Holy Spirit comes in and changes and rearranges things for our good. But the reason we can pray for conditions to change is because of our position, and our position is eternal! We need to be praising and worshiping God that we have been raised up and are sitting with Him in the heavenlies!

When we praise God for our condition, we call attention to today. We get happy about God and what He is doing for us right now. But when we praise God for our position, we call attention to eternity, and we move into a whole new dimension of praise and worship!

## GOD LOVES TO SHOW OFF

After the apostle Paul describes our new position, he tells us the reason for it:

**That in the ages to come he might show the exceeding riches of his grace in his kindness toward us through Christ Jesus.**
**—Ephesians 2:7**

God wants to show off! Do you know that God delights in doing the impossible and He is the best showman who ever existed? P. T. Barnum had nothing on God. Houdini and all these high-tech magicians today can't touch the riches of God's grace expressed toward mankind through the ages. Who can top the parting of the Red Sea or the resurrection of Jesus Christ? When God makes a point, He makes it with style!

But this verse is not only talking about the "big" things God has done. This is about you and me! He wants to show *us* off in the ages to come. Now we must get on our eternal caps and start thinking in eternal terms. That's kind of hard to do because eternity is hard to imagine, and our minds are bound by time and space. We can't even remember things bound in time. You know you don't remember what you did when you were three months old, and I don't remember what I did yesterday! So when we start talking about eternity, it's difficult for the human mind to fathom, but Paul says there are going to be ages to come. We need to quit stressing out about this little moment we're in and realize there is much, much more to come.

**For our light affliction, which is but for a moment, worketh for us a far more exceeding and eternal weight of glory; while we look not at the things which are seen, but at the things which are not seen: for the things which are seen are temporal; but the things which are not seen are eternal.**
**—2 Corinthians 4:17–18**

Paul says that what we are going through now has significance and meaning because we weigh it in light of eternity and not in terms of our present condition and comfort. If we look at our lives through the eyes of God and focus on the eternal things that are not seen by the natural eye, God will work in us a far greater glory in eternity. In the ages to come He will show the riches of His grace by saying, "Look at how I saved them. Look at all they did wrong, how they sinned and were dead, and I saved them." God is going to prove His goodness through our badness!

Now I'm really going to get down into a little groove here, and I hope you can take this! God even means for people to talk about your past! I know you don't want anybody to do that, but it's necessary. You see, God had enough sense to know that when He saved you, somebody would know something about you. And He's going to use what was against you for His glory. Take the lame man who was at the gate called Beautiful in Acts 3:2–10, for example. He sat there all the time, and everybody thought that was as far as he was going to go. Then one day Peter and John came through at the hour of prayer and Peter said, "Silver and gold have I none; but such as I have give I thee: In the name of Jesus Christ of Nazareth rise up and walk" (v. 6).

We all know what happened. That lame man jumped up on his weak, lifeless feet and came walking and leaping and praising God right through the temple. But the first thing everyone said was, "Is this the man who sat outside the gate? Isn't he the same beggar we passed by all those years?" God used that man's past for His glory.

Jesus told one lame man to take up his bed and walk. *Well,* I thought to myself, *if He was going to heal him, why didn't He just let him leave his bed?* If I had been lying in the bed and had been carried in by four men, I'd want to leave the bed and run! But Jesus said, "Take up your bed and walk," because He wanted to use the bed in the man's arms to say that the thing that had carried him, he was now carrying. Are you seeing what I'm saying here? He will use our scars to become His stars!

This concept of God using your past for His glory is for people who have matured enough to see the master plan. Jonah's disobedience and his incarceration in the belly of a whale were what Jesus used as a picture of His death, burial, and resurrection. Jonah was in the belly of the fish for three days as Jesus was in the belly of the earth for three days. Jonah didn't know that one of the reasons he was there was so Jesus could use his failure to preach His message.

"That in the ages to come, He might show the exceeding riches of His glory." God will say throughout eternity, "Look how much I did with so little." If we look back over our lives and examine our successes and all the things we have acquired, we know it is the grace of God in our lives. People think we're smart, but we know we weren't that smart. They think we're so talented and so gifted, but we know that all the creativity and drive they see is being drawn from the very heart of God.

God did so much with so little! After a while He's going to put us in His curio chest and show us off and say, "Look what I did! Look at my workmanship. Can you believe that I made this glorious creature out of clay? Can you believe that is something I scooped up out of the ground, and it wouldn't even hold water when I first picked it up, but I kept on molding it and raising it up until it achieved its destiny."

They tell me that when a potter begins working with clay on a potter's wheel, he never presses down; he always raises the lump of clay up. His hands are continually touching the clay as it spins around, and he is fashioning it into the masterpiece he desires, giving it the form and features that will fulfill its purpose.

For eternity, God will point to us and declare, "Look what I raised up out of nothing! Although their whole life was spinning, I never let go of them, and I raised them up and sat them in the heavenlies. And now these vessels are holding water! They are holding relationships and ministries and concepts and a job and their integrity and getting their life together. They couldn't have done that without my workmanship in their lives. What you heard about them was true—they were a disgrace and a disaster—but my grace was sufficient. And now they are sitting here with me forever."

**And we know that all things work together for good to them that love God, to them who are the called according to his purpose. For whom he did foreknow, he also did predestinate to be conformed to the image of his Son, that he might be the first-born among many brethren.**
**—Romans 8:28–29**

We were raised and seated by the Great Potter of the Universe to be conformed in our inner man to the image of Christ Jesus, and it is our position in Christ that is the source of everything we are and everything we do in the Christian life. From this powerful spiritual position, our spirit man continually breathes the life of God and receives all the spiritual blessings for the moment, for the day, for the time in which we live, and forever.

Whenever we feel the world and the Devil trying to pull us down into that former spiral of death and darkness, we must only remember where we sit!

# 4

# HE GRACED US

When Saul of Tarsus was saved on the road to Damascus, God sent a man named Ananias to pray for him. But because Saul was a well-known persecutor of the church, Ananias was horrified to even go near Saul. So the Lord comforted Ananias with these words: "But the Lord said unto him, Go thy way: for he is a chosen vessel unto me, to bear my name before the Gentiles, and kings, and the children of Israel: For I will show him how great things he must suffer for my name's sake" (Acts 9:15–16).

## STEWARD OF GRACE

From the moment he was saved, Paul knew that he would suffer great things for the Gospel's sake and that God had called him to preach to the Gentiles first, then to kings, and finally to the Jew. Before he was separated by the Holy Spirit for this full-time ministry, however, he spent many years studying the Word of God and being taught by the Holy Spirit. Furthermore, there was one particular revelation Paul received that was essential to his ministry and would truly become the hallmark of his teaching. This was the revelation of the grace of God.

**For this cause I Paul, the prisoner of Jesus Christ for you Gentiles, if ye have heard of the dispensation of the grace of God which is given me to you-ward. . . . Unto me, who am less than**

the least of all saints, is this grace given, that I should preach among the Gentiles the unsearchable riches of Christ.
—**Ephesians 3:1–2, 8**

So passionate was Paul concerning the issue of grace, he nearly came to blows over the matter on several occasions with Peter and the legalistic Jews. In fact, many scholars believe that Paul's thorn in the flesh was actually a faction of religious Jews who had received Jesus as Messiah, and were referred to as Judaizers. They followed Paul wherever he went, endeavoring to turn his Gentile converts from the simple Gospel of being saved by grace to a gospel of being saved by works of the Jewish laws and traditions.

Paul would go into a city, preach the Gospel, and see many Gentiles saved by grace and set free. Then these Judaizers would come in after him and tell the people they weren't really saved unless they observed all the Jewish laws. What Paul had established in the liberty of grace would become a dead, ritualistic work. This totally exasperated the apostle, and he wrote the book of Galatians specifically to eradicate all claims of the law on the Gospel. Galatians is essentially a theological treatise on the importance of grace in both salvation and our Christian walk. He clearly outlines the doctrine of grace once and for all.

Paul takes full responsibility for delivering the dispensation of the grace of God to the church. He is a master builder who is continuously conferring with the Architect to make certain that he is giving the accurate blueprint and specs to the carpenters in his employ. His obligation and joy are to make sure that the church is built according to God's plan of grace. A good Scripture to illustrate this is: "Study to show thyself approved unto God, a workman that needeth not to be ashamed, rightly dividing the word of truth" (2 Timothy 2:15).

The analogy Paul uses here is of a journeyman carpenter who takes a piece of wood that has just been cut by his apprentice and looks down the line to make sure that the cut is straight. Anybody who has ever done any building knows there is a constant conferring back and forth between the architect, the builder, the carpenters, and the journeymen to make sure the master blueprint is being meticulously and faithfully followed. So when Paul talks about being a steward here, he doesn't just pen the words or draw up the specs and then walk away and leave the carpenter on his own. Nor does he cease conferring with the Architect. He continues to communicate with both and have proprietorship over what is being developed to maintain continuity.

When Paul says, "For this cause I am a prisoner," he means, "I can't just walk away from this thing. I am committed to this dispensation of grace and will make sure that it is completely developed and maintains its purity and power." To do that, Paul also made certain that he was imparting this revelation into the hearts of faithful men. These were men who were committed, not fly-by-night people who just wanted to impress people with rhetoric. These were the devout and faithful who had a passion for the truth and the same godly drive Paul had to see the church built according to God's plan.

## MORE THAN UNMERITED FAVOR

For Paul, the grace of God was the most essential component of God's salvation program. Preaching, teaching, and defending the unadulterated, unhampered grace of God was the very mission of his ministry. But what is grace? Those of us who have grown up in church could easily pull out our standard definition of grace: "God's unmerited favor." This cryptic three-word definition is a feeble attempt to explain this grand and glorious aspect of salvation.

Paul was so dedicated to the concept of grace that he used the term three times as much as it is used in all of the rest of New Testament literature! The original definition of grace was "pure joy or pleasure." The idea was that something was done to another person that was pleasurable but undeserved. Out of the utmost and greatest joy, God blesses us for no other reason than that it gives Him pleasure.

Grace, then, is the term that represents the attitude and manner in which God provides our salvation. The flow is as follows: God forms man out of the dust of the ground and breathes into him the breath of life. This breathing and forming aspect of God's creation is significant in that all the other components of God's creation came into existence by His spoken Word. But man is brought into being by intimate and personal contact with God. He invests in His human creation His image and likeness and very Spirit. This is supposed to be a relationship of great fellowship, sharing, and caring. God will display His glory and magnificence, and man, having the ability to observe, experience, and process that kind of information, will worship Him for it.

Instead man blatantly sins against the commandments of God. He dies spiritually and is separated from God, is expelled from the garden of Eden, and begins to suffer the consequences of his actions. While God has all the evidence of the depravity of man to justifiably destroy him, He instead works out an elaborate program of salvation.

The apostle Paul is fascinated by the contrasts found in this history. Humanity is totally incapable of rehabilitating themselves. They cannot produce anything of sufficient value to reverse the sentence of death assigned to them, and they find themselves totally at the mercy of God. At the same time, God is angry with the wicked, and His holy nature will not allow Him to simply overlook their violations and declare man saved. He hates and must destroy sin, but He loves man. The mighty God resolves this problem by offering His Son, Jesus Christ, as a sinless sacrifice to be a substitute for all of mankind. His Son's death satisfies His wrath against sinning mankind, divine justice is served, and through Jesus Christ man has a way back to God and godliness. This is the synopsis of the Gospel message.

As exciting as the substitutionary sacrifice of Jesus Christ is, Paul cannot rest until he has revealed another great facet of this wonderful salvation—grace. Man's totally depraved nature and absolute need for a savior is met with the substitutionary work of Jesus Christ on the cross and through His resurrection. The "pure joy and pleasure" of God himself brought deliverance to the human race. His delight to save and make whole again brought about the atonement through His Son.

**Looking unto Jesus the author and finisher of our faith; who for the joy that was set before him endured the cross, despising the shame, and is set down at the right hand of the throne of God.**
**—Hebrews 12:2**

It was for joy that Jesus endured the cross, and that joy set before Him was you and me! This is the grace with which God brings forth our salvation. The doctrine of grace becomes the backdrop and the framework of our salvation and describes the mindset of God when He brought about our redemption. God's grace is at the very heart of His workmanship in us.

## GRACE REVEALED

One of the best Bible stories to describe grace is the story of the adulterous woman in John, chapter 8, one of my favorite passages. This unnamed woman is forcibly brought to Jesus. She has been caught in the "very act" of adultery. Her prosecutors ask for only one thing from Jesus—His permission to execute her.

What do you think is going on in her mind? She is standing there in front of a man who is going to decide whether she lives or dies. She has no lawyer—not even a character witness to take her side. She is guilty and she knows it. Her prosecutors know it, and it is generally known in her community. The evidence is clear and convincing.

This adulteress has nothing to offer in exchange for her freedom, nothing to say that will persuade the man to exonerate her, and no hope of escaping a terrible death by stoning. She is done for. The prosecutors are hard-nosed and unyielding, the law is clear and precise concerning such a crime, and the man she is facing is known to be meticulously fair and honest. Jesus, it would seem, has no alternative but to agree to her execution.

While she waits for her ears to report what the rest of her being already knows will be the verdict, her eyes show her a strange sight. Her judge stoops to the ground and begins to scribble something on the ground. When He finishes this exercise, all of her accusers disappear. The indictment against her lies on the prosecution table unattended. The judge invites her to join in the search for her accusers, and when she cannot locate them, He says to her, "Neither do I accuse you. Go and sin no more."

That's the grace of God revealed to us! Jesus took her from a position of undeniable guilt and an irrevocable sentence to a totally free and unconditional pardon. That's grace! She did nothing to deserve this kindness; she had nothing with which to purchase this kindness, and she didn't even know that such a thing was possible. That's grace!

"For by grace are ye saved through faith; and that not of yourselves: it is the gift of God: not of works, lest any man should boast" (Ephesians 2:8–9). Paul celebrated this grace, cherished this grace, and dedicated his entire ministry to the cause of presenting the grace message to believers. He wanted us to know that God did what He did for us completely out of the goodness and joy of His heart and without any help from us or even by our request. We are allowed to enjoy forgiveness, restoration into fellowship with God, and an honored place in His family—all without *having* to do anything or without being *able* to do anything. Even the faith with which we receive Jesus Christ as Lord and Savior is given to us by God.

So what is there for us to boast about in ourselves? Was our resurrection from the dead state of sin into the new life in Christ something we did? Was our salvation something we earned, achieved, accomplished, or purchased? No! The quickening of our spirits was just as much God's workmanship as was the resurrection of Jesus! Nothing we did, not any of our efforts, enabled us to be saved.

No good works.

No serving on this committee or that committee.

No helping out this person or that person.

No denying ourselves this or becoming a member of that.

The workmanship of our new life in Christ was and is completely the workmanship of God.

Let's go back to Abraham (originally called Abram), the father of our faith. A very interesting thing happened when God made a covenant with Abram in Genesis 15: Abram slept right through the entire thing! He had obeyed God by slaying the designated animals and cutting some of them in two pieces, then spent the rest of the day shooing the buzzards away from the carcasses. Finally, as night fell, he went into a deep sleep. By the time the smoking furnace of God passed between the pieces, signifying the covenant, Abram was snoring!

Grace means: *The whole Christian life is not about us; it is the gift of God!* It is not about us or our works. Spiritually speaking, it is as though we just kick back, take a nap, and allow God to be God. He then saves us, delivers us, and makes us free forevermore. We have nothing to boast about in ourselves; we only boast in the Lord and what He's done for us. David understood this when he said, "I will bless the Lord at all times: his praise shall continually be in my mouth. My soul shall make her boast in the Lord: the humble shall hear thereof, and be glad. O magnify the Lord with me, and let us exalt his name together" (Psalm 34:1–3).

## GRACE IS NOW

In the last chapter we briefly discussed "for by grace ye are saved." We learned that the Holy Spirit is telling us that we were saved at a point of time in our past, but our salvation continues in the present. Now let's look at this concept in more detail.

Paul weaves the fabric of this grace cloth so intricately, even the words he uses are a blessing. Paul is saying that our salvation was accomplished in the past and we now exist as saved in the present. If we were to translate this passage with the grammar used in mind, it would read: "By grace have you been saved completely in past time, with the present result that you are in a state of salvation which persists through the present time" (Ephesians 2:5 WUEST).

This understanding of grace gives our salvation three primary components. **Justification** is the declaration of God that our guilt and the penalty associated with our sin have been revoked and we are placed in a position of right standing with God. **Sanctification** is the outworking of the internal reality that we are separated from the world and now citizens of heaven, God's eternal work within us. Through time and process, God helps us to develop a lifestyle that embraces a holy manner of living. **Glorification** is the full transformation of our bodies into resurrected, immortal beings. Until then, we will manifest the divine nature of God that has been imparted into our spirit, apprehends our will, and finally, in one grand finale, will one day transform our vile bodies into ones like Jesus' own.

These three words give us a full description of God's grace toward us: We were justified the moment we received Jesus Christ as Lord and Savior; we are being sanctified while we live on this earth; and we will be glorified in the future in heaven. Each one of these aspects of our salvation displays God's workmanship in our lives, but the area we are most concerned with right now is, of course, the ongoing work of sanctification in our present state. Sanctification is the process of becoming like Jesus, of growing in God. If we are to grow in God, we must grow in grace.

"For we are his workmanship, created in Christ Jesus unto good works, which God hath before ordained that we should walk in them" (Ephesians 2:10). As we have stated emphatically in the introduction, God makes us. We do not make ourselves. Our becoming who we were created to be is the full manifestation of His grace in our everyday lives. There will never come a day when God stops pouring His grace into us. Believers grow from grace to grace and from glory to glory!

God's workmanship in sanctification is working to the outside what He has deposited on the inside. We have seen how we received everything we could ever want or desire—all spiritual blessings—at the point of the new birth. When we were quickened and made alive in Christ, we were raised and seated with Him in the heavenlies, receiving our eternal identity and purpose. Now Ephesians 2:10 is telling us the same thing in a more practical way. We were created in Christ Jesus to perform good works.

"Good works" does not refer to helping little old ladies across the street, doling out soup at the homeless shelter once a week, and doing anything that looks like a good deed. Good works are God-ordained works, works God has prepared for us to walk in. In other words, just as He called us out from before the foundation of the world to be His adopted children, He set the paths in which we would walk and the accomplishments we would achieve.

This is why it is so important to listen to God at all times! When you come to the street corner and notice the little old lady standing next to you, if you have peace in your heart, by all means ask her if she needs some help and give her some assistance if she says yes. Because you are listening to God, He will give you a yank in your spirit if you are not to go near her!

What I am stressing here is that a principle of the kingdom we all must live by is that Jesus ministered according to the leading of the Holy Spirit, not according to the needs of the people. You can rest in the fact that if you have no desire or thought to volunteer at the homeless shelter, but you do have a desire to teach the five-year-olds in Sunday school, stay away from the homeless shelter and sign up to teach! Listen to the leading of the Holy Spirit, not to the need of the moment. This is how you discover and know confidently the works God has prepared for you to walk in.

You cannot walk in your best friend's works. You cannot do the same good works your pastor is doing or the teacher on Christian television is doing. You must walk in the works God has prepared for *you* to walk in. They are your unique, individual works, and they were designed specifically for your personality, your gifts, and your abilities. Again we see how God's workmanship in our lives cries to us, "Be yourself! Be who I made you to be, and do the works I've prepared especially for you."

## ENDURING GRACE

**For we are his workmanship, created in Christ Jesus unto good works, which God hath before ordained that we should walk in them.**

**—Ephesians 2:10**

"That we should walk in them" is an interesting phrase. The Greek construction is literally saying that we should order our lives within the sphere of the works God has destined for us to perform, and there is no way to accomplish this but through the grace of God.

The grace of God is the glue that holds this whole scenario together, for it is the grace of God that saves us, supplies the works in which we are to order our lives, and then gives us the ability to do them! In the same way we relied on the miraculous, saving grace of God to quicken our dead spirit and make us alive spiritually, we must continue to rely on this same miraculous, saving grace to walk in the works He has prepared for us.

We are now talking about the workmanship of God as enduring grace, motivating grace, and persevering grace. Through the grace of God, we frail human beings become superhuman vessels through which the power of God can flow to the world! Remember Paul's thorn in the flesh? Regardless of what you believe that thorn to be, the Bible makes it clear that God's grace is sufficient to see us through any attack, trial, temptation, or grievance that might come our way.

Grace is what God gives us to endure circumstances that often do not change. It is that unchanging, unfailing grace that enabled my wife and me to endure long periods of pain and depression as she recovered from a car accident.

As a young man filled with hope for the future, my ears stung at the doctor's words: "She'll never walk again." Then he conceded that there was an outside chance she may walk with a metal brace. My lover, my partner, bone of my bone and flesh of my flesh, had been cruelly crippled. I was heartbroken.

When Serita finally came home, she was in a great deal of pain.

She struggled to take care of our family (two-year-old twin boys) despite the constant misery of her injury. Then came the day she tried to walk for the first time since the accident. She lurched, her foot hitting the floor with a thud, her entire body twisting and contorting. I tried to make sure she never saw the tears that betrayed my confident words of hope and encouragement.

Inch by inch she moved forward as I supported her with my body, soul, and spirit. For a year we persevered through relentless lurching and faltering, with me coaxing and coaching her to continue the fight and believe she would walk again. Then gradually we began to see her gain the slightest trace of strength, then more strength, and finally she began to move about normally.

How did we make it through the long periods of failing miserably? How did Serita tolerate the unmerciful pain day after day? How did we handle the day I came home from work to find the love of my life sitting in front of her closet, gazing through tears at the high-heeled shoes she thought she would never wear again?

It was grace. Grace that enabled Serita to walk again. It was grace that caused us to grow up and get stronger and better than ever. It was grace that encouraged us to survive the struggles before us, to overcome pain and grief and fear as we faced the real possibility of her never walking again.

*Grace is not only a miracle worker, it is a comfort and strength when miracles are delayed.*

No matter how devastating a day may be, we can always expect God's enduring grace to be the undergirding force that keeps our mind from cracking and our feet from stumbling. Whether our test is our children, our finances, or some other dilemma, when God doesn't alleviate the problem, He gives us the grace to endure the process as we trust Him for our deliverance.

Do you see that this is what the world is looking for? People are looking for a way to endure and persevere so they can achieve their dreams. They are looking for a way to get free and stay free. People are desperate for the ability to live in peace and harmony with others. They are looking for a way to grab hold of eternity and live as though they will never die. The exciting truth is that this is a picture of God's workmanship of grace in the believer today.

Through God's grace, believers can get free and stay free. Through God's grace, believers can live in peace and harmony with others. More important, believers can be the living, vital, effective, and productive body of Christ. Through God's grace, believers live as though they will never die because they are alive forever in Christ. They can give their time, energy, talents, and even their lives because they live in the reality that they are eternal beings.

God graced us with eternal life when we were born again, and one day He will grace us with a glorified, resurrected body. But in the meantime, we have the incredible adventure of appropriating His grace to become more and more like Jesus, to walk out the destiny He has set for us, and to be a light in this dark world.

# 5

# HE BROUGHT US NEAR

Before we were born again and quickened by the Holy Spirit, there was a shroud covering us. This sinister shroud of death and darkness kept us from realizing what we were doing and the consequences of our actions. Essentially, we went about our daily activities oblivious to what was happening in the spirit realm. Then when we were saved and made alive in our spirits, we experienced an unveiling. Suddenly we emerged out of darkness into marvelous light, and that light revealed to us the precarious position we once occupied.

We looked back and saw how far we had been from God.

Part of God's workmanship in our lives and one of the great blessings that comes with salvation is the ability to accurately view our former existence. It is much like a person waking up in their car the morning after a drinking binge. Still experiencing the alcohol-induced amnesia, they open the car door, thinking they are parked safely on the side of the road. Only after they get out of the car and look back do they realize, now enjoying the light of day, that their car is resting on the edge of a cliff! Just one more foot of forward motion and they would have plunged to their death. In a similar fashion, believers are allowed to look back and discover just how close they came to eternal destruction.

**Wherefore remember, that ye being in time past Gentiles in the flesh, who are called Uncircumcision by that which is called the**

Circumcision in the flesh made by hands; that at that time ye
were without Christ, being aliens from the commonwealth of Israel, and strangers from the covenants of promise, having no
hope, and without God in the world.
—**Ephesians 2:11–12**

Paul ushers us into a time of historical reflection by saying,
"Remember the facts of your past." He wants to display the grace
of God on the canvas of the Ephesians' former lives by revealing yet
another aspect of their spiritually dead state: As Gentiles, they were
called "Uncircumcision."

## THE UNCIRCUMCISION

The term *circumcision* can only be called vivid imagery! It refers
to a uniquely Jewish practice commanded by God in the Old Testament and was used by God to remind Israel of their covenant with
Him. Dealing with the most private and sensitive part of the male
body, circumcision symbolized that God desired His people to be
honest and forthright with Him in all areas of their lives. He did not
want them to hide anything from Him.

The Bible calls circumcision the cutting away of the flesh, in
this case the foreskin from the male organ. It was a surgical proce-
dure baby boys underwent at eight days old. In the natural, physical world, circumcision is hygienic and helps prevent infection and
disease. In the spiritual sense, the removal of excess tissue symbol-
izes removing the cover from sinful practices. When we lift the
cover of pride, expose our sin, and bring it to God, not only does
He forgive and cleanse us, but He becomes the source of our lives
and our most intimate confidant. In essence, circumcision represents a commitment to living a holy, consecrated life for God.

In his book to the Romans, Paul tells us that when we are born
again, we are circumcised in our hearts. When we surrender to Jesus Christ as our Lord and Savior, we are removing pride from the
most sensitive area of our lives, acknowledging the dilemma regarding our sin, and allowing God to forgive us and give us a new heart.
(See Romans 2:29.) So after we are quickened and made alive by
the Holy Spirit, we see how the shroud of pride that covered our
sin is now lifted and, as Paul instructed us, we look back and understand for the first time how very lost we were.

Although physical circumcision was to be a sign of the covenant God had with the descendants of Abraham, it very soon became a badge of honor or a religious ritual and nothing more. Israel took pride in the fact that circumcision distinguished them from other nations that generally did not practice it, and that pride covered their sin again. Nevertheless, when Paul introduced the Gentiles to the ritual of circumcision in Ephesians, chapter 2, he pointed out the fact that this had been a distinct line of demarcation between Jews and Gentiles.

Being the Uncircumcision meant the Gentiles were cut off from God and His kingdom. When pride rules our heart as a shroud of spiritual death and our spirit is independent from God's Spirit, we live under the following conditions:

**Without Christ.** We must understand that *Christ* in this verse represented the Messiah of Israel, the one whom Israel looked to for deliverance, who would establish them as a prosperous and peaceful nation in the world. God had promised to send a deliverer to the circumcised. Therefore, being "without Christ" meant that the Uncircumcision were without a deliverer.

**Aliens from the commonwealth of Israel.** Personally, I love this word *alien,* especially because of its connotation in our time. Today it carries the meaning of someone from another planet. Similarly, in the biblical sense, *alien* meant someone who was not a citizen, an outsider who was not "at home." The Uncircumcision were excluded from citizenship in Israel as a theocratic nation under the one true God. They were far from God and all He had to offer.

**Strangers from the covenants of promise.** In the Greek text, this phrase actually reads, "strangers from the covenants of *the* promise." In this particular case, *the* promise referred to is God's promise to send the Messiah to deliver Israel. The Uncircumcision did not have an opportunity to participate in a covenant relationship with God, and therefore they had no promise to ensure their future.

**Having no hope.** Being without hope is being without a future, for how can we face the future without hope? The hope of Israel has always been the Messiah. Therefore, the Uncircumcision looked to a future without hope, without the promise of the Messiah.

**Without God in the world.** The Uncircumcision lived in this world without God, literally "apart from God." They had no knowledge of Him or relationship with Him. They were on their own.

How did this all come about? How did Gentiles get into such a precarious position, existing so far from God? The answer is to be found in the Bible's history of mankind.

## THE ORIGIN OF JEW AND GENTILE

In the beginning God created Adam and Eve, who enjoyed the communion of God until they sinned. Because of their sin, God expelled them from the garden of Eden and they were left to live in a cold and cruel world. Made to work by the sweat of their brow, they produced sons and daughters, and the sin nature began to manifest itself immediately. Their son Cain slew his brother Abel. Cain was punished, branded, and banished for his actions. Adam and Eve then produced Seth. At this point we have two lines formed, the family of Seth and the family of Cain.

Neither line produced godly people. Eventually mankind was so depraved and far from God that God decided to destroy man. Only Noah and his immediate family found grace in the eyes of the Lord. So God had Noah build an ark, collect male and female of every animal, and then He flooded the earth. When the earth was cleansed of all evil people, God set a rainbow in the heavens as a covenant that He would never destroy the earth by water again.

Noah emerged from the ark, planted a vineyard, harvested the grapes, made some wine, and promptly got drunk. One of his grandsons "uncovered his nakedness" (performed a sexual act with Noah) while he was passed out, and the human race was off and running in sin again. The Bible declares that the whole world continued to engage in lawlessness on a massive scale. However, God's promise was unshakable. He would never again destroy the earth by water. Instead, He focused His attention on a young man named Abram, the son of an idol maker in Ur of the Chaldees.

Because Abram had a heart that could be touched by God, God made a covenant, or drew up a contract, with him. This covenant established that God would use the life and lineage of Abram to produce a nation of godly people. To establish this covenant, God changed Abram's name to Abraham, which meant "father of a multitude." With this action, God seemed to turn His attention from mankind in general to focus on Abraham and his lineage. He in no way abandoned all of humanity, but intended to use Abraham and his posterity as a tool for evangelizing the whole world. The idea was that God would be so good to Abraham and his descendants that the rest of the world would see His goodness and want God to be their God too.

Out of the loins of this Gentile named Abraham, God started the Hebrew nation. And for the first time in history, the nations were divided by God into two major categories: Jew and Gentile. The Jews were those who had a covenant with God; the Gentiles were the people who had no covenant with God. The Jews began to call on God: Elohim, El Shaddai, Almighty God, while the Gentiles worshiped water and fire and Zeus and Aphrodite and birds and trees. God revealed himself to Abraham and to his descendants, becoming known through the centuries as the God of Abraham, Isaac, and Jacob. Unlike the Gentile nations, the nation of Israel was a theocracy, a God-ruled nation.

## LINE OF THE MESSIAH

The Jewish line was established when Abraham had Isaac, and Isaac had Jacob, who was renamed Israel, which means "he will rule as God." Again, God indicated He had chosen a people for himself who had the opportunity and capacity to rule the nations by His power and Word. The nation of Israel was to bring the light of God to the world. Exodus 19:6 states that Israel was ordained to be a kingdom of priests and a holy nation. Unfortunately, the Bible records how Israel repeatedly went from devotion to apathy to outright rebellion with regard to God. Then when their rebellion led to their near destruction, they would turn back to God and He would deliver them from their enemies. This cycle was repeated over and over through the centuries.

Nevertheless, God would bring His Messiah from the line of the Circumcision. From Jacob (Israel) came Israel, the nation. Jacob had twelve sons, whose families later became known as the twelve tribes of Israel. The nation of Israel fell into bondage to Egypt for four hundred years, until God sent Moses to deliver them. They walked through the Red Sea on dry land, Pharaoh's army being destroyed behind them, and began their journey back to the land God had given them.

During the forty-year trek through the wilderness, God preserved them and provided for them supernaturally in the treacherous desert. A pillar of fire by night kept them warm and a pillar of cloud by day kept them cool. Manna dropped from heaven every morning to feed them, and quail were sent when they complained about the manna. Several times water was made available to them by God's miraculous intervention. They were kept healthy and their clothes and shoes did not wear out. But during this time, God gave the Jewish people something far more precious. He delivered to them what the book of Romans calls the "Oracles of God."

God gave Israel His Law—the principles of His kingdom. He also began to reveal to them His glorious plan of salvation through the form and function of the tabernacle. There were three parts to the tabernacle: the outer court, the inner court, and the Holy of Holies. In each of these sections, there were specific pieces of furniture that represented our redemption through Jesus Christ, the final destination being the Holy of Holies, where God's presence resided.

If you looked down upon the tabernacle from a mountaintop, you would see that it was built in the shape of a cross—long before crucifixion existed. This amazing structure had one objective: to move God's people close to Him. Sadly, it was not long before the meaning and symbolism of the tabernacle degenerated into a religious system. What should have been a glorious age of salvation and deliverance—Israel showing forth the greatness of its God and preaching the Good News of the Messiah to come—became nothing more than a ritualistic and empty series of ceremonies. The most compelling confession of their condition was penned by the prophet Jeremiah: "The harvest is past, the summer is ended, and we [Israel] are not saved" (Jeremiah 8:20).

Undaunted, God proceeded with His plan. He had promised Israel a deliverer, a messiah, a promised one who would bring peace and prosperity. And what a promise it was!

**The wolf also shall dwell with the lamb, and the leopard shall lie down with the kid; and the calf and the young lion and the fatling together; and a little child shall lead them.**
**—Isaiah 11:6**

**But he was wounded for our transgressions, he was bruised for our iniquities: the chastisement of our peace was upon him; and**

with his stripes we are healed. All we like sheep have gone astray; we have turned every one to his own way; and the Lord hath laid on him the iniquity of us all.
                    **—Isaiah 53:5–6**

And I will put a new spirit within you; and I will take the stony heart out of their flesh, and will give them an heart of flesh: That they may walk in my statutes, and keep mine ordinances, and do them: and they shall be my people, and I will be their God.
                    **—Ezekiel 11:19–20**

Unfortunately the Jews only heeded the political prophecies. Their Messiah would make the wolf lie down with the lamb and make warring factions to become friends. They did not expect a Messiah who would die for their sins and make it possible for their dead spirits to be quickened and made alive to the heart of God. They were looking for someone who would make them political rulers in the earth. When the Messiah Jesus arrived on the scene, the leaders of the nation of Israel promptly and maliciously rejected Him.

Never mind that He worked miracles in their midst.

Never mind that He raised the dead and preached the living Word.

Never mind that He lived a sinless, righteous, holy life.

When would He destroy the Roman oppressors and put Israel in power?

Ultimately the leaders of Israel rejected Jesus as their Messiah because He claimed to be God. His intimacy with the Father offended their religious thinking—intimacy rubs religious folk the wrong way! The religious leaders wanted to control the people through law and ritual and tradition. They didn't want the Holy Spirit telling people what to do!

## THE BLOOD OF JESUS

God has the chaos of the ages on His hands. The dispossessed Gentile population—aliens from the commonwealth of Israel and strangers to the covenants of promise—are without hope. The nation with whom He is in covenant—to whom He gave the Law, the sacrifices, the ordinances of worship, divine favor, and the promise of a Messiah—reject their Messiah.

The Gentiles are far from God and don't even know Him.

The Jews who were oh so near don't accept their Deliverer.

"But now in Christ Jesus ye who sometimes were far off are made nigh by the blood of Christ" (Ephesians 2:13). Here we see God's workmanship in bringing the Gentiles to equality with Israel. Through the blood of Jesus of Nazareth, the Uncircumcision "are made nigh"! In the past, the Gentiles had no right to be near God or expect a deliverer, but when Jesus shed His blood on the cross, He brought them near. Jesus destroyed the wall between Jew and Gentile and made clear that the way of salvation was open to all people: "For he is our peace, who hath made both one, and hath broken down the middle wall of partition between us" (Ephesians 2:14).

When Jesus died on the cross as the sacrifice for the sins of mankind, the separation that had existed between God and man since Adam and Eve sinned in the garden of Eden was destroyed. Man could again be in relationship with God directly through believing in and receiving Christ Jesus as Savior. But these verses of Scripture also tell us that Jesus brought Jew and Gentile to equal footing. Now the human race is not classified as Jew or Gentile, but as believer or unbeliever.

If you are a Jew, your Messiah has come and His name is Jesus of Nazareth. If you are a Gentile, the blood of Jesus Christ has now brought you near. You are no longer an alien, a stranger, without the hope of a deliverer. Jesus has broken down the wall between Jew and Gentile and has made both one, calling them all and drawing them all into His body, the church. We must all come to God the same way, through Christ Jesus.

Although many Jews believed in Jesus and were saved, later becoming part of the first-century church, Israel as a nation rejected Jesus as Messiah. Eventually the church was predominantly Gentile. Lest we Gentiles begin to be puffed up with pride, the apostle Paul commands us to look back to the cross and remember that at one time we were afar off and so despicably lost and depraved that we were looked upon as dogs.

What a glorious time to live! Gentiles are near and Jews have their promise fulfilled, which means all of us have the promise of

the Deliverer. The war between us is over! No longer do we squab-
ble and fight over circumcision and washings and feast days and sacrifices—Jesus has fulfilled them all. Through the blood of Jesus
Christ, *all* of us are brought nigh to God!

# 6

# HE IS OUR PEACE

Jesus is our peace. The Bible does not say that He gives us peace or that He sends us peace. He *is* our peace. This is wonderful! That means when we have Him, we have peace. When He becomes our Lord and Savior, peace is ours forever, no matter what situation we find ourselves in. We don't get peace from the things He gives us but from His presence in our lives.

Aside from the Holy Spirit shedding the love of God abroad in our hearts, obtaining His peace that passes all understanding is one of the greatest gifts of God's workmanship in our lives. And it all happened when Jesus destroyed that which caused enmity between God and mankind, and Jew and Gentile.

## ABOLISHING ENMITY

**Having abolished in his flesh the enmity, even the law of commandments contained in ordinances; for to make in himself of twain one new man, so making peace.**
**—Ephesians 2:15**

When Jesus died on the cross, He stopped the law and made it ineffectual. *Enmity* indicates great hostility, likened unto war or extreme conflict. The apostle Paul gives us the root cause of this hostility: the law. You see, the Jewish law was more than the Ten Commandments. It was "even the law of commandments contained in ordinances." This phrase, first of all, refers to the myriad laws pertaining to everything from adultery to agriculture. If you have never read through your entire Bible, then you will probably not have read Exodus, Leviticus, Numbers, and Deuteronomy, the books where all of these judgments and ordinances are given.

The Ten Commandments were the first presentation of God's law to Israel and to mankind at large. They were a kind of paramount overview of His will, with the first four commandments relating to man's relationship to God and the last six relating to man's relationship to man. Then there were the dietary, cultural, and relational laws, which enumerated what to eat and what not to eat, when to plant and when to reap, and how to treat your family and your neighbors. The judgments commanded specific punishments for each violation of these laws. Then there were the ordinances, which dealt with how Israel was to present herself to God as an act of worship or to be forgiven for sins committed, both as individuals and as a nation. These laws included how the priests were to present the various offerings of worship and sacrifices for sin as well as how the ark of the covenant was to be handled.

The nation of Israel took pride not only in the fact that their men were circumcised and they had the hope of a deliverer, their messiah, but also in the fact that they were set apart because God had given them the law. Unlike the Gentile nations, the Jews *knew* what was right and what was wrong because God himself had given the law to Moses. They were experts on the definition of sin, and they were careful not to associate with the Gentile nations that knew nothing about God or His law.

As a result, the Jews considered the Gentiles unclean and treated them as they would treat lepers. They called them dogs, and in those days, a dog was not a beloved household pet! Being called a dog was a great insult. In every area of life, from the daily activities of living to the major feasts and holy days, the nation of Israel ordered their lives according to the "law of commandments contained in ordinances." Their entire way of life and operation as a nation was different from any other nation on earth, and they had great disdain and contempt for anyone who lived differently. Can you see how the law caused enmity between Jew and Gentile?

Now again, we must remember that this was not God's plan. His purpose in giving the law was to reveal to His people that they

127

were sinners in need of a savior. Paul explains this clearly in his letter to the Galatians:

Wherefore the law was our schoolmaster to bring us unto
Christ, that we might be justified by faith. But after that faith is
come, we are no longer under a schoolmaster. For ye are all the
children of God by faith in Christ Jesus.
—**Galatians 3:24–26**

God presented the law to Israel as the standard that couldn't possibly be met in their present unregenerated, spiritually dead state. To reinforce this concept, He also commanded His people to build the tabernacle, and later the temple, not only for a place of worship but as a place to offer sacrifices for their sins. Every time they sinned as individuals or as a nation, the law stipulated exactly what sacrifice had to be made for that particular sin. Then once a year on the Day of Atonement, the high priest would sprinkle the blood of a goat upon the mercy seat of the ark of the covenant— the piece of furniture in the Holy of Holies—and turn a second goat loose to wander in the desert. This annual sacrifice and ritual was the atonement for all of Israel's sin for the year. Most important, it was a type and foreshadowing of Jesus' work on the cross.

And he shall take the two goats, and present them before the
Lord at the door of the tabernacle of the congregation. And
Aaron shall cast lots upon the two goats; one lot for the Lord,
and the other lot for the scapegoat. . . . Then shall he kill the
goat of the sin offering, that is for the people, and bring his
blood within the veil, and do with that blood as he did with the
blood of the bullock, and sprinkle it upon the mercy seat, and
before the mercy seat: And he shall make an atonement for the
holy place, because of the uncleanness of the children of Israel,
and because of their transgressions in all their sins: and so shall
he do for the tabernacle of the congregation, that remaineth
among them in the midst of their uncleanness.
—**Leviticus 16:7–8, 15–16**

And when he hath made an end of reconciling the holy place,
and the tabernacle of the congregation, and the altar, he shall
bring the live goat: And Aaron shall lay both his hands upon the
head of the live goat, and confess over him all the iniquities of
the children of Israel, and all their transgressions in all their sins,

putting them upon the head of the goat, and shall send him away by the hand of a fit man into the wilderness: And the goat shall bear upon him all their iniquities unto a land not inhabited: and he shall let go the goat in the wilderness.
—**Leviticus 16:20–22**

God commanded that a goat be slain on the Day of Atonement because a goat is the biblical symbol of the sin nature, of man in his most depraved state. It's common to see goats eating garbage and all kinds of filth. Furthermore, goats are very independent and will wander this way and that, whereas sheep are dependent upon their shepherd for everything. In the Bible, sheep are a type of the believer and goats are a type of the unbeliever.

When Jesus went to the cross, the Bible tells us that He *became* sin that we might *become* righteous. (See 2 Corinthians 5:21.) Jesus became the goat, crucifying our sin nature on the cross to satisfy God's wrath against it. Then when God was satisfied that our debt had been paid, through Jesus Christ we could be made righteous.

But why did God command a second goat, a live goat, to be used in this ritual? The high priest, in this case Aaron, laid his hands on the live goat and pronounced all of Israel's sin upon it. Then he banished the goat to wander in the wilderness. Jesus also took our sin to the depths of hell and left it there, where it belongs. He threw our sin right back in the face of the Devil himself! Praise God!

You will remember also that when Jesus died on the cross, the veil or large, thick curtain separating the holy place and the Holy of Holies in the temple was torn supernaturally from top to bottom. (See Matthew 27:51.) God did that to signify that the final sacrifice had been made for all sin for all time. No more goats were to be sacrificed on the Day of Atonement! No more spotless lambs during Passover! All violations against the law were paid as the blood of Jesus poured to the ground. From that moment on, every believer could be born again, forgiven of their past, present, and future sins, and have the law written in their heart!

And I will put a new spirit within you; and I will take the stony heart out of their flesh, and will give them an heart of flesh: That they may walk in my statutes, and keep mine ordinances, and do them: and they shall be my people, and I will be their God.

—**Ezekiel 11:19–20**

There is no more enmity and hostility between Jew and Gentile, and there is no more enmity and hostility between God and man because Jesus abolished the law on the cross. The issue today is not keeping the law, and if you don't succeed, making the proper sacrifice at the temple. The issue today is following the leading of the Holy Spirit. Today, *believers* are the temple of the Holy Ghost! We are living sacrifices unto our God.

## IT'S ALWAYS BEEN FAITH

**And that he might reconcile both unto God in one body by the cross, having slain the enmity thereby.**
**—Ephesians 2:16**

Paul changes directions in verse 16 because the enmity being slain on the cross here is not the hostility between Jew and Gentile, but the hostility between all mankind and God. Although God had made covenant with the Jews, and they were considered near to God, the Jews needed to be born again as much as the Gentiles. When a Jew is born again, they become a part of the new body, the church, just as the Gentiles do.

"And came and preached peace to you which were afar off, and to them that were nigh" (Ephesians 2:17). Jesus preached peace to "you which were afar off" (Paul is referring to the Ephesians, who were Gentiles), "and to them that were nigh" (the Jews). He went first to the house of Israel in His three years of ministry, because the Jews were near to God. What we are seeing in Ephesians 2:11–17 explains a passage of Scripture that many of us don't understand or even want to deal with because it portrays Jesus being uncharacteristically rude and uncompassionate.

And, behold, a woman of Canaan came out of the same coasts, and cried unto him, saying, Have mercy on me, O Lord, thou son of David; my daughter is grievously vexed with a devil. But he answered her not a word. And his disciples came and besought him, saying, Send her away; for she crieth after us. But he answered and said, I am not sent but unto the lost sheep of the house of Israel. Then came she and worshipped him, saying, Lord, help me. But he answered and said, It is not meet to take the children's bread, and to cast it to dogs. And she said, Truth,

Lord: yet the dogs eat of the crumbs which fall from their masters' table. Then Jesus answered and said unto her, O woman, great is thy faith: be it unto thee even as thou wilt. And her daughter was made whole from that very hour.
**—Matthew 15:22–28**

Can you see the enmity that existed between Jew and Gentile? And yet in the very midst of this hostility and tension, Jesus smashes the law to smithereens and wipes out the enmity with God's grace, mercy, and compassion! He responds to this Gentile woman's faith and even commends her for it. We are struck with the fact that it is truly faith in the Lord Jesus Christ that fulfills all the law! (Read Galatians 3:24–26 again.)

This woman was a Canaanite, and Canaanites were the most depraved of Gentile nations. Even archeologists have found abounding evidence of the rampant and terrible immorality among this people. She was *unclean,* and yet Jesus accepted her! Why? Because of her faith. She recognized the Deliverer and refused to let go of Him, no matter what it cost her. She didn't care if He called her a dog! She was not moving until He became *her* Lord and healed her daughter.

Of course, the disciples did not understand why Jesus even spoke to the Canaanite woman because they were still entrenched in the law. They did not catch on to the fact that Jesus was demonstrating salvation by His grace, through faith. Later, when the Jews cried that the law came from God and the law was the way of salvation, the apostle Paul would argue, "You remember your father Abraham? Was he righteous because of the law?"

They would say, "Well, no. Abraham lived before the law was given."

"Well then," Paul would ask, "Was he righteous because he was circumcised?"

"Uh, no. He was justified before God commanded circumcision."

"Okay, I see. Was Abraham a Hebrew then?"

"No, he was a Gentile."

"Yes," Paul would agree, "Abraham was a Gentile who by faith believed God and it was counted unto him as righteousness." (See Romans 4:3.) Abraham became a Jew only when he surrendered his life to God.

For he is not a Jew, which is one outwardly; neither is that circumcision, which is outward in the flesh: But he is a Jew, which
is one inwardly; and circumcision is that of the heart, in the spirit,
and not in the letter; whose praise is not of men, but of God.
—**Romans 2:28–29**

## A NEW WAY

In a practical sense, the "law of commandments contained in
ordinances" covered three areas of life. First, it set up the theocracy,
the government of God over the nation of Israel. This contained
the judgments, which dealt with how the people related to one another. If anyone committed a crime, or there was a conflict between two people, the law told them how the situation should be
handled. For example, if your neighbor stole your ox and was
caught with the goods, the law commanded your neighbor to return to you twice what he stole: "If the theft be certainly found in
his hand alive, whether it be ox, or ass, or sheep; he shall restore
double" (Exodus 22:4).

Second, the "law of commandments contained in ordinances"
commanded what sacrifices were to be offered for what sins, also
commanding various washings, cleansings, and absolutions. Essentially, these were outward practices that symbolized the forgiveness
and cleansing of sins committed. The following verse tells people
how to wash themselves if they eat something that is unclean.

**And every soul that eateth that which died of itself, or that
which was torn with beasts, whether it be one of your own
country, or a stranger, he shall both wash his clothes, and bathe
himself in water, and be unclean until the even: then shall he be
clean.**
**—Leviticus 17:15**

Third, the law dealt with how to worship. There were specific
feasts (Feast of Tabernacles, Feast of Unleavened Bread, Feast of the
Firstfruits) and holy days, such as the days of Purim (remembering
Queen Esther's act of courage to save Israel from destruction) and
the Day of Atonement, which we have already described. Then
there were various offerings, such as peace offerings, drink offerings, and heave offerings. These were to remind the children of Israel that the source of all wealth and prosperity was the Lord.

And the Lord spoke unto Moses, saying, Speak unto the children
of Israel, and say unto them, When ye come into the land
whither I bring you, then it shall be, that, when ye eat of the
bread of the land, ye shall offer up an heave offering unto the
Lord. Ye shall offer up a cake of the first of your dough for an
heave offering: as ye do the heave offering of the threshingfloor,
so shall ye heave it.

**—Numbers 15:17–20**

Now, I don't know about you, but all these laws and judgments
and ordinances do not sound like a life of peace to me! Being consumed with the law and ordinances and washings and sacrifices and
offerings does not bring peace but is a constant reminder of the enmity and conflict between God and man. God is righteous and man
is not, so for the two to have any kind of relationship, man must
continually be washing and cleansing and working and working to
keep God satisfied.

How would you like to wake up every morning and go to bed
every night studying the law to make certain you hadn't broken any
of it? Then if you had broken a law, you would have to find out
what you needed to do to be made clean. Can you see yourself on
Saturday night, running all over town trying to find the perfect goat
to sacrifice at the altar the next morning?

And if any one of the common people sin through ignorance,
while he doeth somewhat against any of the commandments of
the Lord concerning things which ought not to be done, and be
guilty; or if his sin, which he hath sinned, come to his knowledge: then he shall bring his offering, a kid of the goats, a female without blemish, for his sin which he hath sinned. And he
shall lay his hand upon the head of the sin offering, and slay the
sin offering in the place of the burnt offering.

**—Leviticus 4:27–29**

How would you like a church service like that? Thank God, Jesus fulfilled and abolished all of the law and the sacrifices! Now we
have peace because He is the ultimate, final sacrifice and our complete redemption from sin. He is our feast of unleavened bread. He
is our Passover Lamb. He is our drink offering and our wave offering. Do you understand what I'm saying?

Jesus is our Sabbath, and when we come to Him we have entered into complete and total rest. He is our scapegoat, and because of Him our sins have been carried into the wilderness and forgotten forever! The wine that we drink represents His blood, and the bruising of His body is our health and healing. His flesh is the veil in the temple rent from the top to the bottom, and He is our peace!

Jesus is the fulfillment of everything the Old Testament law and ordinances foreshadowed. He is the concrete reality of every abstraction found in the tabernacle and temple design and furniture. When we receive Jesus, God's workmanship in our hearts sees that we keep the Sabbath holy. In fact, we keep every day holy!

**Surely his salvation is nigh them that fear him; that glory may dwell in our land. Mercy and truth are met together; righteousness and peace have kissed each other. Truth shall spring out of the earth; and righteousness shall look down from heaven. Yea, the Lord shall give that which is good; and our land shall yield her increase. Righteousness shall go before him; and shall set us in the way of his steps.**

**—Psalm 85:9–13**

God opened David's eyes, and he looked through time to see Jesus bringing mercy and truth together. He saw righteousness and peace in one. He saw the fulfillment of the law in his Messiah. He saw that in Christ Jesus were all blessing and honor and glory and power! David was looking at a new thing that was based purely on faith in Jesus Christ. He saw us, the church, enjoying peace with God through the blood of Jesus.

Whether Jew or Gentile, God's workmanship has made peace available to all men, women, and children on the earth through Jesus Christ. Eternal, unfathomable, life-transforming peace comes from simply being in right relationship with God, and that is what Jesus' death and resurrection offers us. Peace is knowing Jesus as our Lord and Savior. Peace is being quickened and made alive in our spirits. And this is not a peace that disappears when life starts spinning in chaos and confusion or the bottom drops out from beneath us! Yes, when storms come we will feel them strike our flesh and we may even experience some fear, but on the inside we have a peace that passes all understanding.

Jesus *is* our peace, and He will never leave us or forsake us.

# 7

# HE IS BUILDING US

The apostle Paul was God's appointed steward of the revelation of grace, but he was also intensely preoccupied with building the church. The more I study about him, the more I'm fascinated because he was a Hebrew man whom God called to minister to Gentiles. Before he was born again his Hebrew name was Saul, reminiscent of the fact that he came from the lineage of the tribe of Benjamin, because the first king of Israel was also named Saul, a Benjamite. But Paul was also a citizen of Rome, which brought many privileges. So today we would say that he was multicultural. Wherever he went, he would adapt to the culture and customs and language of the people he was with in order to win them to Christ.

**Give none offence, neither to the Jews, nor to the Gentiles, nor to the church of God: Even as I please all men in all things, not seeking mine own profit, but the profit of many, that they may be saved.**

**—1 Corinthians 10:32–33**

There is no doubt that Paul had one of the deepest understandings of God's vision of the maturing, increasing, growing church. More than any other, he expounded on the coming together of Jew and Gentile and the one way of salvation through Jesus Christ, which was open to all mankind.

## HEAVENLY ACCESS

A wonderful reality sets in when we realize that we all have access to God through Jesus Christ: "For through him we both have access by one Spirit unto the Father" (Ephesians 2:18).

*Access* depicts a formal entree into the presence of a king or deity, a "royal audience," so to speak. Furthermore, it also denotes a confidence and boldness to enter the presence of that dignitary. The book of Hebrews expresses it perfectly: "Let us therefore come boldly unto the throne of grace, that we may obtain mercy, and find grace to help in time of need" (Hebrews 4:16).

Being in Christ gives us the position and legal right to enter the heavenly throne room, but the Holy Spirit who lives inside us is the one who ushers us into the presence of God with confidence and boldness. We all have access by one Spirit, our Comforter, our Teacher, our Guide. He is in all of us, and His job is to unite us with the Father and unite us with one another.

We are *commanded* by the Word of God to come boldly into the throne room of God to obtain mercy and grace in our time of need. This is an awesome, mind-boggling privilege! Moreover, in the context in which Paul is speaking to us in Ephesians, he is saying that even though I come from generations of heathen, I have just as much access to the Father as the Jew who has known and served Him for centuries!

Whether we are black, brown, white, yellow, or red, we now have access to the Father's house! How do you get into your house? You have access. If you didn't have access, you couldn't get in. You must understand what Paul is saying here. *All* of us heathen were wrong. The black man was doing something crazy in Africa; the white man was doing something crazy in Europe; the yellow man was doing something crazy in China; the brown man was doing something crazy in South America; and the red man was doing something crazy in North America—and God just snatched all of us out of that craziness with the glorious Gospel of Jesus Christ and gave us all *access*. He looked us straight in the eye, pointed to His Son, Jesus, and said, "Here's your key—your access—into my house. Please come in." Thank you, Lord!

Let me give you a practical, everyday example of the power and peace found in the fact that we have access into the heavenly realm. Do you remember when the storm was raging on the Sea of

Galilee, the disciples were about to drown, and Jesus was asleep at the back of the boat? (See Mark 4:35–41.) The lightning was flashing and the thunder was roaring and the ship was tossing to and fro *when Peter spoke to Jesus.* And when he spoke, his words did something the storm couldn't do. Peter's words woke Jesus!

The storms of life don't disturb God or incite His compassion to move in our behalf—we do! He is listening for the voices of His children who call on His name in faith. When we open our mouths, address Him as Father, and come in the name of Jesus, we have access to Him. We are immediately present with Him in His throne room of mercy and grace.

We don't have access to only part of Him.

We don't have access for a limited time.

The fullness of God is made available to us and is present with us whenever we call upon His name. Our access is an eternal fact—proof positive that we have been raised and are now seated with Jesus. Our heavenly Father expects us to come into His house and into His presence confidently and boldly.

There is no "access denied" when we pray.

There is no "limited availability" clause.

There is no "except in certain cases" rule.

There are no "time limits" in the contract.

We have eternal access to the presence of God with no geographic limitations. We can be in a gymnasium and have access to the presence of God. How can this be? Because we *are* the house of God, the dwelling place of His presence. The precious Holy Spirit dwells in us. Wherever we are, that place can be filled with the glory of God and become His sanctuary because we bear His presence inside of us at all times and in all places.

Are you enjoying to its fullest capacity the privilege you have to access God at will? Do you recognize that the angels of the Lord are encamped around you and that the presence of God is nearer than your own breath?

## WE'RE IN THE HOUSE!

Now therefore ye are no more strangers and foreigners, but fellow-citizens with the saints, and of the household of God.
**—Ephesians 2:19**

We are no longer strangers and foreigners. We are part of the family and household of God. We have access to Him and His home, and we are to "come home" confidently and boldly at all times and in all places and under all circumstances. If we approach God like a foreigner, we approach Him in unbelief, timidly crying and begging, "I hope you don't run me out. Please let me in." And God will stare at us incredulously, wondering, *What's wrong with you?*

What would you think if one of your children came to your house like that? Wouldn't you think it ludicrous if you were in your house and one of your kids came up to the front door and started ringing the doorbell? You'd say, "What's wrong with you? You know you don't have to ring the doorbell. You live here. You're not one of the neighbors who live in another house. You're not a stranger from across town. You're not a foreigner who is just visiting from another country. You are my child, my flesh and blood!"

So God is standing there with His arms folded, saying, "What are you doing ringing the bell when Jesus died to give you the key? You can come in and out and find green pastures whenever you want. You're one of my kids now. My Spirit dwells in your spirit, and I have drawn you near to me, to live in my house forever."

"I know," you say, "but you don't know what I've been going through." You are into your condition again and have forgotten your position! If you ever get a grip on your position—that you are of the household of God, living in His miracle-producing, peace-inducing presence—you're going to break through your condition! You're no more a stranger! You're no more a foreigner! You are a fellow citizen with the saints of the household of God. God's workmanship has placed you in His house!

## THE BODY IN THREE FORMS

Now therefore ye are no more strangers and foreigners, but fellow-citizens with the saints, and of the household of God; and are built upon the foundation of the apostles and prophets, Jesus Christ himself being the chief corner stone; in whom all the building fitly framed together groweth unto an holy temple in the Lord.

**—Ephesians 2:19–21**

Paul gives us three illustrations in these verses of what the body of Christ is. First, we are "fellowcitizens with the saints." Second, we are "of the household of God." And third, we are a "holy temple in the Lord." As "fellowcitizens with the saints," we are citizens of the city of God and of heaven. I'm not certain many of the saints, particularly in America, understand that today. Most of the church is more in love with the world than who they are in Christ. They are more concerned about what's going on in the earth than what they are supposed to be doing here.

**To wit, that God was in Christ, reconciling the world unto himself, not imputing their trespasses unto them; and hath committed unto us the word of reconciliation. Now then we are ambassadors for Christ, as though God did beseech you by us: we pray you in Christ's stead, be ye reconciled to God.**
**—2 Corinthians 5:19–20**

Every believer should remember at all times that they are not of this world, but merely sojourners on this earth and ambassadors for Christ to this world. Before salvation, we were aliens to God and citizens of earth; after salvation, we are aliens to this world and citizens of heaven. We are not of this world! We are citizens of heaven used by God to preach the Gospel and make disciples of all nations. That is the ministry of reconciliation that all believers have and that Paul reminds us of in these verses.

Then Paul tells us that we are "of the household of God." We have talked a lot about what it means to be a member of God's family, having complete access to His throne room and the privilege of walking in His presence at all times. As His dear children, we can walk, talk, and fellowship with Him continually, all day and all night if we wish. He is our loving Father forever.

It's very hard for me to speak about God being a Father today because so many people had no father in their home. Or if they did have a father in their home, he was nearly the opposite in character and behavior to our heavenly Father. If you are one of these, don't be afraid to open your heart to God and allow Him to be the father you always hoped existed and yearned with all your heart to know! In the most powerful way, you will see His workmanship of restoration and peace in your life!

Believe me when I say that our Father God is the one you have been dreaming of, who loves you no matter where you've been, what you've done, or who you've been with. You are the child He wanted, and if you have any doubt of His wanting you, look to the cross. That's how much He wanted you! As you let Him love you and heal you, you will become secure in His household and secure in the plan He has for your life.

Finally, Paul says that we are "a holy temple in the Lord." If you think you are excited about being a citizen of heaven and a member of God's family, just wait until you get a glimpse of being His holy temple! Now we are confronted with something that goes even farther beyond our imagination and natural understanding, something magnificent in every sense of the word.

## FITLY FRAMED TOGETHER

The Ephesians had built one of the biggest and most elaborate temples ever constructed on earth—a temple to the pagan goddess Diana. Even today, this temple is considered one of the most incredible edifices of the ancient world. Now Paul is writing to the believers who live in the shadow of that temple, saying, "*You* are now the temple of the Lord! And you are far more magnificent in beauty, far more masterful in construction, and far more holy than the greatest temple human beings have ever built."

To understand God's supernatural construction of this holy temple, we must begin with the foundation, which the Bible tells us is the apostles and prophets. The prophets represent the Old Testament and the apostles represent the New Testament. Paul is saying, "Jesus is the fulfillment of the Old Testament, and the New Testament is the revelation of Him and His body, and both must be treated as the inerrant Word of God."

Our foundation is, was, and always will be God's Word. It is the Word that gives us stability and understanding to stand strong and to be effective in our calling. It is the Word that is the rock of our salvation, the rock that holds us together and empowers us when the storms of life rage against us. It is the Word of God that keeps us from being deceived and wandering off the path God has set for us. It is the Word of God that builds our faith, gives us revelation and understanding, and enables us to carry out God's will for our lives.

Paul says, "Jesus Christ himself being the chief corner stone." Who is the Living Word? Who fulfilled the Old Testament prophecies and satisfied every jot and tittle of the law? Who appointed the twelve apostles, continues to appoint the ministry gifts, and places all believers in their callings today? Whose blood abolished the enmity between God and man and Jew and Gentile? That would be our chief cornerstone, the one who holds this building called the church together.

The cornerstone, by definition, brings two walls together. When a building is constructed, a large stone is placed at the corner, which will join two walls, usually perpendicular to one another. Each of these walls is going in a different direction and has a specific function, but the cornerstone joins them, and together they form a new building. No longer two separate walls serving different purposes, they unite to form an entirely new structure, one that has infinitely more space, strength, power, and potential than the walls had by themselves. Do you see the multiplying, unifying, supernatural power of Jesus, the chief cornerstone?

Now that God has laid such an excellent and eternal foundation, with a cornerstone that has stood every stress test known to man, we begin to build upon this firm foundation, "all the building fitly framed together." By "fitly framed," the apostle Paul describes the work of a master craftsman stonecutter who chisels away at each stone, smoothing the rough edges, cutting away the excess, and filling in the holes. The elaborate process of stone cutting makes each stone unique, able to fulfill its particular function and to fit with every stone around it.

"Ye also, as lively stones, are built up a spiritual house, an holy priesthood, to offer up spiritual sacrifices, acceptable to God by Jesus Christ" (1 Peter 2:5). Each of us are lively, or living, stones, and in order for us to fit together, God works on us, continually growing us up and maturing us into the living sacrifice He has ordained us to be. We must also remember that He places believers in every generation and in every nation on that solid foundation so that we are all one building, consisting of the saints who have gone before us and those who will follow us, made up of every race and nationality.

Every stone is fitly framed—shaped, molded, and formed—to do its part in the building. Some of us are pretty rough stones when we are brought to the building site! But we're in the hands of the Master, the one who knows just how to chisel and shape us and set us into the building in a way that we fit.

We hear a lot today about independent ministries and independent churches and independent believers. How are you going to be independent in a body? If you tie a finger off from the hand, it dies! If your knees decide to leave and join an army of knees, your body collapses (and the army of knees is not going to go far either!). Only the body where each part fulfills its function will stand healthy and strong. And when we truly become fitly framed together, we will be a fortress that the Enemy cannot get over, get around, or go through! We will become a habitation in which God is fully present and His glory fills us and flows through us and overflows from us to others.

## GROWING IN HOLINESS

The Greek language in Ephesians 2:21 indicates that this building is continually growing. This building we know as the church is not made with hands but of lives fitted together by the Spirit and created for growth. It is created for outreach. It is designed to be continuously "added on to" by the Holy Spirit. Paul writes that we are a giant temple continuously under construction. If we're not growing, we're not healthy, and we're not becoming more holy.

It is important to know that Paul chose a word, when he spoke of our being a temple, that means inner sanctuary, or Holy of Holies. This is where the ark of the covenant was placed and the presence of God resided. By using this word, Paul is saying, "We are a building which, as we mature and multiply under the direction of the Holy Spirit, will rise up to become a holy place, a place where the presence of God resides at all times."

In the Old Testament, the ark of the covenant was the sign of God's presence. It was kept in the tabernacle, a temporary tent-like structure. Long gold-covered poles of wood, called staves, were put through rings on each side of the ark so that it could be carried on the shoulders of the priests whenever it was moved. The tabernacle is a picture of the individual believer. We live in "tents," our bodies, as we move through this earth, and the ark, or presence of God, moves with us. God's anointing rests on us, just as the ark rested on the shoulders of the priests who carried it.

But as the church, corporately we become the temple, stationary and holy and immovable. No longer are we moving about as tents; we are living stones, fitly framed together and increasing and growing into the holy temple of the Lord. When the ark was placed in the temple in Jerusalem, the staves were removed from it. It was now in its permanent home! The anointing and glory of God filled the entire temple, and the cloud of God's presence was so strong that the priests could not stand up and minister—they fell prostrate in worship. (See 1 Kings 8:1–11.)

When the Lord sees us come together in corporate worship, He pulls out the staves and says, "I'm staying here in the midst of my people. I will walk up and down in the midst of them. I will pour out my anointing on them and make them a holy people, full of my grace and glory!"

It is at this point that the eternal attributes of God and the *position* we have in Christ Jesus break through and have direct bearing on our *condition*. We become "a holy temple in the Lord." The word *holy* paints a picture of who we are and how we operate. We are consecrated and set apart for God's exclusive use; He alone is the one we follow and serve. We love Him with all our heart, and when God has our whole heart, He has our whole life. Now we begin to see His workmanship in bringing us into unity and the power of becoming one.

# 8

# HE MADE US ONE

Paul was called primarily to minister to the Gentiles, but he had a passion for the Jewish believer and the Gentile believer to understand that they were now one in Christ Jesus. If he were in America, he would perhaps be dealing with black Christians and white Christians, because he was on a mission to tear down any kind of division in order to bring unity to the body. Interestingly enough, the first instance of Gentiles coming into the body of Christ did not happen to Paul but to Peter.

## ONE DOOR FOR ALL

In Acts, chapter 10, an unusual and unprecedented event occurred at the house of a Gentile named Cornelius. God had commanded the apostle Peter to go to this man's home and share the Gospel with him. When Peter spoke the truth of Christ Jesus, the Holy Spirit fell on all those who heard him speak, and Peter and the other Jews who were with him were astonished that the gift of the Holy Spirit was poured out on the Gentiles. In this intense and historical moment, the Jew and Gentile came together as one to form the church—the Holy Spirit united them in the body of Christ.

The church has only one door, and both Jew and Gentile have to stoop to get in that door. By stoop, I mean they must bow their knees to Jesus and acknowledge Him and Him alone as their Lord.

The Jew has to humble himself from legalism and traditions of men and accept the door of faith. The Gentile has to repent of his heathen ways and come in the same door of faith. Jesus said: "I am the door: by me if any man enter in, he shall be saved, and shall go in and out, and find pasture" (John 10:9).

When we pass through that door we are renouncing our allegiance to everything else and joining ourselves to this new workmanship that is created in Christ Jesus unto good works. The Jew had to go through the door of their Messiah, Jesus, to get in. The Romans had to go through Jesus to get in. And every nationality on earth has to enter through this one solitary door, no matter whether you are male, female, educated, or illiterate. There are no big "I's" or little "you's." There is only one way in, and that is through faith in Christ Jesus.

Paul states that Jesus "hath made both one." This new thing is not a Jewish thing or a Gentile thing. He has made both one as they believe on the Lord Jesus Christ and are saved: "There is neither Jew nor Greek, there is neither bond nor free, there is neither male nor female: for ye are all one in Christ Jesus" (Galatians 3:28).

The church is to be a meeting ground for both genders, all nationalities, all social levels, all races, and all cultures. The church is a fusion place. It is a place that has its own ethnicity—that of being a royal priesthood, a holy nation, a new people.

God has never cared about differences in skin tones and hair colors and facial features. Only one thing matters to Him: whether we are in covenant relationship with Him. And the only way to be in covenant relationship with Him is through Christ Jesus. God sees only two categories of people: saved and unsaved, believers and unbelievers, born again and not born again. Either we know God through Jesus Christ or we don't. Even in the Old Testament, God did not care if a Jew married a Gentile as long as that Gentile was a believer in Him.

The master will of God is that all things come together in Christ—divisions healed, breaches mended, sins wiped out—and righteousness reigning.

## TOGETHER FOREVER

If Paul were here today, after he got through tearing down the walls of racial prejudice, he would be jumping on denominationalism because his whole mission was to make believers understand that the church is one entity. When we join it, we pledge allegiance to every single brother and sister who is a part of the body of Christ. We are literally raised up together, not one dominating the other, not one controlling the other.

Now, if you think Paul would have had a difficult time trying to bring people together today, just imagine dealing with the Jew and Gentile believers of his time. When the Bible says there was enmity between them, it's talking about war! Why do you think Paul spent so many verses of Scripture saying in so many ways that the blood of Jesus Christ abolished the enmity?

After centuries of being God's chosen people, of being the only nation with whom God would communicate, of course the Jews would want to lead the way when their long-awaited Messiah appeared. They were the only ones who knew about Him. They had been steeped in religious traditions and ceremonies while the Gentiles were worshiping the sun and birds or the Greek or Roman gods. And the Gentile idea of worship was the Jewish idea of depravity! So of course the Jews would believe that they should be the leaders and dominate the Gentile believers. But Paul contended: "But God . . . even when we were dead in sins, hath quickened us together with Christ, (by grace ye are saved;) and hath raised us up together, and made us sit together in heavenly places in Christ Jesus" (Ephesians 2:4–6).

God didn't quicken and raise the body in parts! He raised the whole body up *together*. There are some blessings that you and I will never get until we see everybody with whom we are associated come into that same level of blessing. I'm talking about corporate blessings! We must see the church as one unit, one body. We must begin to understand that the greater blessing is not on us as individuals but on the whole corporation for whom Jesus died.

If you ever understand that, it will make an evangelist out of you! You will become obligated and committed to my deliverance because you will realize that you will not be totally whole without me. Why? God has raised us up together! We are intimately and sensitively connected forever in spirit. I am a living stone connected to you, another living stone, and God will work on us until we fit together!

There is a wonderful illustration of this in Numbers 32, just before the children of Israel were going to cross the Jordan River and take the Promised Land. Two of the tribes of Israel wanted to settle where they were and did not want to cross the Jordan and fight with the rest of their brothers and sisters. This was Moses' response:

**And Moses said unto the children of Gad and to the children of Reuben, Shall your brethren go to war, and shall ye sit here? And wherefore discourage ye the heart of the children of Israel from going over into the land which the Lord hath given them?**
**—Numbers 32:6–7**

When Moses confronted the tribes of Gad and Reuben with their sin, they immediately turned around and came back into the position of unity. They said: "We will not return unto our houses, until the children of Israel have inherited every man his inheritance" (Numbers 32:18).

The tribes of Gad and Reuben were saying, "We've got to leave our inheritance, cross over to the other side, and fight with our brothers. We will not rest and cannot enjoy what we have until they have theirs. If we are one, all of us have to walk in the faith and the unity of the Spirit to embrace and obtain the inheritance God has given us all."

I can't enjoy my healing while you're sick. I can't enjoy my victory while you're a victim. There's something about my receiving a blessing that makes me have to minister to you and say, "The same God who brought me through can bring you through!" He quickens us and raises us up *together*. We are His workmanship—corporately.

## A HABITATION OF GOD

**In whom ye also are builded together for an habitation of God through the Spirit.**
**—Ephesians 2:22**

Notice: We are "*builded together* for an habitation of God." Paul is not talking about each of us as individuals in this context. He is speaking of corporate realities. There is a place in God that the church will never know until we lay aside our petty differences and allow the Holy Spirit to make us one. But there is no way the body of Christ can come together and be one without allowing the Holy Spirit to move on us as a corporate body. Do you see that?

If the church could have been united over doctrine, our many learned and respected theologians and seminaries would have accomplished that by now. If we were going to be united by a Christian celebrity, don't you think powerful and dynamic ministers like Billy Graham or John Wesley or Dwight Moody would have achieved unity by now? No, the Word of God tells us that no celebrity will unite us, nor will the great programs and ideas of man. Only the Holy Spirit can unite us, and Paul clearly understood that.

Jesus also understood that, which is why He told the disciples not to go anywhere or do anything after His ascension until they received the Holy Spirit. (See Luke 24:49.) This is why He spent His last hours before His crucifixion telling the disciples all about the Holy Spirit, the one who would come and be to them exactly what He had been to them. And before He went to the cross, Jesus prayed a long, beautiful prayer for the church, which would be formed after His resurrection. The theme of that prayer was unity:

**Neither pray I for these alone, but for them also which shall believe on me through their word; that they all may be one; as thou, Father, art in me, and I in thee, that they also may be one in us: that the world may believe that thou hast sent me.**
**—John 17:20–21**

The cry of Jesus' heart for His church is the same today as it was when He prayed this prayer: that we might be one as He and the Father are one. But this concept of unity and oneness—this kind of togetherness—is unfathomable to the natural mind! We can read that verse a million times and nod and say, "Yes, amen, we must be one." But then we look at all the denominations that are at war over this doctrine and that doctrine, and we look at all the saints we can't stand to be around because they're not living holy enough for us or they just plain do stupid things. Then we look at all the preachers who have fallen and given the church a bad reputation. How can we ever be one with all these crazy, mixed-up people?!

That's what Ephesians 2 is all about! Paul says, "Lest you become too good to be fitly framed together with your brethren, just remember how you were once dead in your trespasses and sins. Remember how you walked according to the course of this world and Satan was your spiritual master. Then consider how the Jew and Gentile were at war and how the blood of Jesus abolished that war.

And once you see how only the gracious workmanship of God brought you to salvation and is continuing to save you and make you holy, consider the reality that you were raised and seated with your brothers and sisters—all of them! Now, I know you cannot accomplish this unity in your own strength and ability, and that's why you have the Holy Spirit. That's His job—so let Him do it! When you do, you will see a move of God's power that will shake the world."

It is only the supernatural workmanship of God by His Spirit that will bring us into true unity and oneness. And we are seeing this happen all over the world today. Believers and their leaders are praying and seeking out relationships with believers and leaders from all denominations, all races, and all nationalities. God is moving as never before to bring the body of Christ together because there is a power in corporate worship, in being of one mind, one heart, and one spirit that will blast through the gates of hell like no nuclear weapon ever demolished a natural site!

Within the hearts of believers across the globe lies more potential power than the world has ever seen, and it is called the love of God in the unity of the Spirit. When we as individual believers simply begin to allow the Holy Spirit free reign in our lives, giving Him permission to clean us up, blow away the cobwebs of our past, and bring forth His righteousness, peace, and joy in our lives, we will love one another! We will be fitly framed together! And Jesus told us that it is this love for one another that will show the world that God sent Him to be their Lord and Savior.

We will be one with the Father as Jesus is one with the Father. We will be one with each other as we are one with Jesus. Then there is no limit to the surge of God's power that will flow through us to touch those who are lost, broken, hurting, and without hope. This is God's masterful and magnificent workmanship in the church today. Hallelujah!

# PART THREE

*Intimacy With God*

# Introduction

---

When we speak of worship, what usually comes to mind is the segment of our church services when the congregation sings songs of praise and worship to the Lord. We begin with praise songs that move to a strong beat and cause us to shout and dance with joy. During praise, while we are rejoicing, our focus is on everything God has done, is doing, and will do for us. Then there comes a point where the Spirit of God moves us to slow down, quiet down, and focus our attention entirely upon Jesus himself. Now we leave all temporal things behind, enter into the Holy of Holies in the heavenlies, bow our hearts to the ground, and see and hear only Him. We are consumed by our Lord and Savior, worshiping Him with our whole being.

When we speak of worship in this way, it is a most sacred experience, and the beautiful thing is, we can have this experience anywhere and at any time. We don't have to wait until Sunday morning, which leads to my main point. As exhilarating, burden-lifting, and life-transforming as worship in our services can be, this is only a part of the meaning of worship for the believer. Worship comprises the very essence and foundation of our life in Christ. Worship is the complete consecration of our lives to God. It is the attitude we walk in, speak from, and meditate in at all times. Our life is completely His.

The attitude and place of worship we walk in each day is the classroom of the Holy Spirit. The more we cultivate and develop a worshipful manner of life, the more He can teach us about the thoughts and ways of God. As we grow up in the Lord, we know more, see more, understand more, and surrender more!

Remaining faithful to God's Word and following the leading of the Holy Spirit means we give up any idols, turn over any obsessions, put off sinful thinking and habits, and crucify our flesh again and again. We renew our minds and cast down every vain imagination and lie of the Enemy. We immerse ourselves in a life of worship unto our God.

Through this continuous purification and progressive sanctification, we have more and more capacity to love, to be thankful, to step out in faith and power, and to worship our Creator with our whole heart. More than that, we have the maturity to commune with Him on a higher level. We are restored to the place Adam and Eve enjoyed as they walked and talked with Him in the garden of Eden.

Worship is falling down before the Lord in complete submission and humility *on the inside* at all times, making ourselves available to whatever He would have us say or do. It is inviting the Holy Spirit to transform us and make us into the fullness of the image of Jesus Christ. It is yielding all we have and all we are to the refining power of God so that He might use us and flow through us to bless others. Worship is giving to the Lord the honor and glory due His name twenty-four/seven.

Worship expands our intimate knowledge of our Creator and deepens our faith in Him. And our worship is never ending. What we do in worship on earth today is only a prelude to what we will be doing throughout eternity. In this world, we worship as once-lost creatures who bow before the God who has found them, quickened them, and made them alive forever.

We can never fully comprehend all that God is, but the more we worship Him, and the more we love and understand His thoughts and ways, the more we love to worship Him with every breath. With each new revelation about our incredible God, the richer and deeper and higher our worship becomes. To know Him is to worship Him. When we truly know Him, we can't help but worship Him. He is our all in all, our beginning and ending. He is Alpha and Omega. He is Lord of all. He is King of Kings. In Him we live and move and have our being!

When we consider worship in light of the book of Ephesians,

we see clearly why the apostle Paul waits until the first verse of the third chapter to declare that he is nothing more than a prisoner of Jesus Christ. Worship is different from praise because the worshiper has stepped beyond thanking God for altering their *condition* to worshiping Him for their *position* as His children. They love Him for who He is, and they are forever humbled by whom He has made them to be.

In Part One, "Loved by God," we explored the first chapter of Ephesians, which describes in detail the incomprehensible reality of who God is and all He accomplished in His redemptive work through Jesus Christ. In Part Two, "Experiencing Jesus," we dug into the second chapter of Ephesians, where God mercifully quickens us with Christ, raises and seats us together with Him and with each other, and makes us a holy temple in which He dwells forever. By chapter three, Paul falls upon his face and cries, "I am undone by the revelation of my Creator and all He has done for me. I am nothing but a prisoner of the Lord Jesus Christ! All I can do is worship Him!"

Paul was not forced or made to be a prisoner of Jesus Christ. He *chose* to be His prisoner. Believers choose to allow Jesus to save them and heal them and set them free, but few choose to become His prisoners. The Greek word Paul uses here means not only to be held captive, but to be bound. Paul not only allowed the Lord Jesus Christ to take him captive when he was saved on the road to Damascus, but he bound himself to Jesus in his daily life.

To Paul, worship was not something he did occasionally as a ritual; it was something he did continually. Following his example, worship of our God must not be something we do with one aspect of our being, such as our voice; it is something we must do with all that we are. Worship of our God is not accomplished in services from time to time; *worship is our service.* Nor is worship something we do only when we are happy and blessed. We worship God in all situations and circumstances.

Worship flows from our spirit in power, infuses our soul with understanding, gives divine expression to our body, and causes illumination of our countenance. Believers in Christ Jesus don't have to stop to think about worship. We don't say, "I think I'll pause to worship God now." Rather, we *live* in a state of worship and give

# 1

# FOR THIS CAUSE

---

"For this cause I Paul, the prisoner of Jesus Christ for you Gentiles . . ." (Ephesians 3:1). The apostle Paul was a man of purpose. He understood who he was in Christ and he knew his role in God's plan for the church. Much can be said about him, but I believe it is important to know three things about his former life, as Saul of Tarsus, which formed his character and ultimately produced a life that graphically and dynamically expressed complete surrender to Jesus Christ—the epitome of worship.

*First, Saul of Tarsus was an extremely intelligent man.* He had the ability and intellect to readily adapt himself to whatever audience he happened to be addressing or company he was keeping. He knew enough about the Greek culture to preach effectively to the Greeks. As a Roman citizen, he was thoroughly familiar with the Roman way of life. Yet he knew the Scriptures inside and out and could speak with ease on any scriptural matter with the Jews. He was affluent, influential, well-known, and highly respected by all the scholars and theologians of his day—until he became Paul, the Christian!

You must understand that the Gentile intellectuals and highly religious Jews of that time considered Christians insane. After all, they believed in a God who had become a man, died, and then rose from the dead. They believed in a Messiah whom most of Israel had rejected. It was acceptable for a rough, superstitious fisherman like Peter to preach Christ, but not Paul the scholar! Christianity was associated with those who were unlearned and not very religious. Once Paul became a Christian, he was an oxymoron. He was an "intelligent Christian." He didn't fit the mold. He was highly educated and had always been zealously religious. He had an impeccable heritage that should have never led to his conversion to this ludicrous worship of a Jew by the name of Jesus of Nazareth.

*Second, Saul of Tarsus was a truly multicultural person.* We hear a great deal today about multicultural churches, but let me assure you of this: You cannot have a multicultural church just by mixing cultures and races together. The people in the church must be multicultural in their *thinking*. To be multicultural is to be able to walk in another person's culture without trying to alter it. It is to have an appreciation for diversity. Because Saul was well-traveled, well-read, and spoke several languages, he was as at ease and accepted among the intelligentsia of Rome as he was among the Pharisees of Jerusalem. This made him truly multicultural. By the time he was converted, he was well aware of the traditions and thinking of all the people to whom he would minister.

*Third, Saul of Tarsus had the best of ancestry and heritage.* If any Jew had confidence and pride in his natural lineage and upbringing, it was Saul of Tarsus. Let's read the apostle Paul's own description of himself:

**Though I might also have confidence in the flesh. If any other man thinketh that he hath whereof he might trust in the flesh, I more: Circumcised the eighth day, of the stock of Israel, of the tribe of Benjamin, an Hebrew of the Hebrews; as touching the law, a Pharisee; concerning zeal, persecuting the church; touching the righteousness which is in the law, blameless.**
**—Philippians 3:4–6**

You would think Saul's intelligence, his multicultural acumen, and the high regard he carried as a Jew would never allow him to bow before Jesus Christ, and yet he did. What was it that brought him to the place where his paramount objective in life was to embrace this Jesus of Nazareth as Messiah and to reveal Him to others in all His splendor? How did God strip Saul of Tarsus of all reliance upon his brilliant mind, his multicultural identity, and his heritage as a Roman citizen and a righteous Jew? He made him a prisoner.

## THE PRISONER

And as he journeyed, he came near Damascus: and suddenly
there shined round about him a light from heaven: And he fell
to the earth, and heard a voice saying unto him, Saul, Saul, why
persecutest thou me? And he said, Who art thou, Lord? And the
Lord said, I am Jesus whom thou persecutest: it is hard for thee
to kick against the pricks.
### —Acts 9:3–5

Saul of Tarsus was on his way to the city of Damascus in Syria
to kill any believers he could find there when he ran into Jesus of
Nazareth—the very Jesus he hated. In one statement, Jesus completely turned the tables on Paul and he was locked up forever as a
prisoner in His service. He declared to Paul that by persecuting
Him and His followers, he was fighting God and literally kicking
"against the pricks."

In the Middle East in that time, oxen were controlled by farm-
ers who used a sharp instrument to goad or prod them into motion
in the right direction. Pens in which oxen were kept were lined
with these "pricks" to keep the oxen in place, as moving against
them would cause the oxen great pain. By using this illustration, we
can see that there was no enticement in the Lord's call on Saul's life.
He didn't tease him or coax him with blessing plans. He didn't say,
"I'm going to make you wealthy" or "I'm going to make you famous and important." He simply said, "Saul, you are completely
out of the will of God. You are fighting me like a stubborn ox kicking against the pricks."

Saul responded in an instant and humbled himself. Trembling
there on the ground before the Lord, he said, "What wilt thou have
me to do?" (Acts 9:6). Later, in Damascus, the Lord showed him
what he was going to suffer for the Gospel. The message was direct:
"You are my chosen vessel, and you will suffer many things for this
cause I give you." Did Saul take three days to consider the matter?
No, he went immediately to the believers there and presented himself for service. No longer was he the dreaded and cruel Saul of Tarsus, but Paul, the prisoner of Jesus Christ.

The apostle Paul worshiped Jesus with a total abandonment of
all his natural credentials and lived in complete compliance to the
Holy Spirit. When he desired to travel to certain cities and he felt

the Holy Spirit constraining him, he didn't go. When others warned him not to go to certain places and he felt the Holy Spirit compelling him, he went, regardless of threats to his life. He identified himself simply as "a prisoner of Jesus Christ."

To be a powerful, effective Christian means that you must be a prisoner, a slave to Jesus Christ. When God says to do something, you do it, with no regard for what people may think about you or say about you. You obey Him regardless of how you feel at any given moment or about any given thing. To be a prisoner of Jesus Christ is to be chained to Him, which means you automatically go where He goes, say what He says, and do what He does. It is to comply with His will fully and to allow the Word of God and the leading of the Holy Spirit to rule your heart and mind.

The time has come when we must stop confusing preachers with politicians. Shaking hands and kissing babies is not what being a preacher is all about! Being a preacher is solely about obedience to God and saying what God wants said. And this applies to all believers! Whether we are clergy or laity, full-time or part-time, on staff or a volunteer—we are all ministers and prisoners of Jesus Christ.

Paul knew that eventually he was going to be killed for the Gospel he preached. Nevertheless, he preached it—passionately and joyfully. How many Christians today would be willing to go to a city and preach the Gospel if they knew the result of their obedience could be imprisonment or death? I suspect very few. And yet that attitude and lifestyle of worship is what is required of us if we are going to be useful to God as witnesses of the Gospel. *All of us may not have to die for Christ in the physical sense, but we all must die to self in the spiritual sense.*

Those who are prisoners of Jesus Christ know that the message they proclaim is far more important than themselves as a messenger. The message takes center stage. The messenger is just a backdrop on which the message has been painted with brokenness and pain, surrender and submission, and utter joy of their salvation. Prisoners of Jesus Christ have yielded fully to God's call on their lives and continually put off the world, their flesh, and the Devil in their daily lives.

Just before he was beheaded on the Appian Way, Paul wrote to Timothy from his prison cell in Rome, "I have finished my course. I have kept the faith" (2 Timothy 4:7). He knew the time of his departure was at hand. From the first moment on the Damascus road to a prison cell in Rome, Paul was the prisoner of Jesus Christ. And the question he asked the moment he received Jesus Christ was the question of his heart for every moment thereafter: "What wilt thou have me to do?"

## WHAT WILT THOU HAVE ME TO DO?

There was nothing in Paul's career as a minister of the Gospel that was prestigious. Although he was equipped by education and experience to debate the law with the most intellectual Jewish scholars in Israel, to whom did the Lord send Paul? The Gentiles.

Not only was Paul the prisoner of Jesus Christ, but God locked him up with the idolatrous, whoremongering, homosexual-practicing Gentiles! If being knocked off his horse by a bolt of lightning didn't shake Paul up, this should have. This was the ultimate in public humiliation for a Jew with his background and abilities.

Paul was not sent first to the pristine halls of the temple in Jerusalem to proclaim the name of the risen Messiah. Nor was he sent first and foremost to the courts of kings and noblemen to preach Jesus Christ. No, God gave Paul the primary objective to reach the unclean, immoral, idol-worshipers of the Roman Empire. And one of the sleaziest cities in the world was Ephesus, a city filled with debauchery, polygamy, incest, orgies, and degradation, where men were lovers of themselves and where pride reigned supreme. Paul was directed to preach the Gospel and teach the mysteries of Christ Jesus to people he probably wouldn't even have spoken to before he received Jesus.

Could it be that the following passage in Ephesians, chapter 2, was not merely Paul's knowledge of the truth about Jew and Gentile coming together as one in Christ Jesus, but literally born from his spirit as he struggled with and conquered the issue himself?

**Wherefore remember, that ye being in time past Gentiles in the flesh, who are called Uncircumcision by that which is called the Circumcision in the flesh made by hands; that at that time ye were without Christ, being aliens from the commonwealth of Israel, and strangers from the covenants of promise, having no hope, and without God in the world: But now in Christ Jesus ye who sometimes were far off are made nigh by the blood of**

Christ. For he is our peace, who hath made both one, and hath broken down the middle wall of partition between us; having abolished in his flesh the enmity, even the law of commandments contained in ordinances; for to make in himself of twain one new man, so making peace; and that he might reconcile both unto God in one body by the cross, having slain the enmity thereby: And came and preached peace to you which were afar off, and to them that were nigh.

**—Ephesians 2:11–17**

Paul had a revelation from God about the Gentiles and the church, and without that revelation, he would never have been able to fulfill his calling. God had revealed to him the mystery of the church, and he was consumed with it. He became the greatest expositor of God's blueprint for the church who has ever lived. If you pulled all of his epistles out of the New Testament, the church would be lost, because Paul defines and articulates the functioning of the New Testament church. Without the apostle Paul, we never would have understood how we were to function as the literal body of Christ.

For example, Jesus empowered the church by giving us the Holy Spirit at Pentecost, but in his epistles, Paul enumerates specifically and thoroughly how we are to operate in the power of the Holy Spirit as individuals and as a corporate body. First Corinthians 12–14, in particular, calls the local church body and the individual believer to a place of love, order, and integrity with regard to moving in the supernatural power of God.

You can always tell when a local church body is operating in the power of God but has not studied the Word of God, specifically the New Testament epistles, and followed the New Testament pattern and order. They are like powerful ships with no rudder. They pump out steam and their smokestacks are blowing great gusts, but they sail in circles—never going anywhere—never growing up and maturing in the operation of God's power.

Some of the foundational principles Paul teaches the church about flowing gracefully in the power of the Holy Spirit are:

- We are all members of one body, and there are different administrations, but we are of one Spirit, and each member is equally vital.
- Prophesy one by one, not everyone at the same time! And if

you have word in a different tongue for the church body, it should be interpreted.
• The gifts of the Spirit are given as the Holy Spirit wills.

Paul's mandate from God was to bring the revelation of Jesus Christ to the Gentiles and then bring understanding, order, and truth to the churches they formed. To accomplish this, he traveled extensively and wrote prolifically. The church must be forever indebted to his faithfulness to carry out his mission, for the epistles of Paul lay the foundation for who we are and how we are to function as the body of Christ.

## PAUL'S CHARGE TO OUR GENERATION

In his epistles, Paul unveils before our eyes God's glorious church. Pulling away the curtain of ignorance and darkness, he reveals to believers what the church really is and how the body of Christ is ordained by God to operate in this earth. Our generation desperately needs to embrace this heavenly understanding and vision of who we are as the church, because the Enemy is sending every deception and evil work against us to destroy that understanding and neutralize our vision. We must be defined by God's Word and led by the Holy Spirit—nothing more and nothing less.

If we don't understand what the church is and ignore the New Testament epistles, humanism will pass for the church, psychic readers will pass for prophets, mind-power and familiar spirits will pass for the Holy Spirit, positive thinking will pass for faith, and Satan's supernatural ability will pass for God's presence and power. The glory of God will be replaced with Satan's "aura." And his pale, flimsy, ultimately life-destroying spiritism will deceive many to turn from the true abundant life offered through Jesus Christ.

Do you remember what Paul's final warning to the Ephesian leaders was in Acts 21, before he left them? The wolves are coming! Don't be deceived! Don't let anyone or anything redefine who we are in the kingdom of God. Being a worshiper is not singing and jumping and shouting with reckless abandon at meetings. Being a worshiper is submitting fully to the Word of God and the Spirit of God at all times. Only the true worshiper will spot the wolves and have the power to dispel them. Only the true worshiper will grow up into the image of Jesus Christ.

As the church, we are the only ones on the planet who are spiritually born into this body through the death, burial, and resurrection of our Savior God, Christ Jesus. As individuals, our past is buried and we have newness of life. As a corporate body, we are an awesome entity without precedent. No carnal, unregenerated mind can comprehend us because we are *the mystery*.

# 2

# THE MYSTERY

Not too long ago, there were articles in the paper reporting statements made by a certain denomination about marriage, specifically a wife's submission to her husband and her role in the family. Immediately, secular minds began arguing against that statement, and leaders of the church began to "dialogue" with them. Suddenly we heard statements from church leaders like, "No, that's not what we really meant. What we really meant was . . ."

**But the natural man receiveth not the things of the Spirit of God: for they are foolishness unto him: neither can he know them, because they are spiritually discerned.**
**—1 Corinthians 2:14**

If we are not careful, we are going to allow unconverted human minds to redefine the New Testament church God has established. If the natural mind does not comprehend the things of the Spirit of God, and the things of the Spirit include divine understanding of God's Word, why is the church entering into this fruitless biblical debate with unbelievers? Most important, why are we backing down from God's Word? The church must come to grips with the reality that the world will never accept us. We are a mystery!

There are two realities we must understand as the church. First, we need to continue preaching the Gospel without apology and without shame, and if unbelievers reject Jesus Christ and call us crazy, then so be it. Second, we need to face the fact that the epistles were not written to the unbeliever, but to the believer. Submission of a wife to a husband in the godly, righteous, holy sense of the New Testament is not a concept the worldly mind can grasp. Unbelievers are supposed to think these teachings are ridiculous! They have no spiritual capacity to receive them, and Paul exhorts us that these truths are "foolishness" to them. The unregenerated person cannot comprehend that submission can bring freedom and joy, because this is "spiritually discerned," and they are spiritually dead.

Paul's letters were written specifically to us, this new, unique mystery called the church. We are the ones who are filled with God's Spirit, the Teacher who gives illumination, divine empowerment, and comfort. With the Holy Spirit living in us, we are alive to God, have the spiritual capacity to comprehend Paul's letters and teachings, and possess the grace to obey the Word of God. It takes the Holy Spirit in us to be able to live the life of a worshiper of Jesus Christ. Paul understood this.

## MADE KNOWN BY REVELATION

"For this cause I Paul, the prisoner of Jesus Christ for you Gentiles, if ye have heard of the dispensation of the grace of God which is given me to you-ward . . ." (Ephesians 3:1–2). After expounding on the wealth and workmanship of God in chapters 1 and 2, Paul finally gets around to explaining his credentials to the Ephesians and the church at large in chapter 3. In verse 1 he declares that he is a prisoner of Jesus Christ sent to the Gentiles. Then in verse 2 he begins to talk about the message God has given him to deliver, which he first refers to as "the dispensation of the grace of God."

Now, the word *dispensation* used here does not mean a period of time as is the usual usage by believers today. It is translated from the Greek word that means "administration" or the management or oversight of something. It describes the work of a servant who has been given considerable responsibility over his master's household. So Paul is saying that the responsibility or oversight of the doctrine of the grace of God has been given to him to deliver to the Gentiles. Paul then goes on in verse 3 to explain how he received this mandate:

How that by revelation he made known unto me the mystery;
(as I wrote afore in few words, whereby, when ye read, ye may
understand my knowledge in the mystery of Christ) which in
other ages was not made known unto the sons of men, as it is
now revealed unto his holy apostles and prophets by the Spirit;
that the Gentiles should be fellow-heirs, and of the same body,
and partakers of his promise in Christ by the gospel.
—**Ephesians 3:3–6**

It was by revelation that Paul received the understanding of the
mystery. The Greek word for *revelation* here means "an unveiling,
a revealing." In the same way God tore the veil of the temple when
Jesus died on the cross to reveal the Holy of Holies, He pulled aside
the curtain of darkness and ignorance that had hidden the mystery
of the church for ages past and revealed the truth to Paul and to
others.

The *mystery* here literally means something we cannot possibly
know without God telling us, something we cannot possibly see
without God showing us. God has set this whole thing up so that
we cannot truly know who we are and how we are to operate except by coming to Him and hearing it straight from Him. It is imperative that we fellowship with the Father in order to understand
Him, to understand ourselves, and to comprehend His plan for us.

Paul received the revelation of the mystery directly from God
and relates that revelation to us in his New Testament epistles, but
we must then open our hearts in faith toward God and receive His
Word directly from Him—just as Paul did.

The very creation of the church and workmanship of God in
the church baffles the natural mind. How can anyone be born *again*?
How can a believer be totally transformed by the renewing of their
mind to God's Word and then grow into the full stature of Christ
Jesus? We cannot fathom the mystery of godliness and holiness and
perfection in Christ without operating from our spirit. We must
forsake the vain reasonings of our natural mind and dive fully into
the revelation flowing from the mind of Christ within us.

A mystery is also something that on the surface is not only baffling but may appear to be ridiculously confusing. As I mentioned
before, the entire concept of the church is just that to the unbeliever. Unbelievers cannot begin to understand how God could

create the church through crucifixion on a Roman cross and resurrection from a Jewish tomb.

And talk about ridiculous, from the Jewish perspective, just what would you think if one of your distant cousins stood up in the synagogue one day and declared that he was the Messiah? Worse yet, if later he taught that he would die, and like a seed planted in the ground, rise again bringing a mighty harvest with him? You would say just what they did: "Isn't this Jesus, the carpenter's son? What is he thinking?!" The Jews weren't waiting for a Messiah who would be born in a manger and wrapped in swaddling clothes. They certainly weren't looking for someone who came out of Nazareth, the town where Jesus was raised. (They didn't remember that he was born in Bethlehem in accordance with Old Testament prophecy about the Messiah.)

The Jews of that time were expecting a noble king, riding on a white horse, to secure their independence from Roman rule. But this Jesus of Nazareth was an embarrassment to the Jews, who saw Him as a rabble-rouser and troublemaker. He could bring great harm to them by aggravating Rome. If He did not have the supernatural power to defeat Rome, He should be quiet and stop agitating everyone. Nothing Jesus did made sense to them, and yet He was amassing an incredibly large following. Finally the only thing that made sense to them was to cry, "Crucify Him. Get Him out of the way!"

Saul of Tarsus was one of those who held this opinion. He had actually been one of the leaders who believed that all Christians should be eliminated. He held the coats of those who stoned Stephen in Acts 7:58–60. And now here we are reading Paul's letter to the Gentile Ephesians, declaring the very thing he had once considered to be not only ridiculous but dangerous!

What made the difference in Paul's life? Revelation. On the road to Damascus, his natural eyes were blinded while his spiritual eyes were opened. Paul's spirit had been illuminated by the truth concerning the grace of God, and this revelation caused a complete conversion in his life.

## THE LEAST OF ALL SAINTS

Can you imagine God whispering in your ear the meaning of a mystery, and then when you proclaim that meaning, everybody thinks you're crazy? That's the situation in which Paul found himself. People generally thought he had lost his mind when it came to talking about a crucified Messiah and a resurrected Lord. Moreover, the people who knew Jesus best—the apostles—also questioned Paul because of his past. As a result, Paul was often an isolated and controversial figure in the early church. He was called by God to preach something for which he had very little Old Testament validation. Because the church was a mystery from ages past, God had only hinted about its existence in the Old Testament.

Let's look at some of the aspects of the mystery of the church that Paul brought to us by way of revelation from the Holy Spirit. The life of Jesus Christ himself was a mystery hid in God, and something our natural mind cannot comprehend. How can a young virgin conceive and bear a child and still be a virgin? How can the death of one man qualify to pay for the sins of the entire human race? How can someone die, be buried, and then come back to life in an immortal, corporeal body? Who is this resurrected Lord who takes the time to remove His graveclothes and leave them neatly folded in the tomb?

So here was Paul, sent to the Gentiles to preach something no one had ever heard before, including the Jews. To make matters worse, there was very little Old Testament Scripture to confirm what he was teaching. Yet there can be no doubt that Paul understood and skillfully and powerfully delivered the message of the mystery, the revelation of the church, the body of Jesus Christ.

**Whereof I was made a minister, according to the gift of the grace of God given unto me by the effectual working of his power. Unto me, who am less than the least of all saints, is this grace given, that I should preach among the Gentiles the unsearchable riches of Christ.**
**—Ephesians 3:7–8**

Paul received the revelation of the mystery from God and delivered that message to the Gentiles the same way he received salvation: by grace, through faith. His faith and trust in God opened his heart to receive the vision of this unique new entity called the church. Then, filled with a passion to see this glorious church raised up, he marched out to proclaim it to the world and become one of God's master carpenters. In verse 7, Paul is referring distinctly to the moment when he was saved on the road to Damascus:

"Whereof I was made a minister . . . by the effectual working of his power." It was the grace of God that saved him, it was the grace of God that gave him his calling, and it was the grace of God that enabled him to fulfill his calling.

Then Paul continues by calling himself "the least of all saints." He is saying, "Yes, I have been given this awesome responsibility to bring the revelation of the mystery, the understanding of who and what the church is, to you Gentiles. But just in case you start thinking I'm so much smarter and greater than you are, I want you to know that I received this call and this revelation the same way you did: by grace, through faith. And the supernatural power that is working in me, 'the effectual working of his power,' is in you too!"

**For I am the least of the apostles, that am not meet to be called an apostle, because I persecuted the church of God.**
**—1 Corinthians 15:9**

**This is a faithful saying, and worthy of all acceptation, that Christ Jesus came into the world to save sinners; of whom I am chief.**
**—1 Timothy 1:15**

There is no arrogance left in Paul as he writes to the Ephesians. He genuinely regards himself as the "least" among the saints. After his conversion on the road to Damascus, he was convinced that he was the chief of sinners and not worthy to be called an apostle because as Saul of Tarsus he had persecuted and murdered Christians with zeal and satisfaction. I believe the reason Paul possibly understood and appreciated the message of God's grace more than any other believer of his time was because he considered himself completely unworthy of God's mercy and grace. Everything in his being cried out in sheer awe and gratitude that Jesus even saved him, let alone made him a minister of the Gospel.

Today there are many Christians who think they did God a favor by allowing Him into their lives. We don't see many who are willing to proclaim themselves to be the "least" among the saints! But this spirit of genuine humility is required if we are to truly worship God and fulfill His plan. If we don't have an attitude of being least among the saints, we will never be great in the kingdom of God. Paul's attitude of humility was the key to his receiving the revelation of the church.

## A HUMBLING TRUTH

Which in other ages was not made known unto the sons of men, as it is now revealed unto his holy apostles and prophets by the Spirit; that the Gentiles should be fellowheirs, and of the same body, and partakers of his promise in Christ by the gospel.
**—Ephesians 3:5–6**

Few of us today can begin to comprehend the intense hatred that the Jews had for Gentiles in the time of Paul. If a Gentile sat at the table with a Jew, the Jew would break his plate, get up, and leave. Even the idea of breaking bread with a Gentile was mind-boggling to a Jew. So intense was the dividing line between Jew and Gentile, we witnessed Jesus' refusal at first to even speak with the Syrophoenician woman in Mark 7:24–30. Yet now Paul is asking Jews and Gentiles to sit down at the same Communion table and partake of the Bread of Life, Jesus Christ. Can you see the incredible act of humility it took for Paul to carry out his calling?

Jesus told a parable that foretold how this scenario would unfold:

A certain man made a great supper, and bade many: And sent his servant at supper time to say to them that were bidden, Come; for all things are now ready.

And they all with one consent began to make excuse. The first said unto him, I have bought a piece of ground, and I must needs go and see it: I pray thee have me excused. And another said, I have bought five yoke of oxen, and I go to prove them: I pray thee have me excused. And another said, I have married a wife, and therefore I cannot come.

So that servant came, and showed his lord these things. Then the master of the house being angry said to his servant, Go out quickly into the streets and lanes of the city, and bring in hither the poor, and the maimed, and the halt, and the blind. And the servant said, Lord, it is done as thou hast commanded, and yet there is room. And the lord said unto the servant, Go out into the highways and hedges, and compel them to come in, that my house may be filled.

For I say unto you, that none of those men which were bidden shall taste of my supper.
**—Luke 14:16–24**

The first call of God was to Israel—an elect group, chosen by Jesus himself during His earthly ministry. The invitation was as old as Abraham, an invitation to "come and dine." But when God served the Bread of Life and sat Him down at the table, the nation of Israel made excuses about why they could not partake, and they walked away.

The second call was to the Gentiles—the halt, lame, deaf, dumb, and blind. The Master was saying, "Let anybody come to the table." The *anybody* includes US! All of us unclean, uncircumcised Gentiles came to the Master's house to partake of a formal, sit-down dinner with white linen. The church is a "spread" that was prepared for aristocrats and eaten by common folk like us. This is where Paul entered, center stage, to proclaim the mystery of the church, which would be predominantly Gentiles.

The third call is the challenge for the end of the age, because there is still room at the Master's table for all those who will come. And since no man knows the day or the hour, we are all a part of this call. We are to go and compel the final harvest to come in before the entrance is closed to the Master's house. What a marvelous grace! What a privilege is ours!

It's little wonder the Jews in Paul's time didn't know what to think. God had broken all protocol in saving the Gentiles. He had broken the generations-old "religious etiquette" in calling for these formerly heathen believers to be filled with His Holy Spirit. A humbling message, to be sure, for a Jew with the heritage and background of Saul of Tarsus! But Paul the apostle realized that he was one of the Master's servants going into the highways and byways, compelling guests to come to the table and share in Communion with the Lord and with one another. He knew the Gentiles, who once would never have been allowed near the holy things of Israel, were now being invited by the Holy One of Israel to have intimate fellowship with Him.

Delivering the mystery of the church was a monumental responsibility and all-consuming task. We are a spiritual body born from God through the shed blood of Jesus Christ. We are the coming together of Gentile and Jew, bond and free, male and female. We are citizens of heaven who operate on earth according to our spiritual position, transcending and overcoming our natural conditions. We are a holy nation, a peculiar people, set apart exclusively for God's use.

It was because Paul was continuously overawed by the manifold grace of God toward him that he could humbly deliver the revelation of the mystery first to the Gentiles, then to the Jew, and finally to kings. His gratitude and heart of worship toward God is what allowed and enabled him to carry out God's plan for his life.

# 3

# UNSEARCHABLE
# RICHES

Unto me, who am less than the least of all saints, is this grace given, that I should preach among the Gentiles the unsearchable riches of Christ.

—Ephesians 3:8

Paul was given grace by God to proclaim to the Gentiles the "unsearchable riches of Christ." The Greek word for *unsearchable here* literally means these riches cannot be searched out or tracked. The contemporary meaning for the word would be something that could not be explored or examined. However, here Paul invites us to do all the exploring of Christ's riches we can. Then, when we are finally exhausted from our search, we will discover that we have only begun to enjoy what He has for us. No matter how much we search and no matter how much we find in Him, we will never come to the end of His riches.

How big is the God you worship?

"He's infinite, omnipotent, awesome," you might say.

But how big is God to *you*? Is He big enough to meet all your needs? Is He big enough to handle all your problems? Is He big enough to fulfill all your desires? Is He so big you cannot even begin to comprehend how big He is?

One of the words used as a synonym for *unsearchable* is *unfathomable,* which alludes to a search mission in the open sea. When seafarers want to determine how deep the water is, they emit

174

sounds into the water. Then they measure the time it takes to hear the sound reflected off the bottom of the ocean. The nautical unit of measure for this sounding is called a fathom, which is about six feet in length. When something is unfathomable, it means the ocean depth is so great that when the sound is sent down it never returns. What a powerful word picture of the full measure of Christ's riches in our lives! There is no tracking the end of them. We can spend all we want of His riches and still not put a dent in His supply.

Understanding that Christ's riches are unfathomable frees us from many of the hazards of riches. Normally, when people have access to riches, they remain secretive, protective of their find, and selfish. They will hire an elaborate security staffs and change their daily habits in an effort to protect and hoard their wealth. Excessive wealth often destroys relationships and can cause extensive personal problems. But the riches of Christ are inexhaustible, so we are free to share them and spend them without worrying about poverty tomorrow. These riches mean we are freed from jealousy, envy, and strife. And we are free to love, to rejoice in our salvation, and to impart this good news and grace to others.

Unsearchable riches mean that a person can know Jesus Christ their entire lifetime and never discover all of His wealth and glory. The riches of Christ Jesus are beyond full exploration, beyond full discovery, beyond full experience, and beyond full knowing. Paul—highly educated, speaking several languages, multicultural in thought, an excellent communicator—would be the first to admit, "I can't even articulate how much I've discovered in Christ." As worshipers of God, this is great news! There is no place to go but higher and deeper in spirit and in truth.

## FELLOWSHIP OF THE MYSTERY

**To make all men see what is the fellowship of the mystery, which from the beginning of the world hath been hid in God, who created all things by Jesus Christ.**
**—Ephesians 3:9**

Now Paul gets very specific about what, exactly, the unsearchable riches of Christ are. The fellowship of the mystery is described with two words that we discussed in the previous chapter. Paul is to make all men see the *administration* of that which can only be known by *revelation* from God. Literally, he is to explain to us how God brought forth and oversaw the creation of the church and reveals the workmanship of God in the body of Christ. Then he goes on to say that this has been hidden in God from the beginning of the world.

God laid out the blueprint of His great plan from the beginning of the ages, from the very foundation of the world. He had a plan to redeem mankind, which included a special time period when predominantly Gentiles would be redeemed. We call this the Church Age. That plan was hidden for thousands of years because the first stage of God's plan was to pull out the Hebrews and bring them into covenant with Him. They were the firstfruits, and the Gentiles were the latter-day harvest.

Only a few clues were given to the prophets in the Old Testament about this aspect of God's plan, but when Jesus began to preach, He made mention of the Gentiles often and demonstrated how they were redeemed by grace, through faith, just like Abraham, Isaac, and Jacob. Once He reminded the people that in Naaman's day all the lepers who were in Israel died of leprosy, except Naaman, who was a Gentile. He recovered from this dread disease because he sought out God's prophet Elisha and obeyed his commands, showing his faith in God. (See Luke 4:27 and 2 Kings 5:1–14.) A Gentile succeeded where the Jews had failed because he had faith in God and obeyed His prophet's instruction.

Jesus also reminded them that it was a Gentile widow who received a miracle of provision when she was hospitable to the prophet Elijah and obeyed his commands, while the widows of Israel died in famine. (See Luke 4:26 and 1 Kings 17:1–16.)

Jesus even ministered to Gentiles on occasion. When a Roman centurion came to Him seeking healing for his servant, Jesus healed the man. This centurion said to Him:

Lord, my servant lieth at home sick of the palsy, grievously tormented. And Jesus saith unto him, I will come and heal him. The centurion answered and said, Lord, I am not worthy that thou shouldest come under my roof: but speak the word only, and my servant shall be healed. For I am a man under authority, having soldiers under me: and I say to this man, Go, and he

goeth; and to another, Come, and he cometh; and to my servant, Do this, and he doeth it.
—**Matthew 8:6–9**

Jesus marveled at this man's statement and said, "Verily I say unto you, I have not found so great faith, no, not in Israel" (Matthew 8:10). He then went on to proclaim this great word about the Gentiles:

**Many shall come from the east and west, and shall sit down with Abraham, and Isaac, and Jacob, in the kingdom of heaven. But the children of the kingdom shall be cast out into outer darkness: there shall be weeping and gnashing of teeth.**
—**Matthew 8:11–12**

There are a few mentions of Gentiles coming into closer relationship with God. But now Paul is telling the Ephesians that the intent of God from the beginning has been revealed fully. One of the unsearchable riches of Christ is that all men, Jew and Gentile, can be saved by simply calling upon the name of the Lord Jesus Christ. We are invited to see and to know the truth of Jesus Christ, the plan of redemption God had for us from the beginning of time, and to enjoy all of His unsearchable riches.

## THE POWER OF THE WORD

"And to make all men see what is the fellowship of the mystery, which from the beginning of the world hath been hid in God, who created all things by Jesus Christ" (Ephesians 3:9). Another unfathomable treasure we have obtained as believers is the revelation of the immeasurable power of God's Word. This revelation begins with understanding that God "created all things by Jesus Christ." Like the "fellowship of the mystery," in these few words we are presented with a truth that is foolishness to the natural mind. All of creation is the work of Jesus Christ because He is the living Word of God, and God created all things by His Word. John the apostle began his account of the Gospel with this same truth:

**In the beginning was the Word, and the Word was with God, and the Word was God. The same was in the beginning with**

God. All things were made by him; and without him was not any thing made that was made.
—John 1:1–3

And the Word was made flesh, and dwelt among us, (and we beheld his glory, the glory as of the only begotten of the Father,) full of grace and truth.
—John 1:14

Jesus is the Word incarnate, and God continues to create all things through His Word, Jesus Christ. As John says, "Without him was not any thing made that was made." When God spoke, it was the Word, Jesus Christ, who caused God's intent to come into being, and that is true today. When God speaks, it is the Word who causes miracles to happen, the sick to be healed, the sinners to be forgiven, the demons to flee, and the weak to be made strong.

"Through faith we understand that the worlds were framed by the word of God, so that things which are seen were not made of things which do appear" (Hebrews 11:3). God speaks from the invisible realm and the Word brings forth a visible reality. We were not a people—not a church—until Jesus Christ spoke the intent of God into existence and said, "Let there be . . ." The same creative Word that created light in a dark void created salvation in a heathen heart!

To those who marveled and wondered, *How can this be that God would include Gentiles in His plan?* Paul said, "It is by the same power that God created the world out of nothing. The Gentiles were brought in and the church was born out of the mouth of God." God sends His Word, and His Word causes things to come into existence that were not previously seen or known. God sent His Word in the form of flesh-and-blood humanity into this world, and by Christ Jesus' life, death, and resurrection, He caused a church to be birthed that had not existed before.

God spoke in your heart the truth of Jesus Christ, you believed in Him, and you were born again in your spirit. God spoke and the Holy Spirit filled your being so that you entered a new realm of existence—you in Christ and Christ in you forever.

When God speaks, reality happens! His Word is full of grace and power, fully effectual to bring about anything He desires.

One of the main reasons we praise and worship God, one of

our motivations and greatest joys, is this fact that God continues to create life and wholeness and purpose out of things that seem dead and broken and void of purpose. We are what we are today because God spoke His Word and made us and remade us and continues to remake us. Everything we need, desire, hope for, and believe for is created and will be created by the power of His Word.

Nothing is beyond the power of God, and that power is expressed and manifested through His Word. Whatever He desires to exist, He *speaks* into existence! And we partake of the unsearchable riches of Christ when we speak and proclaim His Word in the earth today. When we think and act and speak in accordance with God's Word, all the forces of nature, every demon, and even the angels of heaven must obey because God's Word is the final authority in all matters and in all situations! Every knee must bow to the name of Jesus, who is the Living Word.

If you are grasping this truth right now, your heart is bursting and your mind is spinning and your feet are dancing! In Hebrews 1:3, we read that Jesus Christ is, even today, "upholding all things by the word of his power." When God speaks, His Word has power embedded within it to do what God sends it to do, and it will sustain that work forever.

For as the rain cometh down, and the snow from heaven, and returneth not thither, but watereth the earth, and maketh it bring forth and bud, that it may give seed to the sower, and bread to the eater: So shall my word be that goeth forth out of my mouth: it shall not return unto me void, but it shall accomplish that which I please, and it shall prosper in the thing whereto I sent it.

**—Isaiah 55:10–11**

When you speak what God speaks and you speak according to His will, His Word prevails and destroys any obstacle the Enemy throws up. When you live according to God's Word and believe, all things are possible. Now, that is unfathomable wealth!

## WE TEACH THE ANGELS

To the intent that now unto the principalities and powers in heavenly places might be known by the church the manifold

wisdom of God, according to the eternal purpose which he purposed in Christ Jesus our Lord.
**Ephesians 3:10–11**

These verses of Scripture are filled with the unsearchable riches
of Christ! Paul begins by telling us why God created the church. In
verse 11, he says that this was an "eternal purpose" or intention. In
other words, this was on God's heart and in His mind throughout
eternity past and through all the ages of time into eternity future.

Paul goes on to say that the intention of God is to use the
church to show the principalities and powers His manifold wisdom.
The Greek language used in this verse tells us clearly that the principalities and powers spoken of here are not the demonic forces of
Satan roaming the earth but the angelic beings of heaven. The word
*heavenly* depicts the highest celestial realm, the third heaven, where
God sits and the cherubim and seraphim reside. So God has chosen
us, mortal vessels of clay, to be filled with His Spirit and His Word
to display His manifold wisdom to the angelic population of the
universe!

This is a mind-blowing concept! Human believers, the body of
Christ, are literally teaching and imparting revelation about the
mystery of the church and the plan of salvation to Michael and
Gabriel and every angelic being of heaven. Moreover, we are revealing the "manifold wisdom of God."

First Peter 1:12 talks about how the angels have a passionate desire to understand what God has done, that the cherubim gaze at
the mercy seat in heaven, sprinkled with the precious blood of Jesus Christ, pondering the intent of the Father in this great work
called the redemption of mankind. Paul has placed before us the
baffling and awesome truth that God is using *us* to display His multifaceted wisdom in His plan of redemption and the creation of the
church, and that we are teaching the angels what was in the mind
and heart of God from eternity past.

For some reason God has chosen to honor us with this awesome
responsibility and, like Paul, we must humbly declare that we are
the least of all saints, that we are completely unworthy of such a
privilege. We are overwhelmed by the unsearchable riches of
Christ. And only in this attitude of worship and humility are we
able to show the magnificent glory of God, even to angels.

# 4

# TIMING IS
# EVERYTHING

**But he answered and said, It is written, man shall not live by
bread alone, but by every word that proceedeth out of the
mouth of God.**

**—Matthew 4:4**

Jesus told us that our life, our deliverance, our hope, and our fu-
ture are found in the words that proceed from the mouth of God.
His words are the truth by which we worship Him in spirit and in
truth. And the first and final words that proceed from the mouth of
God and that form the very foundation of our lives are found in the
Holy Scriptures.

## OUT OF GOD'S MOUTH

God's Word is eternal, beginning in eternity past and extending
to eternity future. God's Word is absolute. Nothing can be added to
it and nothing subtracted. Jesus, as God's Word, is Truth. Nothing
more needs to be said for our salvation and our full redemption. He
said of himself, "I am the way, the truth, and the life: no man
cometh unto the Father but by me." (See John 14:6.)

God's Word, being eternal, is also ongoing and perpetual. A
wonderful example of this is when God said, "Let there be light."
He set into motion a chain of light—unending in time and space.

The words He spoke are still going out. Light is filling the dark souls of men and women.

The Bible also tells us that all things are upheld by God's Word. He does not create and then say to His creation, "Fend for yourself." He upholds what He creates. When God speaks, we can stand on His Word and know that He will be faithful to perform what He has spoken.

However, God is not through speaking to His people! His written Word is the foundation upon which we build our lives, but He also speaks to us by His Spirit. If we are true worshipers of Him, our eyes on Jesus and our ears constantly listening to the still, small voice of the Holy Spirit within us, we know that He is speaking to us continuously throughout our day, leading us and guiding us and giving us revelation, wisdom, and insight into the future. He is also speaking to us today as individuals, as churches, and as the church at large through words of prophecy.

The problem with many people is that they experience a "word" from the Lord and then go off by themselves to build an entire movement on that one word. The prophetic word of God's wisdom and knowledge is ongoing and must be continually weighed in light of the Holy Scriptures. God will not speak today in contradiction to what He has written in His Word. Nevertheless, we have to keep our spiritual ears wide open to catch the daily and seasonal leading of the Holy Spirit as well as the prophetic directions and instructions to the body of Christ at large. God wants to talk to His people!

## THE PROGRESSIVE WORD

"To the intent that now unto the principalities and powers in heavenly places might be known by the church the manifold wisdom of God" (Ephesians 3:10). What was hidden before is *now* revealed. God's Word is progressive. He does not reveal all truth to us all at once but in stages and increments as we need to know and can handle it. The apostle Paul is keenly aware that God is the master of time and that His timing is perfect. He has a particular time for the release of all things toward those who love Him and worship Him. Solomon expressed this truth in these words from the book of Ecclesiastes:

To every thing there is a season, and a time to every purpose
under the heaven: A time to be born, and a time to die; a time
to plant, and a time to pluck up that which is planted; a time to
kill, and a time to heal; a time to break down, and a time to
build up; a time to weep, and a time to laugh; a time to mourn,
and a time to dance; a time to cast away stones, and a time to
gather stones together; a time to embrace, and a time to refrain
from embracing; a time to get, and a time to lose; a time to
keep, and a time to cast away; a time to rend, and a time to sew;
a time to keep silence, and a time to speak; a time to love, and a
time to hate; a time of war, and a time of peace. . . . He hath
made every thing beautiful in his time: also he hath set the
world in their heart, so that no man can find out the work that
God maketh from the beginning to the end.
**—Ecclesiastes 3:1–8, 11**

There is a perfect time for every detail of your life, and God
knows those times. When you praise and worship Him faithfully
and sincerely, He will reveal the times and seasons of your life, but
God's Word to you is always *progressive*. It is planted in your heart,
it buds, it grows, it develops, and finally it yields a harvest in your
life. In His mercy and understanding, God gives you only as much
revelation as you can handle at that time of your life.

If He had told you ten years ago what He would have you doing now, your mind could not have taken it in. You would have
run! You wouldn't have been ready for all that lay ahead for you.
Thank God that He reveals His plan, His will, and His Word to us
in progressive stages. We could not contain all the revelation at
once. The fact is, as much as God has done for us and through us
and in us in the past, He has that much and more to do for us,
through us, and in us in the future. Right now, many things are a
mystery to us, but we can take comfort and have the security of
knowing that the blueprint has been drawn. The plan is already in
effect and is unfolding before us in the fullness of God's timing.

## THE REVELATION OF THE LAMB

Consider for a moment the revelation of God regarding Jesus.
Our first type and shadow of Him is found in the book of Genesis.
After Adam and Eve sinned, they realized they were naked before

God and sought to cover themselves with leaves. But we cannot cover our sin. Only God can do that. It was the Father who walked through the garden in the cool of the evening, found an animal, killed it, and used its skin to cover the nakedness of Adam and Eve. God initiated the first blood sacrifice to cover the sin of man. That first nameless animal made it possible for Adam and Eve to relate to each other in a new way and to stand before God without shame. God began with the simple truth that only the shedding of innocent blood can cover the shame of man's sinful condition.

Then God told Adam and Eve's first two sons, Cain and Abel, to bring Him a sacrifice. Abel brought a blood sacrifice of a lamb, and Cain brought a sacrifice of grain. God rejected Cain's offering and received Abel's. Cain became jealous of Abel and killed him. (See Genesis 4:1–8.) Here is the first mention of a lamb sacrificed for the sin of mankind and God's acceptance of it.

Later, when God is delivering the children of Israel out of Egypt, He commands the sacrifice of a lamb for the Passover. The lamb was to be a male without spot, wrinkle, or blemish. The blood of the lamb was applied to the doorpost and lintel of the house to provide protection from death. It was at that point that man began to understand that the blood of a sacrificial lamb had a personal benefit. As believers, we apply the blood of Jesus to the door of our hearts.

Then, through the prophet Isaiah, God revealed that the Lamb was a man. The ultimate blood sacrifice would be the sacrificial death of a spotless, innocent man for the sins of the world.

**He is despised and rejected of men; a man of sorrows, and acquainted with grief: and we hid as it were our faces from him; he was despised, and we esteemed him not. Surely he hath borne our griefs, and carried our sorrows: yet we did esteem him stricken, smitten of God, and afflicted. But he was wounded for our transgressions, he was bruised for our iniquities: the chastisement of our peace was upon him; and with his stripes we are healed. All we like sheep have gone astray; we have turned every one to his own way; and the Lord hath laid on him the iniquity of us all. He was oppressed, and he was afflicted, yet he opened not his mouth: he is brought as a lamb to**

the slaughter, and as a sheep before her shearers is dumb, so he openeth not his mouth.

—**Isaiah 53:3–7**

It was centuries later before God revealed who this man was. When John the Baptist was baptizing believers in the Jordan River, he looked out at the crowd, saw his cousin, Jesus of Nazareth, and said, "Behold the Lamb of God, which taketh away the sin of the world" (John 1:29).

After Jesus insisted that John baptize Him, John saw the Holy Spirit descend from heaven like a dove and rest on Him. The next day John confirmed the truth about Jesus again, "Behold the Lamb of God!" (John 1:36). In His perfect time, God revealed who the Lamb was. He held back the revelation of His Word until that precise moment in history. In the fullness of His timing, God sent forth His Son, born of a virgin: "That in the dispensation of the fulness of times he might gather together in one all things in Christ, both which are in heaven, and which are on earth; even in him" (Ephesians 1:10).

In the fullness of times God performed His Word. Has the Lamb been slain? Yes. When Jesus died on the cross, He died as the one, true, definitive, and eternal Lamb sacrificed for the sins of the whole world. The sacrifice was made in at the perfect time according to the plan of God from the beginning. As we read in Revelation, Jesus is the "Lamb slain from the foundation of the world" (Revelation 13:8).

## BE ALERT!

Be on the alert for God's timing. Timing is everything! Look for God to unveil something from His Word that has been hidden to you before. There are some things God couldn't tell you until now for your sake. If He had told you that some of your friends were going to leave you when you decided to live for Jesus, you might not have been able to go to the next level of spiritual discernment and holiness. God holds everything until the time is right for you to receive it and act on it: "For therein [in the gospel of Christ] is the righteousness of God revealed from faith to faith: as it is written, the just shall live by faith" (Romans 1:17, brackets mine).

We are always to walk by faith and not by what we see and experience. Our faith tells us, "God has more to reveal to me, and He will reveal what He desires for me to understand in His perfect timing. God is doing an eternal work in me. The more I believe and grow into the likeness of Christ Jesus, the more God is going to reveal to me. And as I experience new revelations and walk in them, I am going to grow in Christ and grow strong in faith to receive even more."

Paul tells us in Romans 10:17 that it is God's Word that builds our faith. We must immerse ourselves in His written Word and keep our spiritual ears attuned to the voice of His Spirit by living a life of worship. Worship establishes our faith and trust in God that "Father knows best." Then we will live our lives and carry out our calling according to His perfect timing.

# 5

# THE FAITH OF HIM

In whom [Christ Jesus] we have boldness and access with confidence by the faith of him.
　　　　　　—Ephesians 3:12 (brackets mine)

In chapter 2 of Ephesians, we explored the workmanship of God in our lives and the fact that we have this fabulous access to come boldly into the throne room of God to obtain mercy and grace in time of need—anytime, anywhere. Now Paul tells us that this "boldness and access with confidence" comes only "by the faith of him." Notice the phrase "of him." We spend so much time being concerned about our having faith *in* Jesus Christ that we often fail to move into the deeper revelation of what it means to have the faith *of* Jesus Christ. This is the faith by which we worship God from the innermost core of our being.

Do you think Jesus Christ ever lacked faith? Did He have any problem trusting God the Father? Did He receive all that He asked of the Father? Did He ask only what He knew the Father desired to grant? Was His faith perfect? Our answer to these questions must be an unqualified yes!

Does Jesus Christ continue to receive all that He asks of the Father? Is His faith still perfect? And will it be perfect tomorrow, and every tomorrow into eternity? Again, we must say yes!

Now let me ask you this: Who lives in you and will live in you forever? Is it not this same Christ Jesus?

I am crucified with Christ: nevertheless I live; yet not I, but Christ liveth in me: and the life which I now live in the flesh I live by the faith of the Son of God, who loved me, and gave himself for me.

**—Galatians 2:20**

Our boldness doesn't lie in our own faith, which can quickly melt into fear. Our confidence to move into deeper spiritual waters and take on spiritual adversaries rests in the faith of Jesus who lives and abides within us. We must continuously and diligently tap in to and draw upon His bold, active, dynamic faith, a faith that never shrinks back or cowers in the face of evil. There is such a thing as holy boldness that is beyond our own courage, and that boldness is rooted in the faith of Jesus Christ, who dwells in us and in whom we live and move and have our being.

The same thing applies to our having access to the throne of God with confidence. Our confidence to come before the Father with our requests and petitions is confidence shed abroad in our hearts by the presence of Jesus Christ. Is Jesus fearful or intimidated by coming into the presence of God the Father? Does He cower before God's throne? Is He reluctant to turn to God the Father and make known His requests? Absolutely not!

The confidence we have to come boldly before God's throne is a confidence born of the faith of Jesus Christ in us. Because He dwells within us as our high priest, we are able to hold fast our profession of faith and to know with certainty that He will never fail us or forsake us.

Now, there is a divine faith that comes into our spirit that is beyond our human ability. It is called the *gift of faith,* identified by Paul to the Corinthians as a gift of the Holy Spirit. This gift is bestowed upon us as the Holy Spirit wills and as we require that supernatural faith to do what God has called us to do. (See 1 Corinthians 12:9.) But whether we are given the gift of faith or are walking in the everyday "faith of Him," there is one thing we can count on with certainty when it comes to the faith of Jesus Christ: His is a tried and proven faith. It is perfect faith. And it is always within us to draw upon.

## PROVEN FAITH

You will recall that when Jesus prayed in the garden of Gethsemane, He wrestled with His own human will in those hours of agony. Finally He submitted himself fully to the Father in His flesh and said, "Abba, Father, all things are possible unto thee; take away this cup from me: nevertheless not what I will, but what thou wilt" (Mark 14:36).

What was it that Jesus desired to be taken from Him? What was the cup He didn't want to drink? Jesus wasn't only wrestling with the idea of going to the cross, the pain of the scourging, and the crown of thorns on His head, or the nails driven into His hands and feet. Jesus was wrestling with becoming *sin*. In all of eternity, He had never known sin. In His earthly life, He had lived without sin or guile. Now the Father was asking Him to take on the sins of the whole world and to *become* sin. It was such a deplorable concept to Him that He prayed, "Pass this bitter cup from me!"

In all of eternity, the Son of God had never been separated from the Father, not even for the twinkling of an eye. In His walk on earth, He had lived in complete communion with the Father, saying and doing only what the Father led Him to say and do. Now the Father was asking Him to become sin, which meant being separated from the Father. Jesus was facing the reality of being smitten by the Father, who had never shown Him anything but the most tender, abiding love. He was in agony at the thought of facing even a moment of alienation from Him.

For Jesus to pour himself out completely—to be stripped of all glory and honor and to die as a common thief, and then to go down into the depths of the grave and face hell in our place—was an act of supreme faith. Everything Jesus faced in the hours and days after the garden of Gethsemane required a complete faith that the Father would accept the sacrifice of His life on the cross, resurrect Him from death, defeat the Enemy, and unlock the gates of hell so that He might take captive what the Devil held captive. Furthermore, He had faith that the Father would fully restore Him to His position in heaven, seated at the Father's right hand.

Jesus knew the reality of what was ahead of Him. Nevertheless, He had to walk through it by faith. Through the days leading up to His trial and crucifixion, Jesus spoke His faith:

Destroy this temple, and in three days I will raise it up.
—**John 2:19**

I lay down my life, that I might take it again. No man taketh it
from me, but I lay it down of myself. I have power to lay it
down, and I have power to take it again. This commandment
have I received of my Father.
—**John 10:17—18**

For as Jonas was three days and three nights in the whale's
belly; so shall the Son of man be three days and three nights in
the heart of the earth.
—**Matthew 12:40**

On the cross Jesus cried out to the Father, "Eli, Eli, lama
sabachthani?" which is to say, "My God, my God, why hast thou
forsaken me?" (Matthew 27:46). There was no agony greater than
being forsaken by the Father. Then Jesus hung His head and said,
"It is finished."

The sun could not look on the death of God's only begotten
Son. The ground began to tremble. The veil of the temple split
from top to bottom. Law had a head-on collision with grace. The
heavens roared, and graves opened all over Jerusalem. The most
awesome moment in all of history—past, present, or future—shat-
tered time and space and echoed through eternity.

The prophet Isaiah's voice from centuries past was no doubt
ringing in Jesus' ears, "Surely he hath borne our griefs, and carried
our sorrows: yet we did esteem him stricken, smitten of God, and
afflicted" (Isaiah 53:4). Jesus was struck by His Father so that we
might know what it means to have His everlasting arms wrapped
around us. Jesus felt the wrath of the Father fall upon Him so that
His righteousness might fall on us.

What did Jesus have to hold on to in those darkest moments?
His faith in God's Word. His friends vanished into the anonymity
of the crowd. His disciples cowered in fear in a locked upper room.
His strength ebbed from His muscles. His blood flowed from His
wounds. His breath left His body. The Father turned away at the
sight of the sin He became. All that remained was His faith in God's
Word.

The only thing that was alive when Jesus was buried in the
tomb of Joseph of Arimathea was His faith-spoken words. What

God says is eternal. His Word does not end. The faith of Jesus Christ was God's faith and the words He spoke were God's words. So His faith went on believing and speaking. It could not end. The crucified and buried fleshly nature of Jesus didn't know that faith because His physical body was dead. But His faith was alive because His Spirit remained alive. His eternal Spirit bore His eternal faith, and that faith kept believing—past His being taken down from the cross, past His being wrapped in burial cloths and spices, past His being laid in a tomb, a stone being rolled in front of it, and a watch being set.

On the third day, when the earth shook, the stone rolled away, the soldiers fainted as if they were dead, and the Son of God came out of that tomb in victory, it was by one force alone: His faith in God's Word. Jesus went to His death, the grave, and hell believing that the Father would raise Him up. He rose from the dead and ascended to His Father because of His faith and the Father's response to it.

## THE POWER OF THE RESURRECTION

"If Christ be not raised, your faith is vain" (1 Corinthians 15:17). If the resurrection had not occurred, we would have no proof that faith in God's Word works, that faith in God's Word is eternal, and that faith in God's Word conquers all. Worship would be without foundation! But because of the resurrection, we know faith in God's Word works and we have something incredible and miraculous to shout about!

**If in this life only we have hope in Christ, we are of all men most miserable. But now is Christ risen from the dead, and become the first-fruits of them that slept.**
**—1 Corinthians 15:19–20**

How is it that we become the firstfruits of His resurrection? How is it that we can know with certainty that we will live in eternity and be raised from death to rule and reign with Jesus forever? It isn't because of who *we* are. It isn't because of our own human faith. It's because we now have Jesus Christ dwelling in us, and it is by *His* faith and *His* Word that we will be raised. The faith within us today is not our faith alone but His faith, His most excellent, proven, perfected, enduring, dynamic, eternal faith! No doubt Paul could hardly keep from shouting as he proclaimed, "In Him I live! In Him I move! In Him I have my being!" (See Acts 17:28.)

Jesus' faith has been proven. We look at the resurrection today and say, "His faith works! His faith conquers death!" It is His faith that operates inside us and will never cease to operate. It will go on believing past our moment of death to the moment of our resurrection! We would have nothing to preach if we did not have the resurrection to back us up. If Jesus hadn't risen from that grave, we would have no hope, but because He rose, we have everlasting hope!

The power of the resurrection, knowing Jesus is alive forevermore, gives us rock-solid confidence and faith that what God has spoken will come to pass. This revelation gave Paul the boldness and the confidence to proclaim: "Death is swallowed up in victory. O death, where is thy sting? O grave, where is thy victory?" (1 Corinthians 15:54–55).

When you and I received Christ Jesus as our Savior, the Spirit indwelt us. The faith of Jesus Christ is the driving force of His Spirit. It is His faith that motivates us to keep on. It is His faith that overwhelms us with the knowledge that His Word is absolute, unchanging, and eternal. It is His faith that allows us to be immovable, steadfast, abounding in the work of the Lord, knowing that Christ in us is greater than anything we encounter on this earth. (See 1 John 4:4.)

We can worship God because of the faith of Jesus Christ in us! It is resurrection faith! It is unshakable faith! It is faith that abounds and overflows and conquers. It is faith that produces and continues to produce. It is faith that continues to believe because it is the faith of God himself!

# 6

# TRIBULATIONS
# OF GLORY

For ye shall go out with joy, and be led forth with peace: the
mountains and the hills shall break forth before you into
singing, and all the trees of the field shall clap their hands.
Instead of the thorn shall come up the fir tree, and instead of
the brier shall come up the myrtle tree: and it shall be to the
Lord for a name, for an everlasting sign that shall not be cut
off.

—Isaiah 55:12–13

This passage of Scripture describes the life of a worshiper. Because God inhabits our praises (see Psalm 22:3), when we continually make melody in our hearts to the Lord (see Ephesians 5:19), His
presence is continually with us. And when His presence is continually with us, we "shall go out with joy, and be led forth with
peace." Our hearts are filled with joy and our minds kept in peace
because we are safely hidden in the secret place of the Most High,
warm and secure under the shadow of the Almighty (see Psalm
91:1–2)—no matter what comes our way.

## FAINT NOT!

Worship sensitizes our hearts and minds to the voice of the
Holy Spirit, who carefully leads us and guides us through the quag-
mire of darkness and evil in this life that seeks to destroy us at every

turn. Worship gives us the perspective and attitude that we are not going from battle to battle and trial to trial, but from revelation to revelation and victory to victory. Maintaining an attitude of worship is vital to carrying out God's plan for our lives and overcoming the onslaught of the Enemy. No one understood this better than the apostle Paul: "Wherefore I desire that ye faint not at my tribulations for you, which is your glory. For this cause I bow my knees unto the Father of our Lord Jesus Christ" (Ephesians 3:13–14).

For what cause did Paul bow? He was requesting strength and perseverance and courage for the Ephesians that they would "faint not." The word *faint* here can mean to be frightened, discouraged, weary, or to lose hope, but the preferred meaning is "to lose heart." Paul was concerned that when the believers saw what he had to endure for the Gospel's sake, they would lose heart, lose their passion for the kingdom, and become self-preservationists. He did not want his difficulties to frighten or discourage believers from fulfilling God's call on their lives. He wanted them to continue in steadfast prayer, reach the lost, and make disciples regardless of the trials and tribulations he endured.

When we see other believers, especially in other countries in the world today, being persecuted, tortured, and even executed because they refuse to deny Jesus as their Lord and Savior, we can lose heart and become afraid. We begin to wonder, *Could I be tortured or even die for Jesus?* Paul wants to put our hearts and minds at rest immediately by making the astounding statement that the tribulation he suffers on our behalf is for *our* glory! Only a prisoner of Christ Jesus could make such a bold proclamation and have the lifestyle and testimony to back it up.

What is Paul trying to say? I believe he is telling us, "Look, there is more to this than meets the eye. Tribulation of this kind, which is being persecuted for our faith, brings the glory of God on the scene. In the end, the one who is going through the tribulation experiences the glory of God; in fact, the whole body of Christ experiences the glory of God, and God himself is glorified and magnified. Moreover, when any one of us suffers by refusing to deny our Savior and Lord, it brings honor and glory to the entire church."

The word *tribulation* can mean anything from torture to extreme pressure to difficult living conditions. However, Paul's meaning of tribulation in this context is specific and definite: This is tribulation for the Gospel's sake. You are being persecuted, treated badly, or abused because you stand tall for Jesus Christ and refuse to deny Him in any way, at any time, or under any circumstances. Tribulations are definitely not something we enjoy, but they bring eternal rewards and the glory of God into our lives.

Even so, where and how does the goodness of God enter in? Surely He takes no pleasure in seeing His children suffer pain, but God's goodness does not mean that no Christian will ever suffer. And Jesus told us we would be persecuted for our faith in Him.

**If the world hate you, ye know that it hated me before it hated you. If ye were of the world, the world would love his own: but because ye are not of the world, but I have chosen you out of the world, therefore the world hateth you. Remember the word that I said unto you, The servant is not greater than his lord. If they have persecuted me, they will also persecute you; if they have kept my saying, they will keep yours also. But all these things will they do unto you for my name's sake, because they know not him that sent me.**
**—John 15:18–21**

God's goodness toward us is that when we suffer for His name's sake, He will use that suffering to produce a great, eternal benefit for us and for the body of Christ at large. He will bring glory and honor to our lives and to the lives of all believers throughout eternity.

Paul could worship the Father in the midst of his tribulations because he knew without any doubt that what the Father called him to do, the Father would equip him to do. And what the Father equipped him to do, he could successfully accomplish. And what he successfully accomplished in obedience to the Father and by the power of the Spirit, the Father would reward. Then the Father would use what Paul did to bring about a successful, productive, reward-producing benefit in the lives of others.

Paul knew that no matter what difficulties and obstacles and trials he faced, the glory of God would be seen upon the church because of it. He exhorted us strongly to faint not when we saw other believers go through tribulations for the Gospel's sake. This is the time when we ought to go into even higher gear to pray, study God's Word, reach the lost, and make disciples. And the Bible promises us in Galatians 6:9 that if we do not faint, at just the right time, we will reap a tremendous harvest for our faithfulness. In this case that harvest is the glory of God!

## GOING BEYOND

Let this truth sink into you: *You can't do anything in your own strength and power that has any eternal benefit or lasting goodness.* The Father always calls us to move just beyond what we can do in our own strength and power and to trust Christ in us to do what we cannot do. He calls us to trust and then obey, knowing full well that in our own strength, we'll fail, but in Him, we will be able to do "all things through Christ which strengtheneth [us]" (Philippians 4:13).

When Peter and John met a lame man at the Beautiful Gate to the temple, Peter said to him, "Silver and gold have I none." In other words, Peter said, "I don't have enough money to get you from where you are sitting right now to where God wants you to be, which is standing and praising Him inside the temple. What I have in my own strength and ability isn't enough."

But then Peter went on to say, "But such as I have give I thee." And what did Peter have? He had the same power that raised Jesus from the dead living in him! He had the faith of Jesus surging through his being, a never-fail, eternal, always-productive faith. And when Peter relied upon what he had by the Spirit, he said to that lame man, "In the name of Jesus Christ of Nazareth rise up and walk." (See Acts 3:1–6.)

But Peter didn't stop with bold words. He reached down, took the man by the hand, and lifted him up. Peter did for this man what the man could not do in his own strength. The man couldn't rise on his own power, so Peter lifted him to a standing position. And as this man believed, taking into his being the power of the name of Jesus Christ, "his feet and ankle bones received strength" (Acts 3:7).

Peter moved beyond what he could do in his own ability and faith and moved into what he could do in the power of the Spirit and the name of Jesus. The lame man moved beyond anything he had ever been able to do into what he could do when he believed.

What the Father commands us to do and equips us to do is *done*. Nothing can stand in the way of the Father's will. Nothing can stop it, cut it off, keep it locked up, or cause it to be turned aside. When the Word goes forth, it doesn't return void. When we speak His Word by His faith and in His name, we will always accomplish what He wants accomplished!

Paul faced such a situation when he went to Jerusalem. He tells us that he was "bound in the spirit unto Jerusalem" and that he did not know what would happen to him there. (See Acts 20:22.) Here is Luke's account:

And as we tarried there many days, there came down from Judaea a certain prophet, named Agabus. And when he was come unto us, he took Paul's girdle, and bound his own hands and feet, and said, Thus saith the Holy Ghost, So shall the Jews at Jerusalem bind the man that owneth this girdle, and shall deliver him into the hands of the Gentiles.

And when we heard these things, both we, and they of that place, besought him not to go up to Jerusalem. Then Paul answered, What mean ye to weep and to break mine heart? for I am ready not to be bound only, but also to die at Jerusalem for the name of the Lord Jesus. And when he would not be persuaded, we ceased, saying, The will of the Lord be done.

**—Acts 21:10–14**

Ultimately, because of his visit to Jerusalem, Paul was imprisoned in Rome. He knew that Jesus helped him endure the journey that led him to Rome and the years of imprisonment that followed. He knew that what he suffered had been authorized by God and that God, by His Spirit, was equipping him to accomplish all that He commanded him to accomplish, including the strength to endure the tribulations. He saw before him a great reward for his trials, which were at the command of God, in the will of God, and which he was endured by the grace of God. He wrote to Timothy:

Remember that Jesus Christ of the seed of David was raised from the dead according to my gospel: Wherein I suffer trouble, as an evil doer, even unto bonds; but the word of God is not bound. Therefore I endure all things for the elect's sakes, that they may also obtain the salvation which is in Christ Jesus with eternal glory.

It is a faithful saying: For if we be dead with him, we shall also live with him: If we suffer, we shall also reign with him: if we deny him, he also will deny us: if we believe not, yet he abideth faithful: he cannot deny himself. Of these things put them in remembrance, charging them before the Lord that they strive not about words to no profit, but to the subverting of the hearers.

**—2 Timothy 2:8–14**

Paul saw a great reward ahead: The believers on whose behalf he was suffering were going to obtain "the salvation which is in Christ Jesus with eternal glory" (v. 10). And he saw that he would be reigning with Jesus for eternity, crowned with His righteousness forever. At the end of his life, when he knew it was time for his life on earth to end, he wrote:

**For I am now ready to be offered, and the time of my departure is at hand. I have fought a good fight, I have finished my course, I have kept the faith: Henceforth there is laid up for me a crown of righteousness, which the Lord, the righteous judge, shall give me at that day: and not to me only, but unto all them also that love his appearing.**

**—2 Timothy 4:6–8**

Paul saw a crown of righteousness going to all those who believed as he did, those who were eagerly awaiting the Lord's return. He saw a reward for his faith and obedience, and it was a reward that benefited not only himself but the Ephesians. His tribulations were also for their glory.

## IT'S NOT ABOUT YOU

Your tribulations for the Gospel's sake are not only for you. They are not only so you can grow in faith and experience more of the promises of God in your life. They are not only so you can defeat the Enemy and walk in victory. What you do in being a prisoner of the Lord Jesus Christ is also for the benefit of others. Your works impact people. What you say touches them. Paul said in 2 Timothy 2:14, it is for "the subverting of the hearers." It is so that all arguments and unprofitable words and silly quarrels can be put to rest once and for all. Our tribulations for Christ Jesus have a higher purpose and a more noble cause: They bring glory to God and to His church.

Even though we may suffer, be in bonds, or even die, the Word of God is not bound by our circumstances. It continues to speak about the glory of God. It continues to speak of our salvation in Jesus Christ, our eternal life in Him, our reign with Him, and our bringing glory to Him. No matter how we may suffer, the Word of God in us continues to prosper, bless, produce, and bring eternal life.

Have you ever stopped to think about all that Paul wrote from prison? Not only did he write the letter to the Ephesians but also the epistles to the Philippians and Colossians, as well as pastoral letters to Timothy (1 and 2), Titus, and Philemon. Furthermore, it was while Paul was in prison that Luke went about doing all of the research he did to write an "orderly account" to Theophilus, which we know as the gospel of Luke and the book of Acts. How much less would the church know if Paul had not suffered on our behalf?

If Paul had not been imprisoned and undergone tribulations, would we have had the great teaching and encouragement of these books? Furthermore, his imprisonment and suffering bring authenticity to his words, cause them to ring true in the heart, and convict believers to stand strong in Jesus Christ as he did.

I would that ye should understand, brethren, that the things which happened unto me have fallen out rather unto the furtherance of the gospel; so that my bonds in Christ are manifest in all the palace, and in all other places; and many of the brethren in the Lord, waxing confident by my bonds, are much more bold to speak the word without fear.
—**Philippians 1:12–14**

God hath not given us the spirit of fear; but of power, and of love, and of a sound mind. Be not thou therefore ashamed of the testimony of our Lord, nor of me his prisoner: but be thou partaker of the afflictions of the gospel according to the power of God; Who hath saved us, and called us with an holy calling, not according to our works, but according to his own purpose and grace, which was given us in Christ Jesus before the world began.
—**2 Timothy 1:7–9**

Paul's suffering was indeed for the glory of the believers who read his letters, both in his time and today. What a great ongoing reward is Paul's! Have you ever stopped to think that he is still drawing reward from what you and I do in response to the truth we read in his epistles? His reward goes on and on. Why? Because it is an eternal reward from the Father for his obedience and trust in doing the Father's work by the Father's power!

Even in our suffering and tribulation, God makes certain that His Word goes forth to produce the result for which He sent it. Our part is to trust, to believe, and to obey. God's part is to use our trust and our efforts and our faith to do what He desires to do. In Paul's case, He brought forth a lasting work in the hearts of men and women around the world, not only in his generation, but in the generations following.

Paul set a remarkable, supernatural example for us, and that's the greatest point to be made here. He did not do what he did in his own strength, and neither can we. He bowed his knees to the Father to receive divine ability and capacity to run the race set before him. Thank God, the same strength and courage and perseverance and grace that Paul received from God are available to us. So now it is our turn to bow our knees to the Father!

When our families and neighbors and associates at work see us go through tribulations trusting and believing God, acting on His Word, and worshiping Him in the midst of the greatest persecution and ridicule, our rewards will continue for generations. But more than that, our tribulations glorify God and reflect glory upon the body of Christ at large. Most important, as a result many will come to know the Lord. There is no more powerful witness to this perishing, lost generation than a believer who brings glory to God and His church through tribulations for the Gospel's sake.

# 7

# THE WHOLE FAMILY

For this cause I bow my knees unto the Father of our Lord Jesus Christ, of whom the whole family in heaven and earth is named" (Ephesians 3:14–15). God will eventually pull everything He has created together under one name—the name of Jesus: heaven, earth, the whole family. As believers in Christ Jesus, we are to worship God with an awareness of that reality. In writing to the Ephesians about the "whole family" of God, Paul is making reference to the "holy convocation" that awaits us in eternity. This holy convocation is God's master plan for all things that were, are, and ever will be. It is also the culmination of His master plan for the church.

## THE CHURCH OF THE FIRSTBORN

For ye are not come unto the mount that might be touched, and that burned with fire, nor unto blackness, and darkness, and tempest, and the sound of a trumpet, and the voice of words; which voice they that heard intreated that the word should not be spoken to them any more. . . . But ye are come unto mount Sion, and unto the city of the living God, the heavenly Jerusalem, and to an innumerable company of angels, to the general assembly and church of the firstborn, which are written in heaven, and to God the Judge of all, and to the spirits of just men made perfect.
—Hebrews 12:18–19, 22–23

The church is so much bigger than most Christians think it is! We tend to think of "church" as the building we go to on Sundays or the body of believers with whom we meet on a regular basis. If we think bigger, we think the whole church is comprised of believers between California and New York, and maybe a few in Alaska and Hawaii. In our arrogance, we think "our few and no more" make up the church. But the "church of the firstborn" is bigger than America, much bigger! It is the church of the whole world throughout time. Any person who has bowed, is bowing, or will bow to the name of Jesus is part of "the general assembly and church of the firstborn, which are written in heaven . . . the spirits of just men made perfect" (Hebrews 12:23).

The church is bigger than today, encompassing yesterday and tomorrow as well—all of then and all of forevermore. When God sees the church, He sees the church that is and was and will be. He sees people who are going to believe in Christ Jesus who haven't even been born yet. God always sees things from the perspective of eternity.

God knows precisely what He needs from you today that will have an impact on a believer whom you will never meet on this earth, who lives halfway around the world, but who will be blessed by what you do and enabled to bless others in his own ministry. He knows precisely what He wants you to say today that will be repeated down through the generations to touch someone who is born a century from now, should He tarry. He knows how to use your whole life—your prayers and your giving and your words and your deeds—to bless people you don't know and will never know in this life, but who are people with whom you will live forever.

It is because God sees everything from an eternal perspective that we can say things happen now that were predestined before the foundation of the world. It is because God sees all of eternity that we can know that the Lamb was slain from the foundation of the world on our behalf. God fixes His purposes in eternity, and He manifests His purposes in time.

When you are going through trouble and times of tribulation, you can know with certainty that God is going to bring you through that experience and that He is going to work all things together for your good. Why? Because He sees your eternal future. Your eternal future is with Him, and that means your eternal future is not only good, but it is glorious beyond your imagination! As part of the "church of the firstborn," you are viewed in light of eternity at all times, and God wants you to view yourself that way too.

## THE GREATEST WORSHIP EVER

The greatest worship experience you will ever have isn't going to happen in your local church next Sunday, no matter how great that worship experience may be. God has an even greater one planned in eternity. It is a worship service in which the whole family is gathered—not only Jews and Gentiles worshiping together, and not only several denominations worshiping together. It will be a time when you join with believers from every background and corner of this world, from every generation past and every generation future. All of us will be worshiping God around His throne with the innumerable host of angels. In one accord we will cry, "Holy, holy, holy" to our Father.

Anytime we begin to worship the Father, we need to catch a glimpse of the heavenly convocation that is also worshiping Him. We need to see with spiritual eyes that we are worshiping God with a vast congregation of saints, that we are "compassed about with so great a cloud of witnesses" (Hebrews 12:1). We need to see with spiritual eyes we are worshiping God in the midst of countless angels—the very host of heaven—who join their voices with ours in crying, "Thou art worthy."

And when he had taken the book, the four beasts and four and twenty elders fell down before the Lamb, having every one of them harps, and golden vials full of odours, which are the prayers of saints. And they sung a new song, saying, Thou art worthy to take the book, and to open the seals thereof: for thou wast slain, and hast redeemed us to God by thy blood out of every kindred, and tongue, and people, and nation; and hast made us unto our God kings and priests: and we shall reign on the earth.

And I beheld, and I heard the voice of many angels round about the throne and the beasts and the elders: and the number of them was ten thousand times ten thousand, and thousands of thousands; saying with a loud voice, Worthy is the Lamb that was slain to receive power, and riches, and wisdom, and

strength, and honour, and glory, and blessing. And every creature which is in heaven, and on the earth, and under the earth, and such as are in the sea, and all that are in them, heard I saying, Blessing, and honour, and glory, and power, be unto him that sitteth upon the throne, and unto the Lamb for ever and ever.
—**Revelation 5:8–13**

John writes in Revelation that our voices join those who are singing a "new song" to the Lamb with the angels and the elders. When we worship, all of those in heaven fall down at His feet and join our worship, crying a loud "Amen!" to every word of praise and worship we utter.

Have you ever been in a house of prayer or in your home, worshiping the Lord by yourself, when you suddenly felt deep in your spirit, *I'm not alone*? You were right! You are never alone in your worship of the Father. You are just one voice of the whole family of believers on heaven and earth that have worshiped, are worshiping, and will worship Him forever. Your voice not only joins the vast host of saints and angels in heaven, but their voices join yours here on earth.

Are you aware that when you begin to worship the Lord in the quiet of your house, angels move into your house and worship Him right along with you? The Bible tells us that the angels of the Lord encamp around those who worship the Lord. The angels don't just sit there in their worship. They worship along with you. Their job is to deliver you. David wrote, "The angel of the Lord encampeth round about them that fear him, and delivereth them" (Psalm 34:7).

The word *fear* encompasses several realms of thought and emotion. It means a deep love, an abiding reverence, and the utmost respect for the absolute authority and sovereign rule of the Creator God. This abiding respect includes a holy fear of a God whose holiness and righteousness will destroy evil as well as give life. We definitely do not want to be standing in a place of opposition to our God! But the great news is, when we stand with God and our hearts are pure before Him, He will take care of the evil that attempts to destroy us. To fear God means to worship Him fervently, and fervent worship releases the angels to deliver us and put us into a position to receive the full blessings and provision of the Lord.

Open your spiritual eyes today as you worship the Lord! See the great host of angels camping about you, strong and glorious and countless in number. See the great host of saints, some who are the Old Testament saints who died in faith, not yet having seen the promise of Jesus Christ yet embracing Him from afar. See those who come from denominations other than yours, who perhaps don't know hymn number 856! See believers who are from other centuries, who are of other colors, customs, and cultures. You are going to have to take off the blinders of your prejudices and biases and doctrines and organizations and movements to see your whole family!

The worship of the Lord is for the whole family together, not the family separated into little cliques gathered in this corner and that corner, some standing, some sitting, and others on their faces. No—the whole family is united and intermingled as one family, in heaven and earth, and all are bowing before the Lord. God desires for us to be one because it is only in a unified body that His power can be released. It is only when we see ourselves bonded together under the authority of the divine Chief Executive Officer, who gives us a vision for this "mystery corporation" called the church, that we can begin to experience the fullness of the Holy Spirit's power in our midst. Paul is adamant about unity: "There is one body, and one Spirit, even as ye are called in one hope of your calling; one Lord, one faith, one baptism, one God and Father of all, who is above all, and through all, and in you all" (Ephesians 4:4–6).

When we come together with the whole family, we are in a position to receive a greater blessing from God. There are blessings that are not poured out by God on individuals but on the whole family. It is only as we are fully a part of that whole family and see ourselves as being in fellowship with the whole family that we can receive those blessings.

# 8

# LOVE THAT PASSES
# KNOWLEDGE

Many Christians today stand like stones or merely go through the motions during worship because they live beneath their privileges as children of God, and the greatest privilege of being God's child is receiving His love and joy. God's unconditional love and exceeding great joy are the security and strength we must have to fulfill His plan for our lives and enjoy it.

We must draw upon the warmth and comfort of our most valuable friend and resource, the Holy Spirit who lives within us. The Spirit is always available to pump the Father's unconditional love, strength, and truth into the part of us that counts the most—our inner man.

## MIGHT BY HIS SPIRIT

In our text, Ephesians 3:16, "That he would grant you, according to the riches of his glory, to be strengthened with might by his Spirit in the inner man," I first want you to notice the phrase "in the inner man." Paul did not say in the inner *child,* but the inner *man.* Paul was expecting the Ephesians to mature and to grow up in Jesus Christ. So many believers today see themselves as weak spiritually, and many of them are weak. Why? They have not grown up in Christ, because they are still living as malnourished and underdeveloped children on the inside. They have not received the "riches of his glory," neither have they been "strengthened with might" by the Holy Spirit.

The Greek word translated *strengthened* means an infusion of that which invigorates and energizes; in this case it is *might,* the energy to do work, or the enabling power that flows from the riches of God's glory. This verse paints a vivid and powerful picture of the Holy Spirit flooding our spirits with His ability and wisdom. We understand that the Holy Spirit lives in us to empower us to succeed at whatever God calls us to do.

"The heir, as long as he is a child, differeth nothing from a servant, though he be lord of all; but is under tutors and governors until the time appointed of the father" (Galatians 4:1–2). A baby boy may be born to a king, but that little boy, even though he is a prince destined for a throne, is still going to be told what to do, where to go, and how to live—just as if he were a servant or a butler. Even though we are destined to rule and reign with Jesus Christ as joint heirs, many of us have not yet obtained the maturity to receive our inheritance. We still rely heavily on the pastor or a friend in the Lord to guide us and correct us instead of forming an intimate relationship with the Father ourselves. We continue to require other believers to tell us what to do, where to go, and how to live, and we live as little children, weak and ineffectual. The only thing that will enable us to grow up in Christ is to tap in to the power of the Holy Spirit within.

The problem is, many believers are only desiring outer strength—a strength that can be measured in terms of things and possessions and titles and associations and power and prestige, even biceps! I'm not interested in teaching you how to get another designer tie or how to get a house with a three-car garage instead of a two-car garage. Things we own are not a proof of faith or of spiritual strength. I'm not against prosperity, and I believe in being healthy and blessed, but let me also assure you that the people listed in Hebrews 11—the great giants of faith—didn't prove their faith by the things they acquired or by how much they possessed at the time of their death!

No chapter in the Bible defines faith more than Hebrews 11, and when we read through that chapter, we find that Noah lost everything that he couldn't take into the ark and Abraham lived in tents and died looking for but never seeing a "city which hath foundations, whose builder and maker is God" (Hebrews 11:7–10).

We find that the mighty in faith—people such as Gideon, Barak, Samson, Jephtha, David, Samuel, and the prophets—"wandered about in sheepskins and goatskins; being destitute, afflicted, tormented" and that they "wandered in deserts, and in mountains, and in dens and caves of the earth" (Hebrews 11:37–38). The mighty in faith went through all kinds of crises and turmoil. Some were tortured, others were mocked and scourged, others suffered bonds and imprisonment; some were stoned, sawn asunder, or slain with the sword. (See Hebrews 11:35–37.) So why do we in the church today evaluate faith on the basis of temporal things and temporal power? God has something far greater in mind for us! He wants us to be strong in the inner man.

I'm not talking about giving up things. Thank God He has given you things! Things can be wonderful, but ultimately, they are not a big deal. Everybody's got *things*. But that isn't where our strength lies. Things rust, rot, wear out, get eaten by moths, are destroyed by fire and tornadoes and hurricanes and floods. The same goes for prestige, fame, and worldly power. Politicians get elected and then get defeated. A person can be number one today and forgotten tomorrow. A leader might command an army or a nation one day and not even be mentioned five years later. Nothing of this temporal world produces lasting strength. Only the Holy Spirit can give that kind of strength because only the Spirit is eternal and omnipotent.

I've never met a wino or a prostitute who got saved by having more things. I've never met a person possessed of the Devil who was delivered by receiving things. I've never known a dope dealer whose life was turned around as soon as he acquired more things. The only true strength and power for changing human lives are found in the Spirit of God.

People who are strong on the inside—strong in the inner man, strong in the Spirit—can live with things or without things. Things matter very little. Things can be enjoyed, but they aren't the reason for living. Those who are strong in the Spirit live for Jesus, worshiping Him with their whole heart.

## JESUS AT HOME

**That Christ may dwell in your hearts by faith; that ye, being rooted and grounded in love, may be able to comprehend with**

all saints what is the breadth, and length, and depth, and height; and to know the love of Christ, which passeth knowledge, that ye might be filled with all the fulness of God.
—**Ephesians 3:17–19**

Paul now reveals why he is praying for the Ephesians "to be strengthened with might by his Spirit in the inner man." It is "that Christ may dwell in your hearts by faith." The word *dwell* is the key here. It comes from a compound word that means "to live in as a home," with a sense of finality. Paul is revealing a great truth to us. Although we are saved and have asked Jesus into our hearts, when we allow the Holy Spirit to infuse us with His power, Jesus settles down and is completely at home in our hearts. This verse is talking about Jesus not only living in our hearts but also feeling at home there! And the reason Jesus feels at home in us is because we are filled with and walking in the same power that He is filled with and walking in. We have allowed the Holy Spirit to fill us with himself. Oh, that our Savior would feel as comfortable in our hearts as He is sitting with His Father in heaven!

Now, what happens when Jesus is at home in our hearts and we are infused with the power of the Holy Spirit? We become "rooted and grounded in love" (v. 17). We are securely fixed and permanently immersed in God's love. The Holy Spirit is flooding our hearts with His love (see Romans 5:5), and thus His love flows through us to others. Furthermore, in this attitude and perspective of love, we are "able to comprehend with all saints what is the breadth, and length, and depth, and height; and to know the love of Christ, which passeth knowledge" (Ephesians 3:18–19).

The love of God is not reserved for just a few fortunate believers. It is for *all* saints. God desires that all believers know the immense and vast love He has for His children—the breadth, length, depth, and height of His compassion toward us. No group of believers today has a corner on God's love! God's love is for black saints, white saints, Hispanic saints, Catholic saints, Baptist saints, Charismatic saints, and all saints of every description. When Jesus is at home in all of us through the power of the Holy Spirit, and we are rooted and grounded in God's love, there is no limit to what God can accomplish in the church.

## PAST KNOWING

The love of God is not something we can "know" with our mind. It is something that "passeth knowledge." It is beyond our ability to comprehend. The love of God is something we have to accept by faith in our hearts, accept as a fact of God's nature, and open our hearts to experience just as we accepted and experienced our salvation. As surely as we know we are saved by the blood of Jesus, we know we are divinely loved and eternally cherished because of the blood.

I've traveled across the United States and halfway around the world, and I've preached in just about every kind of church you can name to many types of people, through many interpreters, in countless situations. And let me tell you, one of the hardest things to preach to this generation is the love of God. I can stare Christians right in the face and preach about the love of God and get blank looks!

Now, if I ask a person, "Do you believe God loves you?" that person is likely to say yes, but deep down inside, he has doubts. He is thinking: *I hope He loves me. I've heard He loves me. I don't see how He could love me, but if you say so, maybe He does love me.* As a whole, we Christians do not fully believe that God loves us, and so few of us have experienced His love.

Why are so many believers starved for the love of God? Most of us have not been taught how to accept the love of God by faith. We have been taught to obey God and that if we disobey Him, He'll chastise us. We've been taught His Word, His will, and His purpose. We have been taught seven steps to this and three steps to that and five steps to something else. But we have not been taught that God loves us and that we are to accept and receive His love by faith.

Statistical reports say that approximately one in four adult women in our nation today are molested between the ages of five and fifteen. And what is coming out now is that the number of men who were molested as boys in that same age range has grown at an alarming rate as well. Countless others who have not been sexually abused have been physically abused—beaten by drunken fathers and drugged mothers, by uncaring stepparents, and by exhausted and impatient grandparents. Those who are not physically or sexually abused have often been emotionally deprived. They have grown up in situations in which they were never fully certain they were loved, wanted, appreciated, or valued.

The church puts up a sign and says, "All hurting people are welcome here," but when these broken, wounded, tattered, and torn people who have never fully known the unconditional love of a human being come walking through the front doors, the first thing the church does is tell them the rules of their doctrine, the words to the hymns, and the commandments God expects them to obey. We rarely wrap our arms around the loveless, broken, wounded, and hurting and say, "God loves you, and I love you too."

The wounded in our midst rarely open up to bare their secrets for fear of being rejected, ostracized, or left out in the woodshed again. They may participate in the life of the church as Sunday school teachers and choir members and worship dancers and actors in church dramas, but deep inside they are bleeding, hurting, and aching. And only one thing can ever satisfy that longing and that pain in their hearts: the unconditional, infinite, unending love of God. The breadth and length and depth and height of the love of God is what they need the most and often what they receive the least.

We bring hurting ones to Jesus and we tell them that God is their Father, but their only image of a father is linked to abuse. We say to them, "Welcome to the family," but family is where they were rejected and alienated. We teach them about authority, but authority to them is stained by pain. We tell them to submit to their mentors, but in their hearts submission is linked to a total lack of value.

Those who have been wounded by their fathers, whether sexually, physically, or emotionally, are people who are afraid of their heavenly Father. They fear His presence. They fear His knowing their innermost thoughts. They fear He will never love them. They fear they will never be good enough, clean enough, talented enough, or valuable enough to be accepted by Him in His kingdom.

Any time a child doesn't know that his father loves him, he is destined to be dysfunctional. That's why Paul said, "I pray that you might know the love of Christ." This is a love that "blows the mind" because it's beyond anything we can *know*. It cannot be compared to anything we grew up with, experienced in the past, are married to, or have given birth to. The love that God has for us is infinitely pure, infinitely accepting, infinitely patient and kind, infinitely generous, infinitely *more* than any other kind of love. It's so high, you can't get over it. It's so low, you can't get under it. It's so wide, you can't go around it. It's so deep, you can never get to the bottom of it. And what you cannot fathom with your mind, you can never exhaust!

The love of God must be accepted by faith. How do we do that? In the same way we accept the salvation of our souls by faith. We choose to believe with our will that God is true to His Word and that His nature is love and that when we are in Christ, we are His beloved. (See Ephesians 1:6.) Then we look at the cross. The death of Jesus Christ on the cross is the ultimate expression of God's love. He was God's only begotten Son! And to show us how much He loved us, God required that His Son extend His arms on the cross, an invitation that says, "This is how much I love you." John tells us this in the most well-known verse in the Bible: "For God so loved the world, that he gave his only begotten Son, that whosoever believeth in him should not perish, but have everlasting life" (John 3:16). Paul expressed it this way: "God commendeth his love toward us, in that, while we were yet sinners, Christ died for us" (Romans 5:8).

In receiving Christ as our Savior, we receive the full expression of God's love toward us. There is absolutely nothing that we have to do—or can do—to earn God's love. God loves us through Jesus Christ. He loves us because He desires and chooses to love us. We experience His love only as we accept all that Jesus Christ did for us on the cross and open our hearts to Him in faith. John also wrote, "We love him, because he first loved us" (1 John 4:19). He gave himself as an offering and a sacrifice for us. "And we have known and believed the love that God hath to us. God is love; and he that dwelleth in love dwelleth in God, and God in him" (1 John 4:16).

The love of God is not something we can acquire simply by knowing. We must experience it, which is made possible by the indwelling of the Holy Spirit. Paul wrote this to the Romans: "The love of God is shed abroad in our hearts by the Holy Ghost which is given unto us" (Romans 5:5). It is the Holy Spirit who convinces us of God's love, infuses us with God's love, and who causes us to experience God's love. The fruit of the Spirit is first and foremost love. (See Galatians 5:22.)

## HOW TO RECEIVE GOD'S LOVE

You will begin to feel the love of God flowing in you when you decide to accept by faith that God loves you, accepts you, and values you. You must pray, "Father, I receive your love. I believe you love me. Help my unbelief. Help me to accept your love. I open my heart to you. I open my life to you."

Then you need to walk in the love of God. Say to yourself a thousand times a day, if you need to, the truth of God's Word to you: "God loves me. My heavenly Father loves me. He truly loves me." Pause and open your heart to Him. Let Him comfort you and hold you in His arms. He will never withdraw His love from you! His love is unconditional and eternal and it is His nature. He doesn't change just because you have a bad day. His love toward you goes on and on forever.

It is never enough to know the truth or even believe the truth. In his letters, Paul repeatedly calls for those who believe in Christ Jesus to *walk* in the truth. To walk in love is to respond to life as if we truly believe we are loved by God. How do we act when we are in love? Most people who are in love walk with their head up and shoulders back and they have a bounce in their step. Their eyes are twinkling and they have a smile on their face. They have a confidence and a glow about them that is contagious because they know they are loved. There is no dysfunction in a child who knows they are loved!

Do you know you are loved by God? Have you accepted the fact by faith? Then walk in that love! Act as if you are loved by God. "But what if I don't feel like He loves me?" you may ask. Walk like it anyway! There are lots of times when we don't feel like the person God says we are. We are to walk as He sees us, not according to our feelings. We walk by faith. There is no place in the Bible where it says we are to walk by our feelings.

The beauty of walking by faith is that there will come that moment in time when, if we faint not, what we have been believing and acting upon will be manifest. Eventually we will begin to experience and feel God's love for us. And it is the love of God that heals us, bathes us, washes us, cleanses us, restores us, builds us up, and makes us whole. It is of critical importance that we experience the love of God if we truly are to have an identity as His son or daughter.

God's love is what heals us from the inside out and enables us to enter into healthy, whole relationships. His love destroys and dispels any desperate clinging to another person or need to manipulate others. So many believers today are basing their relationships upon the idea that a spouse will heal and restore everything inside them. No human being is capable of doing that! Only the Lord can heal us by His love.

Those who know God's love and are walking in God's love are not desperate people, turning to this one and that one in the hope that someone will value them and love them. They aren't people who are continually changing their hairstyles and clothes in the hope of attracting someone who will love them. They aren't desperate for attention or continually questioning whether they are acceptable in the eyes of others. To know the love of Christ is to know the most awesome love a person can ever know. It is to be forever satisfied and content and fulfilled.

Always remember: God's love for you never fails. It "beareth all things, believeth all things, hopeth all things, endureth all things" (1 Corinthians 13:7). God never gives up on you. He bears with you when you are serving Him with your whole heart and even when you aren't. He believes the highest and best for you, even when you can't believe that for yourself. He hopes, with the assurance of eternity, that you will be blessed beyond measure, even when you are so swallowed up by circumstances that you don't feel hope. He endures all things, even your doubts and rejection of Him. God's love is kind. It is patient. It is *perfect*. (See 1 Corinthians 13.)

Those who have truly experienced God's love and who walk in the full understanding of God's love are those who never have to be enticed to worship. They don't need professional praise singers to get them to enter into praise and worship before the Father. They have a fountain of love inside of them that bubbles up continually and never runs dry, because they walk in the full assurance that the Father will never reject them, leave them, bring up their past, or scorn them. They are filled with His love and overflowing with praise and worship to Him at all times.

# 9

# A FINAL CALL
# TO WORSHIP

---

Paul closes his prayer for the Ephesians with praise to God: "Now unto him that is able to do exceeding abundantly above all that we ask or think, according to the power that worketh in us, unto him be glory in the church by Christ Jesus throughout all ages, world without end. Amen" (Ephesians 3:20–21).

"Unto him be glory" refers to our God, who loves us infinitely and is omnipotent. Paul says that He is "able to do exceeding abundantly above all that we ask or think," and the Greek language here indicates that the ability of our God transcends the highest measure we could imagine. This is one of those phrases in Scripture where we intensely search for some English word that might even come close to portraying the fullness of God's power. The translators working on the King James Version settled on "exceeding abundantly."

God wants us to know that He is *able*. No matter what we face in life, He is able to handle it—and He is able to empower us to handle it. If God only loved us and didn't have the power to hold us up, we might be encouraged, but we would fail. On the other hand, if God only had power and didn't love us, we might be delivered, but we would feel crushed in our spirits. With both the love and strength of God together, we have an unbeatable combination.

The might of the Spirit is beyond our comprehension. None of us can fathom the power of God in creating this entire universe and upholding it moment to moment. The love of Christ is beyond our knowing. None of us can ever fully fathom why God loves us, how much God loves us, or the countless manifestations of God's love toward us. Put them together—might and love—and there simply is no way we can take in all that truth and ecstasy! So how do we experience the full expression of God's might and love? Paul says this vast resource of God's love and might is experienced by us "according to the power that worketh in us" (Ephesians 3:20).

## ACCORDING TO . . .

In the first two chapters of Ephesians, the word *according* always refers to something God did. But in this verse in chapter 3, Paul is telling us that the degree to which we experience God and the success we achieve as Christians depends on the degree to which *we allow* the Spirit of God to fill us, empower us, illuminate us, and move us. And the way we allow the Spirit of God to transform us in this manner is to be a worshiper of God, to be completely His.

When we worship God, we open the floodgates of God's love and might toward us. We begin to understand the unsearchable riches of the wealth He has given us in Christ Jesus. We begin to understand how to walk the walk He has placed before us. We start knowing things that are unknowable, doing things that are not doable, having things that were not ours to have, reaching things that are unreachable, touching things that are untouchable—according to His power that worketh in us. We can *know* He is able and loves us exceeding abundantly, beyond our imagination and reason, as we allow His Spirit free reign in our hearts and minds.

Paul wrote to Timothy that God had not given us the spirit of fear—He did not give us a spirit of doubt, low self-esteem, or weakness—but rather *love* and *power* and a *sound mind*. (See 2 Timothy 1:7.) When Jesus was just about to return to heaven, He told His disciples not to go anywhere or do anything until they had received the power of the Holy Spirit: "And, behold, I send the promise of my Father upon you: but tarry ye in the city of Jerusalem, until ye be endued with power from on high" (Luke 24:49).

Let's read Luke's account of this in the book of Acts:

**The former treatise have I made, O Theophilus, of all that Jesus began both to do and teach, until the day in which he was**

taken up, after that he through the Holy Ghost had given com- mandments unto the apostles whom he had chosen: To whom also he showed himself alive after his passion by many infallible proofs, being seen of them forty days, and speaking of the things pertaining to the kingdom of God: And, being assembled to- gether with them, commanded them that they should not depart from Jerusalem, but wait for the promise of the Father, which, saith he, ye have heard of me. For John truly baptized with wa- ter; but ye shall be baptized with the Holy Ghost not many days hence.

When they therefore were come together, they asked of him, saying, Lord, wilt thou at this time restore again the king- dom to Israel? And he said unto them, It is not for you to know the times or the seasons, which the Father hath put in his own power. But ye shall receive power, after that the Holy Ghost is come upon you: and ye shall be witnesses unto me both in Jerusalem, and in all Judaea, and in Samaria, and unto the utter- most part of the earth. And when he had spoken these things, while they beheld, he was taken up; and a cloud received him out of their sight.

## —Acts 1:1–9

Of the hundreds of disciples who heard and saw Jesus at this time, only 120 remained to receive the power of the Holy Spirit in the upper room in Jerusalem, but what a time those 120 saints had! On the Day of Pentecost, they also experienced the fullness of the power that had calmed the stormy seas, cast a legion of demons from a raging man, and raised Lazarus from the dead.

When Jesus, true to His Word, poured out the Holy Ghost on them, a mighty, rushing wind swept through the upper room, tongues of fire appeared on their heads, and fiery tongues of every kindred and tribe came out of their innermost being. They hit the streets, and Peter, who days before had denied the Lord three times and proved himself a coward, preached a passionate, tradition- breaking, Holy Ghost message. In one day the same power that res- urrected Jesus from the dead swept through the streets of Jerusalem and brought three thousand people into the kingdom of God! (See Acts 2.)

This is what God wants us to be walking in right now, this power to witness boldly and bring in a mighty harvest of souls, but it is "according to the power that worketh in us." According to . . . We must have the power of the Holy Spirit operating full force and without hindrance in our lives to fulfill the mandate God has given us in these last days.

## AMEN

"Unto him be glory in the church by Christ Jesus throughout all ages, world without end. Amen" (Ephesians 3:21). How often do we hear the saints cry, "All the glory goes to God!" and "Glory to God!" But do we really understand there is no other place for the glory but on God? The glory belongs exclusively to Him. Worshipers have that settled in their minds and hearts, and if an issue or situation arises where they are tempted to give glory elsewhere, they settle it again. God alone gets the glory.

The phrase "throughout all ages, world without end" actually means "all the generations of all the ages." There is no moment in time when God does not receive glory! The fact that we must remember is that He does not receive glory from the world, the secular media, the movies, or unbelievers in general. God receives glory from us, His church. We have that privilege, honor, and responsibility throughout eternity—and if we haven't begun, we can begin right now!

If you have not set your will to be a worshiper of God, a prisoner of the Lord Jesus Christ, don't waste another minute! Make that decision now. Allow the magnificent power of the Holy Spirit to fully inhabit your life and endue you with God's ability and love. Let Him transform you to reach higher and higher heights of joy and revelation in Christ Jesus.

Paul ends his prayer with the simple word *Amen*. It is another word we say all the time and never think about what it means. But I can tell you that if we did, we'd keep our mouths shut a whole lot more than we do! *Amen* means that everything we just declared is absolutely, unequivocally true. There is no arguing with a statement that has an amen at the end of it! Therefore, when Paul says amen, he means, "Everything you have just read is true. Don't even think about doubting it. The Word of God will stand forever, and you can build your life upon it without the slightest hesitation or anxious thought."

## IN SPIRIT AND IN TRUTH

The last amen truth I want to put you in remembrance of about our worship is what Jesus told the precious Samaritan woman at the well: "The hour is coming, and now is, when the true worshipers will worship the Father in spirit and truth; for the Father is seeking such to worship Him. God is Spirit, and those who worship Him must worship in spirit and truth" (John 4:23–24 NKJV). Did you hear that in your spirit? God is *seeking* worshipers! He is searching the earth for those who will worship Him in spirit and in truth. When I read that, my heart leaps up and says, "Here I am, Lord! Find me! I want to worship you in spirit and in truth!"

In the fifth chapter of Ephesians, Paul admonishes them to be filled with the Spirit (v. 18), and the Greek language there indicates that they are to be continually filled with the Spirit. He likens our being filled with the Spirit to being intoxicated with wine: "Be not drunk with wine, wherein is excess: but be filled with the Spirit." We are to be "under the influence" of the Spirit at all times!

When we drink of the Spirit, He energizes and activates and causes the nature of Christ to rise up in us. We do things we wouldn't normally do, say things we wouldn't normally say, and the more we drink of Him, the more we want to drink of Him.

It is very obvious when a believer is drunk in the Holy Spirit. Their spiritual sight is affected, their reactions are different, their judgment reflects the wisdom of God, and the boldness they exhibit makes any complacent, lukewarm believer turn red with embarrassment. The cold, nod-to-God, Sunday morning Christian will quickly label the drunk believer a fool, but this is what the Bible calls a fool for Christ. (See 1 Corinthians 3:18.)

A believer with knowledge of the Word who is not completely under the influence of the Holy Spirit is living in a legalistic, joyless religion. A real fool for Christ gives all control to the Holy Ghost and studies to show himself approved, a workman not ashamed, rightly dividing or understanding the Word of God. (See 2 Timothy 2:15.)

Being a worshiper in spirit and in truth simply means being completely dependent on the Holy Spirit and studying the Word of God continually. We drink of the Spirit and eat of the Bread of Life. We come to Jesus and say, "I love you, Lord. Tell me whatever you want to tell me. Let me know what's on your heart and mind. All

I want to do is love you and be with you. Fill me up with you, Lord."

That's the kind of relationship God desires from us in our worship. He longs for us to come into His presence, tell Him we love Him, and let Him know how much we delight in Him. We don't need a problem, an agenda, or even a good reason to worship Him. We are just happy to be with Him, and our very life hangs on every word He speaks. Have you ever been so happy that you just couldn't help whistling and humming and singing little songs to yourself? That's the quality of joy we are to have in our worship. Worship is not drudgery, obligation, chore, or tedious duty. It is joy and light and love and intimacy with a holy God!

Have you ever noticed how newly married couples are always trying to talk their unmarried friends into getting married? Nothing is better, nothing sweeter, nothing more enjoyable than passionate, ecstatic, joyful, blissful love! People who are in love don't go around picking fights. They don't have time or inclination for arguments. They aren't critical of others. They are floating along on "cloud nine" pretty much oblivious to the flaws, faults, and failures of others. They are so wrapped up in loving they have no room for hating.

That is the position of the believer who is lost in worship of their God. They have no room for rebellion, bitterness, anger, or hatred. They have no desire to manipulate or control others. They desire only that everybody feel the same glorious way they feel—completely and utterly consumed and ecstatic about Jesus, their Savior, their Lord, and their dearest, forever Friend.

Worship is intimacy with God. It is spending time alone with Him. It is singing to Him and talking to Him and sitting in His presence, communing with Him and listening to Him. Worship is reading the Bible and waiting for Him to give instruction and revelation and wisdom. It is praying in the Spirit and allowing Him to fill you up to overflowing with faith, love, and joy. It is delighting in His presence, completely at peace and at rest.

Our worship is loving Him more than anything else in life. Amen and glory to God!

# PART FOUR

## Life Overflowing

# Introduction

The book of Ephesians reveals to us the mystery, the majesty, and the beauty of the church. In the beginning, the apostle Paul arrests our attention with the Holy Spirit's description of who we are and what we can and should do as the bride of Christ. In the end, we are overwhelmed and blessed to be a part of such an exquisite union, yet intensely sober as Paul drills into us our responsibility to protect the reputation of Jesus Christ in our walk with Him.

The apostle Paul is an interesting personality in the kingdom of God. Credited with writing approximately two-thirds of the New Testament, he is best known for his unshakable zeal for God. His intense allegiance to the will of God is awe-inspiring, but embedded in all of his teaching is his passion for developing and maturing believers. His mission in life is to prepare us to represent Jesus Christ on the earth. It is not enough for us to enjoy our salvation; we must also appreciate and respect the responsibilities associated with it.

Our actions, lifestyle, and the manner in which we relate to people are of paramount importance to Paul. He demands that we "walk worthy of the vocation [calling] wherewith ye are called" (Ephesians 4:1). In other words, we should conduct our lives in such a way that the Lord would not regret having saved us. At this challenge, many questions arise:

How willing are we to accept responsibility for our actions?

How committed are we to protecting the reputation of God?

Are we genuinely walking with the Lord, or are we stumbling through life?

Our walk with Christ is not a stroll around the block—it is a power walk! We do not walk in our own strength or wisdom, but in the power of the Holy Spirit, who speaks only of Jesus, continually revealing His goodness, His justice, and His grace. Thus we walk with integrity because we feel responsible to represent Him well. The way we choose our steps demonstrates to all who watch us that we walk with divine, inspired purpose. He died for us, He called us, He loves us—and we will not let Him down.

We walk with an erect posture, looking toward our future. We are not wandering aimlessly as though we have no place to go and nothing to do. He has called us out of our dull and sinful lives into the glorious kingdom of God to fulfill His purpose and plan for our lives.

Jesus saved us, and in so doing He gave us a new nature. Now we are new creatures in Christ. Old things passed away the day we were convicted, convinced, and converted. And so we walk in dignity, strength, and—most of all—love. Energized by His Spirit, motivated by His love, and guided by His wisdom, we walk into life overflowing.

Prepare yourself now to discover the joy of power-walking with God. Don't forget your stretching exercises of prayer and faith! Be sure to wear some comfortable shoes, because you are about to negotiate your way through rocky terrain. And there's no need to be afraid, because it is not your walk or my walk, but our walk with God. Now, let's get started!

# 1

# WALKING RESPONSIBLY
# IN CHRIST JESUS

---

The church represents Jesus to the world. We are the *body* of Christ, which means we are Jesus Christ's physical presence in the earth today. But what is our specific responsibility to God as His individual children? Paul brings us right to that point in Ephesians 4:1: "As a prisoner for the Lord, then, I urge you to live a life worthy of the calling you have received" (NIV).

How many books are on the market today telling people how to set goals and reach them? How many people are giving talks about how to dream big dreams and fulfill them? How many plans are there for mapping out the future and achieving great things? They are beyond counting! Yet most of those books, talks, and plans are based upon man's ability to set his own agenda, map out his own life, determine his own goals, and then reach those goals on his own effort, using his own intelligence and skills and exerting his own strength and power. That's *not* what God has for the believer! The believer is to walk out *God's plan*.

## WALKING OUT GOD'S PLAN

The Holy Spirit is not committed to any plans other than those of God the Father and of the Son, Jesus Christ. We are dead wrong when we come to God and say, "Here's my idea. I'm asking you to put your stamp on it and help me do it." No, we are "His workmanship, created in Christ Jesus unto good works, which God hath before ordained that we should walk in them" (Ephesians 2:10).

Our position must always be, "Lord, show me your plan. Teach me the way I am to walk. Give me your instructions." And then when we know with certainty in our hearts and minds what God desires for us to do, we are to do the walking. He isn't going to walk for us; He empowers us as we walk in Him. He helps us, encourages us, counsels us, and comforts us with His presence.

The Lord is committed only to His plans and purposes. He is committed to us always in His love, but He is committed to the fulfillment of our plans and purposes only if they are in alignment with His. We are called by God to walk in a very specific way and in a specific direction. In essence, that is our calling. We don't just walk around aimlessly in this life; our walk accomplishes God's plans and purposes. Some believers seem to think that only pastors, evangelists, and missionaries are called by God; but the fact is, every believer is called: "As a prisoner for the Lord, then, I urge you to live a life worthy of the calling you have received" (Ephesians 4:1 NIV).

The phrase "prisoner for the Lord" here is more than a statement of fact. It refers to the actual state of confinement Paul endured. Paul calls this incarceration "prisoner for the Lord." You would expect him to say, "prisoner *of* the Lord." By using the word *for*, Paul signifies that from his perspective, he was not a captive of Nero but a prisoner for Jesus' sake.

There is a metaphorical meaning to the word *prisoner* here as well. It can mean "binding as with a spell." Paul is captivated by Jesus Christ and counts his imprisonment as nothing more than a symbol of his position in Him. Therefore, Paul cherishes and glories in his confinement. Theodoret, a fourth-century theologian, put it this way: "He glories in his chains more than a king glories in his crown."

When Paul wrote this, he was under house arrest in Rome, but he didn't regard himself as a prisoner of the Romans. He was a prisoner of Jesus Christ—a voluntary slave—totally in subjection to Jesus. He goes where Jesus tells him to go, he endures what Jesus puts before him to endure, he walks where Jesus tells him to walk, he says what Jesus tells him to say. He is *completely committed* to Jesus' call on his life.

Through the years Paul's commitment brought him to a level of intimacy with the Lord. It began on the road to Damascus, when he was extraordinarily beckoned to the service of God and arrested by a blinding light. He was summarily repudiated by believers, which only strengthened his resolve to pursue his Lord. Thus he was driven into the Arabian desert to be forever yoked with the Lord.

After years of intense study and infusion of divine truth at the foot of Jesus, Paul bursts into the church at Jerusalem and confronts them with kingdom principles. He risks relationship with the apostles to champion the true Gospel—that where the Spirit of the Lord is, there is liberty. The church is to walk in the freedom of the Spirit and is no longer in bondage to the rules of religion.

Paul pays a severe price for his submission to the will of God and ultimately bears in his body the marks of Christ Jesus. By the time he writes to the Ephesians, he is seasoned, tempered, and has been refined like gold. All of his trials and experiences have brought him to compel the Ephesians to walk in a way that is worthy of their calling, to be completely committed and fully submitted to Jesus in every area of their lives.

The call of God is ever before us, driving us to the place God desires us to go and propelling us into the position where we will fulfill His purpose for our lives. Every believer has a call on their lives. Some are called to preach; others are called to establish businesses. But no matter the particular assignment, we all contribute to God's grand design for the kingdom.

## THE CALL SHATTERS LIMITATIONS

The call of God is continuously tugging on our hearts to go forward, propelling us to the next level of what God has for us. We cannot say that we have attained, but rather that we pursue the call of God. It is a feeling that extends itself ahead of us and motivates us to move forward. A true call of God is always beyond our grasp. It is what causes us to grow, to excel, to seek—to reach out beyond ourselves. And it is in this impossible place that we are humbled, knowing that we are being assigned a task that exceeds our ability.

God's call resonates in our potential, not in our present reality or natural capability. He never stops calling us to take one more step, do one more thing, engage in one more act of faith. We are always in a position to *pursue* the call of God. As we reach to attain that calling, we excel and are humbled at the same time. We are perpetually in a position where we must become more like Jesus in order to succeed. Thus the pursuit of excellence and humility of spirit coexist as we walk in our calling.

Years ago I preached that God never asks people to do something they can't do. The more I studied God's Word, however, the more I realized that God often asks people to do things they cannot do. He asked Peter to walk on water. He asked the lame man to take up his bed and walk. He asked Lazarus to come out of the grave. The very essence of God's calling on us is to challenge us to do something that is humanly impossible.

What God does is this: He endows us with His rich grace so that we might attain those things that are beyond our human comprehension or effort. When we say yes to His call and move in obedience and faith, He imparts the ability we lack to perform His will. The Lord does not impart His ability first and then call us. He calls us, and *as we step out in faith and obedience,* He imparts His ability.

The challenge each of us faces is to walk as if we have already arrived at the point to which God is calling us. We must first understand who we are in the body, what God has in His plan for us, and then *walk as if we were there.* Our walk should be a divine reflection of our calling. We should be able to look at our walk—its worthiness, preparation, and influence—and be able to recognize our calling. In other words, our walk will reflect our call.

I saw a television program about economically poor students who were attending an excellent high school in which the teachers and principals believed in them, held high goals for them, and challenged them to excellence. One of the students said, "When I come here, it's as if I'm coming to work. I have a job to do, and my job is to graduate from this school with the best grades possible, to get a scholarship, to go to college, to make something of myself, and to change this community for the better." That student spoke with conviction. Her head was held high. She had a gleam in her eye, a strength to her being. She was already walking in her future! She was walking as if she had already achieved all that was put before her.

Like this student, we must operate in God's vision for us. We must walk according to the portrait He has painted of our future. More than that, each of us must know that to fulfill God's plan, our lives must epitomize our call. The splendor of God's call must be reflected by our steadfast faith and obedience.

## THE POWER OF WALKING "IN SYNC"

"As a prisoner for the Lord, then, I urge you to live a life worthy of the calling you have received" (Ephesians 4:1 NIV). The word *walk* in the King James Version, or *live a life* in the New International Version, does not refer to a meandering stroll. It means to walk or live in step with the Lord, to catch the beat of the Holy Spirit, and to move precisely as He moves. When God acts, we act. When God pauses, we pause.

We must never think we can compartmentalize our life to the point where we say, "In this category, in this season, in this circumstance, I am operating on my own. In this other category, other season, and other circumstance, I am operating according to the power of the Holy Spirit in me." The Holy Spirit does not come and go from our lives!

Our entire life, our entire walk is in Christ. Paul preached to a crowd in Athens: "In him we live, and move, and have our being" (Acts 17:28). Every step of our walk, every day, must be synchronized with the Holy Spirit.

Now, to walk to the beat of the Holy Spirit means that you will *not* be walking to the beat of the world! What you hear in your spirit will be different than what you hear all around you. Unfortunately, some believers are so enthralled and impressed by the world, they never get quiet enough to hear the Holy Spirit inside them. As a result, they miss all God has for them.

Let me assure you of this: Once you begin to walk to the rhythm of the Holy Spirit, nothing is going to matter as much to you as keeping pace with Him. You will find that the direction He moves is always the right direction. His timing is always the right timing, and the results are always the best results.

The Holy Spirit challenges us, inspires us, empowers us, helps us, and causes our efforts to be effective. He works through us as we engage our minds, open our mouths, move our feet, and use our hands according to His will. Most of us have not begun to move into the fullness of all that the Holy Spirit has prepared for us, however, and the apostle Paul is continually challenging us to do so.

**And to know the love of Christ, which passeth knowledge, that ye might be filled with all the fulness of God. Now unto him that is able to do exceeding abundantly above all that we ask or think, according to the power that worketh in us, unto him be**

**glory in the church by Christ Jesus throughout all ages, world without end. Amen.**

**—Ephesians 3:19–21**

This passage of Scripture is the last part of Paul's prayer for the Ephesian believers in chapter 3, and it prefaces his call to walk worthy of our calling in Ephesians 4:1. These verses are so rich we must consider them in more detail. Paul begins by praying that believers would become intimately aware of the love of Christ. He is convinced that a believer's excitement about the work of the kingdom is in direct proportion to their working knowledge of how much Jesus loves them.

Paul characterizes Jesus' love as a love that is beyond our knowledge. What he is saying is that the love of Jesus for us is a love that cannot be fully understood. The Greek word here is a compound word meaning "to exceed or go beyond" and "to throw." In other words, the love of Jesus exceeds the goal. Whatever our need for love is, Jesus' love for us goes beyond that requirement.

Some people might take exception to the concept of anything that is so great it cannot be fully known. However, Paul is not diminishing the believer's ability to discover the love of Jesus. Rather, he is describing the expansive dimensions of that love and declaring that even if a lifetime were devoted to the pursuit of this knowledge, the task could not be completed. Clearly, then, Jesus Christ has so great a love for us that we cannot conceive of its height, width, or depth.

In Ephesians 3:20, Paul brings his prayer to its natural conclusion. If Jesus has so much love for us that we cannot fully comprehend it, then what kind of help can we expect to receive from Him? Paul's answer is that the help Jesus provides for the believer is "exceeding abundantly." Most literary people would frown on Paul's use of both *exceeding* and *abundantly,* but both of these words together are still not sufficient to express Paul's original thought.

"Exceeding abundantly" in the English text represents one word in the original Greek text. That word is literally translated "quite beyond all measure." But even this expression is not enough for Paul. He further defines the quality of Jesus' help by stating that what the Lord will do for His loved ones is too great to imagine. He challenges the believer to prescribe their own deliverance, spend quality time making sure that they have covered all the bases.

Then, when you have come up with a plan, formula, and strategy, you will still fall short of anticipating how great Jesus' deliverance will be for you.

The Lord says to His people, "I love you with a love that passes your ability to comprehend it. I believe in you far more than you believe in yourself. I have unfathomable riches in glory for you. I am come that you might have life, and that you might have it more abundantly." (See John 10:10.)

Everything the Lord does, He does in abundance, an overflowing outworking to facilitate and enable us to fulfill our purpose and our walk. And when it comes to our walk, it is also far greater and more awesome than most of us recognize, believe, or can even imagine.

What we each must do, of course, is to train our ears to respond only to the call of God and to react only according to the beat of the Holy Spirit. Paul gives us instruction about how to do this in the next verses. He says, "Walk with all lowliness and meekness, with long-suffering, forbearing one another in love, endeavoring to keep the unity of the Spirit in the bond of peace" (Ephesians 4:2–3 NKJV).

We cannot step out in faith and obedience to fulfill an impossible calling without knowing the unfathomable love God has for us, that He will not fail us in any way or leave us stranded in our own abilities. And then, as we walk according to His call on our lives, we are intertwined with one another and He calls us to love one another as He has loved us. "Forbearing one another in love" is one of the keys to our being able to fulfill our calling, and we accomplish this through an attitude of lowliness and meekness.

## LOWLINESS AND MEEKNESS

The call of God is always a high calling. We must never think of it as a call to a low position of authority, strength, or spiritual power. God's call challenges us to go from strength to strength and from glory to glory, to move up the mountain to ever greater heights. But the paradox of God is this: The higher the calling, the lower we must become in our own eyes. Jesus said about John the Baptist, "Among those that are born of women there is not a greater prophet" (Luke 7:28). John the Baptist, however, said of Jesus and his relationship to Him, "He must increase, but I must decrease" (John 3:30).

The apostle Paul had one of the greatest callings this world has ever known. He contributed more to the New Testament than any other apostle. Without his epistles, we would know far less about how the church is to function. We would have far less understanding about the mystery of our faith in Christ Jesus. Yet Paul said of himself, "Christ Jesus came into the world to save sinners; of whom I am chief" (1 Timothy 1:15).

If you believe God has called you to greatness, your response to that call should be to fall on your face before Him. As best I can tell, every great man and woman of God responded to God's call on their lives by falling prostrate on the floor before the Lord. When an angel of the Lord appeared to Zacharias and told him he would have a son named John, Zacharias fell prostrate on the floor and didn't move, to the point that people wondered if he was dead.

The prophet Ezekiel said that in the presence of the Lord and at the vision the Lord gave him, he collapsed on the floor. The voice that called to him had to tell him to get up, saying, "Son of man, stand upon thy feet, and I will speak unto thee" (Ezekiel 2:1).

On the isle of Patmos, John said that he looked and saw Jesus standing in the midst of seven golden candlesticks. His voice sounded like the voice of many waters and His feet looked as if they were burning with fire. John wrote, "And when I saw him, I fell at his feet as dead" (Revelation 1:17).

Those who exalt themselves are humbled by the Lord.

Those who humble themselves before the Lord are those whom the Lord raises up.

Paul begs the Ephesians to prostrate themselves before the Lord, to recognize that the more gifted they are, the more humble they must be. They must be continually aware and acknowledge fully that the power working in them is not their own human power or ability, but the power of the Holy One of God.

Most of us do not desire a position of lowliness. It goes against our human nature. And that's precisely God's point. Anything we achieve or accomplish in this life as a believer in Christ Jesus is *not* something we do on our own. It is the Holy Spirit who dwells in us and works through us to accomplish *His* purposes. The more we are humble before the Lord and recognize that the work is His work, the accomplishments are His accomplishments, and the rewards are His rewards, the more God can and does use us.

As lowly as Paul was in his spirit, he felt even more lowly because of a "thorn in the flesh" that the Lord allowed the Enemy to place in his life. Paul clearly saw this thorn as something that kept him from exalting himself. After Paul had prayed three times for the Lord to remove this thorn from his life, he heard the Lord say to him: "My grace is sufficient for thee: for my strength is made perfect in weakness" (2 Corinthians 12:9).

Paul responded to this word from the Lord by saying:

**Most gladly therefore will I rather glory in my infirmities, that the power of Christ may rest upon me. Therefore I take pleasure in infirmities, in reproaches, in necessities, in persecutions, in distresses for Christ's sake: for when I am weak, then am I strong.**
**—2 Corinthians 12:9–10**

None of us know exactly what that thorn was in Paul's life. What we do know, however, is that life has thorns. They come in many shapes and forms. The thorn may be a problem child, a restless marriage, an affliction in the body. God seems to tailor-make thorns for various personalities. And while it is our privilege to pray for the removal of thorns—and in many cases God removes them—we must also recognize that at times God has a purpose for the thorns. That purpose is to keep us lowly and meek so that He can manifest himself through us.

The thorn is painful enough and disturbing enough that we are reminded always that *God* is working in us and through us. We are not succeeding or achieving anything in our own power. That thorn deflates all the air that other people will try to pump into our heads. That thorn allows us to receive a compliment and yet not become exalted by it. In this way, we remain meek and humble and pliable in the hands of God.

## THE ULTIMATE GOAL

Paul presents to the Ephesians the goal of our walk in Christ Jesus: As we walk in the unity of the faith and the knowledge of the Son of God, we will mature "unto a perfect man, unto the measure of the stature of the fulness of Christ" (Ephesians 4:13). Certainly this is a precise definition of what it means to walk responsibly in Christ Jesus.

But what is a perfect man? The world has its definition of the perfect man or the perfect woman. God's definition, however, is that the perfect person acts just as Jesus Christ would act in any given situation or circumstance. The word *perfect* in this verse means mature, developed, and brought to the full manifestation of divine purpose expressed through humanity.

God is never content with the status quo. He is always making us, calling us, developing us, and growing us up into a greater and greater likeness of Christ Jesus. We aren't just walking through life for the sake of walking. We aren't on an aimless stroll. We are going somewhere!

We are being called to be like Jesus.

We are being developed so that our ministry to others will be like that of Jesus.

We are being given experiences and put into situations so that we might mature to the point where we have the same attitude, perspective, and discernment as Jesus.

Every day, in countless ways, God is designing methods and ways of bringing us to full maturity in Christ. God is building us up so that we are a more accurate reflection of His Son. When we know this, pursuing the call of God takes on new meaning. We are stunned by the wisdom of God: As we follow His call we become conformed to the image of His Son, and our walk becomes holy and pleasing in His sight.

Our walk in Christ Jesus is the only walk that satisfies the human soul. It is the only walk that fulfills our purpose for being on this earth and brings us ever closer to our Lord. Our walk in Christ is the reason we were created. When we accept this truth and live it, we bring glory to God by walking responsibly in Christ Jesus.

# 2

# WALKING AS A NEW PERSON IN CHRIST JESUS

As believers in Christ Jesus, we have the privilege of displaying the nature and characteristics of Jesus to people who do not yet know Him. It is an honor, but it is also a serious responsibility. In many instances, all people will know about Jesus is what they see as they observe our lives. Just telling people *about* Him is not enough. We are called to be witnesses *of* Him. It is how we act and react to situations that gives our neighbors and co-workers a negative or positive impression of Jesus.

I am always fascinated by how much unbelievers know about how Christians should live and act. If you don't believe this, just listen to what they say when believers behave badly, exhibit ungodly character, or act immorally. These worldly observers will say things like "I thought you were saved" or "I thought born-again people didn't . . ."

Our blessed position in Christ is a distinctive one. Believers cannot do, act, or say things like everyone else. We represent the Lord and His message of salvation. Understanding and accepting this reality can be difficult for some believers who do not like to be different.

## WE ARE DIFFERENT

Being different causes you to be noticed and exposed to scrutiny. Many people feel safe when they can hide in the crowd and be one of the gang, but hiding in the crowd is exactly what Jesus doesn't want us to do. In Matthew 5:16, He commanded us to let our light shine, and a shining light draws the attention of everything and everyone.

Believers walk in downtown areas and on Main Street, wearing the bright clothing of righteous living. However, for many, hidden underneath their clothes are struggles with desires and passions held over from their worldly life. Too often it is assumed that all is well with them because they look wholesome.

Some believers become comfortable living the double standard, enjoying the reputation of righteousness while continuing to dabble in the sins of the world. Of course, the common observation is that "everybody is doing it," but the truth is that *not* everyone is doing it—whatever *it* is. It doesn't matter if everybody is having sex with everybody else, everybody is cheating on their taxes, everybody is gossiping about their neighbors, or everybody is lying about nearly everything. We are called to live by a higher standard. We are no longer part of "everybody." We are part of the body of Christ Jesus.

All of us want to be liked by others. All of us want to be understood, welcomed, appreciated, and embraced by others. But if we are in Christ, we are going to have to face the fact that people in the world aren't going to understand us and many aren't going to like us. We are going to have to become disengaged, dislodged, and even disloyal to some people.

This has nothing to do with unity within the body of Christ. With other believers we are to become like-minded and of one heart. But with unbelievers, who are living apart from Christ Jesus and are walking in darkness, it is impossible for us to be unified with them in their lawless thinking, attitudes, and practices. Paul exhorts:

This I say therefore, and testify in the Lord, that ye henceforth walk not as other Gentiles walk, in the vanity of their mind, having the understanding darkened, being alienated from the life of God through the ignorance that is in them, because of the blindness of their heart: Who being past feeling have given themselves over unto lasciviousness, to work all uncleanness with greediness.

—Ephesians 4:17–19

Paul gives us a thorough and insightful description of how unbelievers walk. He says they walk "in the vanity of their mind," which means their minds are devoid of truth. When it comes to the Gospel and the kingdom of God, they are incapable of making an appropriate decision. Because they have hardened their hearts to God and are alienated from Him, we can have no spiritual fellowship with them.

## WALKING IN THE LIGHT

Paul draws a strong comparison between ignorance and darkness and also between light and knowledge. To be ignorant in spiritual matters is to live in darkness, which results in nothing but groping, grasping, and aimlessness. The person who walks around in the dark is a person who doesn't know where he is going or what he is about to trip over. Such a person is likely to be filled with frustration, confusion, and fear.

There are countless people on the earth today who have the capacity to be brilliant. They could be building spaceships and curing diseases and establishing companies, but they are ignorant. They haven't been taught what must be known in order to build a spaceship, cure a disease, or establish a successful company. Because they don't know, they live in a condition that is far less than their capacity.

So it is with those who live in spiritual darkness. They don't know they can have purpose and direction in their lives. They don't know all the wonderful things God has planned and prepared for them. They don't know the purpose God has for them, or how to walk in that purpose. The reason they don't know is because they have chosen *not* to know. It isn't a matter of no one teaching or preaching, or of no one available for wise counsel. It is because they have decided they simply don't want to know. Furthermore, this state of not knowing is not benign. It is a malignant arrogance that says, "I don't need to know." Their influence is so pervasive that even some believers are caught up in the web of deceit they spin.

How many people who control the airwaves and wield great influence over the media and technology are people who are actually blind when it comes to why they are alive? Those who are alienated from God are not some sort of neutral entity that can be avoided. Paul says we are *not* to walk as these spiritually blind people walk. We are to avoid their influence. We are to reject the dark messages they launch against our minds.

Too many times we hear people say, "Well, everybody believes that," or "Everybody is saying it," and the conclusion that is drawn is this: "Everybody must be right." But everybody might be absolutely *wrong* if everybody is walking in spiritual darkness!

## WALK WITH RESTRAINT

I am a great proponent of the idea that it's time some Christians moved behind enemy lines. We need more truly saved Christian reporters. We need more Christian magazines, more Christians creating television programs, more Christians involved in the leadership of companies and working as our representatives at all levels of government. But they are not to walk as the Gentiles walk. After Paul describes the incredible darkness in which those who do not know Jesus walk in Ephesians 4:17–19, he exhorts us: "But ye have not so learned Christ" (Ephesians 4:20).

It's time for Christians to speak up when evil raises its ugly head and attempts to steal our minds and destroy our homes with sexual immorality and mindless violence. It's time for us to refuse to be intimidated by those who don't know anything about spiritual reality and truth. We are to walk among the Gentiles, but we are not to be like them.

Nobody wants to be led by a blind guide. Nobody wants to follow an ignorant person. And yet daily millions of Christians choose to be led by the blind guides of this world, those who are spiritually ignorant and who choose not to open their hearts to the Gospel of Christ Jesus.

Paul wrote to the Ephesians that these blind Gentiles are "past feeling" and have "given themselves over unto lasciviousness, to work all uncleanness with greediness" (Ephesians 4:19). *Lasciviousness* is unbridled lust, excess, and shamelessness—which all lead to unrestrained appetite. It is saying that we can do whatever we feel like doing whenever we feel like doing it without consequence.

Multiple sexual partners. Bisexual and homosexual relationships. Lust out of control. Husbands hitting wives. Wives murdering husbands. Children suffering from all kinds of abuse. Anger out of control. Drugs sold at every intersection, not only in the projects but in the suburbs and in the school corridors. Everybody high on something or addicted to something. A desire to escape reality gone out of control. That's unrestrained appetite.

Paul also states that the Gentiles have given themselves "to work all uncleanness with greediness" (Ephesians 4:19). The darkened, spiritually blind mind is a mind that is obsessed and addicted to things that are unclean before God. Furthermore, they see great gain and profit in the business of sin. For example, they earn a living by making pornographic films, selling drugs, getting involved in prostitution, or engaging in any kind of illegal, immoral, or unholy activity just because the money is good. To do so is to "work all uncleanness with greediness."

I have heard Christians say, "Well, I'll make money selling liquor and then give my profits to the church." That's a blind Gentile way of thinking! The same is true for those who bring injury to other people solely for the sake of gaining great profit for themselves. An honest profit does not bring harm or perpetuate sin.

In Ephesians 4:20, Paul says plainly that we have not learned this from Jesus. Jesus did not walk this way, and we are to be like Him. We are to restrain ourselves from these evil ways as He did, by the power of God's Word and the Holy Spirit within us. As believers, we have been taught and are continually being taught by the Holy Spirit. Jesus called the Holy Spirit the "Spirit of truth," and He said that the Spirit would lead us into every remembrance of His Word that we needed to make wise decisions.

Some may say, "Well, I don't know that much about the Bible. I'm a new believer. I haven't known Jesus very long." No matter how long you have known Jesus Christ, there are some things you are going to *know* immediately as being right or wrong through the leading of the Holy Spirit. There is an immediate awareness once a person has received Jesus Christ as Savior that certain behaviors and certain attitudes are no longer appropriate to our new way of life. Then, as we continue to study God's Word, we will discover that the leading of the Holy Spirit is always in complete concert with His Word, that the Word of God is not a dead letter filled with impossible demands but is alive and full of life-transforming power.

The Holy Spirit makes alive in us an understanding of what is corrupt, deceitful, lustful, and sinful. And as we renew our mind with the Word of God, our senses become more keen to discerning and differentiating between good and evil.

**For every one that useth milk is unskilful in the word of righteousness: for he is a babe. But strong meat belongeth to them**

that are of full age, even those who by reason of use have their senses exercised to discern both good and evil.
**—Hebrews 5:13–14**

In certain areas of vulnerability and weakness, we can insulate ourselves from failure only by submitting ourselves to the ministry and teaching we need to be set free and stay free. There's no excuse for any believer to remain blind to God's truth or to live like an unbeliever. If God has called us to restrain our flesh, then He has provided the means by which we can do it.

## PUT OFF THE OLD NATURE

A believer should never say, "I am now a part of the redeemed and forgiven, but I am living the same way I lived before I accepted Jesus Christ as my Savior." Our lives are to be different than that of blind sinners. There are some things that we *put off* when we come to Christ.

If so be that ye have heard him, and have been taught by him, as the truth is in Jesus: That ye put off concerning the former conversation the old man, which is corrupt according to the deceitful lusts.
**—Ephesians 4:21–22**

The phrase "put off" is a vivid picture of a person taking off their filthy rags of sin and self-righteousness and burning them. They do not take them off and hang them in the closet for a rainy, difficult day; nor do they toss them on the floor to be tripped over daily. That is a perfect illustration of deceitful lusts. For example, we cannot go drinking with our associates from work while claiming we are being a light to them. The truth is we are walking in darkness.

No, when we take off our filthy rags, we are to rid ourselves forever of all thinking, attitudes, and behavior associated with our existence apart from Jesus Christ. This is an outward manifestation of the inward transformation, what the Bible calls the fruit of righteousness. (See Hebrews 12:11 and James 3:18.) Earlier we discussed believers who walk on Main Street with clothes of righteousness but underneath are filled with turmoil. The process whereby they rid themselves of this contradiction is the putting off and burning forever the undergarments of sin.

God does not automatically remove every evil thing from our lives the moment we receive Jesus as Lord and Savior. We still have baggage and bondage left over from our former life that we must remove and destroy. It is our responsibility to put off those things. We may not want to acknowledge that we have them in us, clinging to us, or flowing from us. We may not even want to talk about them. But eventually we are going to have to face them, *because we cannot put on the new man and be the new person we are in Christ if we are holding on to the old man.*

There are many believers who have old habits they need to break. Some of those habits are prejudices and old ways of thinking. Some of those habits are so common to a person's life that they aren't even aware they have them. But one by one, those habits must be changed. Some believers have broken their old habits, but they are still tormented by the thoughts related to them. These thoughts have to be put off just as the habits are.

**Finally, brethren, whatsoever things are true, whatsoever things are honest, whatsoever things are just, whatsoever things are pure, whatsoever things are lovely, whatsoever things are of good report; if there be any virtue, and if there be any praise, think on these things. Those things, which you have both learned, and received, and heard, and seen in me, do: and the God of peace shall be with you.**

### —Philippians 4:8–9

We can only successfully and permanently put off thoughts by replacing them with godly thoughts. We must reassure ourselves of God's unfailing commitment to our future by becoming extremely familiar with His promises in His Word. We must train our minds to think about things other than the sin in which we once lived. We need to start building new habits of thinking that will then help us to establish godly attitudes, behavior, and reactions: "And be renewed in the spirit of your mind; and that ye put on the new man, which after God is created in righteousness and true holiness" (Ephesians 4:23–24).

There are some rich nuggets of thought in the phrase "renewed in the spirit of your mind." The word *mind* is not the word for brain but rather refers to the manner in which a person comes to conclusions. It is the ability to perceive and understand, and to feel, judge, and determine things. Paul says that we are to make new or young again the attitude of our thinking. How we process information and the manner in which we come to conclusions must be subject to the will of God.

When a person starts thinking new thoughts or putting on new habits, they may feel a little strange at first. They may think, "This is just a put on!" Just as a new coat or a new pair of shoes may not be immediately comfortable, so our new thoughts and new habits may not immediately feel natural to us. What we must do, however, is to continue putting on those new thoughts and new habits that we know are right before God again and again until they are comfortable!

We have to practice being nice until we are automatically nice.

We have to practice going to church every Sunday morning until anything but church on Sunday morning seems strange to us.

We have to practice giving our financial gifts in the offering until giving to God is as natural as buying a new outfit at the mall.

We have to practice speaking the truth until a lie tastes bad in our mouths and telling the truth is our automatic response when we are questioned in any situation.

We must practice speaking good of others until our cynical, sarcastic, negative, bitter, and angry remarks are completely purged from our conversation.

"But," you may say, "isn't this hypocritical—feeling one way and speaking and doing something else?"

No. It's *retraining* yourself to walk the way the Lord desires for you to walk and *restraining* yourself from lasciviousness. You are declaring to Him, "It's no longer a matter of anything goes in my life. It's a matter of what you say and what you command and what you direct me to do."

## FOUR THINGS WE MUST PUT OFF

In Ephesians 4:21–24, Paul tells us flat out that any change in our behavior requires our will. What we do is our choice. Paul is very specific with the Ephesians—and us—about what must be put off and what must be put on:

**Wherefore putting away lying, speak every man truth with his neighbor: for we are members one of another. Be ye angry, and sin not: let not the sun go down upon your wrath: Neither give**

place to the devil. Let him that stole steal no more: but rather let him labour, working with his hands the thing which is good, that he may have to give to him that needeth. Let no corrupt communication proceed out of your mouth, but that which is good to the use of edifying, that it may minister grace unto the hearers.

**—Ephesians 4:25–29**

**No More Lying.** Lying has to go. In its place we must put on truth. Lying is conscious and intentional falsehood, a deliberate attempt to deceive, to convince a person of something that is not true or of a feeling that is not genuine.

Lying is anything that is not the "whole truth and nothing but the truth" in both content and intent. It includes those little lies that some people are so quick to justify. Lying includes leading others to a false conclusion, even though we may not actually have spoken false words. It includes setting up a pretense or an illusion that is false. In the place of lying we must become truth seekers and truth speakers.

**No More Sinning in Anger.** Unrestrained anger that results in sinful behavior has to go. In its place, we are to reach for reconciliation and peace.

Paul is not talking about righteous indignation or being angry at sin and taking a stand for what is right. Nor is he talking about ignoring evil and refusing to do anything about it. God has given us the ability to feel anger so that we will get angry at the same things that anger Him—the misuse and abuse and *use* of people for evil.

We are to be angry whenever and wherever we find sin in operation and the Devil in charge. But we are to respond to those situations that make us angry by engaging in the spiritual warfare necessary for bringing down the strongholds of Satan. We are not to seek revenge for ourselves or those who have been hurt or offended. Paul is very clear that anger isn't a sin in and of itself. What is wrong is being angry and then sinning in our anger.

We are to go immediately to those with whom we have quarrels and disagreements and to reconcile our differences—even before nightfall. We are to give the Devil absolutely no place to hang his hat in our lives. We are to give him no toehold, no crack in the door of our soul. We are to completely turn a deaf ear to any temptation the Devil whispers to entice us to sin in anger.

**No More Stealing.** "Let him that stole steal no more" (Ephesians 4:28). In the place of stealing, Paul says, "Get a job. Do something good. Earn so that you have something to give away."

Paul knew that Ephesus was a major trade city of the world. It was a city where everybody was out for a deal and out to gain as much profit as possible. It was a city with great wealth, a lot of buying and selling, a lot of caravans and ships bringing their wares. It also saw a lot of corruption and greed.

There's a big connection between stealing and hoarding. Those who steal from others, which includes those who cheat, are dishonest and underhanded, are me-centered people. They want everything flowing their way. Once they have obtained something from others through immoral and illegal means, they are very unlikely to let it go. They consume what they steal or they spend what they steal on themselves. Why? Because they are continually trying to prove to themselves that they deserve what they have stolen. They are continually trying to possess it in order to lay rightful claim to it. The more they steal, the tighter they hold on to what they steal in order to make sure they are in possession of it. The truth is, of course, that they can never lay full claim because what they are seeking to claim is not rightfully theirs.

There's a similar link between earning and giving. Those who earn things through honest means know that what they have is rightfully theirs to do with as they desire. They are much more likely to give extra to those in need whenever they can.

They also know that whatever they have earned is by the grace of God. God helps those who are engaged in honest labor. He rewards those who labor "as unto Him." Those who work honestly are in a position to obey the command of Jesus, "Freely ye have received, freely give" (Matthew 10:8). They know they can trust God to continue to help them earn and work and give.

Paul is not only trying to clean up thievery and dishonesty, he's trying to turn around the entire way the Ephesians think and behave toward one another. He's preaching a spirit of generosity to the church—a free-flowing sharing of gifts.

Why is this spirit of generosity so important in the church? Because it relates to far more than practical gifts of money and material possessions. It includes the gifts of the Spirit, ministry to others, and sharing the Gospel. If you are truly a generous person, you are going to be willing to turn yourself and your pocketbook inside out for other people. You'll turn your schedule upside down so you have time to give. You'll open the doors of your home so you can give hospitality. You'll open up every treasure chest of talent or skill you have been given to enrich the lives of others.

A truly generous person is a person the Holy Spirit can use. A generous person is an open vessel, an open conduit through which He can move. The generous person is a person through whom the Holy Spirit can pour His gifts and manifest His fruit.

Are you committed to earning honestly as much as you can so that you can give as much as you can to others in the name of Jesus? Imagine what a blessing could be poured out to our churches, our neighborhoods, our cities, and to needy areas around the world if all believers were this generous!

**No More Corrupt Communication.** Paul says, "Stop talking like you used to talk. Stop engaging in anything that causes decay or destruction in another person's life. Instead, speak good to and about others."

Corrupt communication is not only swearing and telling dirty jokes—neither of which have a part in the walk of a believer. Corrupt communication means communication that has become twisted, polluted, or invalid. It is lying. It is any form of communication that leads to an end that is contrary to God's highest and best desires for another person.

Are you aware that cynicism, sarcasm, and negative criticism are all forms of corrupt communication? This kind of talk tells only your opinion about a matter, which is never the genuine truth from God's point of view. Negative comments tear a person down just as much as a blatant lie can tear down their reputation or self-esteem.

Paul tells the Ephesians to speak only "that which is good to the use of edifying, that it may minister grace unto the hearers" (Ephesians 4:29). Edifying means "to build up." It doesn't mean false flattery or praise, but to build up another person in the spirit. It means to speak God's Word to them without any overtones of self-righteousness or condemnation. It means to give genuine compliments because we recognize that they are the workmanship of God and someone to whom God has poured out His grace, love, and mercy.

To edify is to recognize that another person has just as much claim to the grace of God as we have. The attitude behind edification is that another person is in just as much need of forgiveness and has just as much access to forgiveness as we have. To edify is to say things that will help a person hold his head higher, walk straighter, and act better than before.

We should never justify hurtful conversation just because it is the truth. Never does the Bible instruct us to tell everything we know! In fact, many of the proverbs are adamant that only a fool tells their whole mind all the time. If the telling of a fact is going to tear up the unity of the body or bring down another person, it's wrong to voice that fact. Let it stay with you and allow God to do what He desires to do without your adding the fuel of your words to a verbal bonfire.

There's no room in a believer's walk to say, "Well, I have to say what I think." The fact is, what you are thinking may not be true. James says, "Whoever controls the tongue controls the whole movement of the body." (See James 3:3–5.) To a great extent, what you say determines the extent of your ability to act. It puts a boundary on what you can do and will do, and it sets limits on your witness.

We think, we speak, we act. That is the usual progression of human behavior. But it is not only ourselves that we influence when we speak. We are also putting limits on others, and ultimately upon the body of Christ as a whole. What we say exerts influence upon the entire body of believers with whom we are in association!

A little statement of gossip not only corrupts the speaker of that gossip, but it brings damage to the ears of the persons who hear it and to the reputation of the person about whom the gossip is being spread.

A little lie not only brings damage to the soul of the liar, but it causes the hearer of that lie to be damaged and infected with falsehood. The person who hears a lie may act on that lie, believing it to be true. Those actions will also be false. They, in turn, will impact other people, and bit by bit the entire community or church will be infected with an element of falsehood and decay. What we say has a ripple effect that reaches beyond us to the lives of others.

In contrast, to give an edifying word is to say something that will help a person see Jesus more clearly, desire a deeper relationship with the Father, and be more open to the Holy Spirit. To give an edifying word causes a person to open herself up to all that God desires to do in and through her life.

Edifying words also have a ripple effect that can bring about good. Flowing through a body of believers they can bring about a greater outpouring of love, acceptance, forgiveness, and reconciliation. Spoken frequently in a group of believers, edifying words produce unity and greater spiritual power. They also create an atmosphere where lives are changed and blessings are poured out.

## WE CAN DO IT!

Paul would not have begged the Ephesians to give up lying, stealing, anger, and corrupt communication if this manner of life was impossible for us to achieve. The fact is, we *can* live this way. We don't have to tell lies in order to advance our position, steal from others to be prosperous, or be dishonest in order to gain what we need. We do not have to be angry in order to exert control or engage in corrupt communication to get our way. Simply put, we do not have to give place to the Devil!

We can walk in "righteousness and true holiness" (Ephesians 4:24). It's a choice we make daily as we pray, "Holy Spirit, lead me. Help me to guard my tongue. Help me to earn and to give. Guide me in the right ways to express my anger at injustice and evil. Help me to become a mighty warrior against the gates of hell."

When we choose to live this way, according to God's Word and by the power and leading of the Holy Spirit, an exciting and world-changing reality occurs. We are literally *being* the new person we are in Christ Jesus. We are living from our true essence and eternal identity, and our walk with Jesus becomes a daily adventure in faith and power!

# 3

# WALKING IN STRENGTH

The book of Ephesians was written from a prison cell in Rome several years after Paul's last meeting with the church leadership from Ephesus. Paul had lived and worked in Ephesus for three years, and for two of those years he had taught daily in the school of a believer named Tyrannus. (See Acts 19:8–10.) He was no stranger to the Ephesians and they were no strangers to him. He knew them and the issues that faced them.

Paul had enjoyed a powerful ministry among the Ephesians and many miracles took place. This is where handkerchiefs and aprons were taken from Paul and were laid on those who were sick and they were delivered from diseases and evil spirits. (See Acts 19:11–12.) It was in Ephesus that so many were converted to Jesus Christ that a vast number of pagan scrolls and instruments of magic were burned. (See Acts 19:17–19.) There were so many that received Jesus that the silversmiths who made shrines to the goddess Diana incited the city to riot because they were so upset at their loss of sales. (See Acts 19:23–41.) Despite the persecution and rioting, the Gospel flourished. In Acts 19:20 we read, "So mightily grew the word of God and prevailed."

## PAUL'S FAREWELL: DEFENSIVE STRATEGY

In Acts 20:16, Paul was on his way to Jerusalem to celebrate Pentecost when he stopped at the port of Miletus to meet with the elders of the church at Ephesus. During this last and brief time with them, Paul reminded them of many things, but when we examine this passage of Scripture in detail, we see clearly how Paul leaves the Ephesians with a word from God on how to defend themselves and stand strong in the faith at all times, "at all seasons." He reminds them that for the years he lived among them, he overcame every temptation and trial he faced and how he accomplished this super-human feat.

**And from Miletus he sent to Ephesus, and called the elders of the church. And when they were come to him, he said unto them, Ye know, from the first day that I came into Asia, after what manner I have been with you at all seasons, serving the Lord with all humility of mind, and with many tears, and temptations, which befell me by the lying in wait of the Jews: And how I kept back nothing that was profitable unto you, but have showed you, and have taught you publicly, and from house to house, testifying both to the Jews and also to the Greeks, repentance toward God, and faith toward our Lord Jesus Christ.**
**—Acts 20:17–21**

First, the *manner* in which Paul served the Lord and the Ephesians was "with all humility of mind." This is the attitude of lowliness and meekness Paul exhorts us to have in Ephesians 4:2, which we discussed in chapter 1. When we maintain an attitude of humility, the Holy Spirit can teach us and strengthen us. We will have the wisdom and God's supernatural power to prevail over the temptations and trials that come against us. But if we are proud and arrogant, the Holy Spirit can do nothing with us and we are left to our own thinking and ability. It is inevitable that we will fail and fall.

Second, Paul said he "kept back nothing that was profitable unto you, but have showed you, and have taught you publicly, and from house to house." Not only did he teach them everything they needed to know to succeed as Christians in a very hostile, dangerous world, but he lived it in front of them twenty-four/seven. Paul didn't preach one thing on Sunday and then live contrary to his message on Monday. He went from house to house and *showed* them what it meant to live victoriously for Jesus Christ.

More than that, when Paul messed up, when his carnal thinking or fleshly desires overtook him or the Devil's craftiness succeeded in distracting or deceiving him for a time, he was quick to repent, "testifying both to the Jews, and also to the Greeks, repentance toward God, and faith toward our Lord Jesus Christ." This third point cannot be overemphasized!

When men and women of God who are leaders in the body of Christ are overtaken by a fault before those they lead, when fathers and mothers miss the mark in their families, and when employers sin against God and against their employees, it is absolutely imperative that they come to repentance before those who follow them. Why is this so vital? When a standard of purity and excellence is lifted up by leaders, parents, and employers, it can then be passed down through the ranks of leadership in the body of Christ so that every member maintains purity and excellence. Then the whole body can be "fitly joined together" and "every joint supplieth." (See Ephesians 4:16.)

Your physical body is not going to be able to do much if your shoulder or your knee or your elbow is out of joint, and the body of Christ is no different in a spiritual sense. If we are going to succeed in the calling God has given us, if we are going to reach the lost, heal the sick, cast the Devil out, and make disciples, we must be healthy and all our joints must be supplying.

**And now, behold, I know that ye all, among whom I have gone preaching the kingdom of God, shall see my face no more. Wherefore I take you to record this day, that I am pure from the blood of all men. For I have not shunned to declare unto you all the counsel of God.**
**—Acts 20:25–27**

Paul now makes a monumental statement: He is pure from the blood of all men because he has not neglected his most sacred duty and holy responsibility before God, which is to declare the whole counsel of God. In other words, Paul was careful to feed the flock of God with a balanced diet of the Word.

There is a tendency in the contemporary church for pastors and leaders to specialize in one area of the Gospel or the kingdom. While it is exciting to see God operate in certain areas like healing, prosperity, or worship, a congregation must also be nourished by the principles of righteousness, spiritual warfare, and holiness. It is balanced and comprehensive teaching in the Word of God that equips believers with the strength and overall stability to successfully withstand the assaults of the Devil as they walk with God. Satan is cunning and does not only attack in one way. He uses different strategies and weapons to penetrate our greatest weakness at just the right moment.

Our revelation and practice of worship from yesterday may not overcome and defeat the forces of darkness that will come against us tomorrow. Healing Scriptures alone may not keep our house built on the rock when the storms of deception rage against us. We must continually grow in the Word as the Spirit of God leads us to study the whole counsel of God. And pastors and leaders must be diligent to teach the whole counsel of God as the Spirit leads. Only the Holy Spirit knows what we need to learn today that will sustain us tomorrow.

Paul then went on to give a strong warning:

**Take heed therefore unto yourselves, and to all the flock, over the which the Holy Ghost hath made you overseers, to feed the church of God, which he hath purchased with his own blood. For I know this, that after my departing shall grievous wolves enter in among you, not sparing the flock.**
**—Acts 20:28–29**

Paul knew that the church would always be opposed by somebody, over something, at some time. No local church founded on the shed blood of Jesus Christ has ever been established without facing opposition. No body of believers has ever become so mature in the faith that all opposition has disappeared. The wolves are out there . . . ravenous and vicious. Paul's desire is that the believers in Ephesus and believers today be protected.

What counts is not the fact that we live without adversity, but rather that we have the strength to stand strong in the face of it. That is the real crux of the matter. Paul is determined that his ministry will outlive him, and in order for that to happen, the church at Ephesus must remain strong when opposing voices rise up.

Our concern today is that we be so rooted and grounded and established in the truth that *we* will stand when opposition comes our way. If we rely upon the crutches of fantasy and a false sense of well-being, when the adversary attacks, we will be quick to crumble because our crutches are flimsy. Only the truth of God's Word will hold us steady and steadfast when the storms come.

It is never realistic to think that a person can do anything for God—including living a steadfast Christian life in the midst of daily challenges—and not face intense opposition on a regular basis. The church must build a strong line of defense with God's Word to stand strong against the wolves from within and without. Paul said to the Ephesians:

**Also of your own selves shall men arise, speaking perverse things, to draw away disciples after them. Therefore watch, and remember, that by the space of three years I ceased not to warn every one night and day with tears.**
**—Acts 20:30–31**

Opposition is not only from the outside but also from inside the church. A split in a church is nothing new. From the very beginning, Paul anticipated divisions, "isms," and schisms. He said to the Ephesian elders, "I've got to prepare you for those things before they arise so you will be strong. Please remember how I tearfully and continuously warned you of these things for the three years I was with you."

Paul labored among the Ephesians for their benefit, even to the point of weeping before God both for them and with them that they might grow strong in the Lord Jesus Christ. He was determined that they have sufficient enduring strength to sustain their faith after he was gone. Paul was not a man who spewed religious rhetoric from cold lips and an indifferent heart. He had passion for his students. He made himself available to them day and night: "And now, brethren, I commend you to God, and to the word of his grace, which is able to build you up, and to give you an inheritance among all them which are sanctified (those who are set apart for His use)" (Acts 20:32, parenthetical phrase mine).

Paul had absolute confidence that the Word of God was able to equip the church with all it needed to withstand any assault. He had so much confidence in the strengthening power of God's Word that he was able to leave the elders of Ephesus on the dock at Miletus with full assurance and every confidence that they would be all right. He knew he would never see them again on this earth, but that the Word of God would continue to build them up in his absence.

Paul closed his comments to these elders of the early church by saying, "I have showed you all things, how that so labouring ye ought to support the weak" (Acts 20:35). He wanted them to follow his example—to teach, to build up, to support, to give all that they had to the challenge of remaining strong in Christ. And after he had spoken his heart fully to them, he prayed with them and said goodbye in a very emotional parting.

**And when he had thus spoken, he kneeled down, and prayed with them all. And they all wept sore, and fell on Paul's neck, and kissed him, sorrowing most of all for the words which he spoke, that they should see his face no more. And they accompanied him unto the ship.**

**—Acts 20:36–38**

These people loved Paul and Paul loved them. It was out of his great love for them that he pleaded with them, "Continue in God's Word always. The Word is your only line of defense in this world. It will keep you strong and allow you to prevail over every evil thing, including the wolves who come to your door or perverse deceivers who rise up among you. Don't waver from the truth!"

## RETAKING OCCUPIED TERRITORY

Walking in strength is not only a defensive measure, but it is also an offensive tactic. We explored how to use the strength of God to protect ourselves from the ravages of wolves; now we are prepared to march forward and offensively and aggressively take back what the Enemy has stolen.

When it comes to walking in strength, Ephesians and Joshua are companion books. The book of Joshua presents a story of conquest. Armed with the anointing of God and His mandate to take the Promised Land, Joshua and the Israelites exercised their freedom and calling to be kingdom builders for the first time. In the same way, Paul beseeches the Ephesians to do more than just "hold the fort." He commends them "to God, and to the word of his grace."

We are set apart for His use and we have an inheritance to obtain! We do not merely sit and count our blessings and expect everything we need and want to fall out of heaven. We are to rise up on our most holy faith and march forward to take back what the Devil has stolen and to take hold of that which God has already purchased for us through the blood of Jesus Christ. Like the Israelites in Joshua, we must garner all our strength and courage from the knowledge that God is on our side and what He says we have, we can have.

After Paul builds us up in the first chapters of Ephesians, expounding on the truths of our calling, election, and intimacy with God, he then stirs the nest like a mother eagle, prompting us to take wings and fly. Otherwise, we will never realize the majestic heights to which we have been called, the destiny that awaits us.

Believers were never intended by God to be the recipients of salvation alone. While it is true that we have been saved from death, we have also been saved to life—abundant life. Being saved from death is a simple case of rescue, but God is interested in more than rescuing us. He has chosen to make us partners and joint heirs of all that He intended for us to share with Him from the beginning, that we might move out in His power and reclaim the bounty of those riches that lay strewn on the fields of the Promised Land.

From our perspective as New Testament believers, the book of Joshua is a picture of people who have ceased from wandering in desert places, who have come to know God, who have embraced the promises of God, and who are now ready to seize the things that God has promised to them.

The book of Joshua is not a book for wimps, and Ephesians is not for wanderers—those who wander from this conviction to that, murmuring and complaining along the way, backsliding as much as they are moving forward, always with one eye looking back to Egypt. If you still have a desire for life in Egypt, a life of sin and compromise, then you are not ready to march in and seize the Promised Land!

Let me be very practical here. I have met people who tell me that they have no problem watching certain television programs that are filled with lustful and violent messages. As far as I am concerned, these people are giving the Devil the sofa in their living room. They are allowing him to occupy that place. They may have shut the Devil out of every other place in their lives, but they allow him to reside and rule there.

I have met other people who say, "Well, business is business, and business is cutthroat. It's highly competitive. Certain tactics are required to succeed." These people are giving the Devil a place in their office. They are allowing the Devil to sit across the desk from them and to conduct his business there, his way. They may have claimed every other area of their lives as a place for righteousness, but not their office.

I have met other people who say, "Church is church, but then there's my sex life." These people put on holy clothes on Sunday morning and are just as quick to take them off on Sunday night with someone who is not their spouse. They don't see any relationship between their sexuality and their spirituality. They have allowed the Devil to claim this territory in their lives.

It is God's desire that we take back ALL that the Devil has occupied!

When Joshua prepared to enter the land of Canaan, he had a full awareness that every square inch of that land was held by the Enemy. Not one city, not one acre had been claimed by the Israelites. God had promised it to them, but it was not theirs. It could only be theirs if they took it.

Just as Joshua and the Israelites had to drive back the Hittites and Jebusites and other people who represented the worst sins of mankind, so you are going to have to drive the Devil out of every square inch of the territory of your life. While you were living in a state of sin, the Devil took over vast areas—in some people, he took over just about every area! Now that you are saved, whenever the Devil has an opportunity, he is going to move in and take control in those areas. He is going to occupy your sexual desires, your desires for things, your desire for power, and your desire for wealth.

John wrote that we are to stop loving the world and "all that is in the world, the lust of the flesh, and the lust of the eyes, and the pride of life" (1 John 2:15–16). When we begin our walk as believers in Christ Jesus, God gives us the strength to *remove* the Devil from our lives and take back every inch of territory he has occupied.

Taking over the territory of the Devil means . . .

- kicking the Devil out of your house—every room, every bookshelf, every cupboard.
- kicking the Devil out of your car and refusing to let him ride with you.
- kicking the Devil out of your neighborhood and out of your church.
- kicking the Devil out of the place where you work so that you do your job as unto the Lord.
- kicking the Devil out of your social life, refusing to associate with those who influence you to commit sin.

- kicking the Devil out of your marriage relationship; no longer pattern your marriage after the world but after God's Word.
- kicking the Devil out of your love life, putting an end to illicit affairs and ungodly romances.
- kicking the Devil out of your family, not allowing the devil control or influence over your children.
- kicking the Devil out of your viewing habits, reading habits, spending habits, and consumption habits.

Now, the Devil is not going to just roll over and give up! He is going to fight you for every bit of territory. He desires to rule this world, both its territory and its systems. He doesn't care about people! He destroys those he influences, steals from them, lies to them, kills them.

The good news is that once God has liberated us, we are given the power to drive the Enemy out of our land! The Bible says that we have the authority to say to the Devil, "You may not occupy this place anymore. You have no authority here. You have no right to be here. Get out in the name of Jesus!"

Once you are a believer in Christ Jesus, you are called to walk out the land that God has promised to you and to regain every aspect of your life in Christ. Just as Joshua and the Israelites were given the authority, power, and ability to take Jericho, you have been given the authority, power, and ability to cause certain walls to tumble down in your life. You have the ability to tear down the strongholds of Satan and to declare, "I no longer belong to you. I belong to Jesus Christ."

It's time we say:

"You can't have my rest and my peace; God gives His beloved sleep." (See Psalm 127:2.)

"You can't have my healing and health; by Jesus' stripes I am healed." (See 1 Peter 2:24.)

"You can't have my mind and my imagination; I cast down every thought that exalts itself against the knowledge of God." (See 2 Corinthians 10:5.)

Nervous breakdown? No! I can do all things through Jesus Christ! (See Philippians 4:13.)

Marriage breakdown? No! Jesus is the author and finisher of my faith! (See Hebrews 12:2.)

Communication breakdown? No! God gives me wisdom! (See James 1:5.)

Our offensive weapon is the same as our defensive weapon— the sword of the Spirit, the Word of God. (See Ephesians 6:17.) Wherever and whenever you tell the Devil he has to get out of your way and get off your land by speaking the Word of the Lord in the power of the Holy Spirit, he must go. You have the authority, power, and ability to successfully expel the Enemy from your territory, which is anywhere you place your foot. God has called you to walk in His strength today!

# 4

# WALKING IN UNITY

---

**I therefore, the prisoner of the Lord, beseech you that ye
walk worthy of the vocation wherewith ye are called, with all
lowliness and meekness, with longsuffering, forbearing one
another in love; endeavouring to keep the unity of the Spirit
in the bond of peace.**

**—Ephesians 4:1–3**

Immediately after admonishing the believer to dignify the divine vocation with an appropriate lifestyle, Paul continues without pause to set the attitude in which we are to walk and the manner by which we walk. We don't walk alone. Not only do we have the Holy Spirit in us, but we have both the privilege and the responsibility of walking with others. There is no place in the Scriptures where we are called to live in isolation as individuals or to think we are the only group of people worthy of Christ. We are to "keep the unity of the Spirit in the bond of peace."

Paul is consumed with the importance of relationships, which comprise unity, and that is why he goes right into this issue after begging us to walk worthy of our calling. The truth is, fulfilling our calling is inseparably tied to our allegiance to one another. In chapter 4, he calls the Ephesians to be longsuffering toward one another, forbearing one another in love. This is the attitude we are to have as we walk. And for what purpose? "To keep the unity of the Spirit in the bond of peace." He is continually trying to bring about a oneness in the church by encouraging believers to care for one another, be patient with one another, yield to one another, and bear one another's burdens.

Let's consider the word *longsuffering*. In the Greek text the word is used primarily for patience. The word also expresses the attitude of an endurance test. It suggests that the person having this kind of longsuffering remains calm while going through a test, storm, or struggle because their passion is directed toward something beyond, something that transcends and outweighs any present discomfort.

We must have a passion for unity in the church because unity has a cost attached to it. It doesn't happen automatically or without effort. So often we think that if we just come together and love God, we are going to get along. But getting along takes effort. It takes a willingness to be patient with one another, to diffuse our selfish ambitions and cast them on God so that unity and peace can be sustained. It requires a conscious decision to stick together and not leave a group when things get difficult or when we encounter someone we don't like.

## THE HOLY SPIRIT'S ROLE

*Unity apart from the Holy Spirit is impossible.*

In ourselves, we don't have enough love to be united in spirit with another person. We don't have the patience, the goodness, the kindness, the joy, or the self-control required. Those are fruits of the Holy Spirit. It is only as we consciously decide that we are going to live and walk according to the Spirit that we can begin to achieve unity with other believers.

Why is it so important that we work for unity in the body of Christ? Because it is only in a unified body that the power of God can be released. It is only when we see ourselves tied together under the authority of the divine Chief Executive Officer that we begin to experience the fullness of the Holy Spirit's power flowing freely in our midst. It is the power of God that destroys the yoke of bondage—of sin, sickness, and oppression—and if there's one thing we need in the church today, it is more of God's saving, delivering, and healing power!

**Behold, how good and how pleasant it is for brethren to dwell together in unity! It is like the precious ointment upon the**

head, that ran down upon the beard, even Aaron's beard: that
went down to the skirts of his garments.
—**Psalm 133:1–2**

This is a perfect picture of unity in the body of Christ. In your
mind's eye you can see the oil as it is poured over the head, streams
down the face and beard, makes its way to the hem of the garment,
and drips upon the feet until they glisten. This is the oil of gladness
for the corporate body of believers. There is a joy and peace that
come when believers are synchronized by the unifying power of
God's anointing. Earlier we discussed walking in synchronized fashion with the Holy Spirit. Now we take this one step further and see
that as we walk in this manner with the Spirit, we can walk in unity
with one another.

When the leader of a particular church in the body of Christ is
anointed with the Holy Spirit, that oil is to run from head to toe in
that church without becoming the least bit diluted or polluted by
individual agendas or fleshly desires in the church body.

Any time you begin to inject your feelings, your opinions, your
agenda, your goals, or your desires into the pure agenda of the Holy
Spirit, you dilute and pollute what the Holy Spirit is attempting to
do in you and in others with whom your life is linked. When that
happens, unity corrodes and ministry becomes less and less effective. The presence and power of the Holy Spirit dissipates because
He is grieved and is leaving.

How do we go about achieving and maintaining the Holy
Spirit as the central life force in the body of Christ? It happens only
when each believer is willing to submit himself to the Holy Spirit
and say, "What the Spirit is doing and what the Spirit is saying are
far more important than my personal image, reputation, influence,
or identity." We must see the unity of the Spirit as being essential to
the power of God being released in us so that we can heal the brokenhearted and set the captives free. We must be willing to fall face-
down before God and give up our individual agendas for the greater
good of the kingdom, that all may come to the saving knowledge
of Jesus Christ. Walking in unity is key to the Gospel being
preached effectively throughout the earth.

## BEING ONE

There is one body, and one Spirit, even as ye are called in one hope of your calling; one Lord, one faith, one baptism, one God and Father of all, who is above all, and through all, and in you all.

### —Ephesians 4:4–6

I have a problem with people who say that their church is *the* church. Their view and perception of the body of Christ is much too limited, narrow, and misinformed. The church is not one local church body. It is not one denomination. It is not even all the believers in one generation. The church is, was, and is to come. The bride of Christ is as eternal as Christ himself. The whole church—the saints which are, the saints which were, and the saints which will be—are one church espoused to one Lord.

Along these same lines, Paul says there is one Spirit. Now, why does he say something that is so obvious? He must have visited our churches today! How many times have we endured the tongue-lashing of a believer who is supposedly speaking by the Spirit but is actually releasing personal frustrations or pent-up anger resulting from unresolved wounds and offenses? Then there is the believer who desires attention and uses the gifts to get it, touting their special revelation from "the Spirit" in our midst. This does nothing but cause confusion and erode the confidence believers have concerning the validity and work of the Holy Spirit.

Now, I don't want to get off in a ditch here! Every word spoken in the congregation does not have to be perfect. When well-meaning but unlearned believers step out in faith and courage to give what the Holy Spirit is saying, we must encourage them and correct them when necessary. This is how they grow and develop their gift. What we must always remember, however, is that when the Holy Spirit speaks through a vessel, *He will never contradict the Word of God or himself.*

The truth will be confirmed by the mouths of two or three, and all that is spoken will flow in a stream of edification and comfort. This is the "one Spirit" Paul is referring to. The Holy Spirit is not fragmented or schizophrenic. He is consistent and reliable, and what He says to one, He says to all. When He fills a room and speaks, He draws us to and lifts up Jesus. He unifies us in a powerful corporate anointing where yokes are destroyed and captives set free.

Then Ephesians 4:4 speaks of the hope of our calling. What is the hope of our calling? The resurrection! Paul takes us to the ultimate outward expression of unity—the resurrection—which, again, is supernaturally brought about by Jesus. Think about it: No believer who precedes us in death will go before us, and those of us who remain will not lag behind. When Jesus comes for us, He will come for us *all*. In one split second, we will all be caught up to meet Him in the sky!

"One Lord, one faith, one baptism, one God and Father of all, who is above all, and through all, and in you all" (Ephesians 4:5–6). There is *one* Lord who calls us, one faith that unites us, and we are all baptized into Christ when we are born again. Whatever our color, cultural background, race, doctrinal persuasion, or gender, there is one unifying force for us as believers, and that is Jesus Christ. There are not two Gods—one for Jewish believers and one for Christian believers. God is not a black God or a white God, a Japanese God or a Hispanic God. He is one God, above all, in all, and through all.

If you are not baptized into Christ, these verses do not apply to you. The *all* to whom God is Father in verse 6 is exclusively the body of Christ and not the world at large. The church is the body of Christ, a living, breathing organism functioning under the direction of her Head, Jesus Christ. But no matter how you describe the church, the most significant feature is her oneness. That we understand this point is a major concern of Paul's.

**For as the body is one, and hath many members, and all the members of that one body, being many, are one body: so also is Christ. For by one Spirit are we all baptized into one body, whether we be Jews or Gentiles, whether we be bond or free; and have been all made to drink into one Spirit.**
**—1 Corinthians 12:12–13**

Oneness among believers is not plain or homogeneous; it is a dynamic oneness. God has chosen to take different individuals and join them together to make one whole. As a picture, the church is like a jigsaw puzzle. Each piece alone has a strange shape and can even sometimes appear to be distorted. However, each piece is cut to fit perfectly with another piece of the puzzle, and when all the pieces are joined together (fitly joined), then and only then can the powerful, life-changing picture be seen.

Some of the most wonderful stories about unity seem to be associated with times of war. The dividing forces of prejudice and bigotry seem to disappear in the heat of battle. If you are in a foxhole with a guy, you don't care what color his skin is. You care whether he's on your side or not. So it is with the kingdom of God and our warfare against the Devil. We are on the same side as other Christian believers, and we have a common enemy, a common problem, a common conflict. If we are going to win the battles we face against Satan, we must come together.

Ultimately, we all have the same need to be forgiven by God and accepted into His beloved. We all need the same divine medication for our souls: God's love. If I have a deadly disease it makes no difference to me whether the anointed one praying for me is yellow, red, black, or white. I will gladly allow him to lay his hands on me! If my heart is broken and I need restoration, it makes no difference to me that I didn't grow up in the same neighborhood as the one who is preaching the healing of old wounds and offenses from the past. I must be willing to say, "Your God is my God. I am trusting the God whom we both serve to deliver me and make me whole."

The gifts of the Holy Spirit are distributed by Him into the body of Christ through people from all walks of life with diverse kinds of talents and abilities. We need to recognize our own unique gifts and develop them as part of our walk in Christ Jesus, but we must never separate our gifts from the whole body. We must never see our administration or talent as being better than or apart from the church as a whole. We have one God who gives each of us gifts, and He is the one who orchestrates how they will all fit together in a powerful whole.

Our walk truly becomes a power walk when we put away all our offenses and disagreements and come into the unity of the faith. We will never agree on every doctrine, but we can agree on the essentials. Jesus is our Lord and the Head of the body of Christ of which we are members. Through the Holy Spirit who lives within each of our hearts, we become one.

When we walk in unity with one another, our walk puts the unity achieved at the tower of Babel to shame! Those who were building that miraculous structure at Babel were commended by God for their achievement of unity. However, their agenda was a selfish, self-serving one that was of no use to His kingdom. Thus

God was justified and even compelled to confuse them and destroy that powerful unity.

However, when God's mandate is being carried out by joyful spirits in the church who are in love with Him and each other, the Bible says that nothing will be withheld from them. There is no issue of confusion to be reckoned with, because God's will is the only consideration of His body. As this occurs, the church will literally tear down the gates of hell and establish righteousness, peace, and joy on this earth.

# 5

# WALKING IN
# THE SPIRIT

Grieve not the Holy Spirit of God, whereby ye are sealed
unto the day of redemption.
—Ephesians 4:30

Paul *commands us* to stop grieving the Holy Spirit, so it must be
of paramount importance to him and to us. The word *grieve* here
means to outrage and humiliate, as a king who has been deposed by
his subjects. Even though it is not possible to depose Jesus Christ,
we are still capable of dethroning Him from our hearts and turning
our passion and zeal toward people or things that distract us from
God's will and truth.

Grieving the Holy Spirit is to say or do things that prohibit His
participating in our lives to the extent He desires. The chief cause
of grief to the Holy Spirit is walking in the lusts of the flesh. When
we walk in the flesh, doing what we want to do, when we want to
do it, and the way we want to do it, apart from God's truth and
commandments, the Holy Spirit simply says, "I can't go there. I
can't help with that. I can't participate." We shut off the Spirit's
function in our lives when we choose to sin and to engage in behaviors that are contrary to God's purposes.

Now, this does not mean that the Holy Spirit leaves us. Paul is
very clear on that point. He says, "Ye are sealed unto the day of redemption." When we believe in and receive Jesus as our Savior, the
Holy Spirit moves into our lives and seals us. He infills us and He

resides within us until the day of redemption—the day we enter God's presence in eternity.

"For he hath said, I will never leave thee, nor forsake thee" (Hebrews 13:5). The Holy Spirit never leaves us or forsakes us. He seals us unto the day of redemption. *Seal* means "to mark as a means of identification." This mark denotes ownership and carries with it the protection of the owner.

*Redemption* has a narrow and specific definition. It means "to pay the price for, to buy back from, to take ownership of by paying the ransom price." This word picture is awesome. Paul is showing us our state of being before salvation, when we were held captive by a cruel master. But then Jesus came and redeemed us, paying the price for our release from the Enemy and the bondage in which he held us. We became Jesus' property, and He marked us as His. We are sealed by the Holy Spirit as a sign to all that we have the protection of Jesus.

Therefore, because we are sealed unto the day of redemption by the Holy Spirit, we are able to walk in this world and not become a part of it. We are able to walk and not be destroyed by the destroyer. We are sealed, marked, secured, and protected. We have been bought with a price, freeing us from Satan's grip and setting us securely in the arms of Jesus, able now to serve our Lord and Savior with gladness.

However, when we choose to follow the dictates of our own fleshly desires, we disconnect ourselves from the Holy Spirit's favor in our lives. He cannot manifest himself in anything that is contrary to the will and goodness of God.

The Holy Spirit will not help you lie or avoid the consequences of lying. He will manifest himself only as you tell the truth, confess your lies, and obtain forgiveness.

The Holy Spirit will not help you cheat another person, or help you avoid the consequences of getting caught. However, the Holy Spirit will manifest himself when you seek to treat others honestly and make restitution to those you have cheated.

The Holy Spirit will not help you seduce another person's spouse or help you cover up that seduction or act of adultery. However, the Holy Spirit will help you to resist the temptation to sin and/or help you terminate an illicit love affair. He will help you to live in sexual purity.

The Holy Spirit desires to be on our side! He delights in helping us—in giving us the information and discernment we need, in leading us into right decisions and right actions, in giving us the inspiration and motivation to act righteously and courageously, and in strengthening us to withstand evil and to speak and act in truth. The Holy Spirit wants to see us grow in Christ Jesus, manifest His fruit, and operate in His gifts.

When we choose to act against God's desires and do things our own way, the Holy Spirit is grieved. Paul says, "Don't do it!"

## SIX THINGS THAT GRIEVE THE HOLY SPIRIT

"Let all bitterness, and wrath, and anger, and clamour, and evil speaking, be put away from you, with all malice" (Ephesians 4:31). Paul identifies six things that he knows with certainty grieve the Holy Spirit:

- bitterness
- wrath
- anger
- clamor
- evil speaking
- malice

Look at this list closely. Most of these things can be held internally for a fairly long period of time without others knowing what is going on inside. Eventually, however, what is festering inside us is going to erupt, and these vile wounds will make us offensive to the Holy Spirit and those we are sent to serve. The way to grieve the Holy Spirit and destroy unity is to operate in these six things; the way to please Him and preserve unity is to avoid these six things at all cost.

**Bitterness.** A person can live with bitterness for years, but eventually that bitterness is going to leak out. It is going to manifest itself in acid remarks that corrode relationships, weaken the mettle of our peace, and ultimately cause depression or illness. More insidiously, it is going to manifest itself in unforgiveness. And when we choose not to forgive others, we limit the forgiveness of God toward us. Jesus said, "Forgive, and ye shall be forgiven" (Luke 6:37).

The Holy Spirit loves to reveal himself as God's mercy and love in an atmosphere of forgiveness. When we forgive, the cancer of bitterness cannot take hold of our soul and the Holy Spirit is free to flood our lives with the blessings of God.

**Wrath.** Wrath is rooted in a spirit of revenge—it is a strong desire to get even, to destroy one's enemy, and in the process to advance one's own personal power and position. A person can plot revenge for years and never act on it. What eventually happens is that they become so consumed with revenge that they no longer have the time or inclination to think about ways of advancing the Gospel or of speaking the name of Jesus to bring healing to another person. The person who is consumed with revenge cannot witness to the person they desire to see destroyed.

"Oh," some say, "I'm leaving vengeance up to the Lord." And in the next breath they are whispering, "I just wish God would hurry up and deal with them!" That's a spirit of wrath at work. Any time you desire something bad to happen to another person rather than to see that person come to experience the fullness of God's forgiveness and mercy in their life, you are captivated and obsessed with wrath.

The Holy Spirit flows through people who have yielded themselves to Him in love and overcome their desire to be vindicated. They have chosen to see people experience God's healing balm instead of His painful judgment.

**Anger.** Anger is actually rooted in a desire for power, being denied something that we want or think we deserve. When we feel this acute sense of losing control over a situation, we lash out and become abusive. One of the things we have to understand about abuse is that those who abuse are not acting out of hatred. They are acting out of a desire to show or to regain power. They are reacting to someone's put-down, rejection, or refusal to be controlled. Anger is saying, "I'm going to get mine," "I deserve more," "I'm not being treated fairly," "I'm not being shown the dignity and respect I deserve."

Some expressions of anger are not sinful, such as righteous indignation, a zeal for the things of God when they are maligned, and a disdain for satanic victories over families and governments. When anger at injustice, unrighteousness, and evil is turned toward acts of ministry and giving, it becomes the hot fuel for the flame of the Holy Spirit to work miracles of deliverance.

However, most anger is rooted in selfishness and it is dangerous for us to justify it or rationalize it. When we do this, we are deceiving ourselves and "do not the truth," because in reality we are serving our selfish lust for power. (See 1 John 1:6.) If we allow anger to fester in us, eventually it will manifest in an unrighteous, unholy way. We will lash and gash and crash, rather than seek out a solution that is strong and effective and righteous. When anger boils over, it burns and destroys.

Anger can reside in a person long before it manifests itself, and all the while it will grieve the Holy Spirit and hold us back. While we are grasping and striving for personal power and control over any or all areas of our lives, we are cutting off the power of God to work in and through us.

The Holy Spirit is waiting for the body of Christ to empty itself of personal lust for power so that He can fill us to overflowing with God's power. Then we can do mighty exploits for the kingdom in Jesus' name.

**Clamor.** To clamor is to make noise or to shout in a way that is disruptive. Clamor is rooted in a general restlessness because something is perceived to be missing or lacking. A person clamors to be heard when he feels left out or unnoticed. He clamors for more when he feels cheated, shortchanged, or deprived. Inside, clamor is a feeling of frustration.

Have you ever met a person who just couldn't be satisfied or was never at peace with herself? There are people who always seem to be stirring up the pot, bringing up past hurts, nagging for more, or agitating for something else—it might not even be something better, just different.

Clamoring is the opposite of being content. Paul wrote to the Philippians, "I have learned, in whatsoever state I am, therewith to be content" (Philippians 4:11). That doesn't mean that Paul was content with the status quo at all times. Rather he had learned to have a peaceful spirit regardless of outward circumstances. The person with a *clamoring* spirit is a person who hasn't fully learned to trust God.

"Though I speak with the tongues of men and of angels, and have not charity [love], I am become as sounding brass, or a tinkling cymbal" (1 Corinthians 13:1). Sounding brass and tinkling cymbals are the noise of clamor! To clamor is to say, "Pay more attention to me."

**Evil Speaking.** Evil speaking is injuring another's good name, slandering or uttering a defamatory statement or report. We may explode, lashing out at others close to us and even at those we love deeply. Or we may seethe, always on the verge of saying something we know we'll regret, always trying to hold ourselves in check. Whether thinking it or actually saying it, evil speaking will destroy our lives.

Eventually evil speaking will keep a believer from thinking the thoughts of Christ and witnessing to the love of Jesus. The renewal of our mind is thwarted every time we speak evil of someone else, and we will fail to grow spiritually.

**Malice.** To have malice is to be motivated by hatred. It is the ultimate in moral inferiority and decay because it is the exact opposite of love. Malice can be directed toward an individual, a group of people, or a type of person. Malice is at the root of disharmony. It gives rise to prejudice, bigotry, and many forms of retaliation, hurtful words, and harmful deeds.

Malice is a close associate of each of the other things Paul says grieve the Holy Spirit, because it is simple hatred. Hatred and bitterness go together. Hatred and wrath are companions. Hatred and anger are often linked. Hatred and clamor work hand in hand. Hatred and evil speaking are brothers.

Malice is at the other end of the spectrum from love and brotherly affection. It is contrary to the very nature of the Holy Spirit. The Holy Spirit cannot manifest himself where hatred exists, because the foremost fruit of the Holy Spirit is love.

In summation, when the Holy Spirit is grieved by one or a combination of these six things, not only is the individual believer's life affected, but unity in the body of Christ is seriously disturbed. Therefore, it is essential for us as believers to guard our hearts and minds and avoid at all cost the entanglements of these things.

Does the Holy Spirit create, nurture, produce, or cause bitterness? Absolutely not. The work of the Holy Spirit is mercy.

Does the Holy Spirit generate wrath and vengeance in a person? Never. The work of the Holy Spirit is reconciliation and unity.

Does the Holy Spirit inspire anger at a loss of personal power and pride? Never. The work of the Holy Spirit is to help us yield to the will of God and to praise God humbly in all things.

Does the Holy Spirit bring about clamor in us? No. The work of the Holy Spirit gives peace and joy.

Does the Holy Spirit initiate or encourage evil speaking? No. The work of the Holy Spirit is forgiveness, blessing, and edification.

Malice and all of the other attitudes and behaviors that grieve the Holy Spirit grieve Him because they are the opposite of His nature and the work He desires to do.

## KINDNESS AND TENDERNESS

**Be ye kind one to another, tenderhearted, forgiving one another, even as God for Christ's sake hath forgiven you.**
**—Ephesians 4:32**

What is it that Paul says we *are* to do? In our terminology, Paul says, "Be nice to one another."

We all know what it means to be tenderhearted. Just think for a moment of a mother who lovingly cradles and rocks her child, kissing him and holding him close and singing softly to him. Now, that child may have just fallen in the mud, been in a fight with another child, or won a prize at school that day. It makes no difference to the tenderhearted mother. She loves that child and cares for that child with just as much tenderness. Any error the child may have made, and any correction that may have been given, has no bearing on the amount of tenderness the mother feels or expresses toward her own child. God feels the same way about His children, and it is His supreme desire that we are as tenderhearted to one another as He is to each of us.

We all know what it means to be kind. Just think for a moment of the person who gently and generously helps another person who is in need, suffering sickness, sorrow, or is in any kind of trouble. The cup of water to the thirsty person. The meal to the homeless man. The warm shawl to the homeless woman. The visit to the lonely person in the nursing home or to the prisoner in the county jail. The kind person offers no condemnation to anyone for being thirsty, homeless, old, sick, or in jail. There's only respect, affirmation, and genuine concern. Again, this is how God treats us and how He desires that we treat one another.

What is done in tenderness and kindness is done quietly, simply, and genuinely. It isn't intended for show. It is intended as an expression of selfless love.

"Be tenderhearted and kind," says Paul.

"But," you may say, "I don't feel tenderhearted toward all people." Ask God to help you change the way you feel. And until you feel tenderhearted, act tenderhearted anyway!

You may not know what to say to the person who is grieving in the funeral home. Just go and sit quietly with her. That's *being* tenderhearted.

You may not know what to say to the person who is sick in the hospital. Just go and say a prayer for his healing in the name of Jesus. That's *being* tenderhearted.

You may not know what to say to the person who is scared about a doctor's appointment. Just go with that person and hold her hand while she sits in the waiting room. That's *being* tenderhearted.

The more you perform kind and tenderhearted acts, the more you are going to find your heart opening up to others and the more you will desire to show tenderness. The same goes for kindness. We all know the kind thing to do for a person in need. Do that kind thing! You may not *feel* kind, but Paul didn't say anything about feeling kind. He said, "*Be* kind." Pick up that person who needs a ride to church. Hold that crying baby while that mother deals with her crying toddler. Secretly leave a sack of groceries on the back porch steps of the family you know is going through a hard time. Call and give a word of encouragement to the person you know has just lost his job. *Be* kind.

If you have any doubt about what the kind or tenderhearted thing may be, ask the Lord to reveal it to you. The Holy Spirit will probably remind you of something Jesus did. Any time you have a question about what to say or how to act, look to Jesus. Do what He did.

Jesus preached good news to the meek.

He bound up the brokenhearted.

He proclaimed liberty to the captives.

He opened the doors of the prison to those who were bound.

He proclaimed what was acceptable to the Lord.

He comforted those who were mourning.

He replaced ashes with beauty.

He substituted sadness with joy.

He replaced a spirit of heaviness with a garment of praise. (See Isaiah 61:1–3.)

The Holy Spirit is always pleased whenever we act like Jesus!

## FORGIVENESS

**Be kind and compassionate to one another, forgiving one another, just as in Christ God forgave you.**
**—Ephesians 4:32 NIV**

When we truly begin to see others as God sees them—people in need of forgiveness, transformation, renewing of their minds, mercy, and grace—we can't help but forgive them and show kindness and tenderness toward them. When we think that somehow we *deserve* the forgiveness of God, we look down on others and deny them the grace by which we are forgiven.

The fact is, none of us deserves the goodness of God! None of us is worthy of God's love and mercy. None of us could claim salvation on our own merits. We are saved because God first loved us, sent His Son to die for our sins, and chose to indwell us with His Spirit. The only way any person ever got into the true church is by way of forgiveness.

If God had not forgiven you, you would have no relationship with Him. You would not have the promise and hope of eternal life. You would not have the Holy Spirit residing in you. You would not know what it means to lay down guilt and shame and move into a new life of purity and wholeness. All people are in need of forgiveness, and when we keep that fact in mind we are going to find it much easier to resist the things that grieve the Holy Spirit and be kind and tenderhearted toward others.

Jesus taught His disciples:

**Forgive us our debts, as we forgive our debtors. If ye forgive men their trespasses, your heavenly Father will also forgive you: But if ye forgive not men their trespasses, neither will your Father forgive your trespasses.**
**—Matthew 6:14–15**

It doesn't get any plainer than that!

To be forgiven is to be set free of guilt, shame, and recrimination. It is also to be set free to love others and to do good to them. When we forgive others, we are not saying that sin doesn't matter. Sin is deadly and it is a deadly serious issue to God. God never winks at sin. But to forgive others is to say, "I am not going to heap guilt, shame, and recrimination on you. I am not your judge or your jury. I free you so God and God alone can deal with you. I set you free in *my heart* and in *my mind*."

To receive forgiveness from God is to take the same approach: "I receive God's forgiveness for my past. I am not going to hang on to guilt, shame, and recrimination. I am not going to remind myself continually of what I once was or once did. I am going to free my mind to think about those things that God desires that I think about!"

Some believers I know haven't forgiven their own children for doing things that aren't half as bad as things they once did. Forgive your children! Don't continue to lay guilt and shame on them. As long as you take on the role of judge and jury, you are not going to be free to do what God truly wants you to do with and for your children. Furthermore, you will self-destruct and short-circuit the power of God in your own life.

Some believers have not forgiven their parents. Even if you were abandoned, your parents divorced, or you were abused by them, you must forgive your parents. Refuse to continue to place blame on them. Free them from your judgment. As long as you are holding resentment and bitterness, you cannot receive the joy of the Lord or be used by God to set others free.

Whatever we do not forgive, we are destined to repeat. If you do not forgive that abusive parent, you will repeat the pattern of abuse in your life. It is inevitable. If you do not forgive the person who hurt you in a past relationship, you will strike out at every person who comes into relationship with you. You will not be free to love and to be loved.

Your past is tied to you through the umbilical cord of unforgiveness. When you forgive, you cut the cord. But if you do not forgive, you continue to be tied to that sin or that hurt and you will repeat it. That's the way curses are passed from generation to generation. Something is held on to that should have been forgiven, cleansed, changed, or let go.

Our Christian experience begins with repentance and forgiveness but is sustained by continually purifying our hearts and our motives. Maturity is reached as we submit ourselves to a lifestyle of obtaining forgiveness from God and those we have offended and then by turning around and granting forgiveness to those who have offended us. When we live according to the law of forgiveness, our hearts remain pure and tender, our spirits are light, our minds are free, our vision is clear, and our manner and speech will be kind—filled with the power of the Holy Spirit to save, heal, deliver, and set free.

Forgiveness—from God to us, toward others, and to ourselves—is the key to avoiding and conquering any temptation to fall into the things that grieve the Holy Spirit. We then, being free from all spiritual hindrances, are unified in our purpose and position and empowered by the Spirit to conquer the Enemy, possess our promised land, and glorify our Savior.

# 6

# WALKING IN LOVE

Be ye therefore followers of God, as dear children; and walk in love, as Christ also hath loved us, and hath given himself for us an offering and a sacrifice to God for a sweetsmelling savour.
—Ephesians 5:1–2

Have you ever seen a little boy strut about a room just like his daddy? He swaggers and holds his head and swings his arms just like his father—and he doesn't even know he's walking like him. And what about the little girl who walks just like her mama walks? She tilts her head and puts her hand on her hip just like her mother. She hasn't decided to do that, she has just copied what she has seen without thinking about it. She is an exact duplicate of her mama.

Paul wrote to the Ephesians, "Walk like your Father. You are His child, so walk like Him." As believers in Jesus Christ, we are God's children, and that is an overwhelmingly awesome concept to any human being. We are born of His Spirit, which means that spiritually speaking, we are His direct offspring. Paul is exhorting us to grab this truth and live it by imitating the One who gave us new birth. But how do we attempt this? By walking in love in the same way that Jesus loved us.

We are to walk, talk, think, and behave like Jesus. Now, if Paul had written to the Ephesians, "Walk in love," it would not have been nearly as challenging as what he actually says: "Walk in love, *as Christ also hath loved us.*" Our challenge is not to love in our own strength, but to love *as Christ loves*. There is a vivid example of this concept in 2 Corinthians:

**Blessed be God, even the Father of our Lord Jesus Christ, the Father of mercies, and the God of all comfort; who comforteth us in all our tribulation, that we may be able to comfort them which are in any trouble, by the comfort wherewith we ourselves are comforted of God.**

**—2 Corinthians 1:3–4**

Paul reminds us how Jesus comforted, delivered, and encouraged us and how He continues to do so whenever we go through a difficult or even tragic time. He instructs us to minister to and help each other in the same way Jesus ministers to and helps us.

Remember how you were blessed by that special word from the Lord, the one He impressed on your heart just at the moment when you were about to lose hope? Do you recall the enormous relief that flooded your soul when you expected a rebuke for your flawed behavior, but instead He encouraged you and strengthened you to stand strong, ready to overcome at the next temptation?

If we just think about how much His kindness, grace, mercy, and love meant to us then and mean to us today, we can understand what kind of effect being kind, gracious, merciful, and loving will have on someone else who is going through a trial. Believers who extend grace and compassion are imitating Jesus as much as those who seek to raise the dead or multiply fish and bread to feed a multitude. Jesus' ministry on earth was marked by spectacular displays of power as well as spectacular displays of love.

Forgiving the woman caught in adultery, sending her home redeemed and restored, is also a hallmark of Jesus' work on earth. If we are going to be just like Him, we must find people who are hurting, abused, and broken and minister to them until they become healed, restored, and mended. Ultimately our walk is going to be a manifestation of love.

**This is the message that ye heard from the beginning, that we should love one another. . . . We know that we have passed from death unto life, because we love the brethren. . . . My little children, let us not love in word, neither in tongue; but in deed and in truth.**

**—1 John 3:11, 14, 18**

It was John who said that the very nature of God is love. All that He does is motivated by love, grounded in love, and displayed in love. (See 1 John 4:8.) John 3:16 tells us that God loved mankind so much, He gave His only begotten Son to die for our sins and provide the way back to God. The motivation for God's every act was and is love. Therefore, we are to walk in the high calling of Jesus' love for others. Our challenge is to walk through every day in such a way that we reflect the love walk of Jesus.

If you want to walk as a Christian, imitate Christ. Any time you wonder what the loving thing to do is, look at what Jesus did. Love people the way Jesus loved and the way He loves you.

## SACRIFICE OF SELF

Paul calls Jesus' love "a sacrificial offering." One of the definitions of *sacrifice* is "victim" and the word *offering* could be rendered "presentation." Jesus allowed himself to be presented as a victim on our behalf. See Him at Calvary, being mauled and tortured for evil, despicable thoughts and acts that He never experienced. He accepts our guilt and pays the price for it so God can love us and be loved by us without restraint. His is a sacrifice born of a desire to bring the love of God to a lost and dying world and restore to the Father His lost children. Jesus went to extraordinary lengths to ensure our access to God.

Paul says that the sacrifices we make in love are a "sweet-smelling savour" to God—they are like wonderful aromatic incense rising up to Him. God delights in our expressions of love to other people. We give Him pleasure through our acts of genuine Christlike love. But it isn't easy to love like that! Paul doesn't make any claim that such love is easy or automatic. He calls such love a sacrifice—something we must choose to do willfully and consistently, and it goes against our fleshly nature. We have to *choose* to empty ourselves on behalf of others. We have to *choose* to die to self so we can love others more genuinely.

We have a tendency to think that some people are simply more loving than others, that some are just a "natural" at showing love or doing the loving thing. But the Bible says love is always a choice and that it is a choice that costs us something—our pride, our worldly reputation, our preoccupation with self. No person can be loving toward others while staring into a mirror. No person can give to others while clutching his wealth in his hands. To genuinely love, we have to put ourselves aside—and that is painful. It goes against our human nature, which desires to be number one. Genuine love is always a form of self-denial, because we are putting someone else—their care, interests, and well-being—before ourselves.

Many people are waiting for the love of God to envelop them to the point where they become some sort of divine being who walks around doing wonderful loving things for others. That isn't the way it works! There is no instant formula.

To be loving, we must choose the cross. We must die to our own selfish desires and ambitions. We must make loving others a priority that is right next to loving God. Jesus spoke of two commandments that fulfill all the others:

**Thou shalt love the Lord thy God with all thy heart, and with all thy soul, and with all thy mind. This is the first and great commandment. And the second is like unto it, Thou shalt love thy neighbour as thyself. On these two commandments hang all the law and the prophets.**
**—Matthew 22:37–40**

Everything we say and do is to be a reflection of our love for God and our love for others.

## LOVE IN ACTION

**But fornication, and all uncleanness, or covetousness, let it not be once named among you, as becometh saints; neither filthiness, nor foolish talking, nor jesting, which are not convenient; but rather giving of thanks.**
**—Ephesians 5:3–4**

Walking in love and holiness is not automatic with conversion. Our spirits are converted from old creature to new creature, but our actions are still subject to our will and are the outcome of choices we make. Nobody is immediately or instantly moral because they accept Jesus as Savior. Immoral acts of the past are forgiven, but salvation is not an *automatic* vaccination against all immoral acts in the future.

All Christians must pray for the guidance of the Holy Spirit in everything they think, say, and do. At the same time, they must seek to have their minds renewed by the Word of God. Otherwise, it is possible for them to give their hearts to Jesus and continue to smoke and drink and curse and chew and run around with those who do—and not even see any line of distinction between what is right and wrong in these areas! Without the enlightenment and discipline that comes from God's Word and the Holy Spirit, no believer can be trained in godly behaviors, of which love is the highest.

In Ephesians 5:3–4, Paul is making it very clear that sexual immorality, uncleanness, and covetousness are *not* acts that coexist with the love of God. For example, those who practice fornication are out for their own pleasure, seeking only to use another person, without any thought to God's commandments or love for that person.

Those who are "unclean" are into perversion, a vicious immorality that flaunts itself in the face of God's love and commands. Being unclean is a blatant rejection of all that is holy and pure and righteous. Where fornication is sexual activity outside of the law of marriage, uncleanness is practicing every extreme and deviant unnatural behavior.

Those who covet are manipulators, always trying to see how they can get what someone else has. They are takers. Jesus is a giver.

Paul also speaks of filthiness. Ephesus was a city where orgies related to the false goddess Diana took place. Hallucinogenic drugs and excessive drinking were a part of those ungodly feasts connected to the Temple of Diana. Have you ever seen the aftermath of a party of drunks or drug users? The result is filth.

Finally, Paul condemns foolishness and jesting, which are the exact opposite of being sober-minded. Being sober-minded is holding those things that are important to God as dear and precious. Foolishness and jesting are making light of the things that are important to God, teasing about things that are eternal, and joking about God and the work of God in people's lives.

**This ye know, that no whoremonger, nor unclean person, nor covetous man, who is an idolater, hath any inheritance in the kingdom of Christ and of God.**

**—Ephesians 5:5**

The truths Paul is conveying to the Ephesians in this passage of Scripture are foundational truths about character, morality, and personal discipline, truths that are essential to the Christian love walk. However, Paul is also giving a highly sober warning to the believer: Do not practice these things or you will not receive your inheritance in the kingdom.

When we love God and respect and love others, we will not practice fornication or perform unclean acts. We will not covet or fall into filthiness or foolish talking and behavior, because our life belongs to Jesus Christ. As a result, God can open the windows of blessing in our lives and pour out our inheritance. Peter describes our inheritance most succinctly: "His divine power hath given unto us all things that pertain unto life and godliness" (2 Peter 1:3).

When we choose to walk in love, all the power of God backs us up and goes into action to pour His abundant life into ours. We triumphantly and humbly experience our inheritance in Christ— prosperity of every kind—spirit, soul, and body. The *result* of love in action is moral and selfless behavior, but the *reward* of love in action is the manifestation of our inheritance in the kingdom.

## A THANKFUL HEART

Paul puts one main thing on the ledger sheet opposite fornication, uncleanness, covetousness, filthiness, and foolishness and jesting: giving of thanks. Thanksgiving is the beginning of our praise and worship. It is also the beginning of morality and forgiveness.

When you are truly thankful for another person's life before the Lord, you won't want to engage in fornication with that person.

When you are truly thankful for what the Lord has given to you and what the Lord has given to others, you won't covet what others have.

When you are truly thankful for your own salvation from sin and for the freedom God gives you not to sin, you won't want to engage in sin.

When you are truly thankful for the goodness and blessings of God, you won't want to engage in filthy behavior.

When you are truly thankful for your eternal life and for your salvation from eternal death, you won't want to make light of God's mercy and forgiveness.

The loving person is first and foremost a thankful person. She is a person who knows, "We love him, because he first loved us" (1 John 4:19). If God had not loved us first and reached out to us in His mercy and love, we could not have become His children. If He had not sent His Son, Jesus, to die on the cross, we could not have been spared the consequence of spiritual death for our sinful nature. Love flows freely from a thankful heart!

## LOVE IN THE CHURCH

Making a commitment to walk in love sounds very noble and grand when we declare it, but walking it out is another matter, and Paul knew that firsthand! The fact was, the church in Ephesus was a mixed bag. There were mature believers and brand-new believers. Some needed to be taught and some needed to be reminded of what they had been taught already. We're no different today.

Some of the believers in the church today have come out of lifestyles that were just as bad as anything found in Ephesus—orgies, drugs, incest, idolatry, and prostitution. Other believers have followed the traditions of the church all their lives and they are so uptight about the rules and rituals that they have totally overlooked the joy of salvation and what it means to be led by the Spirit.

Variety and differences are part of the challenge of our walk in love. We are called by God to love all kinds of people from all walks of life and at all levels of maturity. We aren't given the privilege of walking only with people who are like us. Some of the people who are walking with us know things we need to learn. Others need to be taught, discipled, and trained in the things of God. We are to love all people: those who are over us in authority and lead us by their example; those who are, spiritually speaking, brand-new babies; and those who are seeking, striving, and determined to overcome their weaknesses and please their heavenly Father.

**A new commandment I give unto you, That ye love one another; as I have loved you, that ye also love one another. By this shall all men know that ye are my disciples, if ye have love one to another.**

**—John 13:34–35**

Jesus said that the world would know the church by the love we have for one another, and that love is a supernatural, heavenly love that comes straight from the heart of God: "The love of God is shed abroad in our hearts by the Holy Ghost which is given unto us" (Romans 5:5).

Walking in love is a miraculous, divine way of life that can only be realized as we yield ourselves fully to the Holy Spirit, completely abandon our selfish concerns, and obey Jesus' command to love with every fiber of our being. If every member of the body of Christ would follow Jesus' words in John 13:34–35, not only would the church be transformed and transcend the power and potency of the early church, but it would once again turn the world upside down!

# 7

# WALKING IN WISDOM

---

Let no man deceive you with vain words: for because of these things cometh the wrath of God upon the children of disobedience. Be not ye therefore partakers with them.
—Ephesians 5:6–7

Paul was aware that there were men roaming about the various churches of his time teaching that certain types of sin and disobedience were either acceptable or didn't matter to God. This was a Greek way of thinking, for many of the Greeks held to the opinion that they could do anything they wanted in their bodies because the body didn't really matter, only the spirit mattered. This was not the wisdom of God!

Know ye not that ye are the temple of God, and that the Spirit of God dwelleth in you? If any man defile the temple of God, him shall God destroy; for the temple of God is holy, which temple ye are. Let no man deceive himself. If any man among you seemeth to be wise in this world, let him become a fool, that he may be wise. For the wisdom of this world is foolishness with God.
—1 Corinthians 3:16–19

Paul stood 100 percent against the Greek teaching that excused bodily sins and warned us that judgment comes on those who choose to continue in fleshly sins once they know better. We are to avoid such behavior and avoid people who believe such behavior is acceptable. We are not to listen to man's wisdom, which is foolishness to God. We are to walk in God's wisdom. He goes on to remind us:

**Ye were sometimes darkness, but now are ye light in the Lord: walk as children of light: (For the fruit of the Spirit is in all goodness and righteousness and truth); proving what is acceptable unto the Lord.**
**—Ephesians 5:8–10**

If you have questions about what is good and right before God, ask a mature believer. Study what the Bible says and pray for revelation from the Holy Spirit. Seek godly counsel. If you have any doubt whatsoever about whether you are acting in a wise manner, search for an answer from godly sources and do not act until you have complete peace.

## BE THE LIGHT!

To have the Light of the World within you and then to choose to walk in darkness is to obliterate your witness for Jesus Christ. When you choose to sin or act upon man's wisdom, you deny the Holy Spirit any opportunity to work through you. If you need a standard, Paul says to look to what is good, right, and true. The Holy Spirit will always produce fruit that is marked by goodness, righteousness, and truthfulness. Anything else is not of Him.

Paul doesn't leave it at that. He doesn't just say, "Don't sin." He goes a step further and says, "Don't associate with those who do. Speak out against their sin." Those are strong words.

**Have no fellowship with the unfruitful works of darkness, but rather reprove them. For it is a shame even to speak of those things which are done of them in secret. But all things that are reproved are made manifest by the light: for whatsoever doth make manifest is light.**
**—Ephesians 5:11–13**

Does this mean we are never to be around sinners? No. The fact is, you must be around sinners to have the opportunity to share the Gospel of Jesus Christ and to lead an unbeliever to salvation. What Paul says is that we are not to have "fellowship with the unfruitful works of darkness." We are to avoid sinning. We are not to seek out, go along with, party with, or associate routinely with the sinful activities of unbelievers. We are to have absolutely no ties with sin.

Furthermore, we are not to dismiss sin or to attempt to justify it, either in ourselves or in others. We are to *reprove* sin. We are to stand against it, speak against it, and in the face of sin, do the very opposite—display the love and righteousness of God.

Finally, we are not even to speak about works of darkness. When we speak about something, we intensify it, call attention to it, diminish its shame, and even glamorize it. That's one of the major flaws in our world today. Sin seems to be discussed and paraded about in movies, on talk shows, and in every prime-time program on television. The more sin is talked about, the less shameful it becomes. Children grow up thinking, "Everybody does this. Everybody talks about it. There's nothing wrong with something everybody talks about and everybody does."

Nothing could be further from God's truth!

When we put sin on center stage, we are giving it permission to become familiar. We are giving permission for others to study it, gawk at it, become accustomed to it, and eventually say, "It's all right." That's why Paul strongly admonishes us not to talk about the shameful things done in secret. Instead, he tells us to choose to be innocent of those things and be a light. When darkness is around us, we should shine even brighter!

When someone wants to tell you a dirty joke, say, "I'd rather not hear it." If they persist in their effort, walk away.

There's no good fruit from sin. That's why the works of darkness are called *unfruitful*. Sin has consequences that are deadly, and they are not fruit. Fruit is pleasant, good, nourishing, and life-giving. Although sin is pleasurable for a season, in the end it produces the exact opposite. It is unpleasant, evil, depleting, and life-destroying.

"Awake thou that sleepest, and arise from the dead, and Christ shall give thee light" (Ephesians 5:14). For some of the Ephesians and for many believers today, these words of Paul are a wake-up call. Paul knew that many were aimlessly walking along, so tied up in worldly things and sin that you would never know by looking at them that they were believers. Paul could not have made this plainer: If you are born again but persist in the works of darkness, you will be asleep among dead people. Although you are spiritually alive, you have repressed and suppressed your spiritual life and light by your acts of disobedience and are nothing more than a reflection of the darkness you are walking in. If you put a sleeping person in a room of dead people, you would have to get very close to the one sleeping to tell he was alive.

If this is you, WAKE UP! Look where you are going. Open your spiritual eyes. You are about to sleepwalk right over a cliff! Move far away from sin and those who encourage you or entice you into sin. If you do this, the Word of God promises that Jesus will give you light, and that is the wisdom of God. From this moment on, if you have any doubt about what is right, ask Jesus. He'll show you. He'll guide you into the truth of what is pure, holy, and righteous before God.

In reality, the only way to be a light and walk in the light is to walk with wisdom. The Bible says Jesus is wisdom to us. (See 1 Corinthians 1:30.) He is the Living Word. (See John 1:1 and 14.) When we walk with Jesus, have fellowship with Him, seek His counsel at all times, and love and worship Him as we go about our day, we will walk in the light and grow in the light.

**This then is the message which we have heard of him, and declare unto you, that God is light, and in him is no darkness at all. If we say that we have fellowship with him, and walk in darkness, we lie, and do not the truth: But if we walk in the light, as he is in the light, we have fellowship one with another, and the blood of Jesus Christ his Son cleanseth us from all sin.**
**—1 John 1:5–7**

It is very simple: When we walk in the light, we will be the light!

## THE PRINCIPAL THING

**Wisdom is the principal thing; therefore get wisdom: and with all thy getting get understanding. Exalt her, and she shall promote thee: she shall bring thee to honour, when thou dost embrace her. She shall give to thine head an ornament of grace: a crown of glory shall she deliver to thee.**
**—Proverbs 4:7–9**

When Solomon became king of Israel, he was just a young man, but God told him He would give him anything he wanted. What would you do if Jesus appeared to you today and said, "I'll give you anything you desire. Just name it, and it is yours right now"? Solomon did not ask for the fastest chariot in the world, the most beautiful wife in the land, or even the wealth of kingdoms. This incredible young man asked God for wisdom.

As a result of his request, God granted Solomon wisdom and everything that comes with wisdom: riches, wealth, and honor such as no other king had possessed or ever would possess after him. (See 2 Chronicles 1:7–12.) Every blessing in life rested upon the foundation of wisdom. Therefore, it is not surprising that Paul sums up the walk of the believer by writing to the Ephesians: "See then that ye walk circumspectly, not as fools, but as wise" (Ephesians 5:15).

The word *circumspectly* is a very interesting word in the Greek. It depicts perfection in the sense of being exact, careful, and accurate, and it leaves no room for any quality or characteristic of life that is undisciplined, untrained, unholy, ungodly, or unrighteous. To walk circumspectly, we must be entirely focused on what *God* desires to accomplish in us, through us, for us, and around us. We must be careful, accurate, making certain that our lives—thoughts, speech, actions, and motives—line up perfectly with God's Word and the guidance of the Holy Spirit at all times. A circumspect walk is a walk in which we pay attention and "take heed."

The message here is that our wandering stage in sin and distraction from God's will is over. It's time to cross over the Jordan River and enter into the fullness of what God has promised us, our inheritance as His children and believers in Jesus Christ. If we truly are going to walk in victory, claiming every bit of territory that the Devil seeks to possess in our lives, we are going to have to walk focused squarely upon the truth of God, shunning anything that would lead us astray or cause us to veer from the path God has set for us.

"Redeeming the time, because the days are evil" (Ephesians 5:16). There must be no delay! No more wasting time in foolish talking, ungodly fantasy, and carnal appetites. It's time to know our calling, our purpose, our hope, and the will of God—and appropriate all He has promised!

"Wherefore be ye not unwise, but understanding what the will of the Lord is" (Ephesians 5:17). Wisdom is intimately connected with understanding. When we walk in God's wisdom, we have His understanding of a situation. We may not know all the details or even see the outcome in the beginning, but we have a deep sense of God's eternal plan and purpose in every action He directs us to take. Inevitably, as we walk out God's plan, He enlightens us with understanding and we see how each piece of the puzzle fits perfectly. Biblical scholar Zodhiates states that understanding is the ability to "put something together and make sense of it," and in the experience of the believer, it is a divine, eternal, all-knowing sense that emanates from God himself. Understanding is something believers have the privilege of walking in while the world around us stumbles in darkness, ignorance, and confusion.

Paul does not leave us out there, wondering how in the world we are to get wisdom and walk in understanding in our practical, everyday lives. He goes on to give us very specific instructions: "And be not drunk with wine, wherein is excess; but be filled with the Spirit; speaking to yourselves in psalms and hymns and spiritual songs, singing and making melody in your heart to the Lord" (Ephesians 5:18–19).

There has been a lot of controversy in the church concerning the consumption of alcoholic beverages, but I believe that debate is almost a distraction and a tangent from the message God is bringing to us in these verses of Scripture. The point is that we are to be filled with the Spirit. Nothing else in life should satisfy, motivate, or drive us but being filled with the Spirit. Not only is being filled with the Spirit the only way we will be able to walk in the wisdom of God's Word and will, but it is the only way we will have a magnificent and joyful experience in doing so!

In order to be filled with the Spirit, however, we must *speak to ourselves,* and we must speak the right things: psalms, hymns, and spiritual songs. We must make melody in our hearts, praising and worshiping our Lord at all times. This is God's simple prescription for a healthy, happy, fulfilling, and successful Christian walk, and yet we spend most of our time doing something else.

How many people do you know who are consumed by their work?

How many people spend every spare minute on a hobby or pastime that is of little consequence?

How many people do you know who are wasting precious time reading books or watching TV shows or movies that have no eternal benefit, that actually draw them away from the things of God and pull them down?

How many people do you know who spend every weekend at the lake, in the mountains, at the beach, or any place other than the house of God?

Paul says to us, "Don't let anything consume your time, attention, or energy but the Spirit!"

There is nothing wrong with working, resting, playing, and growing, and certainly the Word of God encourages us to do these things. However, the great thing about being filled with the Spirit is that you can be filled with the Spirit wherever you are and whatever you are doing. You may not be able to sing psalms, hymns, and spiritual songs while you are working, but you can make melody to the Lord in your heart! There is no activity in which we cannot at least have a heart filled with praise and worship to God.

How is all this connected to wisdom? When you have a heart filled with the Spirit, making melody unto the Lord, you are plugged in to wisdom himself. You are connected to the Divine Revelator of Truth and the Power of the Universe. You are walking hand in hand with Jesus, the King of Kings and Lord of Lords, who is the Alpha and the Omega and knows the end from the beginning.

The surest way to know whether you are in God's will and walking in His wisdom and understanding is whether or not you are making melody to Him in your heart. If you feel uncomfortable doing that or are not doing it, something is wrong and you are heading for the cliff like someone who is asleep among the dead! But the good news is that in one moment of time you can be right back on track by simply repenting, turning your heart back to God, and beginning to sing psalms, hymns, and spiritual songs to Him.

Wisdom is the principal thing because it is the key to everything good, holy, and worthwhile in life. By being filled with the Spirit and walking in God's Word, we will not only accomplish the call of God on our life, but we will experience marvelous adventures and great blessings along the way!

# CONCLUSION: OUR MANDATE

In the book of Ephesians, God gives the church the mandate to cross the Jordan and take the land. There's no justification for refusing to walk forward in the fullness of His promises. To choose to continue wandering in the wilderness, staying in sin, delaying our growth, avoiding our call, denying who we really are, and focusing on things other than the Word and the Spirit is to choose death. That is not our walk or our mandate from God. We are to be the light, expel the darkness, and bring prosperity and peace to the hearts of mankind. When the hearts of men are filled with the prosperity and peace that come through knowing Jesus Christ as Lord and Savior, every aspect of their lives becomes beautiful and fruitful.

But to achieve our mandate from God, we must walk His way. Our walk is to be a responsible walk, always giving honor and glory to the One who saved us, healed us, and set us free, by staying on the path He has designed for us. We are to walk as the new creature we are in Christ, showing forth His character and compassion to everyone we meet. Our walk is a walk of supernatural strength, continually relying on our Father God's ability and not our own to exceed and shatter all expectations for our lives. Our walk is not alone but hand in hand with Jesus and with each other, in unity and in love, which gives us power to reach and transform the world. And finally, our walk is a wise walk, based not on our human, foolish ideas and perceptions, but on the very mind and heart of God, which is revealed to us by His Word and His Spirit.

Our walk is powerful, and it brings results and rewards that reach far beyond our own sphere of influence—in this life and in the life to come.

# PART FIVE

*Celebrating Marriage*

# Introduction

Everybody loves a wedding! A wedding is considered great cause for celebration, not only by the bride and groom, but by family members, friends, and even those who don't know the happy couple. When a man and woman pledge their entire lives to one another, it is one of the most sacred and cherished moments for them and for all who stand with them. They are making vows of fidelity and love to each other for life.

We all know the love story of the ages: Man and woman meet, they fall in love, they marry, and they live happily ever after. But we must remember that weddings are God's idea. From the beginning, God anticipated that man and woman would be joined together in a holy union, or holy matrimony. He called this sacred covenant becoming *one flesh* (see Genesis 2:24), and this joining in marriage became His most vibrant illustration to fallen mankind of the intimate relationship He sought with them.

Why did God choose to describe His love relationship and lasting commitment to a union with His people through the experience and significance of a wedding and a marriage? Throughout the Old Testament we find references to God being the Bridegroom of His people, who are His bride: "As the bridegroom rejoiceth over the bride, so shall thy God rejoice over thee" (Isaiah 62:5).

In the New Testament, the Holy Spirit gives us the crowning joy of the mystery. Jesus, our Savior and Lord, is the bridegroom of the church, and we are His beloved bride: "There came unto me one of the seven angels . . . and talked with me, saying, Come hither, I will show thee the bride, the Lamb's wife" (Revelation 21:9).

The apostle Paul gracefully addressed this issue in writing to the Ephesians. His teaching on this subject in the epistles is one of the most beautiful and yet practical about how we are wedded to the Lord Jesus Christ. This teaching is at the very heart of what it means to be loved and cherished by God and to be one with Him.

I believe God chose the wedding and marriage to illustrate His relationship with His people because it is the most intimate and personal relationship we experience in our natural lives. And when our hearts and minds begin to see and understand the depth and richness of this revelation—we are forever loved by and married to Jesus Christ—the ecstasy of our position and condition in Him is beyond expression!

# 1

# OUR KINSMAN-REDEEMER

In the book of Ruth, God gives us a beautiful example of how Jesus becomes our Bridegroom and we become His beloved. As a Moabite and former idol worshiper, Ruth represents the church. Like her, we once lived under the rule and influence of Satan and a world system that is totally opposed to God's kingdom. As Ruth's deliverer, Boaz represents Jesus. Jesus is our kinsman in the flesh who loves us, pays the price to redeem us from our spiritual poverty, and then takes us as His bride. Throughout the Bible, God repeatedly uses weddings and marriage to reveal to us His pursuit of us, His love for us, and His desire to be with us forever.

*Marriage is a God-created relationship.* In spite of what many people think, marriage has never been a secular institution. In fact, those who follow the dictates of the world, the lusts of their flesh, and the lies of the Enemy have very little use for marriage. They would just as soon be single so they can fornicate and commit adultery with whomever they choose. It doesn't bother them to father children and never be a father to those children. It doesn't bother them to have children by several different men and never have contact with those fathers again. The world has little regard for the demands of fidelity and "until death do us part" vows, and it has a high degree of tolerance for marital infidelity, separation, and divorce.

However, marriage is holy and divine in its very definition and nature. That's because God created the wedding and marriage to be a picture of how Jesus would pursue, commit to, and love His bride and how His bride should love and cherish Him in return. When a man and woman come together at a wedding, it is a sacred, spiritual act. Where the world views marriage as a partnership, like a merger between two companies, the church views marriage as the divine, sacred uniting of a man and a woman for life: "Therefore shall a man leave his father and his mother, and shall cleave unto his wife: and they shall be one flesh" (Genesis 2:24).

In marriage, male and female are fused and bonded into one flesh. Furthermore, what God reveals about Adam and Eve—and about the relationship between a husband and wife—illustrates what the church is ultimately to be to Jesus. Paul speaks of this sacred relationship to the Ephesians: "This is a great mystery: but I speak concerning Christ and the church" (Ephesians 5:32).

Although Paul writes only ten verses about marriage between husband and wife in this epistle, those verses are so rich that an entire marriage seminar could be taught from them. And when we finish studying Ephesians 5:22 to 5:31, teaching about wives submitting to their husbands and husbands loving and cherishing their wives, we come face-to-face with the reality of our marriage to the Lamb. Ultimately, natural marriage is an illustration Paul uses to show the depth of our relationship with the Lord.

There are those who call the church the *body* of Christ, and there are those who call the church the *bride* of Christ. Some modern teachers have argued over which is correct. They say, "If the church is His body, which is male, it cannot be His bride, which is female." The fact is, in the first marriage between Adam and Eve, Eve was both Adam's body and his bride. She was bone of his bone and flesh of his flesh, yet she was separate from him in form and inseparably bound to him in spirit. As believers in Christ Jesus, we are inseparably bound and eternally married to the Lord Jesus Christ in spirit. Yet on this earth, we live out His life in our flesh. We are body and bride simultaneously.

## ADAM AND EVE

In order to understand more fully what Paul is teaching the Ephesians and us, let's take a look at the marriage of Adam and Eve. The first man, Adam, was created in the likeness and the image of

God. He was the picture God wanted to display of himself on the earth in fleshly form.

Now, Adam did not look like God physically because God is Spirit in His essence, and spirit has no form or physique. Nor did Adam look quite like me or any man alive on the earth today. Adam was a *created* man, created by God without blemish or defect. I don't have any idea how Adam looked—I wasn't there! But I know this. He was *like* his Creator. His Creator is Father God, and Adam was like God. Adam was distinctive from all other created beings. He had self-awareness, creative thought, and the ability to communicate with God in a personal way.

"Male and female created he them; and blessed them, and called their name Adam, in the day when they were created" (Genesis 5:2). God called their name Adam—male and female created He *them*. Adam was a perfect person and he had complete dominion over everything. He had a position granted to him by his Creator and an image that reflected his Creator. When Adam stood up and began to walk about this earth, he was a different person than you and I. I'm not talking about the color of his skin, the color of his hair, the features of his face, or the build of his body. He walked about this earth and had total dominion over every aspect of the earth.

How long did Adam exist in this state of wholeness and perfection in God's image? We don't know. We only know this: He was alone. Then one day God said that his state of aloneness was no longer suitable. For the first time in the act of creation, God proclaimed, "It is not good." And then he said, "I will make him an help meet for him" (Genesis 2:18).

When God said, "It is not good for man to be alone," the word *alone* here is a Hebrew word, which means to be by oneself, the only one. This word lends itself to the concept of being the only one of a species. To illustrate His point, God brought every living creature before Adam and he named them, including the fish of the sea, the fowl of the air, the beasts of the field, and all creeping and crawling things. In every species, Adam encountered male and female. Male and female bluebirds. Male and female dolphins. Male and female ants.

Finally, God took Adam and put him to sleep and said, "I don't have to reach down in the dirt to create anything for you, because you are so much like me that I need only reach inside you, pull something out of you that is already in you, and use it to create a helpmeet for you."

God reached into Adam's side and pulled out a rib and from that rib constructed a woman. Adam knew she was of his body. He could become one with her because she came from him. And the two became one because they were one before they were two.

It is a great mystery to our minds that two can become one, and this is the mystery of the church in its relationship to God. As human beings we have the potential to become one with God. Because God created us and gave us a portion of His nature, even in our sinfulness, we can respond to Him, be restored to Him, be reconciled to Him, be reunited with Him, and be one with Him. No longer are we man or woman separated from God, but man or woman infused with the very presence and Spirit of God. We enter into oneness with Him.

In the physical, Eve was a composite of different chromosomes, all of which were related to Adam and which could unite with his chromosomes. When Adam and Eve coupled with one another, all of Adam's masculinity and all of Eve's femininity found full expression and fulfillment, and in their union multiplication and growth came forth.

This is the mystery of Christ and the church. It is as Jesus finds expression for His Spirit in our flesh and through our flesh, and as we find expression in Jesus for all that we are, that we become one with Him and together produce the spiritual fruit of souls for His kingdom. Hallelujah! No wonder the angels and all of heaven shout with joy whenever another soul comes into the kingdom of God!

## SATAN'S ATTACK

After we encounter the powerful yet wholly beautiful experience of becoming one both in marriage and with our Lord, is it any wonder that Satan attacked the union of Adam and Eve and continues to attack marriage today? Is it any wonder that Satan continues to attack our union with Christ Jesus? He is trying to put a stop to two things: oneness—complete union, cohesiveness, unity—and the production of fruit!

Satan's entire effort is aimed at the overthrow of God. He seeks the destruction of the believer's union with Christ Jesus and with other believers. He hates oneness and unity among believers and within the church. Why? Because he hates the production of spiritual fruit. The last thing Satan wants is for sinners to be born again, for the oppressed to be delivered, for the demon-possessed to be set free, for new believers to grow into maturity to the full stature of Christ, for the church to be strengthened, and for the kingdom of God to be established.

Satan is quick to slip into any group, union, marriage, or church. And he started his attack in the garden of Eden with the woman. He doesn't start with Jesus because he already battled Jesus and lost! Remember Jesus' description of Satan's fall before man was created: "And he said unto them, I beheld Satan as lightning fall from heaven" (Luke 10:18). He lost when he was Lucifer and rebelled against God, he lost the definitive battle at the cross and the resurrection, and he continues to lose to Jesus every time a believer takes authority over him in Jesus' name. Satan is a defeated foe, so his attacks are aimed at the believer, and his attacks on the believer ultimately target Jesus Christ.

When Satan came to Eve, his final destination was not Eve but Adam. Both Adam and Eve had dominion over the earth (see Genesis 1:27), but Adam was the head. Satan intended to destroy Eve on his way to destroying Adam and as a means of gaining the earth for his own possession. The Bible tells us that before his fall, Lucifer's throne and dominion were on the earth. He is referred to as the king of Tyrus:

Son of man, take up a lamentation upon the king of Tyrus, and say unto him, Thus saith the Lord God; Thou sealest up the sum, full of wisdom, and perfect in beauty. Thou hast been in Eden the garden of God; every precious stone was thy covering, the sardius, topaz, and the diamond, the beryl, the onyx, and the jasper, the sapphire, the emerald, and the carbuncle, and gold: the workmanship of thy tabrets and of thy pipes was prepared in thee in the day that thou wast created. Thou art the anointed cherub that covereth; and I have set thee so: thou wast upon the holy mountain of God; thou hast walked up and down in the midst of the stones of fire. Thou wast perfect in thy ways from the day that thou wast created, till iniquity was found in thee.
**—Ezekiel 28:12–15**

When Adam fell and bowed his knee to Satan, Satan gained dominion over the earth again and he keeps his dominion through fallen mankind. But then Jesus, the Second Adam, did not bow His knee to Satan. And when He redeemed fallen humanity, becoming the door to the restoration of our relationship with God and our dominion on the earth, Satan's rule was threatened again.

Stop to think about this for a moment: Satan cannot destroy Jesus directly. He cannot take on the Son of God in face-to-face combat and win. But what if Satan could destroy every believer in Christ Jesus? He would not be destroying Jesus, who is sitting at the right hand of the Father, but he would be destroying the manifested dominion and expression of Christ Jesus on earth. In seeking to destroy the believer, Satan's ultimate aim is to destroy the work of Christ Jesus and have the earth for himself.

## THE SECOND ADAM

Satan's attack on Eve was intended to test the first man, Adam. After woman had partaken of the forbidden fruit, Adam looked at her as she offered the fruit to him and he came to the conclusion, "I love her so much that if she is going to die, I am going to die with her." He made the first fatal mistake. He loved the *gift* more than he loved the *Giver*.

Eve was *deceived,* but Adam *decided.* The Bible says that Adam "did eat." His decision was an act of his will. The fall of humanity didn't take place when Eve was deceived and ate. It took place when Adam deliberately and intentionally ate. The sins we commit that are borne of deception do not strike at the very nature of our relationship with God. These sins are readily confessed, repented, and cast aside. But the sins we commit out of our will—as a conscious decision and plan of action—are destructive and deadly to our relationship with God. When we say, "I choose to disobey what you have said and to go my own way," we set ourselves up to receive the full wages of sin, which ultimately is separation from God and death.

It was out of Adam's decision to die with his bride that chaos broke out in the kingdom of Eden. When Adam and Eve both entered into a state of death, everything under their domain came under death. That's what a kingdom is—a domain over which you have dominion. It is what you rule and govern. When a king falls, his kingdom falls with him. When a married person falls into willful sin and chooses to become a rebel against God, what he rules is impacted. His children suffer. His home suffers. His family influence in the church and community suffers.

Adam willfully chose sin and fell, so we all fell with him because we were born of his seed. We encounter this principle of the seed in the book of Hebrews: "Levi also, who receiveth tithes, paid tithes in Abraham. For he was yet in the loins of his father, when Melchizedec met him" (Hebrews 7:9–10).

When Abraham paid tithes, Levi paid tithes. Levi hadn't been born when Abraham paid tithes to Melchizedec; in fact, Levi was Abraham's great-grandchild. But because Abraham paid tithes, the practice of paying tithes and the blessing associated with it was built into his seed, Levi. Likewise, when Adam fell, all mankind fell with him. It makes no difference what color he was or what his features were. He was flesh and blood, and when he fell, all flesh and blood fell.

The Scriptures tell us that in the fullness of time God sent forth His Son, born of a virgin. And this Son, whom we call Jesus, is the second Adam. God places Jesus in the womb of a virgin, and He is birthed into flesh on this earth complete in himself. Jesus is a new creation.

Then, for the joy that was set before Him, this second Adam goes through the cross, the crown of thorns being crushed into His skull, the nails being driven into His hands and His feet, the piercing of His side, the agony of death, taking on the sins of the world, and being forsaken by His Father. And He does it for the joy that out of His sacrifice, He is going to receive a wife—a beautiful, exquisite bride. Just as God pulled Eve out of Adam while Adam slept, after Jesus breathed His final breath on the cross, God pierced His side as a sign that His bride was being fashioned.

One man died *from* sin.

One man died *for* sin.

One man passed sin to all mankind.

One man passed righteousness to all mankind.

The first Adam died *with* his bride; the second Adam, Jesus Christ, died *for* His bride.

Being innocent of our sin, Jesus became our kinsman-redeemer. Having come to earth as one of us, our kinsman in the flesh, He gave himself for us, His body and His bride. Now He becomes one with us so He might have a body on this earth that will produce the glorious fruit of the Gospel: many, many children for the Father's heavenly home!

One with our Lord—this is the mystery of the church!

# 2

# A NEW LIFE OF HONOR

One of the most beautiful illustrations of God's love for us is found in the Old Testament book of Hosea. God said to the prophet Hosea, "Go, take unto thee a wife of whoredoms" (Hosea 1:2). Hosea went to the marketplace of prostitute slaves and bought Gomer. He brought her home, made her his wife, and had children with her. He bought her when she was a disgrace and an embarrassment, and he only asked that she be a good wife to him. Hosea offered Gomer a new life of honor before God and man.

God used Hosea to demonstrate how deep and unconditional His love was for Israel. He desired them even when they had forsaken Him, turned to false gods, and had become prostitutes in their worship. Through Hosea, God was saying to them, "Even though you have disgraced me and embarrassed me, I love you and I want you to marry me. I want to give you a new life of honor."

God has always desired a people who would live in a loving relationship with Him: "Thou art my people; and they shall say, Thou art my God" (Hosea 2:23). And that desire found full expression in Christ Jesus. With His sinless blood He "bought" us out of the marketplace of sin and "spiritual prostitution," our worship of false gods and our pursuit of evil practices. Paul wrote about our Savior to the Ephesians: "In whom we have redemption through his blood, the forgiveness of sins, according to the riches of his grace" (Ephesians 1:7).

Jesus redeemed us, purchased us, paid the full price for us, and took us out of the sin market and bondage of the Devil, the world, and our flesh. He purchased us with His life so that we might be free to love Him and become His bride, the church. As slaves to sin, we were ruled by the Devil, who tormented us, lied to us, stole from us, and tried to destroy us with shame. As the bride of Jesus Christ, we are ruled by His love. Our magnificent Lord imparts His righteous nature through the indwelling of the Holy Spirit, who leads us, counsels us, and comforts us. As His bride, He gives us a place of honor, and we are to bring glory and honor to Him.

## WE ARE HIS BETROTHED

As believers in Jesus Christ, we are betrothed to Him, and we are to walk as those who are promised to Him and Him alone. In biblical times, betrothal meant something very different from what it means today. It was not just an engagement but the formal part of the marriage ritual. From the moment the man and woman were betrothed, the two were considered one. However, the marriage was usually not consummated for a year or more.

During the betrothal period, the groom would build a home for the couple and continue courting his bride, getting to know her and allowing her to know him as much as possible. The bride would purify and prepare herself for her groom, and one of the best examples of this is found in the book of Esther. The king chose her for his queen, but she spent many months preparing herself for him. No doubt she learned all she could about him so that she could please him in all respects. Finally, when the groom brought his bride to their new home and they began to physically live as husband and wife, all controversies were laid to rest. They began their new life together in peace.

When we understand the meaning of betrothal, we see that our marriage to Jesus will be consummated physically when we receive our glorified bodies at the resurrection. Yet we are married to Him now. In biblical times, if either the bride or groom had sexual relations with someone else during their betrothal, it was considered adultery. So we must view our betrothal to Jesus as a sacred covenant of marriage, sealed by His blood and the Holy Spirit, who makes us one. Yet we groan for the time when our marriage will be fully consummated at the resurrection and we partake of the Marriage Supper of the Lamb.

Until then, Jesus is fulfilling His part of our betrothal. Before His ascension, He told us He was going to prepare a place for us, and He is always praying and interceding for us. He is continuing to court us, to woo us, to lavish His love upon us, and to bring us into "the knowledge of Him" as much as possible. All His attentions are toward our purification and preparation for His coming.

And what is our part of the betrothal? Remember the parable of the ten virgins? We are to keep our lamps lit with the fire of the Holy Spirit and renew our minds with God's Word. We are to pray without ceasing, rejoice at all times, and love one another as He loves us. We are to be continuously aware that we are Jesus' bride and a reflection of His nature, truth, and glory on the earth.

## DIVINE REFLECTION

**Be ye therefore followers of God, as dear children; and walk in love, as Christ also hath loved us, and hath given himself for us an offering and a sacrifice to God for a sweetsmelling savour.**
**—Ephesians 5:1–2**

Why is it so critical that we follow and imitate Jesus? Because anything we do reflects on Him. We are His betrothed. He gets the glory every time we restrain ourselves from doing and saying what we should not say and do. He receives honor when we humble ourselves and reckon our flesh dead. We present an especially strong witness of His goodness when we love our enemies and those who hate us, persecute us, or reject us. Unfortunately, He also gets a bad reputation when we act badly.

When we walk in the ways of our own fleshly desires and lusts, giving in to selfish ambitions and reactions and behavior, we bring no glory to Jesus, and we certainly do not have His approval or receive His favor. What is worse, we separate ourselves from fellowship with Him. This does not mean He ceases to love us or even loves us less. He loves us with unconditional, merciful, and long-suffering love at all times. Our sinful, unloving actions, however, keep us from the rewards that come from righteous living and loving as He loves.

A single person has only her own reputation to worry about—what she says and does reflect only on herself. But a married person's behavior and words also reflect on her spouse. No man wants his wife running around town, writing bad checks, engaging in filthy conversation, getting drunk and obnoxious in public, or flirting with or dating other men. He wants his wife to refrain from those behaviors because he loves her and wants her reputation to be good, but he also wants his wife to be a godly reflection of him and their family.

A wife doesn't want her husband flirting with or dating other women, getting in trouble with the law, gambling their family income away, smoking dope, or staying out all night at pool halls. She wants him to enjoy a fine reputation and be a man of the highest integrity for his own sake and for her sake and their children's. Every woman wants to be proud of her husband.

We are eternally blessed that our Bridegroom is perfect. His reputation is stellar in all respects, His character unblemished, His strength and courage unmatched, and His love for us beyond our imagination. Our betrothal to Jesus Christ demands that we no longer live for ourselves but for Him. We are to separate ourselves from filthiness or foolishness of any type because what we do reflects upon Him.

## LEARNING WHAT'S HONORABLE

Many newly married couples don't really know how to be married. They continue to think, act, and respond to life as they did when they were single. If this kind of behavior continues for very long, the marriage is in trouble! That's why the Bible directs older, wiser married couples to mentor newly married couples, especially if those newly married couples don't have role models for a good marriage.

If you take two people who come from backgrounds in which daddy was drunk or abusive or mama was running the streets and was rarely home; if you take two people who come from broken homes or whose parents had a frigid, formal relationship; if you take two people who come from homes where manipulation took place, drugs were sold, or where pornography and filthy behavior were manifested, those two people have absolutely no understanding of what it means to have a godly marriage or how to treat each other in a way that pleases the Lord. They need to be taught how to be married.

If a man has a father who was never faithful to his mother, was gone from the home much of the time at the racetrack or the local bar, and who came home only to act in a domineering, manipulative, abusive way toward his wife and children, that young man is going to grow up assuming all husbands and fathers act like this. If he has figured out that this is not honorable, then he still may feel hopeless that he can ever overcome his past and behave differently. He needs the power of the Holy Spirit and the yoke-destroying Word of God, and he needs to be discipled by spiritual fathers who can teach him how to behave toward his new wife. He needs to be taught what is honorable.

If a woman has a mother who cheats on her father, manipulates him for everything she wants from him, and speaks badly about him the minute he's out of earshot, that young woman is going to grow up assuming all wives act like her mama acts. Worse, she may be convicted by the Holy Spirit that these ways are evil, but feel trapped in this generational, cursed behavior. That's when the Word and the Spirit step in, she gets delivered from the curse, and Jesus brings spiritual mothers into her life to teach her how to be an honorable wife.

As Jesus' betrothed, we are no different! When we accept Him as our Lord and Savior, He has purchased us out of the slave market and given us His name, but we need to be taught how to live in an honorable marriage relationship with Him and bring glory and honor to His name. There are those who believe in and love Jesus as their Savior who continue to live impure lives not because they are choosing to sin, but simply because they have never been taught to distinguish between right and wrong in God's eyes.

When a person becomes a Christian, their immorality and sin don't just naturally dissipate. Sin has to be "put away." The old man has to be stripped away and godly behavior has to be put on just as a person might take off old garments and put on new clothes. We read about this in Paul's writings, especially in Ephesians:

**Put off concerning the former conversation the old man, which is corrupt according to the deceitful lusts; and be renewed in the spirit of your mind; and that ye put on the new man, which after God is created in righteousness and true holiness.**
**—Ephesians 4:22–24**

At the time of Jesus' crucifixion, the veil that separated the inner court and the Holy of Holies was rent into two pieces, signifying to all believers that they have direct access to God the Father and may live in intimate relationship with Him. There isn't a moment in our lives when we are not in direct association with the Lord. We are always in His presence—Christ in us and us in Christ.

Any person who is married in her heart and not merely in her words and by the law knows that she is married at all times. There isn't a moment in that person's life when she is not aware of the impact her words and actions have upon her spouse and her family. In our relationship with Christ Jesus, we are His bride at all times, in all situations, in all places, with our whole being. It is our joy to represent Him well and bring honor to His name.

## REVIVAL

Before we go further, I must address the meaning of revival. Many people perceive revival as a mighty move of the Holy Spirit upon unbelievers that brings in a tremendous harvest of souls. This is partially true. But revival is actually a powerful, life-transforming, purifying move of the Holy Spirit upon believers. Then, when the church becomes holy, bold, and passionate about Jesus, He empowers them to bring in a harvest of souls.

Many believers and many churches today need revival because they have no concept of what it means to live as the betrothed of Jesus Christ. They know what it means to live a religious life. They get baptized, go to church on Sundays, put something in the offering plate, own a Bible, and even read it and pray from time to time. They know what it means to "play church." They know when to stand up and sit down during the services. They know how to address the clergy and which day Communion is served. But they don't understand the new life of honor their Savior and Lord has given them. They don't understand their betrothal to Him, and therefore they do not have His purity and power in their lives.

Married life is different from single life in the natural and in the Lord. A single person can go and do pretty much what he wants to do, any time of the day or night. He can spend his money any way he wants to, without consulting anyone. That's not true for a married person. That person is no longer alone but part of a union in which husband and wife hold all things in common and do all things in consideration of each other.

As believers, we must sever all relationship with sin and the world and walk in righteousness, peace, and joy with our Lord. Hosea knew that for the Israelites to come back to God, their husband, they would have to spurn idolatry, the worship of other gods. For Gomer to be fulfilled in her marriage to Hosea, she would have to turn from her form of idolatry—going after other lovers and the money they brought her. Paul wrote to the Ephesians:

**Be ye therefore followers of God, as dear children; and walk in love, as Christ also hath loved us, and hath given himself for us an offering and a sacrifice to God for a sweetsmelling savour. But fornication, and all uncleanness, or covetousness, let it not be once named among you, as becometh saints; neither filthiness, nor foolish talking, nor jesting, which are not convenient: but rather giving of thanks. For this ye know, that no whoremonger, nor unclean person, nor covetous man, who is an idolater, hath any inheritance in the kingdom of Christ and of God.**
**—Ephesians 5:1–5**

We cannot live betrothed to Jesus and continue "dating" this philosophy and flirting with that idol. We must put off the old man and put on the new. We cannot neglect studying the Word of God, and it is essential to the well-being of our relationship with Christ that we are sensitive and obedient to the Holy Spirit. We must engage in intimate prayer and have regular fellowship with other believers. And we must not continue in sin of any kind, whether in our thoughts, our speech, or our deeds.

The honor Jesus bestows upon us as His beloved demands an honorable life in return. Has the church today lived this new life of honor before the world? Only God can judge the hearts of humanity, but as for me and my house, we are seeking revival! We are hungry for more and more of God, and as our Bridegroom illuminates this sin and that oppression and this lie and that error, we are repenting! We are on our faces praying for wisdom and compassion and mercy and grace to walk in this heavenly and totally undeserved gift, this new life of honor. When Jesus returns, we want our lamps to be lit with bonfires of passion for Him and Him alone!

# 3

# SACRIFICIAL LOVE

When we get all dressed up to attend a wedding, we put on our very best clothes and behavior because we are going to take part in a sacred act. A man and a woman are going to give their lives to each other for as long as they live, and we have the honor to stand with them and witness their solemn, sacred pledge to each other. They are going to make a covenant, a holy and irrevocable vow, to be one, to own all things in common, and to love and care for one another for the rest of their lives.

Throughout the Scriptures, the shedding of blood was required for a covenant to be in effect. The covenant on which our relationship with the Lord is based involves the sacrificial shedding of Jesus' blood on the cross. In a marriage, the covenant was fulfilled when the husband and wife had consummated their marriage vows.

The Lord spoke to His people through the prophet Ezekiel about the way He had raised them up to be His bride. As you read through these verses, note that all of the aspects of a covenant marriage are included in this passage of Scripture:

I have caused thee to multiply as the bud of the field, and thou hast increased and waxen great, and thou art come to excellent ornaments: thy breasts are fashioned, and thine hair is grown, whereas thou wast naked and bare. Now when I passed by thee, and looked upon thee, behold, thy time was the time of love; and I spread my skirt over thee, and covered thy nakedness: yea,

I sware unto thee, and entered into a covenant with thee, saith
the Lord God, and thou becamest mine. Then washed I thee
with water; yea, I thoroughly washed away thy blood from thee,
and I anointed thee with oil. I clothed thee also with broidered
work, and shod thee with badgers' skin, and I girded thee about
with fine linen, and I covered thee with silk. I decked thee also
with ornaments, and I put bracelets upon thy hands, and a chain
on thy neck. And I put a jewel on thy forehead, and earrings in
thine ears, and a beautiful crown upon thine head. Thus wast
thou decked with gold and silver; and thy raiment was of fine
linen, and silk, and broidered work; thou didst eat fine flour, and
honey, and oil: and thou wast exceeding beautiful, and thou
didst prosper into a kingdom. And thy renown went forth
among the heathen for thy beauty: for it was perfect through my
comeliness, which I had put upon thee, saith the Lord God.
## —Ezekiel 16:7–14

In our relationship with Jesus, the union that is made possible
for us because of His shed blood is followed by the waters of baptism and the sealing oil of the Holy Spirit on our lives. It is the Lord
who dresses us and makes us presentable as His chosen bride, a
bride dressed in splendor and glory. We are incredibly and remark-
ably blessed as a beloved bride who is bestowed great value.

## PREPARING FOR OUR BRIDEGROOM

Through the centuries, the church has been called the bride of
Christ, and this term is based largely upon a parable Jesus taught in
which He identified himself—the Son of man—as coming for a
bride who is *anticipating* and *preparing* for His coming:

Then shall the kingdom of heaven be likened unto ten virgins,
which took their lamps, and went forth to meet the bridegroom.
And five of them were wise, and five were foolish. They that
were foolish took their lamps, and took no oil with them: But
the wise took oil in their vessels with their lamps. While the
bridegroom tarried, they all slumbered and slept. And at mid-
night there was a cry made, Behold, the bridegroom cometh; go
ye out to meet him. Then all those virgins arose, and trimmed
their lamps. And the foolish said unto the wise, Give us of your
oil; for our lamps are gone out. But the wise answered, saying,

Not so; lest there be not enough for us and you: but go ye rather to them that sell, and buy for yourselves.

And while they went to buy, the bridegroom came; and they that were ready went in with him to the marriage: and the door was shut. Afterward came also the other virgins, saying, Lord, Lord, open to us. But he answered and said, Verily I say unto you, I know you not. Watch therefore, for ye know neither the day nor the hour wherein the Son of man cometh.
**—Matthew 25:1–13**

What a glorious truth that we are the bride of Christ! But how are we to prepare to be Jesus' bride? How do we keep our lamps lit brightly with the oil of the Holy Spirit? Paul answers this in his letter to the Ephesians: "Be ye therefore followers of God, as dear children; and walk in love, as Christ also hath loved us, and hath given himself for us an offering and a sacrifice to God for a sweet-smelling savour" (Ephesians 5:1–2).

Paul tells us to keep our lamps lit with love. We are a part of the greatest love story ever told! As believers betrothed to Jesus we are to think and speak and act with a constant motivation of love and adoration and worship toward Him. But this isn't an emotional head-in-the-clouds or floating-on-air kind of love. Romance in the movies pales in the face of the love of our Savior and Lord! This is *agape* love. The love God has for His children and the love with which Jesus loves us is a sacrificial love.

Agape love is generous, unending, unconditional love. It is loving as Jesus loved us and gave himself as an offering, a "sweet-smelling" sacrifice to God on our behalf. To love others as Jesus loves us is to love not as we desire, but as He desires us to love. This kind of love does not depend upon receiving love in return. Agape love flows from the very heart and character of God because He is love. Agape is a commitment to love, a decision to love regardless of the circumstances.

"It's simple," Paul says. "Just follow Jesus. If you don't know how to be a Christian, imitate Him. Treat other people the way He has treated you, the way He has loved and forgiven you."

Paul wrote to the Corinthians: "Blessed be God, even the Father of our Lord Jesus Christ, the Father of mercies, and the God of all comfort; who comforteth us in all our tribulation, that we may be able to comfort them which are in any trouble, by the comfort wherewith we ourselves are comforted of God" (2 Corinthians 1:3–4).

The Holy Spirit may prompt us to express our love toward another person even when we are going through a trial. Yet we make ourselves available to comfort others at all times with the comfort we are receiving from God. We are sensitive to the Holy Spirit's leading to minister to others in their physical and emotional pain. Then we are a "sweetsmelling savour" to God and He will continue to comfort us as we comfort others.

As we love others and love God, it is important to remember no one becomes a "sweetsmelling savour" without sacrifice. Loving others isn't a great challenge if we can love the people we choose to love, and then love them on our own terms, at the convenient time, place, and occasion, and in comfortable conditions. Loving all other believers, those who may be very different from us in culture, race, background, likes, dislikes, and personality differences—and loving them in spite of their faults, sins, and failures—is a tremendous challenge. The challenge is to display the same kind of sacrificial and unconditional love that Jesus lavishes upon us.

We've said before that we tend to think that some people are naturally loving. We think they are just nice people and we wish we could be like them. Those who follow this line of thinking use this as an excuse for not being loving. They feel absolved of any responsibility to change. But the Bible is very clear when it comes to the way we love God and love others. Jesus said, "A new commandment I give unto you, That ye love one another; as I have loved you, that ye also love one another" (John 13:34).

*Love is a commandment.* Like all of God's principles and laws, we cannot accomplish the love walk without His supernatural ability. Thank God for the Holy Ghost! The Bible tells us that one of the divine purposes of the Holy Spirit is to manifest the love of God in our hearts so that we can manifest that love toward others. In the book of Romans, Paul tells us how this works:

**Therefore being justified by faith, we have peace with God through our Lord Jesus Christ: By whom also we have access by faith into this grace wherein we stand, and rejoice in hope of the glory of God. And not only so, but we glory in tribulations also; knowing that tribulation worketh patience; and patience, experience; and experience, hope: and hope maketh not**

ashamed; because the love of God is shed abroad in our hearts by the Holy Ghost which is given unto us.
**—Romans 5:1–5**

God has given us a divine capacity to love, but we must make the effort to develop that love, to release it, and to walk in it at all times. To love is a choice we make with our will. So many people seem to be waiting for something to happen in their lives so they will automatically feel more love for others, and then out of that feeling, they assume they will show love more spontaneously and generously. That isn't the way it works! The love of Jesus Christ is not going to suddenly envelop us and give us smiles on our faces and wonderful attitudes in our hearts.

Often the greatest sacrifice we make in life is choosing to love. God's love will not only transform our lives but also the lives of those we touch—and we will be a bride whose lamp is lit with His glory!

## THE LANGUAGE OF LOVE

When you observe an engaged couple, you are going to see some things that will tickle you and touch your heart at the same time. They have a way of speaking to each other and showing affection to one another, and there is a certain sparkle in their eyes when they look at each other. This is their language of love.

Since we are betrothed to the Lord Jesus Christ, what is our language of love? How do we express our love for Him? The Bible tells us that our first expression of love is praise and thanksgiving, which can also be a sacrifice!

Thus saith the Lord; Again there shall be heard in this place . . . the voice of joy, and the voice of gladness, the voice of the bridegroom, and the voice of the bride, the voice of them that shall say, Praise the Lord of hosts: for the Lord is good; for his mercy endureth for ever; and of them that shall bring the sacrifice of praise *into the house of the Lord.*
**—Jeremiah 33:10–11 (emphasis mine)**

By him therefore let us offer the sacrifice of praise to God continually, that is, the fruit of our lips giving thanks to his name.
**—Hebrews 13:15**

Every spouse needs to hear how he or she is loved, appreciated, and regarded highly, and Jesus is no exception. He desires to hear from our lips that He is worthy to be praised, deserving of our worship, and valued above all! We express our love in words and in making melody in our hearts. We are to give voice to our love.

How many wives say, "He never tells me he loves me anymore"? And if you ask the husband, he'll probably say, "Of course I love her. Why doesn't she know that? I come home every night, I fix what's broken around the house, I make sure there's food on the table." The fact is, we need to hear words of love from our spouse—and it goes both ways. There are countless husbands today who need to hear words of love, encouragement, and appreciation from their wives. They ache to hear that what they do is valued and that who they are is adored.

When we voice our praise and worship to God, we actually open up the gates of our own souls to receive His love for us. The love relationship we have with Him grows and flourishes as we raise our voices in praise and thanksgiving to our Creator, who loved us even when we were sinners and redeemed us from hell and the curses of death and destruction. He seated us with himself in the heavenlies and took our shame, loneliness, and fear away.

A second way we offer a sacrifice of love to God is by loving what He loves and hating what He hates. Jesus loves what is righteous, true, and good, and hates what is evil, false, and eternally unproductive. We display our loyalty to our Savior and Lord, who bought us back from slavery and bondage by His precious blood, when we submit to His will, His ways, and His wisdom.

Jesus loves only what is "goodness and righteousness and truth" (Ephesians 5:9). He loves the sinner, even as He hates the sin. He stands against and has no fellowship with the unfruitful works of darkness. And what does He love? People! He loves all who are in relationship with Him and all who are not. What Jesus loves, we are to love. We have to get beyond our prejudices, our personality differences, and our petty offenses and embrace what Jesus embraces. To do so is an act of worship. It is an act of love not only for the person we are serving and encouraging and edifying, but it is an act of love and honor toward our Bridegroom.

A third way we offer a sacrifice of love to our Bridegroom is by obeying Him; not only obeying the Ten Commandments and all of the statutes written in the Bible, but by obeying what the Holy

Spirit speaks to our hearts. We are to do what He tells us to do moment by moment.

**If ye love me, keep my commandments. . . . He that hath my commandments, and keepeth them, he it is that loveth me: and he that loveth me shall be loved of my Father, and I will love him, and will manifest myself to him.**
**—John 14:15, 21**

Obedience to the Word and the Spirit is an act of sacrificial love that bears the fruit of the Spirit. Our acts of sacrificial love toward God's people or unbelievers and our obedience to the Holy Spirit's commands and the Word of God manifest the divine nature of Jesus to the world we touch. When anyone comes in contact with us, they come in contact with Jesus.

God's character of love works within us to produce the fruit of the Holy Spirit, the divine language of love. The fruit is God's expressed love, the aftereffect and end result of the working of the Holy Spirit in us. Some Christians see the Holy Spirit as the fruit itself, but the fruit is *of the Spirit.* In the same way that my children are my fruit and they express the essence of my life, the fruit of the Spirit is the essence of the Spirit expressed through us. But you wouldn't say that my children are me, and you wouldn't say the fruit of the Spirit *is* the Spirit. Remember, the love of God is shed abroad in our hearts *by* the Holy Spirit.

Furthermore, the fruit is singular because the essence and nature of the Holy Spirit cannot be divided. However, the fruit is expressed in a multifaceted form, like a diamond of pure agape love with facets that Paul describes as "love, joy, peace, longsuffering, gentleness, goodness, faith, meekness, and temperance" (Galatians 5:22–23). The fruit of the Spirit is one jewel, brightly shining, that catches the light of the Son and refracts His love, beauty, power, and glory.

The Holy Spirit also desires that we reflect all of His nature simultaneously and without classification. The Christian life is not an exercise in being loving at one hour, joyful the next, at peace the next, showing occasional times of patience and self-control, at other times displaying goodness and faith, and at other times being gentle or meek. No! The Holy Spirit desires to refract our Bridegroom's total, unending, and unchanging nature through us at all times. Our love for God is fruitful. It is not a static, abstract thing inside us. It has manifestation. It has productivity. It has expression!

## SEPARATION FROM EVIL

Walking in sacrificial, *agape* love and allowing the fruit of the Spirit to grow and develop in our lives has a flip side to it. We are also admonished by Paul to have nothing whatsoever to do with darkness or with anything that is unproductive in God's kingdom.

**(For the fruit of the Spirit is in all goodness and righteousness and truth;) proving what is acceptable unto the Lord. And have no fellowship with the unfruitful works of darkness, but rather reprove them.**
**—Ephesians 5:9–11**

When we are born again and become Jesus' beloved, the Enemy has no right to reproduce his fruit in our lives anymore. Anytime we give place to the Devil in our lives, we will see the unfruitful works of darkness. And those works are temporal, unsatisfying, unrewarding, and highly limited. There is no eternal value, no lasting fulfillment, and no heavenly reward associated with any work of darkness. In fact, we are commanded to "reprove" them.

The fact that the Holy Spirit uses the word *reprove* says a lot. The Greek word gives the body of Christ clear and definite marching orders when it comes to the unfruitful works of darkness. It means to expose, rebuke, discipline, convict, correct, and expel. There is no compromise with the unfruitful works of darkness! We are to shine the light of God's Word on them and purge them from our lives. Paul goes on to say: "For it is a shame even to speak of those things which are done of them in secret. But all things that are reproved are made manifest by the light: for whatsoever doth make manifest is light" (Ephesians 5:12–13).

Paul says we are not even to talk about the works of darkness because the light will expose them. In other words, we expose and rebuke by simply speaking the Word and releasing the power of the Holy Spirit into that situation. If the Holy Spirit leads us to actually confront the one who is walking in darkness, we simply tell them what God's Word says and pray for them. And remember, the Word tells us to reprove the *works of darkness,* not the one who is blinded and lost in the darkness. Our responsibility is to shine God's heavenly light into their darkness so that they can see!

No wife who truly loves her husband is going to be loving and joyful and edifying in her husband's presence and then turn around and gossip about him and downgrade him to her friends. And yet there are those in the church who display the fruit of the Spirit when they are in the presence of other believers, but get them in secret with a few of their close friends, and listen to how the gossip flows!

There are also those who praise the Lord and worship Him with loud voices inside the church house, but get them in their own house and listen to them complain about what the Lord isn't doing.

To love sacrificially is to love whether we are in public or private. It is to be resolute in mind and heart that God is worthy of praise and thanksgiving whether anybody is listening or not. It is to love and serve God's people whether we are in their presence or not. It is to obey God's commands and to manifest His nature—to bear the fruit of the Holy Spirit—not only in what we say and do, but in the very way we *think* and *believe*. The fruit of the Holy Spirit is to infiltrate and manifest itself in our *attitudes*.

Are you aware that anything you speak, you intensify—not only outwardly but inwardly? This is one of the key principles at work in the corruption of this present generation. In displaying and speaking about sin so freely and so frequently, we intensify it, grow in the knowledge of it, and even become comfortable with it. When we put sin on center stage and talk about it repeatedly, it reproduces because we are having fellowship with the unfruitful works of darkness.

Sin is not normal behavior for the believer.

Sin is never to be routine for the believer.

Sin is not inevitable for the believer.

We have been freed from the bonds of sin!

What we believe is always directly influenced by what we hear. Most believers are very familiar with Romans 10:17, "So then faith cometh by hearing . . ." What we hear influences what we believe.

The rest of the verse is the key for us, ". . . and hearing by the word of God." What we hear influences and establishes what we believe, what we say, and what we do. So our hearing needs to be focused on the Word of God.

# WAKE UP!

What you hear impacts what you believe, and what you believe impacts what you say and do. We either build ourselves up or tear ourselves down in our spiritual marriage to the Lord and our lives in the body of Christ—depending on what we focus upon. So Paul gives us a wake-up call:

**Wherefore he saith, Awake thou that sleepest, and arise from the dead, and Christ shall give thee light. See then that ye walk circumspectly, not as fools, but as wise, redeeming the time, because the days are evil. Wherefore be ye not unwise, but understanding what the will of the Lord is.**
**—Ephesians 5:14–17**

When you are asleep among dead people, you look like a dead person. Paul is saying, "If you act like the world, you are like a spiritually alive person who is asleep among spiritually dead people. So wake up! Shake off your worldly thinking, attitudes, and behavior and stop acting the fool! Walk in the light of Christ and be wise. Then you'll know what you're supposed to do with your life—and you'll be ready when your Bridegroom comes for you!"

Jesus' heart swells with joy and pride when we think like He thinks, feel what He feels, laugh when He laughs, and act as He acts. It gives Him pleasure when we are a living sacrifice for Him, praising and giving thanks for His grace and mercy, obeying His Word and the Holy Spirit's guiding hand, loving and serving others, separating ourselves from all unfruitful works of darkness, and walking in holiness and purity. And the Bible says when we do this, we will be wise, understanding what the will of God is for our lives and in the situations He places us. Walking in the sacrificial love of Jesus Christ is walking hand in hand with our Bridegroom in the light of His glory—fully awake, fully aware, and full of peace.

# 4

# SUBMISSION

As the bride and body of Christ, we must learn how to relate to our Bridegroom and to one another, and God has chosen submission as the principle of the kingdom that sets the tone for all relationships: God and man, husband and wife, parent and child, employer and employee, pastor and congregation, friend and friend. Jesus taught the importance of submission even in the friend to friend relationship: "Greater love hath no man than this, that a man lay down his life for his friends. Ye are my friends, if ye do whatsoever I command you" (John 15:13–14).

Jesus sealed His friendship and became worthy to be our Bridegroom by submitting to the will of His Father and shedding His blood for us, the supreme act of love. When we submit to His Word and the leading of the Holy Spirit, He calls us His friends— and He is not talking about some casual acquaintance we play ball with after school! When Jesus used the word *friend,* He was talking covenant. Everything that is His is ours and everything that is ours is His. His greatest delight is blessing us, and our greatest joy is pleasing Him and knowing Him. Furthermore, He commands us to love one another as He loves us: "A new commandment I give unto you, That ye love one another; as I have loved you, that ye also love one another. By this shall all men know that ye are my disciples, if ye have love one to another" (John 13:34–35).

God has established that the church must operate in the principle of submission—love in action—for the world to see Jesus in us.

However, there are some fundamental truths associated with submission that must be established in our hearts and minds for us to walk this powerful walk. Some of these truths seem hard when viewed on the surface, but when we plumb the depths of them, the truth sets us free.

## SUBMISSION MEANS WAR!

In speaking to the Ephesians about submission, Paul begins with the body of Christ at large:

**And be not drunk with wine, wherein is excess; but be filled with the Spirit; speaking to yourselves in psalms and hymns and spiritual songs, singing and making melody in your heart to the Lord; giving thanks always for all things unto God and the Father in the name of our Lord Jesus Christ; submitting yourselves one to another in the fear of God.**
**—Ephesians 5:18–21**

Notice that Paul introduces the concept of submission in the context of being filled with the Holy Spirit, making melody in our hearts to the Lord, and giving thanks always. This is a big hint: *We cannot possibly submit to one another in our flesh or our own strength!* We must be hooked up to the supernatural love and ability of Christ Jesus to obey this word from God. Also notice that we submit "in the fear of God." Submission now becomes a sacred, holy act of love and reverence unto our Lord. This is not something we can brush aside and take lightly.

The Greek word for *submitting* gives us even more revelation on the concept. It is a term that has a military connotation and indicates soldiers or troops being drawn together in order, none breaking rank, turning on each other, or walking in disobedience to those in authority over them. So the New Testament meaning is that we are to be subject to one another in the divine callings and order in which our supreme commander, the Lord Jesus Christ, has placed us. We are not to assert ourselves or have a self-centered, independent spirit; but we are to accept His commission to serve humbly and in love toward one another. The picture that comes to mind is the mighty invincible army described in the book of Joel:

They shall run like mighty men; they shall climb the wall like men of war; and they shall march every one on his ways, and they shall not break their ranks: Neither shall one thrust another; they shall walk every one in his path: and when they fall upon the sword, they shall not be wounded.

**—Joel 2:7–8**

Paul clearly puts this entire passage of Scripture in the context of war. The body of Christ is in a life-and-death struggle against the powers of darkness that rule this world system. And I have noticed something about people when they are thrown together in a war. All of a sudden it doesn't matter what sex you are, what race you are, what color you are, or how smart you are. We're fighting together against an evil that will destroy us all, and my survival and your survival depend on our working together, submitting to one another in the fear of the Lord. Whether God has placed me as your commanding officer or you as mine, we are united by the cause of freedom and subject to one another through the blood of Jesus.

God loves us equally and is no respecter of persons; He has subjected us to one another positionally. There are generals and there are foot soldiers. There are sergeants and there are medics. There are captains and there are cooks. We are all equally important and come behind in no spiritual gift—God will have intimate fellowship with us and shower blessings on all of us—but we are subject to one another as He has placed us in the body. We submit to one another in the fear of the Lord because the Lord has placed us in our callings and has given us our giftings. Paul describes it as a walk of love where every joint supplies what the body needs:

But speaking the truth in love, may grow up into him in all things, which is the head, even Christ: From whom the whole body fitly joined together and compacted by that which every joint supplieth, according to the effectual working in the measure of every part, maketh increase of the body unto the edifying of itself in love.

**—Ephesians 4:15–16**

In peacetime, as we love and worship the Lord, our equality in Christ is very obvious. It's easy to love one another because His love and grace and blessings are evident in our lives. However, when we are at war, God establishes rank and file, and the tempter comes to say, "You are not being treated as an *equal* because you have to submit to a person who is not as smart, not as hard-working, or not as spiritual as you are. God made you *equal* to this person, so you should not have to submit to him." The Enemy knows that if he can confuse the issues of equality and submission, he can cause us to turn on one another, rebel against authority, and cause our own defeat.

Peacetime does not always require submission. Wartime requires submission. There is no submission when there is no disagreement or conflict. Don't tell me you are submitting when everything is going your way, on your timetable, according to your plan! That is not submission. That is agreement. That is a path with no resistance from anything or anyone. Submission can only occur when there is disagreement, and disagreement comes as a result of the fallen nature. As long as we are living in these bodies that in the flesh work contrary to God's kingdom, we are in a state of war. We must discipline our flesh to submit to the will of God and to one another.

Like it or not, God has placed us in situations where we must submit to win the war. We must reverse the five rebellious "I wills" of Lucifer (see Isaiah 14:13–14), which seek to rule from the old nature of our flesh, and come into line with Jesus' "not my will, but thine, be done." (See Luke 22:42.) We must understand that when we submit to this person or that person, we are submitting to the Lord. We are operating in the fear of the Lord. We are trusting Him and placing our lives in His hands—the only safe place in the universe.

## HOW A WIFE SUBMITS

After introducing the concept of submission in terms of winning the war, Paul then begins to elaborate on three specific areas where the believer must understand and walk in submission: husbands and wives, parents and children, and masters and servants. He tackles husbands and wives first, which is perhaps the most controversial of the three.

**Wives, submit yourselves unto your own husbands, as unto the Lord. For the husband is the head of the wife, even as Christ is the head of the church: and he is the saviour of the body. There-**

fore as the church is subject unto Christ, so let the wives be to their own husbands in every thing.
**—Ephesians 5:22–24**

In writing about submission, Paul is not talking about dominance of gender but about corporate relationship and structure within a family. To submit is to make ourselves vulnerable to the needs and desires of others. It is to yield in the decision-making, problem-solving, directional aspects of a relationship. A husband and wife are in a government relationship—both cannot exert the same degree of authority simultaneously.

By the necessity borne of two people being in one relationship, one person must submit to the governance of the other in facing problems, decisions, and conflicts. The natural minds of people in this generation want to put husband and wife on the same playing field, both playing umpire at the same time. Can you imagine a baseball game with two umpires standing behind the plate? Husband and wife do not play the same position when it comes to making decisions, manifesting authority, or taking responsibility.

Many women believe that to submit to their husbands is to lie down, roll over, and play dead. That by submitting to her husband's decision, she has acknowledged, accepted, and approved his domination of her and sealed her inferiority to him. That she has allowed her identity to be dwarfed or destroyed by his ego and selfishness. This is the lie the Devil would like all wives to swallow because it naturally incites resentment and rebellion.

But understood correctly, submission is a freedom word, a deliverance word, a word of position and function that brings a woman to higher and higher levels of intimacy with the Lord and greater power and influence in her marriage. Submission is about compliance, cooperation, and exceeding influence. And when the kingdom principle of submission is followed, harmony and unity in spirit can be reached even when there is disagreement. Moreover, there are times when a husband and wife, parent and child, or employer and employee can eventually come into full agreement because they are walking in submission.

So much of the time we don't see the whole picture; our spouse has part of it and we have part of it. In the beginning we each may see the situation differently, but as we pray and talk together, sharing what the Lord is showing us, seeking the mind of Christ and the truth, we can see the whole picture and come into agreement. Open discussion, prayer, and progressive revelation often will bring any relationship into harmony and unity.

But what happens if there is prayer, discussion, revelation, and still no agreement? What if the husband is an unbeliever and won't even pray? What if the husband is saved and loves God but spends all his free time in front of the television set or at ball games, neglecting the things of God and refusing to grow up? What if he asks her to do something immoral or illegal?

To me, it is obvious that no believer should ever submit to a request or a behavior that is ungodly, evil, or unholy. If the husband demands that his wife drink or do drugs with him, if he wants her to have sex with someone else, or if he tells her to assist him in committing a crime or telling a lie, she must respectfully say no. The Bible never commands a believer to submit to evil, immoral commands. The apostle Peter does not say, "Rob banks with your husband so he'll see the love of God in you!" No, he says that it is a wife's "chaste conversation," or pure, innocent, modest, and clean behavior that influences her husband to do right and come to God:

**Likewise, ye wives, be in subjection to your own husbands; that, if any obey not the word, they also may without the word be won by the conversation of the wives; while they behold your chaste conversation coupled with fear.**
**—1 Peter 3:1–2**

The most powerful people in the world are wives who know how to submit to the Lord and their husbands! How many men have been won to the Lord through their wives, who treated them like kings and yet refused to do anything that would compromise the Word of God? How many men have seen tremendous success in their business and ministry because they had a praying, godly wife standing with them, giving them wise counsel?

Now, what if the husband is a big, burly carpenter who comes home drunk and punches his wife because he's mad at the world? What if he's a deacon in the church, knows all the religious talk and walk, but when he's home he throws his wife across the room when she aggravates him? No wife should submit to this treatment! If that is going on in your home, go see your pastor and get some counsel immediately—with or without your husband. Jesus does not beat His bride!

Jumping down to verse 33 of Ephesians 5, we see that wives are also to reverence their husbands: ". . . and the wife see that she reverence her husband." This word *reverence* means to respect. This is an attitude, not an action. You can honor your husband's position as your husband and move out of the house to avoid being beaten. You can have a submissive attitude toward your husband and refuse to obey him in an evil act. "Honey, I love you, but I will not do this illegal, immoral thing." Do you see how the husband is impacted by God's love and truth all at the same time? Again, you must never underestimate the powerful influence of a submissive, loving wife who knows how to reverence her husband.

## WHAT ARE WE SHOWING THE WORLD?

Why is this so important in the context of our marriage to the Lord Jesus Christ? A wife represents a typology of what the church is to Jesus. If she rises up and attempts to dominate her husband, she is painting a picture of rebellion against her eternal husband, Jesus, before the world. To rebel is to say, "My way is as good as God's way. I have the right to choose my own destiny and to walk according to my own laws. I am the lord of my own life and nobody rules over me." None of these statements are truth—they are lies that flow from the original lie Satan posed in the garden of Eden: You will be as gods. (See Genesis 3:5.)

There is never any justification for a believer in Christ Jesus to show anything but the utmost respect for Him. After all, He is the *perfect* Husband. His Word is truth; all His ways are perfect; and He is love personified. There is absolutely no reason why a believer should not only submit but also obey the Lord at all times. Believers seem to be almost too casual in their response to the Lord sometimes. He is our Bridegroom and Friend, but He is also our Lord. We are always in a position of submission to Him. We must never assume He exists to serve us or to do our bidding. We exist to serve Him. All things are from Him, and all things are for Him.

The wife's submission is "as unto the Lord." Throughout Paul's writings we find the phrases "as unto" or "like as" or "according to." These phrases are ones he uses to link the practical manifestations of godly behavior to the deeper mysteries of our relationship with the Lord. Everything we do to others is as unto the Lord. There should be a holy fear of God that comes on a wife who entertains the idea of rebelling against her husband when his request does not violate God's Word. And when the request does violate God's Word, there should still be a holy fear of God in her that says, "I do not have to obey, but I still must reverence him." Wives who understand this and practice submission know the awesome reward it brings. God always honors and blesses with incredible favor and influence the wife who submits to her husband.

## ONE LORD AT ALL TIMES

Another vital issue Paul raises in his writings on marriage is that the wife is to be submitted to her husband—not to all men. All women are not to be submitted to all men, but each wife to her own husband. Why? Because they are one. They are fused together, they fit together, they are in a bonded relationship that has an order and structure to it. "Husband and wife" is not the same as "man and woman," neither is it the same as "all men and all women." Paul does not say that a woman is to submit to a man, or all women are to submit to all men. He says that a *wife* should submit to her *husband*.

Submission for the believer is always a covenant relationship, and a wife is called to submit to her husband, the only man with whom she has a marriage covenant relationship. It is the marriage covenant that gives a wife the security she needs to submit. In the same manner, again, believers in Christ Jesus are to be submitted to Christ alone—not to other lords, but to our Lord—because we are His beloved. We are one with Him, we are in a bonded, covenant relationship with Him that has order and structure to it.

"Therefore as the church is subject unto Christ, so let the wives be to their own husbands in every thing" (Ephesians 5:24). Again we see how a wife being subject to her husband gives the world a picture of how the church is subject to Jesus Christ. Then Paul goes on to say that the wife is subject to her husband "in every thing." As we are subject to Christ Jesus in everything, so is the wife subject to her husband in all things. There is no room for rebellion! We cannot fudge on the small things. And there is no room for a rebellious attitude any more than there is room for rebellious words or actions.

When a wife submits to her husband in all things, she is saying to the world, "The church submits to the Lord Jesus Christ in all things. There isn't any facet of the church that is run according to human wisdom, ability, decision-making, or reasoning. All is submitted to Jesus Christ so that His will might be done in all, through all, and for all who are part of His body."

The strongest witness a Christian wife can give to an unbelieving (or rebellious Christian) husband—and to the unbelievers she touches every day—is her character, speaking in love and living a modest life, with a submissive and quiet spirit. A godly wife's submission becomes a testimony to her husband and extends far beyond their home to the world at large. Their family, friends, neighbors, and colleagues at work see that her husband lives with a godly woman, a fine Christian woman, a loving and helpful and exemplary wife.

**Likewise, ye wives, be in subjection to your own husbands; that, if any obey not the word, they also may without the word be won by the conversation of the wives; while they behold your chaste conversation coupled with fear, whose adorning let it not be that outward adorning of plaiting the hair, and of wearing of gold, or of putting on of apparel; but let it be the hidden man of the heart, in that which is not corruptible, even the ornament of a meek and quiet spirit, which is in the sight of God of great price. For after this manner in the old time the holy women also, who trusted in God, adorned themselves, being in subjection unto their own husbands: Even as Sara obeyed Abraham, calling him lord: whose daughters ye are, as long as ye do well, and are not afraid with any amazement.**

**—1 Peter 3:1–6**

Christian wives are to emulate Sara, who obeyed Abraham and called him lord with no fear. When a wife fully trusts the Lord and His plan for her life, submitting to her husband as unto the Lord, she can submit to her husband with great faith. And when a wife submits to her husband in faith, God can move mountains in that husband's life! On the other hand, if she doesn't follow this plan, she brings discredit to the Lord and her testimony becomes tarnished before the very ones she desires most to accept the Lord. More than that, because she is walking in fear and rebellion instead of faith and obedience, she has tied God's hands and He cannot move in her husband's life.

Most rebellion among believers in Christ Jesus isn't what we might recognize as "major rebellion." Most of our rebellion is in the way we think and feel and respond in the little things of life. Likewise, most rebellion we see in Christian wives is not always recognized as rebellion.

When a wife rebels against a husband's wishes, desires, and his position as a decision-maker, she undermines his authority over the family and diminishes his responsibility. Godly authority is always balanced by responsibility. What we have authority over, we are responsible for, and the man who is made to feel or believe that he has no authority over his family is a man who takes far less responsibility for his family.

Many wives seem to want it both ways. They want their husbands to assume great responsibility for what goes on in the family, but they don't want their husband to have any authority over them or over the family as a whole. A godly marriage doesn't work that way! Believers sometimes fall into this same trap. They want God to do all kinds of things for them—blessings and miracles and acts of deliverance of all sorts. They want God to manifest His responsibility for them, but they have absolutely no desire to submit to His authority by doing what He desires them to do and walking in the ways He directs them to walk.

When we submit to Jesus in all things, we will see Him move heaven and earth to bless us in every aspect of our lives. And the same principle applies to a husband and a wife. When the wife submits to her husband and lets everyone know he is the head of the family, that husband will stand up, take responsibility, and bless her and their family—and the world will see it and take note that Jesus is there.

## SUBMISSION IS LOVE

Ultimately every person is required to submit. The husband isn't free of all responsibility to submit, but is commanded to submit to the elders of the church if he is saved, to his boss, or to his board of directors if he's the boss. In addition, every husband is required to submit himself directly to the Lord. Remember, saved or not saved, one day that husband of yours will stand face-to-face with Jesus Christ to give an account of his life!

When we examine the dynamics of submission, we see that it is a choice, just like love is a choice. Because life is not always a bowl of cherries and coming up roses, marriage is not always heavenly bliss! We must choose to love our spouse in the good times and the bad. In the same manner, a godly wife chooses to submit to her husband because she chooses to love him as she loves Jesus. Her husband is her bridegroom on earth; Jesus is her eternal Bridegroom. If she submits to one, she submits to the other, and the love of God is manifest to the world.

In one of Peter's discourses on godly marriages, he concludes with this same overriding theme: "Finally, be ye all of one mind, having compassion one of another, love as brethren, be pitiful, be courteous: Not rendering evil for evil, or railing for railing: but contrariwise blessing: knowing that ye are thereunto called, that ye should inherit a blessing" (1 Peter 3:8–9).

To be "pitiful" is to be tenderhearted. Our love for one another naturally causes us to submit to one another. Submission is a derivative of love. It is part of love and it flows from love.

**Love is patient, love is kind. It does not envy, it does not boast, it is not proud. It is not rude, it is not self-seeking, it is not easily angered, it keeps no record of wrongs. Love does not delight in evil but rejoices with the truth. It always protects, always trusts, always hopes, always perseveres. Love never fails.**
**—1 Corinthians 13:4–8 NIV**

Love is willing to yield. It is not selfish, demanding, or self-centered. Lust, on the other hand, is always based upon self-need and self-gratification. What self wants, self acts to get. Love, in contrast, seeks not her own. It is willing to submit. Love is always more concerned about the care and welfare of the other person in a relationship. And when a wife submits to her husband, she expresses her love and reverence for him and for the Lord Jesus Christ.

# 5

# GIVING YOUR LIFE

After discussing the powerful principle of submission, I hope you wives do not feel like you've been through the spin cycle in a washing machine! Submission is not easy because we human beings do not like to crucify our flesh. But in case you feel you have the hardest part of the bargain by having to submit to your husband, or in case you are a husband thinking, "Yeah, right, she needs to submit to me right now!" let's dive into the husband's role in all of this.

How often, husband, do you crucify your desires, your plans, and your way of doing things in order to love your wife? Do you *tell* her what *your* plans are for the weekend, or do you *ask* her what *she* had in mind? When you come home from work, do you turn the television on and turn yourself off? Is the only reason you touch her to have sex with her? And here's the big one: When was the last time you just sat with her and really *listened* to her?

Paul writes more verses about husbands than wives in his letter to the Ephesians, and I believe there is a good reason for this. Husbands, the question we must all ask ourselves is: What am I giving my wife to submit *to*? Our Lord Jesus Christ has pursued us, showed us how to walk in the Spirit and according to God's will and Word, laid His life down for us, paid our debt of sin, risen from the dead to give us new life, and then raised us and seated us in the heavenlies. He has made us joint-heirs—and that's something to submit to!

Now, as husbands, we come to the stark realization that to play the part of Jesus Christ in a marriage is a superhuman feat, something we cannot possibly accomplish without God's guidance and empowerment. This is a monumental assignment from heaven! So let's take one verse at a time in Ephesians and let the apostle Paul break this down for us.

## SELFLESSNESS

**Husbands, love your wives, even as Christ also loved the church, and gave himself for it.**
**—Ephesians 5:25**

The specific language Paul has chosen in the Greek indicates that husbands are to love their wives *continually*. This is an ongoing process of showing her care and comfort and proclaiming his devotion to her. But is it ever possible for a husband to give his life for his wife as Jesus gave himself for the church? On the one hand, we would have to say no because no man can give his life to save his wife from her sins. Husbands have died so their wives might live, but no man has the capacity to be the savior of his wife or of any other person. Jesus Christ alone is Savior. On the other hand, we would have to say that it is possible for a man to crucify his flesh and *die to self* for the sake of his wife.

Self is difficult to control, and it is even more difficult to sacrifice! We each want what we want, and this seems to be especially true for us men. We don't like having to give up our precious, valuable, very important lives for the sake of anyone. I'm not talking about begrudgingly giving up a little time when our wives ask for a little time, or resenting it when we decide to set aside our personal agendas to accommodate the desire of our wives. Paul describes marriage as total sacrifice of self for love of a wife—willingly. And there's only one way we can do this. We must trust God. Just as Jesus trusted God—for the joy that was set before Him He endured the cross—we must trust God that by giving our lives away we will gain them.

Jesus said, "Whoever clings to his life shall lose it, and whoever loses his life shall save it" (Luke 17:33 TLB). If a husband does not understand this principle or does not practice it, not only will his wife be frustrated, but he will soon become discontent and restless in his relationship with her and look for a way out. Husbands often find it difficult to stay in the confines of marriage. The pressures of lust, frustration, aggravation, irritation, discontentment, misalignment, and miscommunication drive against a man's ability to stay. If he listens to his will, he will seek to break out of the boundaries imposed by marriage. It is only if he is willing to submit to and trust the Lord that he will find the strength to commit fully and love his wife.

Self will always say, "Pass this bitter cup from me."

Self will say, "I love her, *and* her sister."

Self will say, "I'm tired of her, and I want somebody else."

Self will say, "I've been married to her for ten years, and I wonder what it would be like to be with somebody new."

Self must be crucified, and that can only occur when we have an intimate relationship with the Lord.

Self says, "I've been reading the Word daily for years. I think I know it by now. I don't need to read it anymore. I'll just meditate on what I already know."

Self says, "I've been praying for this for a long time, but God doesn't answer, so I think I'll just give up on it."

Self says, "God isn't meeting my needs the way I want Him to. I think I'll try another religion."

If we give in to self, we will see a selfish, self-centered attitude permeate every area of our lives, including our marriage and our church. When people we don't particularly like or with whom we don't agree come into the church, self rises up and says, "Please tell them to go elsewhere."

Self says, "I'm tired of this pastor, and I want to hear somebody new."

Self says, "I've been going to this church for years now. I wonder what it would be like to go to a church down the street that doesn't require so much of me."

Ultimately, the conflict with self always strikes at our relationship with the Lord, and our relationship must be a daily, ongoing conversation. Just as Paul said that loving your wife is an ongoing, continual process, crucifying the flesh and self is not a one-day deal! Paul said in 1 Corinthians 15:31, "I die *daily*." You give your life every day, and that takes sacrifice and endurance. Sacrificial love requires daily giving and a lifetime commitment, but you can do it if you trust God and walk in His ways.

*Selflessness also takes sheer gut-wrenching willpower.*

A husband's sacrificial love is to be a voluntary act of his will.

Husbands are not to wait for their wives to ask or demand their love. God is the one who commands us to love in this way, and sometimes we just don't feel like it, so we have to make ourselves do it. A husband's giving up of self for a wife is not to be the by-product of her constant nagging, whining, or manipulation. Even if she nags, we are to spontaneously give ourselves for her because we are yielding to the will of the Father. And husbands, most likely the nagging will cease when you step up and love her!

No wife should ever demand the love of her husband, just as no husband should ever demand the submission of his wife. Submission is something a wife does "as unto the Lord" (Ephesians 5:22). Loving is something a husband does "even as Christ also loved the church" (Ephesians 5:25). There is no accommodation for rebellion in a wife, and there is no accommodation for anything less than total dying to self in a husband. Crucifixion is not punishment or rebuke or chastisement or torture. It is death! Jesus gave *His life* on the cross. He yielded all of His will to the Father. And He did it so His bride might have her needs met: salvation, redemption, restoration, deliverance, healing, and wholeness.

It is a challenge for a man to be bridled to a marriage! To many men, it becomes a cross because there is something unnatural about being positioned in one place and in one relationship. There is something in the flesh nature of a man that resists being restricted. Does that mean it is difficult for Jesus to love His church? No. But it was difficult for Jesus to give His life, be crucified, be separated from the Father, and literally go to hell and back to gain His bride. He sweat blood over that decision!

Jesus endured agony and torture and pain in His soul and spirit when He made the decision to yield His will to the Father's. He knew in the garden of Gethsemane what awaited Him. He saw then that the Father would turn His back on Him. For the first time in eternity past and present, Jesus would know what it meant to be forsaken by the Father. Perhaps this was the greatest horror of all. And yet He exerted His willpower and chose to do the will of His Father.

Husbands, we forget that we have the same ability! We are empowered by the Holy Spirit just as Jesus was in the garden of Gethsemane. We have His Word to put in our hearts and rule our minds. We have the knowledge that as we obey God's Word and walk in the comfort, direction, and power of the Holy Ghost, we can love our wives as Jesus loves the church. And we also know there is joy set before us when we obey the Lord in crucifying self and yielding to His plan. There is resurrection!

## GETTING CLEANED UP

**Husbands, love your wives, even as Christ also loved the church, and gave himself for it; that he might sanctify and cleanse it with the washing of water by the word.**
**—Ephesians 5:25–26**

In verse 26, Paul gives us a clear, practical, everyday picture of how the husband loves his wife just as Jesus loves us. He is to sanctify and cleanse his wife, which is to say he is to set her apart from the world and its evil system of thinking and behavior (sanctify) and cleanse her mind and heart of all worldly, devilish thoughts and deeds by speaking the Word of God over her and to her.

What is our Bridegroom doing right now? Jesus is interceding for us before the Father. (See Romans 8:34.) He is praying for us, and as He prays the Holy Spirit is speaking His words of love, encouragement, wisdom, and power to us. This is the husband's scriptural model to love his wife. He is to pray for her, pray with her, study God's Word for her and with her, and then speak God's Word over her and to her.

To sanctify is to set aside something as holy. A sanctified vessel is designated for holy purposes or a holy cause. A husband sanctifies his wife as being "set apart" exclusively for God and their marriage relationship. He continually speaks God's words of praise and esteem and value and love over her and to her, cleansing her of any doubt, unbelief, and low self-esteem that she may have.

Husband, tell your wife repeatedly how special she is to you and that you believe she was created just for you. She was fashioned and formed to fit with you, to strengthen you, and to help you. Tell her that you rely on her more than you can express; that other than Jesus, she is the most important person in your life. She is the one with whom you want to share your heart and life. She is the one with whom you want to spend all your days on earth.

One of the reasons a wife is outraged when she discovers her husband has cheated on her is because his promiscuity attempts to defrock her of her self-esteem. She is struck in the face by the fact that she is not exclusive in her exalted position. She feels demeaned and of less value—no longer holy and set apart just for him. She is vulnerable to him because she is submitted to him, and he has allowed another to invade their holy union and tarnish it. If she is not strong in the Lord, this kind of blow can destroy a wife.

When a husband fails to esteem his wife by speaking and behaving toward her in a way that conveys her value and preciousness, he also erodes her ability to submit to him. He gives her nothing to submit to! And he leaves her uncovered and exposed to the negative, unkind, and injurious remarks others or the Devil may speak to her.

Now maybe you are thinking, *My wife is a nagging, manipulating, anxiety-ridden, controlling bag of nerves. What's worse, she doesn't have any respect for me and won't listen to a thing I say.* We must remember the shape we were in when Jesus died for us! The church wasn't the way He wanted the church to be when He died for her.

There are those who seem to think, *I'll get good and then I'll come to God.* It doesn't work that way! Nobody can ever get good enough for God. Nobody can ever cleanse themselves and overcome their own sin nature. The psalmist writes, "I have cleansed my heart in vain. . . . For all the day long have I been plagued, and chastened every morning" (Psalm 73:13–14).

In other words, "Nothing I do delivers me." The truth of God's Word is that only God delivers, saves, redeems, and cleanses completely. We grow in confidence and faith as we are washed with expressions of our new identity in Christ Jesus, as His beloved. So what does a husband do to model Jesus?

In marriage, the husband devotes himself entirely to his wife. A good husband doesn't take a wife and then keep looking for a better one. A good husband doesn't trade in his wife because she isn't all he desires her to be. Why? Because Jesus doesn't leave us or forsake us or have any less commitment to us because we have a lot of cleaning up to do. He did not find a bride who was just the way He wanted her to be when she became His bride. He has been working on His bride for some two thousand years and He's still working on her to become the bride He desires for himself.

A good husband doesn't leave his wife just because she disappoints him in some way. He continues to prepare her for the perfection he desires to see in her. You can pray for her to be delivered of the fear that causes her to be anxiety-ridden and to manipulate.

You can speak words of love and encouragement over her to assure her that she is loved and highly esteemed. She may look at you like you're from the lunatic asylum for a while, but eventually, just as Jesus' love always wins our hearts and transforms our lives, your prayers and love will transform her life too.

## TALK TO ME!

The fact is, it is up to a husband to teach his wife how to please him. That's what Christ Jesus does for us, His bride. He continually teaches us how to please Him. And how does He teach us? He does it by the Word. He talks to us! The problem many husbands have today in their marriages is a lack of talking. Let me assure you husbands of this: If you don't talk, she won't change! We as believers change as we are taught, understand, and begin to apply the Word to our lives. The Word transforms our minds. Over time, we begin to think, speak, and act as the Lord desires us to think, speak, and act.

Husbands, talking with your wife doesn't mean that you lay down the law to her, abuse her verbally, or dictate every detail to her as if you are the emperor of the world. It means speaking to her in love. It means speaking in a loving tone of voice and in gentle terms that assure her continually of your love, support, and care. It means speaking out of a motivation of desiring what is best for her and the family—not only what you desire and want and need.

So many wives have this complaint about their husbands: "I just don't know what he wants!" There's a good reason for that. Their husbands have never told them! Or they have never said what they wanted in a loving tone of voice and with a godly purpose. When a wife truly understands what a husband desires and sees that he loves her completely and sacrificially, she is usually eager to respond and quick to do all she can to meet her husband's desires.

Many wives say to their husbands, "I need to talk to you." That's because wives usually need to talk more than husbands feel a need to talk! But what a wife means when she says, "I need to talk," is that she also needs her husband to listen to her—really hear her—and then talk to her, respond to her. She needs to hear that he loves her, that he understands how she feels, that he longs to meet her needs, and that he recognizes the problems she faces and wants to do something about them. She needs to know what he thinks, decides, feels, and senses, not only for herself but for their children.

The husband who talks to his wife—and who does so often, with love, with openness, and with specificity—is a man who is going to change his wife. If he will change his ways, if he commits to being a godly husband who is rooted in God's Word and is faithful to God's Spirit, what he says to his wife is going to cleanse her. It is going to cause her to separate herself more and more from the evil of the world and the sinful pull of the world. She is going to know how to be his wife, she is going to adore being his wife, and she will have no desire for any other man.

That's the way the Lord cleanses us and washes us. He is always there to have a chat with us! He does it line by line, precept by precept from His Word. He does it by speaking guidance and direction in our hearts. He does it over time, gently, by every means possible. Again and again, He feeds us His Word. He doesn't tell us once what it is that He desires. He tells us again and again, in this story and that, in this lesson and that, in this passage and that, through this experience and that experience. The themes of God's desire run from cover to cover in God's Word and relate to our daily living.

## A TIP FOR WIVES

When a husband talks to his wife, it is extremely important that she listen. That is part of a submissive spirit. Many women do not seem to know how difficult it is for a man to trust a woman with his heart. A man can give his body to almost anybody, but he's very particular about where he gives his heart. The trust that a man feels about matters of the heart is so fragile that it can be destroyed in an instant by one insensitive comment or response. When that happens, a man tends to withdraw into himself like a turtle, harbor the hurt that he feels, and become even more reluctant to open up in the future.

Wives, when your husband opens up to you and discusses how he feels about something, what he dreams of doing, his vision for his own life and the life of your family . . . listen to what he is saying. Hear him out fully. Listen with your heart. Don't interrupt. Don't move in to fill a silence that might occur for a few seconds or even minutes. The more your husband is allowed to articulate to you the vision he has for your family, the faith he has in the Lord, and the desires he has for you as a couple in the Lord, the more secure you are going to feel in your marriage and the more confident and valuable you are going to feel as a wife.

## DEMONSTRATING JESUS

Both the husband and wife are deeply challenged. It is no less difficult for a husband to love his wife, and to do so in a genuinely sacrificial way, than it is for a wife to submit to and reverence her husband. We know that no wife will ever submit perfectly, nor will any husband love with perfect sacrificial love. Nevertheless, Paul sets these goals because the reality is that Jesus is the authority over the church and He loves the church with perfect sacrificial love. Again, as the wife models submission to Jesus to the world, the husband models the love of Jesus to the world. Natural marriage models the spiritual marriage of Jesus and His church.

The wife is to submit to her husband as the church is to submit to the Lord.

The husband is to love his wife as Christ loved the church.

This model requires a great deal of mutuality! I believe a husband finds it much easier to love his wife as Christ loved the church if his wife submits to him and to Christ. Likewise, a wife finds it much easier to submit to her husband if he loves her with a sacrificial love and continually seeks to cherish her and nourish her. However, husbands, whether she is submitting to you or not, the Word of God commands you to love her. You are fulfilling Jesus' role to show the mystery of the church to the world, and Jesus' part of the equation is never in question. He never ceases to be the head of the church. He never ceases to be responsible to God the Father for the body of Christ. He never ceases to love His bride and to offer himself for her completely.

When loving your wife gets tough—and it will get tough—remember the joy set before you. First Peter 3:7 says that if you do this, your prayers will be unhindered! And even if your wife digs in her heels and never submits to you, you are making the most powerful statement to her, your children, your neighbors, your church, and your associates at work: Jesus is our loving, saving, healing, and delivering Lord!

# 6

# AS HE LOVES HIMSELF

Did you know that Jesus loves himself? Think about this for one moment. Never in the Word of God does Jesus put himself down. Never does He insult himself, make a joke at His own expense, or complain that He is nothing but a worm. Does that mean that Jesus was arrogant and prideful? We know that's not true! But Jesus knew who He was and had a healthy, godly love for himself. This is revealed most vividly in this astounding statement of the apostle Paul in his letter to the Philippians:

**Let this mind be in you, which was also in Christ Jesus: Who, being in the form of God, thought it not robbery to be equal with God: But made himself of no reputation, and took upon him the form of a servant, and was made in the likeness of men: And being found in fashion as a man, he humbled himself, and became obedient unto death, even the death of the cross.**
**—Philippians 2:5–8**

We are going to zero in on one phrase in verse 6: Jesus didn't think He was robbing God to be equal with Him, and His reaction to this fact motivated Him to humble himself to the point of death. This seems impossible to our natural way of thinking. How can being equal with God motivate someone to humble himself? Wouldn't being equal with God cause one to get puffed up with pride and arrogance?

Husbands, when you really know who you are in Christ, when

you begin to get a glimpse of all God has done for you in Christ Jesus, when you allow Him to bless you with all spiritual blessings in Christ Jesus, and when you feel the waves of His love and acceptance in the beloved move through your heart and soul, you are going to fall on your face in humility and lay down your life! Knowing all this is what forms the foundation of loving yourself, which is then the motivation for loving others. When we understand and receive His love for us, our first response is to love as He loves.

We can see from Jesus' example that there is a godly love for ourselves that is essential to loving as God loves. The kind of love I'm talking about says what God says about us and thinks what God thinks about us. Because Jesus understood and experienced the love and acceptance of His Father, He desired only to please Him. And the way to please God is to love what He loves.

## NOURISH AND CHERISH

A married couple needs to understand that when they speak to their spouse, they are actually speaking to themselves. Two have become one. What you say to your spouse has a direct reflection on you. Furthermore, what you say to your spouse indicates how you feel about *yourself.*

**So ought men to love their wives as their own bodies. He that loveth his wife loveth himself.**
**—Ephesians 5:28**

Through the years I have counseled numerous couples, among them couples in which the husbands have beaten their wives. In every encounter I've ever had with a wife-beater, I have found the wife-beater to be a man who didn't like himself. He had extremely low self-esteem. He had something in his past that he had not forgiven himself for, and he was angry and disappointed in himself.

When husbands approach their wives, they act out how they feel about themselves. Husband, if you don't know how you feel about yourself, take a close look at the way you treat your wife. The Bible tells us clearly, the degree to which you love your wife, you love yourself.

If you treat your wife with disrespect or anger or abusive behavior, you need to know two things: God commands you to break this pattern of behavior, and He will not reward you as long as you act that way toward your wife. That is why Peter wrote that a man must care for his wife or his prayers will be hindered. (See 1 Peter 3:7.) When a husband acts in anger toward his wife and fails to model Jesus to her, many of the promises that would otherwise have been fulfilled in his life are hindered. But how does this work? And what, specifically, are we to do?

"No man ever yet hated his own flesh; but nourisheth and cherisheth it, even as the Lord the church" (Ephesians 5:29). The Greek words for *nourisheth* and *cherisheth* provide tremendous keys to the revelation the Holy Spirit gives to husbands in these verses in Ephesians. First, the word *nourisheth* means to educate and train in the way a teacher educates and trains a student. This is very easy to see in our Lord and Savior, who gave us the Holy Spirit to lead us into all truth, remind us of His words, and even tell us things to come. But it is a sad commentary on the church that so many men are more like the spiritual babies of their homes than the spiritual teachers of their homes. It's time for men to rise up and take their places as the spiritual heads of their households, to study God's Word and live God's Word before their wives, children, business associates, and neighbors.

Second, the word *cherisheth* means to brood over in the same way a mother hen will brood over her chicks or the Holy Spirit brooded over the earth and brought it to life in Genesis 1. This is a life-giving, Spirit-breathing word! And when we put these two words together, we see a husband who imparts the living Word to his wife, who prays over her in the Spirit, who walks in the ways of God, and loves his wife as he loves himself.

If the first man, Adam, had nourished Eve rather than allowing her to nourish him, the fall never would have happened. Adam and Eve broke the divine order when the one who should have been nourished became the "nourisher." Eve gave to Adam when he should have been giving to her. Adam gave place to the Devil when he failed to give Eve the nourishment she needed. Because Adam didn't nourish her with God's Word, the Devil came in to nourish her with a lie.

It is a husband's responsibility to build up his wife on the inside. The only thing that will give her confidence, courage, purpose, value, and significance is the Word and anointing of God.

So many wives try to drag their husbands to church, seminars, and retreats so they can grow in the Lord. Where are the men who are leading their wives to church and seminars and retreats? So many wives are trying to get their husbands interested in spiritual matters, to read their Bibles and listen to sound teaching of God's principles. Where are the men who are leading their wives to sources that will nourish their spirits?

It's time men faced up to this role in marriage and started patterning their lives and their marriages according to God's Word, not according to the way the world operates. Our role model is Jesus Christ, and the manual for life and marriage is His Word. Ephesians 5:29 says that we are to nourish and cherish our wives "even as the Lord the church." The Lord continually tells His people who they are in Him. They are His beloved children, His people, His delight. He continually feeds His people the revelation of His Word so that He might nourish them and cause them to grow into His image. And the Holy Spirit broods over us, bearing witness with our spirit that we are God's child, that we are loved, that we are cherished by our Bridegroom.

## SERVE, MINISTER, HARVEST

Knowing who we are in Christ Jesus, husbands, means we know we have been made the heads of our homes. We have been empowered and anointed to fill that position. But God not only gives the husband power, He always gives purpose for that power. There is always a vision, a dream, a high calling in Christ Jesus set before us. And in our marriages, the high calling is loving and serving our wives.

If a husband sees only his authority and exercises only his power, his wife is going to be miserable and will find it increasingly difficult to submit. Power without purpose becomes reckless and dangerous. If a husband, however, gets the full picture that his power is for the purpose of serving, he will not abuse his power. His wife will be fulfilled and so will he.

The Lord Jesus always linked authority with servanthood. He exemplified this to His disciples at the Last Supper when He rose from the table, laid aside His outer garments, girded himself with a towel, poured water into a basin, and began to wash the disciples' feet. After He washed their feet, He said:

Know ye what I have done to you? Ye call me Master and Lord: and ye say well; for so I am. If I then, your Lord and Master, have washed your feet; ye also ought to wash one another's feet. For I have given you an example, that ye should do as I have done to you. Verily, verily, I say unto you, The servant is not greater than his lord; neither he that is sent greater than he that sent him. If ye know these things, happy are ye if ye do them.
**—John 13:12–17**

You may love your wife and she may submit to that love, but then her submission should not be met with domination but with ministry. Any person who is called to a position of authority in Christ Jesus must lay down his life and become a servant. When a man marries, his wife becomes his ministry—his number-one ministry. He has the responsibility to nourish and cherish her far more than he has a responsibility for any other person or group of people.

The ministry of the husband to the wife is a ministry of putting her needs before his own needs. Her submission is in all areas of authority; his ministry is in all areas of provision, material and financial as well as emotional and spiritual. The godly husband lives to serve his wife. Being the head of his wife means God has given him the honor and privilege of taking care of a precious treasure, one of His children. The wife truly belongs to God, and He has entrusted the husband with the responsibility to nourish and cherish her, to impart God's life and Word to her. And when you are given responsibility to grow and develop something, you reap a harvest.

When a man takes a wife to himself, he takes her into his total life. She becomes a part of him and he becomes a part of her. They are one. For example, if the husband is a workaholic, the wife will live in a hurricane of work and pressure and stress. If he is not whole in Christ Jesus, she is going to be the recipient of the way he expresses all those areas of brokenness. Whatever he is, she will enter fully into his cycle, his system, his self-esteem (or lack of it), his restlessness, his peace, his degree of wholeness. Whatever he sows into her life will bring forth a commensurate harvest from her.

Thank God Jesus sows wholeness, peace, joy, and love into us through His Word and by His presence. His divine seed produces an eternal harvest in us. And it is Jesus who will reap that harvest.

He is sowing into a church that will become a "glorious bride" without spot, wrinkle, or blemish.

## EMPOWERMENT

**So ought men to love their wives as their own bodies. He that loveth his wife loveth himself. For no man ever yet hated his own flesh; but nourisheth and cherisheth it, even as the Lord the church: For we are members of his body, of his flesh, and of his bones.**

**—Ephesians 5:28–30**

We are now coming to the end of Paul's discussion about the husband's role in marriage, which is a mirror reflection of Jesus' role as Bridegroom to the church. It is obvious that our union with Christ Jesus as our Lord is not a union that is exclusive to the Lord's Day or when we are serving in some capacity or thinking spiritual thoughts. Our union with Christ Jesus makes us one with Him in every area of our lives at all times and in all situations because we are members of His body, even of His flesh and bones. We are Jesus on this earth!

His will should be our will.

His passion should be our passion.

His compassion should be our compassion.

His blessing and honor and power and glory should radiate from our countenance and demonstrate His person to every person we encounter.

As husbands, this is no small task! But men, we must remember that God has not left us without assistance. He has empowered us with everything we need to succeed. We have His Word. We have His Spirit. We have His name. We have His wisdom. We have His love. And He has not only appointed us, He has anointed us to be Jesus to our wives and show forth Jesus to the world.

# 7

# INTIMACY

For this cause shall a man leave his father and mother, and shall be joined unto his wife, and they two shall be one flesh. This is a great mystery: but I speak concerning Christ and the church. Nevertheless let every one of you in particular so love his wife even as himself; and the wife see that she reverence her husband.

—Ephesians 5:31–33

In this final section of Ephesians 5, Paul says that although he has been speaking in practical terms about marriage between a man and woman, he has really been talking about the church's relationship with Jesus Christ, which is a mystery. The issue is not marriage; the issue is the mystery. Marriage between a husband and wife is merely the illustration of the mystery, which is the marriage of Jesus and the church, the relationship of the Head and His body, the Bridegroom and the bride.

In light of this truth, God's infinite wisdom and mercy have established the marriage relationship so that we can only accomplish it by walking hand in hand and face-to-face with Him. The degree to which we pursue intimacy with our heavenly Bridegroom is the degree to which we will enjoy wedded bliss with our spouse on earth. And every aspect of our earthly union reflects the divine design and ecstasy of our heavenly union with Christ Jesus. For example, before we entered into covenant with Him, Jesus was the aggressor. He was wooing us, pursuing us, chasing us down, and courting us. But it is also interesting to note that He was rejected by another before He sought our hearts: "He was in the world, and the world was made by him, and the world knew him not. He came unto his own, and his own received him not" (John 1:10–11).

Jesus became flesh and dwelt among us, but when the time came for Him to take a bride, instead of reaching for an earthly bride, He reached for a spiritual bride—Israel. But Israel rejected Him and, like the first Adam, there was no helpmeet for Him. So He went to the cross, God opened up His side, and out poured the blood that would bring forth His spiritual bride. That is why the cross is referred to as Jesus' *passion.*

When Jesus burst forth from the tomb He began to build His bride just as Eve had been built for Adam. You see, in the Hebrew language of the Old Testament, it says that Adam was created and formed, but Eve was *built.* (See Genesis 2:7, 22.) So it was no coincidence that Jesus declared that He would *build* His church:

He saith unto them, But whom say ye that I am? And Simon Peter answered and said, Thou art the Christ, the Son of the living God. And Jesus answered and said unto him, Blessed art thou, Simon Barjona: for flesh and blood hath not revealed it unto thee, but my Father which is in heaven. And I say also unto thee, That thou art Peter, and upon this rock I will build my church; *and the gates of hell shall not prevail against it.*
    **—Matthew 16:15–18 (emphasis mine)**

The church is a spiritual bride built upon the revelation knowledge of who Jesus Christ is. Jesus gave His life for us, and like a blushing bride who glows with adoration for her bridegroom, we should walk in the glory of the Lord. We are one with Him. We are bone of His bone and flesh of His flesh, members of His body, and walk in the light as He is in the light.

## THE HOLY HUNT

For this cause shall a man leave his father and mother. . . .
    **—Ephesians 5:31**

Jesus had to leave His Father in heaven to come to us and become one with us, and a man must leave his mother and father to become one with his wife. But we must also leave. The church must leave the world that gave us physical birth to be spiritually joined with our Lord and Savior Jesus Christ. Ultimately, at the resurrection, we will also be physically joined with Him.

In marriage, it is the man's role to come to the place of maturity in his walk with the Lord where he says, "It's time I leave mother and father and establish a home of my own. It's time I find a wife." And then the hunting instinct kicks in. The godly man will rely on the Lord to lead him to the wife who is right for him, but he is always the aggressor, just as Jesus is the aggressor.

Although for hundreds of years the vast majority of men on the earth have not fed their families by hunting wild animals, men are still hunters on the inside. A single woman, on the other hand, is the game. She simply goes about her life in purity and holiness before the Lord, knowing that when God gets ready to bring a husband to her, it will be at the right time. A single woman doesn't need to do anything to put herself in a man's way or pursue him. He's supposed to find her and win her heart.

This certainly doesn't mean that women are to be victims of stalkers! It simply means that scouting out a man is not the role of a godly woman. A single woman can pray for God to send the husband of His choice in His timing and for His purposes, but she needs to be about those things that the Lord puts in her heart to do. She doesn't need to go out and run down and tackle a man.

This also does not mean that a Christian woman should accept the first hunter who finds her! She must accept the one she has peace in her heart about, the one she knows God has prepared her for, the one she will joyfully submit to for the rest of her life—and the one who has been prepared by God to love, nourish, and cherish her.

God didn't bring Eve on the scene until the stage was set and Adam was in place to care for her and love her. He didn't birth the church into being until the stage was set and Jesus Christ was raised up to care for her and love her and nourish her. So women, don't say yes to a man who hasn't submitted himself fully to the Lord. Wait until the stage is properly set for you!

In terms of the mystery, Jesus is always on the hunt for His bride. He was on the hunt for us long before we even knew His name or knew anything about Him. He searches continually for those who will turn away from sin and believe in Him. He searches for human hearts that desire to know Him and are willing to do whatever He tells them to do. Jesus is the hunter of the human heart.

Now a word of caution: There is also a supernatural stalker who is after us, and his name is Satan. He is described as our adversary, who operates as a "roaring lion, seeking whom he may devour" (1 Peter 5:8). Jesus said that the Devil comes only "to steal, and to kill, and to destroy" (John 10:10). The Devil is looking for trophies to hang on his wall. He is looking for people he might destroy forever. He tortures his prey and inflicts as much pain and agony as possible before he moves in for the kill.

In sharp contrast, Jesus searches for us so that He might give us life "and that more abundantly" (John 10:10). He seeks us out with all grace and mercy so that we might inherit "eternal glory by Christ Jesus" and that He might "perfect, stablish, strengthen, and settle" us (1 Peter 5:10). If we develop an intimate relationship with Jesus, if we allow this holy hunter to capture our hearts and minds and fill us with His love and light, we will not fall for the dark lies and deception of the Devil.

## HOLY AFFECTION

**For this cause shall a man leave his father and mother, and shall be joined unto his wife, and they two shall be one flesh.**
**—Ephesians 5:31**

After a man has left his mother and father, has found his wife, and she has accepted him as the husband God has for her, they are joined together. They are to be so joined together that they are one. Now, we do not have to have a doctorate degree to understand that when we are joined together with another person we *touch* one another! Affection is holy. It is sacred. And it is something that God ordained between a husband and wife to reflect and illustrate the intimacy Jesus desires with His bride. Furthermore, if affection is not practiced, the covenant becomes very hard to honor.

A number of years ago, an experiment was conducted that tested this very principle. A clinical psychologist was seeking to discover the effects of touch on the pituitary gland and other growth glands of the body. Two groups of babies and nurses were part of the study. One group of nurses was told to take care of only the biological needs of the babies. They were to feed them and change their diapers, but not otherwise touch them or hold them. The other group of nurses was told to handle the babies with a great deal of affection. In addition to feeding them and changing their diapers, they were to touch them, massage them, hold them, and cuddle them.

Both groups of babies were observed over time, and the clinical psychologist was able to chart measurable differences in the two groups. The babies who had not been touched or massaged were dwarfed. They failed to develop normally and to thrive and grow to their full potential. The study pointed to the conclusion that affection enhances and promotes good health and normal growth.[1]

Affection is also one of the barometers of a healthy marriage. An intimate relationship always involves touch. It is normal for a husband and wife to desire to touch each other, to hold hands, to hug and kiss, to caress each other. Show me a couple who doesn't touch very much and I'll show you a marriage that is in trouble. Now, I'm not referring to sex alone, but to affection—skin touching skin, bodies touching bodies, even with clothes on.

And what about touching in the body of Christ? Are you willing to take the hand of that person sitting next to you as you pray and agree on a matter? Are you quick to wrap your arms around another person and love that person in the Lord, even if they just came off the streets and don't smell so good? Is your shoulder always available to receive the tears of a person who is in trouble or who is grieving? Is your hand quick to pat the shoulder of a person needing encouragement? Are you quick to extend your hand in reconciliation and restoration to a person who has hurt you?

There is nothing as chilling as an icy touch or an empty embrace. Nothing produces loneliness like false intimacy. And God knows this! He is a Father who loves to embrace and touch His children, and He loves us to come running into His arms. It grieves Him when we turn from Him and resist His affection, and when we resist receiving His divine touch, we destroy our own ability to express affection and concern for others.

Our affection toward one another must be innocent, pure, and

---

[1] Anna Nidecker, "Maternal Deprivation Reduces Cortisol Levels," Medscope. Web page accessed 1/16/99. *http://womenshealth.medscope.com/IMNB/Pediatric__News/1998/v.32.n01/pn3201.10.01 .htm/.*

genuine. There is no room for hypocrisy in this! There is no place for manipulation or insincerity. If we are to be "fitly joined" together as husbands and wives and as members of the body of Christ, we must submit and love with heartfelt affection. And the only way to express genuine affection is to receive it first from heaven. The way we do that is to stay in communion with God, not only in service at church, but every moment of the day and night.

## HOLY COMMUNION

The bride of Christ was birthed from the blood that flowed from Jesus' side on the cross, and we are forever united in spirit to Him. Yet we are separate in space and in physical form from Him. It is a mystery. We experience intimacy with Jesus in worship, in holy communion with Him. It is in the Holy of Holies in the spirit realm that our spirit and His Spirit realize oneness, where we are fully activated, fully fused, and of one accord. Worship is the consummation of our relationship with the Lord. A wedding is not complete until the union is consummated, and a marriage has no substance without regular intimacy. Our wedding with the Lord is not fully complete until we worship Him as Lord and Savior, and our marriage to Him is only alive and vibrant if we continue to be a worshiper of our Lord.

Nothing is as exhilarating in a marriage as a good sexual relationship. Other things may be as important or as good, but nothing is as euphoric, powerful, passionate, or explosive. And nothing has the same ability to create. In the same manner, our special times of communion with the Lord are the most exhilarating, euphoric, passionate, powerful, and explosive times of our lives. And nothing we do in the church has the same ability to bring forth the harvest of souls He longs for.

We cannot enter into holy communion with the Lord without yielding ourselves completely. In worship, self becomes totally unimportant. The only thing that matters is God. What He desires, what He commands, and what He is totally consumes us. We lose ourselves in His presence, and we do so willingly. It's hard to imagine that anyone could remain puffed up in God's awesome presence. He is everything!

When we lay aside self and love God with all our heart, soul, mind, and strength, He fills us with His presence. Whatever we yield to Him, He occupies. All the areas of our lives that we give to Him, He moves into with all the fruit of the Spirit we need to love and minister and all the gifts we need to do what He's called us to do. Why? Because He inhabits the praises of His people. He moves in where He is welcome and then He redecorates! When we live in a perpetual state and lifestyle of holy communion, everything we touch is blessed and beautified by God.

## HOLY AND GLORIOUS

When a husband and wife become one flesh, it is both reproductive and redemptive. Not only do they produce children, but they produce intimacy with each other that restores and completes and makes whole. Likewise, when the bride of Christ becomes one with her Bridegroom and receives the seed of His Word, intimacy with Christ Jesus restores us, completes us, and makes us whole, and children are born into the kingdom of God.

The foremost thing that is birthed out of worshiping Jesus Christ is souls. Unbelievers who find themselves caught up in the worship of a body of believers find themselves drawn to God in ways they have never felt before. They long for the joy and reconciliation, forgiveness and healing, and total freedom and deliverance they see all around them in worshiping believers.

In addition to souls, we come to the place Ephesians 5:27 describes: "That he might present it to himself a glorious church, not having spot, or wrinkle, or any such thing; but that it should be holy and without blemish."

Jesus makes us glorious!

The blessing He bestows upon His bride is a blessing that makes us the envy of all who see us. It is a blessing that not only nourishes us and beautifies us, but that transforms us into a kingdom of priests unto our God. Nevertheless, it comes with a great price. God is using *our house* to preach to our community, and this responsibility causes our knees to buckle!

Who we are at home cuts to the very root of who we really are. Yet this passage in Ephesians is telling us we must be yielded to the Word and the Spirit to the point that our private lives are open for public scrutiny. That makes us very vulnerable. If He wants to use us from nine to five during the day, we can do that. If He wants to use us from six to nine in the evening for a service, we're available.

But if we are to understand that our *whole life* is the canvas on which He paints the glorious Gospel, then we are intimidated! Most of us feel too weak to be under the world's microscope twenty-four/seven.

Nevertheless, that's what Paul is saying. The most intimate relationship we experience on earth is what God has chosen to illustrate His relationship with His church. He has cast each of us to play a role in His drama without our permission and has challenged us to be conformed to His image. We are not Him, and yet we must put Him on and play the part.

Any actor will tell you that when you play a role on the stage you cannot break character. That means you must exhibit the personality and character of the person you are playing at all times and without exception. Thus we cannot break character; we are bound to exhibit the personality and character of Jesus Christ at all times, in all situations, and with all people.

We are His people and He is our God!

We walk in His glory and emanate His presence!

We become His expression of power and majesty!

We are His resplendent jewel on the earth!

We are the demonstration of His love and the illustration of His redemptive work to every life we touch!

Oh, what a wonder and a marvel to know that the King of Kings and Lord of Lords has chosen us to be His own and we are wedded to Him for all eternity!

# PART SIX

*Overcoming the Enemy*

# Introduction

The book of Ephesians is the New Testament equivalent of the Old Testament book of Joshua. The book of Joshua is a picture of a people who have ceased wandering, come to know their God, embraced the promises of God, and are now ready to seize what God has promised them.

The book of Ephesians translates the natural warfare of Joshua into the spiritual warfare of the believer. It is not the sort of thing we should read and take to heart unless we are ready to pay the price and do what is necessary to possess all God has for us. This is the book where the apostle Paul commands, "Be strong in the Lord, and in the power of his might!" just as God commanded Joshua, "Be strong and of a good courage!"

I believe we are the Joshua generation.

We are the generation who will storm the gates of hell, take the Promised Land, and bring in the last days' harvest of souls. All unrighteousness will fall to its knees as we proclaim the holy Word of the Lord.

But have we counted the cost?

Joshua led Israel to take the Promised Land, but he also served Moses patiently and faithfully for forty years in the wilderness, all the while knowing they could have taken the Promised Land just a few months after leaving Egypt. Joshua was one of twelve spies who came back with a good report after observing the land of milk and honey. This is the report Israel rejected, and because of their unbelief, they wandered in the wilderness for forty years. Only Joshua and Caleb believed God.

The Joshua generation will believe God and obey Him.

The Joshua generation will not murmur and complain.

The Joshua generation will give their lives for the Gospel.

The Joshua generation will lay their lives down for their brothers and sisters.

The Joshua generation will not take the glory for themselves.

If we are not willing to pay the price, we will not survive the time of the Joshua generation! We must be tenacious and unyielding in our love for God and for the brethren—and we must know how to war in the spirit.

Warring in the spirit is much more than standing up from time to time and telling the Devil to stop hindering our finances or making us sick. Warring in the spirit is defeating all the little foxes that would spoil the vine, little foxes such as greed, lust, jealousy, anger, and fear.

Warring in the spirit is getting up an hour early or staying up an hour later to have that intimate time with the Lord, to hear His instructions for the day, to know His heart and mind, to be empowered with His might, and to be fully clothed in His armor so that the Enemy will be driven farther back as we walk in this world.

Warring in the spirit means continually recognizing that we are not warring against people, but the Devil and his demons who work through them. Warring in the spirit takes love, faith, patience, faithfulness, and courage—all the characteristics of Joshua.

Joshua was God's warrior, and because he believed and obeyed God, he took the Promised Land.

The church is Jesus' warrior bride, and when we believe and obey the battle cry of our Lord, we will take the world!

# 1

# LEARNING OBEDIENCE

You need to know something about Joshua if you are going to take the Promised Land: Joshua understood obedience. He lived by God's principle of submission and authority. In fact, every good, effective soldier lives by this principle. No army can wage war successfully without a fighting force that keeps rank and file, respects their officers, and obeys orders. That is why, before Paul dresses us in the armor of God and instructs us in the strategies of spiritual warfare, he explicitly and emphatically tells us in the final verses of Ephesians 5 and the first verses of Ephesians 6 that we must abide in the principle of submission and authority. He explores this vital issue first in the relationship of husband and wife (see Ephesians 5:22–33), which was part of our discussion in part 5, "Celebrating Marriage." I strongly urge you to go back and read our teaching on submission, which will provide more foundation for what we will discuss here with regard to spiritual warfare.

Now, in the first verses of Ephesians 6, Paul continues to talk about submission and authority in the context of the relationship between child and parent and then the relationship between slave and master.

## CHILDHOOD TRAINING

The mature warrior is an obedient warrior. That's what basic training is about—bringing a civilian's will into line with military standards, military codes, military rules and regulations, and a military way of thinking. If the church is going to wage war successfully, she must learn to obey her Commander.

Our submission to Jesus Christ is the only relationship in which we know that at all times, under all circumstances, His commands are right and true. There is never a question about His absolute goodness and righteousness. Therefore, our hearts should be continuously submitted to His Word and His Spirit, and our actions should always carry out His will. However, in human relationships, there are times when we are placed in positions where the authority we are submitted to is not right, just, or gentle. Nevertheless, God calls us to these positions for the purpose of growing in us a submissive heart to *Him*. As we obey those in authority over us and trust *Him*, we grow in our faith.

God's plan is that we learn obedience as children in the home. As parents lovingly demand that their child's will lines up with their will, they are molding and shaping that child's will to line up with the will of the Father for the rest of their lives. Obedience is best learned as a young child. Paul wrote to the Ephesians: "Children, obey your parents in the Lord: for this is right. Honour thy father and mother; which is the first commandment with promise; that it may be well with thee, and thou mayest live long on the earth" (6:1–3).

The adult who was taught obedience by his parents is going to find it much easier to obey the Lord than an adult who was never taught obedience as a child in the home. I firmly believe that a parent who does not teach her child to be obedient is doing her child a great disservice. Structure and order are always much better learned as a child than as an adult. It starts out as simple as setting a rule and holding the child accountable. At eight o'clock Johnny goes to bed—no arguing, no discussion. If Johnny does not obey, he quickly discovers the consequences. If Johnny has an unsubmissive, rebellious, or sour attitude, he finds out immediately that it is unacceptable.

Paul refers to the fifth commandment, found in Exodus 20:12, and tells us that this commandment comes with a promise. When we honor our mother and father, we will live a long and prosperous life. If we want our children to live long and prosperous lives, we must teach them to honor us as parents from the moment they are born. We must give them this vital key to life and fulfillment.

In addition, it will be so much easier for them to submit to Jesus as their Lord if we teach them to submit to us as young children.

Moreover, a child who is required to show respect for authority at home will have a more enjoyable time with teachers and reap the benefits of learning in school. They will have a natural respect for any adult in authority, whether it is a pastor or a policeman. When they go to work as young adults, they will get along well with their bosses and work well with other employees.

We see one main characteristic again and again in our prison system: These inmates failed to learn respect for authority when they were children. They grew up under one of Satan's most vile and destructive deceptions, believing that their rebellion signified strength and power, that they were their own lords and set their own rules. When you have no respect for authority, you believe the lie that you can do anything and get away with it. You have swallowed the serpent's false doctrine that he spoke to Eve in the garden of Eden:

> Now the serpent was more subtle than any beast of the field which the Lord God had made. And he said unto the woman, Yea, hath God said, Ye shall not eat of every tree of the garden? And the woman said unto the serpent, We may eat of the fruit of the trees of the garden: But of the fruit of the tree which is in the midst of the garden, God hath said, Ye shall not eat of it, neither shall ye touch it, lest ye die. And the serpent said unto the woman, Ye shall not surely die: For God doth know that in the day ye eat thereof, then your eyes shall be opened, and ye shall be as gods, knowing good and evil.
> **—Genesis 3:1–5**

Satan's lie is that we can disobey God and not die, that rebellion against His precepts will make us our own gods, strong and independent. But God's Word tells us that only obedience to God, to parents, to all those in authority over us will bring blessing and joy to our lives. As believers, our hearts are submitted to God fully when we make Jesus not only our *Savior* but our *Lord*.

Unfortunately, many Christians today have made Jesus their Savior but not their Lord. They are deceived into thinking they can do what they please without consequences because they are saved and going to heaven. Many Christians find themselves halfway through their lives before they recognize who they are in Christ Jesus or realize that, as believers in Christ Jesus, they are to live in total submission to Him. So many people who call themselves Christians are just playing church—they are going through all the motions and saying all the right words, but they have not truly submitted their entire lives to Him so that they are subject to Him in all things. (See Ephesians 5:22, 24.)

Obedience is the foundation of who we are in Christ, a key to our success in spiritual warfare, and the lesson of obedience is best learned in our earliest years. It is the sapling—still bendable and pliable—that can best be trained to become a strong tree, able to withstand every storm. However, whether or not we were brought up in the counsel and admonition of the Lord, whether or not we were taught the principle of submission and authority as children, right now, before we put on the full armor of God, it is imperative that we submit ourselves completely to Jesus Christ as our Lord as well as our Savior.

Notice that Paul does not command children to *understand* everything their parents tell them to do. He merely commands them to obey. Paul does not command the church as a whole to understand all of the mystery in Christ Jesus, nor does he command the believers in Ephesus to understand all of the profound, prolific concepts he illustrates and presents to them. He does require, however, that they obey the truth of God's Word.

This principle holds true for us in every area of our spiritual growth and development, regardless of our age. We must obey those who are more mature in the Lord. We must do what they teach us and command us to do, especially if they hold positions of authority over us. God is a God of principles and concepts. If you learn these principles and concepts, and the principle of submission and authority is one of them, you can apply God's principles to any situation.

For example, one of my first jobs in the church was not to preach but to play the piano. I figured out right away that once you learned the seven white keys and five black keys, you mastered the entire keyboard. Those twelve notes create an octave that repeats itself over and over to create the keyboard. A similar illustration is our numerical system, which is based upon the numbers zero to nine. If you can count to ten, you can count to a million because the same numbers, with only slight variations in name, repeat themselves over and over.

So it is in the kingdom of God. Jesus taught, "If you are faithful over a few things, I will make you ruler over many things." (See Matthew 25:23.) When God gets ready to teach His people and to raise them up into greater spiritual maturity, He always starts with basic concepts that are readily comprehended and applied. It is for this reason that the Lord admonishes us not to despise small beginnings or the "small things" He does. (See Zechariah 4:9–10.) Anything God originates has the potential to increase, produce a harvest, and be refined into perfection. In Job we read: "Though thy beginning was small, yet thy latter end should greatly increase" (8:7).

If you learn to be faithful on one level, you can be faithful on every level. The person who learns how to tithe faithfully on one dollar is a person who is going to tithe faithfully on a million dollars. Those who say they can't afford to tithe have missed the key issues of obedience and faithfulness. They have missed the principles God wants to teach them.

While God is no respecter of *persons*—meaning that He does not favor one person over another—He is a respecter of *principles*. (See Numbers 23:19.) He always upholds His absolutes, and the principle of submission to the Lord is a foundation principle that must be learned before other principles can be built upon it.

## GOD'S ORDER

Obedience is bordered by rules, routine, structure, and order. Within the heart and soul of every fallen human being, however, is a natural, fleshly tendency to rebel against these things. Some of us become very subtle in our rebellion, claiming that rules, routine, structure, and order are contrary to the flow of God's Spirit. God's Word, however, states clearly that godly rules, routine, structure, and order are not contrary to the working of the Spirit. (See 1 Corinthians 14.) They make it easier for the Holy Spirit to flow through the church and for God's people to obey what the Spirit says. Structure and obedience to God's commandments are essential to the work of the Spirit.

In Acts 6, we read about a dispute that arose in the early church. The apostles responded by appointing seven men of "honest report, full of the Holy Ghost and wisdom" over the practical business of the church. These seven, called deacons, were to make certain that the needs of all the believers were addressed and met with fairness and equity, while the apostles devoted themselves to prayer and the ministry of the Word. (See Acts 6:1–4.) Seven men were appointed for ministry, and the apostles laid their hands on them and prayed for them. The church was getting organized, and here was the result: "And the word of God increased; and the number of the disciples multiplied in Jerusalem greatly; and a great company of the priests were obedient to the faith" (Acts 6:7).

Structure and order caused the Gospel to go forth with greater effectiveness, more souls were added to the kingdom of God, and even the hardest-to-reach souls—the priests in the temple—became convinced of the truth about Jesus Christ! Therefore, we can see that requiring obedience of our children is not going to inhibit their creativity or dreams. On the contrary, it will make their creativity and dreams flourish! They will be more useful and effective in God's hands. Requiring obedience of a child will not make the child resistant to the Holy Spirit; it makes the child more sensitive and compliant to the Holy Spirit.

Rules, routine, structure, and order are required if any person is going to learn these basic principles of God:

- Relationships have boundaries, including the relationship of an individual to the greater group or community. Every relationship has boundaries built into it, and those boundaries have to be learned and respected. For example, if a person says no to your kisses and hugs, respect that and back away; if a store is closed, it doesn't mean you can break in to take what you want.
- Respect must be shown for those who make and enforce rules. Every relationship, every culture, every society, and every church is governed by certain rules, written and unwritten. Those rules must be learned. Thou shalt not lie. Thou shalt not commit adultery. Thou shalt not bring food or drink into the main sanctuary. Thou shalt not run in the halls at school. Thou shalt not talk back to the teacher.
- All behavior has consequences. Good behavior brings reward, even though that reward may be only the good feeling and self-respect that come with knowing we have done what is right. Bad behavior brings discipline, chastisement, and punishment. Those who live in accordance with God's Law put themselves in a position to receive God's blessing. Those who routinely

and willfully break God's Law put themselves in a position to be chastised by God, and if they do not repent, they will eventually withdraw from His presence and protection.

Although the Bible does not state it directly, the command to honor your mother and father clearly implies that your days will be lengthened. Therefore, if a child dishonors or disrespects his father and mother, his days likely will be shortened. As a parent, I would be terrified to train up my children to disrespect me, knowing that because of their disrespect their days would be shortened. We only need to look at the latest edition of any newspaper in this nation to see what is happening to our children when they have no respect or honor for their fathers and mothers. Their lives are being shortened through the violence of the streets and their association with neighborhood gangs that are taking the place of a father and mother in their lives.

I want my children to live and I want them to live in blessing. I want them to experience the promise that their respect and honor will cause it to "be well with them." (See Ephesians 6:3.) Not only do I want these blessings and long life for my own natural children, but I also want these things for every "babe in Christ" in my church. I desire to see the entire body of Christ live long and prosperously on the earth.

Why aren't more of God's people experiencing the full blessings of God? Perhaps it is because as new believers in Christ Jesus they aren't taught to respect their elders in the Lord, their spiritual mothers and fathers, and to have a respect for God's authority over their lives. God cannot entrust the full blessings that go with His kingdom to those who do not submit to Him in their hearts and obey Him in their lives.

## DO NOT PROVOKE

I love the fact that Paul expresses so clearly God's balance. The exhortation for wives to submit to their husbands is followed immediately by the command that husbands are to love and nurture their wives, to lay down their lives for them. Then the charge to children that they should obey their parents is balanced by God's command to fathers that they "provoke not" their children to wrath. Paul writes: "And, ye fathers, provoke not your children to wrath: but bring them up in the nurture and admonition of the Lord" (Ephesians 6:4).

God's plan for His people is filled with checks and balances. A child must learn to obey and to respect his parents, but at the same time, he is to learn that lesson in an atmosphere of love, kindness, patience, self-control, joy, peace, and mercy. A parent must not be unduly harsh, and never abusive. Such behavior only provokes or prompts a child to imitate the harsh and abusive behavior. A child who is treated with anger is a child who is going to respond with anger.

This passage presents a vivid contrast. One of the definitions of "provoke" is to "send away" or "drive away." Paul says that fathers should not drive away their children to the point of wrath but bring them up and nurture them in the discipline and instruction of the Lord. To nurture is to love unconditionally and to instruct is to enlighten. We do not simply make rules and enforce them. We explain them to our children and discipline them in love.

Pastors, teachers, prophets, evangelists—all who function in roles of authority in the church—must admonish God's people with the same attitude as a loving father in the home. Those who provoke their congregations to wrath by man-made teaching and man-made rules that are harsher than God's Law are going to find they are raising up angry, harsh people. We are to win the world through the manifested strength and power of God's love, not the strength and power of men and women seeking to build their own empires.

Notice that Paul admonishes *fathers* to bring up their children in the nurture and admonition of the Lord. So often in our society, we leave the nurturing of children to mothers. As men, we have a tendency to shirk the responsibility of raising children, saying, "That's a mother's duty." Scripturally, however, we fathers are commanded to love and instruct our children, to raise them up to fear, love, and serve the Lord. This does not mean that a father is to replace the role of a mother in a family, but God expects him to actively contribute and oversee the guidance of his children.

The fact is, children ultimately emulate the authority figure in the home. They learn their value system from the head of the household. Mothers often fight a losing battle trying to instill values and godly behavior in their children by themselves. Those children need to see both their mama's tender devotion to the Lord and their daddy's unshakable commitment to biblical values and godly behavior. Fathers need to become strong advocates of good values in the home, and their children need to know that these values are important to them. This means more than just setting high standards of morality for his family. It means that Daddy lives them before his children so that they can learn godly principles by watching him.

In the church, the senior pastor is the final authority figure who embodies the values held by the members of the church. If the senior pastor is lax in character, the church will be permeated with undesirable character, no matter how much good may be going on in the various outreaches. The pastor who teaches his people, both in word and by example, to obey the truth of God's Word and fully submit their hearts in a lifestyle of worship before the Lord is a pastor who is going to raise up his "children" to live long and prosperous lives.

These first verses in Ephesians 6 tell us clearly that God is extremely concerned with the training of our children. He wants them to learn early to serve Him and obey His commands because He wants them to live long and be blessed. He knows that the sooner they learn obedience to His will, the sooner they will become mighty men and women of valor in the body of Christ. Then they will do great exploits in the kingdom of God and bring glory to His name.

# 2

# ONE JOB OPENING

So Joshua did as Moses had said to him.
—Exodus 17:10

I'm certain Moses was a great guy, but do you really think he was always great to work for? He had tremendous responsibility and bore the burden of leading millions of very selfish, independent-thinking people. And he had a temper. This is a man who struck the rock and didn't enter the Promised Land because of it! Don't you think there were times when Joshua was just a little bit frustrated, irritated, or aggravated with Moses? And yet the Bible says that Joshua obeyed Moses without complaint. Why? I believe Joshua knew in his heart that one day he would lead Israel across the Jordan to take the Promised Land. He knew God was preparing him for war.

When God created the church, He gave only one job opening to every member: *slave*. In one New Testament epistle after another Paul declared that he was merely a servant of the Lord Jesus Christ, but the word he used in the Greek meant "slave." The kind of slave we're talking about here is someone who is utterly and completely devoted to their master. Even if they were offered their freedom, they would refuse it because of their lifelong commitment to their beloved lord. In this same sense, we are all called to be servants of the Lord Jesus Christ.

Pastor . . . slave of the Lord Jesus Christ

Engineer . . . slave of the Lord Jesus Christ.
Parent . . . slave of the Lord Jesus Christ.
Construction worker . . . slave of the Lord Jesus Christ.
Spouse . . . slave of the Lord Jesus Christ.
CEO . . . slave of the Lord Jesus Christ.
Usher . . . slave of the Lord Jesus Christ.

If you're too good for the job, I'm sorry. No other openings are available! Jesus made this very clear to His disciples on the night of His betrayal:

He riseth from supper, and laid aside his garments; and took a towel, and girded himself. After that he poureth water into a basin, and began to wash the disciples' feet, and to wipe them with the towel wherewith he was girded.... If I then, your Lord and Master, have washed your feet; ye also ought to wash one another's feet. For I have given you an example, that ye should do as I have done to you.
—**John 13:4–5, 14–15**

None of us has any justifiable excuse for ever saying, "That job is beneath me" or for thinking, *I'm too good for that job,* if we truly want to be warriors for Christ. The only job opening in the kingdom of God is slave!

## PLEASING THE LORD

After explaining the importance of submission and authority as it relates to husbands and wives and children and parents, Paul now begins his discourse on the servant and the master:

Servants, be obedient to them that are your masters according to the flesh, with fear and trembling, in singleness of your heart, as unto Christ; not with eyeservice, as menpleasers; but as the servants of Christ, doing the will of God from the heart; with good will doing service, as to the Lord, and not to men: Knowing that whatsoever good thing any man doeth, the same shall he receive of the Lord, whether he be bond or free. And, ye masters, do the same things unto them, forbearing threatening: knowing that your Master also is in heaven; neither is there respect of persons with him.
—**Ephesians 6:5–9**

Many in Ephesus and other nearby areas had been sold into servitude when Rome invaded their part of the world. In addition to those who were suffering slavery to the Romans, there was a tradition of slavery within the Hebrew community as well. Hebrew men sometimes sold themselves into service in order to repay debts or to acquire something they desired to possess. One of the earliest examples we have of this tradition is Jacob, who became a servant to his uncle Laban in order to gain Rachel as his wife. He worked for fourteen years as a servant in Laban's household to earn Rachel's hand. (See Genesis 29:1–28.)

Both the Hebrews and the Romans had a number of classes—economic, governmental, and social. As a result, virtually everybody in the early church served somebody. In this passage of Ephesians, Paul is essentially saying to them and to us, "Refuse to take advantage of your masters and do not rebel against them. Serve them as if you are serving Jesus himself. And masters, do not abuse or mistreat your servants, because Jesus is watching."

Paul knew a great truth about our relationship with the Lord: Regardless of our outer state or circumstances in life, we are servants to Christ Jesus inwardly and eternally free in Him. This is part of the mystery of Jesus and His church, that as slaves to Christ we are free. Then, because we are called to serve God alone, our service to other people is always "as unto the Lord." We do all of our work for Him, by Him, and in Him. He sees our work and He alone rewards us "according to his riches in glory by Christ Jesus" (Philippians 4:19).

Your employer may be the person who signs your paycheck, but your ultimate Boss is Jesus Christ. He is the one who requires that you be His witness on the job by performing with submission and excellence. He is the one who calls you to the highest standards of morality, integrity, ethics, and godly behavior. He is the one who will convict you that you should not be calling your grandma in Chicago on the company phone and pretending she is a client of your company, that you cannot take an hour and a half for lunch and pretend you were only gone thirty minutes! And He is the one who will see your faithfulness and reward you.

There is an interesting verse of Scripture about Joshua that illustrates this very point:

**And the Lord spoke unto Moses face to face, as a man speaketh unto his friend. And he turned again into the camp: but** *his ser-*

*vant Joshua, the son of Nun, a young man, departed not out of the tabernacle.*

**—Exodus 33:11 (emphasis mine)**

This Scripture indicates that Joshua served Moses, but he looked to God for mercy, justice, blessing, and promotion. Often when we do things for men and women, we naturally expect our reward to come from them. But the Bible says that we are to do all things as unto the Lord and that our reward comes from Him. Nobody may see how much you rehearse for the choir number, but Jesus knows. Nobody may have seen you studying that financial report at 2:00 A.M., but Jesus did. So when you look for your rewards, look to Jesus!

## RECEIVING FROM THE LORD

Paul tells us, "Knowing that whatsoever good thing any man doeth, the same shall he receive of the Lord, whether he be bond or free" (Ephesians 6:8). It is the Lord who provides reciprocity for all we do. He is the one who balances the scales and gives us rewards according to our giving, not according to what others think we are worth.

Many Christians get involved in ministries and after a year or two of active involvement, they begin to lose interest and their participation declines. Some of them even lose interest to the point of leaving the church, and a good number of these people give as their excuse, "They were *using* me. They were asking me to do this and give to that and get involved with this and participate in that." My answer to those people is, "Why did you get involved in the church if you weren't available to be used *by the Lord*?" The Lord uses people, and He uses people by asking them to serve other people!

Joshua easily could have complained that he was being "used" by Moses. When Moses stayed on the mountain praying while Joshua was battling Amalek and fighting for his life down below, Joshua may have been tempted to cry, "Moses is using me!" But Joshua submitted to Moses and received special recognition from the Lord as a result:

**And Joshua discomfited Amalek and his people with the edge of the sword. And the Lord said unto Moses, Write this for a memorial in a book, and rehearse it in the ears of Joshua: for I will**

utterly put out the remembrance of Amalek from under heaven. And Moses built an altar, and called the name of it Jehovah-nissi.

**—Exodus 17:13–15**

God reveals He is our banner of victory in war (Jehovah-nissi) and tells Moses to build the memorial and "rehearse it in the ears of Joshua." He declares that Joshua is the conquering hero of the day. So if anybody comes to you and says you are being "used" in your volunteer work, tell them, "Yes, they are using me! That's what they are supposed to do. I said, 'Lord, I'm available to you and I want to be used.' And the only way He could respond was to use me through someone. I'm doing what I do as unto the Lord!" This is not a faith statement, this is a battle cry!

The problem many of us have is that when we do good to our "masters"—whether that person is our employer, supervisor, or music minister—we want to reap from the one we have served. If we invest in a company or a ministry or a person, we want to reap from the place we invest. If we don't feel affirmed, appreciated, and rewarded by the person who has "used" us, then we become upset. But the Bible says that our reward comes from the Lord: "Whatsoever good thing any man doeth, the same shall he receive of the Lord" (Ephesians 6:8).

Anyone who is intensively involved in ministry must ultimately conclude that no person can ever repay them for the sacrifices they make. Only God can reward them adequately for the selfless acts they do on behalf of others. And He does reward us!

He that cometh to God must believe that he is, and that he is a rewarder of them that diligently seek him.

**—Hebrews 11:6**

[Jesus said,] Give, and it shall be given unto you. . . . For with the same measure that ye mete withal it shall be measured to you again.

**—Luke 6:38**

[Jesus said,] But when thou doest alms, let not thy left hand know what thy right hand doeth: That thine alms may be in secret: *and thy Father which seeth in secret himself shall reward thee openly.*

**—Matthew 6:3–4 (emphasis mine)**

Reward and recognition will come from the Father, and He will determine the appropriate reward for us to receive. Now, if the Father chooses to reward you richly, don't let anybody make you feel bad about it! Accept whatever it is that the Lord provides for you, great or small. Keep giving the same faithful, humble, and excellent service regardless of how much He puts into your hand or how much praise you receive. The more the Lord proves that He can trust you with His blessings, the more He will bless you. And all along the way, whether you are abased or abounding, choose to be content and to serve cheerfully. This is an act of faith in God alone.

When an army goes into battle, all lives are on the line. The sergeants may be making more money than the privates, even though the privates may be taking a greater risk. Not every paycheck in the military is the same. This is also true in God's kingdom. Some receive thirtyfold, others receive sixtyfold, and still others receive a hundredfold. (See Matthew 13:3–8.) The rate of return is up to the Father. Our part is to be grateful for whatever He gives us, to expect His reward, to receive it gratefully, and to stop looking to other people to compensate us for what we sacrifice on their behalf.

Our motivation for serving the Lord must never be the material return we anticipate. Our motivation must be our love for the Lord. Any material return is a fringe benefit He allocates. The real value of what we give is measured in things eternal.

## KINDHEARTED MASTERS

The same balance the Lord gives for husbands and wives or parents and children is stated in the relationship that masters are to have with their servants. Paul writes: "Ye masters, do the same things unto them, forbearing threatening: knowing that your Master also is in heaven; neither is there respect of persons with him" (Ephesians 6:9).

Those who are in a position of authority must never take advantage of the people who serve under their leadership. There is no place in God's kingdom for leaders who are domineering, vengeful, or motivated by anger or hatred for any individual or group of people, at any time or under any circumstances.

I personally believe that no person should ever be appointed to leadership until he has learned to follow. Good leaders are people who are also good followers. They understand the difficulties and challenges of serving someone as unto the Lord. If they have learned to serve people as unto the Lord, when they are at the top of the human leadership ladder they will still follow the Lord's leadership. In this position, more than ever before, they must be able to hear, submit to, and obey the leading of the Holy Spirit.

Joshua was a great leader because he was a faithful servant to Moses for many years. He remembered the difficulties of submitting to a flawed human being when he himself became the leader. Any time a person does not know what it's like to walk in the shoes of another person, the possibility exists for an abuse of power and for abusive behavior. For God to trust us with positions of authority, we must prove first that we know how to control our own desires and lusts for recognition, fame, and power. God-appointed leaders never lead by threat or force but rather lead through the compelling combination of love and righteousness.

What about those who find themselves in a situation where the master is abusive? Should they rebel? No. Paul states clearly that servants should obey their masters "with fear and trembling, in singleness of heart" (Ephesians 6:5). Is that a vulnerable position? Yes! But the person who chooses to remain submissive will be vindicated by God. Joshua learned this when he witnessed the deliverance of Israel from Pharaoh. God will remove any leader who consistently abuses His children.

It is dangerous to rebel against authority. Moreover, you can obey outwardly and still have an unsubmissive heart, which is still rebellion in God's eyes. Remember, God is interested in the heart, because if He has your heart He has *you*. On the other hand, you can submit in your heart and refuse to obey if your employer requests you do something against the Word of God. But you must remain submissive to the one in authority while you respectfully refuse to obey. Why? Maintaining a submissive heart and attitude is simply staying in fellowship with the Lord and doing His will. If you do not remain submissive inwardly, God will have to deal with your rebellious heart, and chastisement will occur not only for the abuser but for you.

Obviously, if the abuse is placing you in danger physically, emotionally, or spiritually, you must pray about quitting. Rest assured, however, eventually God will remove the abusive leader. I have seen

God remove people from leadership in all kinds of ways. When Pharaoh abused the children of Israel and refused to repent, God drowned him. I have also seen Him rescue the abused in all kinds of ways. He removed the Israelites from the abuse of Pharaoh with signs, wonders, and miracles.

Again, I cannot emphasize this strongly enough: It is a dangerous thing for those in authority to abuse a child of God. When a child of God is abused, the Lord will hear and respond to their distress. He will send a strong deliverer to set them free!

## LIKE JESUS

Just as soldiers must obey their commander, every believer is called to obey the Lord—and not occasionally but continually. We do not obey only when the circumstances seem right or when we like the person in authority, but we obey all those in authority over us as if we were obeying the Lord himself. Peter taught us a hard truth in his first epistle:

**Submit yourselves to every ordinance of man for the Lord's sake: whether it be to the king, as supreme; or unto governors, as unto them that are sent by him for the punishment of evildoers, and for the praise of them that do well.**
**—1 Peter 2:13–14**

We are to submit to the laws of men as though God himself had written them. We are to submit to all those in authority over us because God has set them in those positions. To rebel against them is to rebel against God. And if they require anything ungodly or unscriptural of us, we are to disobey outwardly but remain submissive inwardly. In this way our hearts stay pure before the Lord and our obedience to Him is complete.

Unfortunately, most of us probably rebel more for selfish reasons than scriptural convictions. We're in a hurry so we break the speed limit. Our boss is an insensitive tyrant and doesn't pay us what we're worth, so we add an hour here and there on our overtime. We believe the income tax is unconstitutional and oppressive, so we don't report the cash we received for doing odd jobs.

This rebellion and lawlessness is too common in the local church. We don't like the songs the choir director chooses so we quit the choir, even though God has called us there to learn submission to *that* choir director. So then we get involved in outreach, but the director of outreach is disorganized. We get so frustrated with her lack of administrative ability that we eventually quit that too. The truth is, we will go from one endeavor to the next until we learn to submit to authority, stop complaining, and do all things as unto the Lord. We will never be content until we master our selfish whims, put aside our personal agendas, and simply obey God by serving those He has set in authority over us.

When God places us under authority that is not pleasant or does not operate as we would operate, we know He is working on our level of submission to authority! He is preparing us for battle! He is showing us how to lay down our lives! If we are to be like Jesus, we must learn obedience to the point of crucifying our self and our flesh. Jesus poured His life out for us in obedience to the Father, and His example is the model we are to follow. We are to pour our life out for others in obedience to God.

If we are set in authority over others, we must pour our lives out in obedience to God more than ever. God will impart an anointing for us to lead, instruct, and set an example; but we must be even more sensitive and submissive to the Holy Spirit, carrying out our responsibilities with fear and trembling. Our leadership must bear the hallmarks of both the confidence and humility of Christ.

Obedience enables us to be all God designed us to be. It frees our potential and releases our ministries. But most important, when we learn obedience, we learn the foundation for waging war and winning. The Enemy will face a formidable fighting force when our army of Christian soldiers obeys those in authority and our officers model Jesus to those they lead. We will be of one mind, one heart, and one spirit, and nothing will cause us to break rank. The gates of hell shall not prevail against God's obedient church.

# 3

# BE STRONG
# AND STAND

**Finally, my brethren, be strong in the Lord, and in the power
of His might.**
**—Ephesians 6:10**

Finally, Paul has come to the crux of the matter, the place to
which he has been leading us for five and a half chapters. He revealed our incredible wealth in chapter 1, the rich treasury we have
in Christ Jesus. He has shared some of the deep secrets of the kingdom, that we are chosen in Christ Jesus from the foundation of the
world, adopted into the family of God, and accepted in the beloved.
He tells of our marvelous redemption and God's workmanship in
our lives in chapter 2. We are made alive by the blood of Jesus, no
longer bound by guilt and condemnation, and Gentile and Jew are
one in Him. We are saved and being saved every day by His grace,
seated with Him in the heavenlies, and the Enemy is under our feet.

Then, in chapter 3, Paul begins to teach us how we are
strengthened in our inner man by the power of the Holy Spirit, that
our response to all God has done for us is to bow our knees to the
Father. (See Ephesians 3:14.) He addresses our worship unto God
and explains that a constant attitude of worship releases God's holiness, power, and glory in our lives. Then, in chapters 4 and 5, he
turns our attention to our walk, that we are to walk worthy of the
calling God has placed on our lives, not only witnessing *about* Jesus,
but *being* a witness to those around us that Jesus is our Lord.

In chapter 5, Paul explores our role as the submissive bride of Christ and talks about our wedding to Christ Jesus. Then he continues to firmly instruct us in the principle of authority and submission in chapter 6, using the examples of children and parents and masters and servants. By the time we come to Ephesians 6:10, we are perfected for ministry and corporately edified, unified, and made doctrinally wind-resistant. Now Paul is going to tell us the point of everything we have learned and all the training we have been through: God has prepared us for spiritual warfare.

## STRONG IN THE LORD

After Moses died and Joshua became the leader of the children of Israel, God commanded Joshua to take the Promised Land and assured him of victory. Then He proceeded to command Joshua, not once but several times, to "be strong and of a good courage" (Joshua 1:6). The apostle Paul reiterates the same command to the church in Ephesians 6:10: "Finally, my brethren, be strong in the Lord, and in the power of his might."

Being "strong in the Lord" is not an option in the kingdom of God! We are commanded to be strong because every believer is involved in intense spiritual warfare, every day, in all areas of life. The original text translated *finally* means "to the rest" or "as for what remains for you to do." What remains for the church to do? We must "be strong in the Lord, and in the power of his might." We are chosen and prepared to do battle against all enemies of the kingdom of God. Finally—after Egypt and after the wilderness—we are matured and empowered to fight the good fight of faith!

The war in the spirit realm is an ongoing battle between the Lord Jesus Christ and Satan, and we are the body of Christ on this earth. Therefore, Satan is the Enemy of our souls. Before we were saved, he hated us because we were made in the image of God, but we were under his control. Now that we have received Jesus as our Lord and Savior and entered the kingdom of God, we are a threat to Satan's rule on earth. Jesus gave us authority over him! Paul is saying, "Finally, my brethren, it is time to use the authority you have through the blood of Jesus. This is a war from which you cannot and must not back down!"

As the Joshua generation, we are a warring bride, a fighting church, a possessing church that combats the adversary. We are taking back what rightfully belongs to the kingdom of God. There's no escaping the fight, not because we are a vengeful, hateful, warring people, but because the Enemy of our souls is vengeful and hateful and warring in nature. We engage in spiritual warfare because Satan opposes every step we take into the Promised Land. God has given His people a vision and a hope and a future that is sure, but His people must fight to possess all He has given.

At this point you may be asking, "Why does our loving heavenly Father make us fight for the blessing?" I firmly believe there are some things about God we cannot know or understand until we go through some struggles with His help and on His behalf—and He knows it. He knows that we will only learn and appreciate the keeping power of His Word and seek the guidance of His Spirit when we are in the middle of a strong battle. In the crucible of crisis, suddenly something we read or studied weeks or months ago appears in our thinking at just the right moment to give us hope and faith for that particular time and place.

It all begins with a vision, a dream, a word from God that lays the foundation and sets the compass for our life. Just as He sent Joshua into the Promised Land to spy out all that had been given Israel, he gives us a foretaste of the thing He desires to give us, and He shows us how much we will enjoy it. He shows us that He is going to do great and mighty things in our lifetime and that His provision is already on the way. And then all hell breaks loose! We cry out, "Lord, I thought the prophecy was that I was going to fulfill this great calling in your name, that the windows of heaven were opening to me, and that together we were going to do great exploits. Well, I crossed the Jordan like you told me to, but all I see is this great, impenetrable wall!"

If we had to summarize one principle related to the receiving of God's blessings, it would be this: *Not without a struggle.* Whatever God shows us, speaks to us, or puts in our spirit, or whatever has been prophesied to us about our ministry, our life, our finances, our children, our marriage, or our grandchildren, we must understand that it will not happen without a struggle on our part.

The Lord may show us Jericho and tell us it is ours, but we still must march around seven times, shout, and then defeat the inhabitants once the wall is down. (See Joshua 6.) The Lord may show us a land flowing with milk and honey and say to us, "This is yours," but it will still be up to us to rid the land of God's enemies before we can settle down and eat the grapes. (See Numbers 13:1–14:25.)

We can learn about the full wealth that belongs to us in Christ Jesus, but in order to obtain it, we are going to have to learn the skills of spiritual warfare. We are going to have to roll up our sleeves and do some hand-to-hand combat with the Enemy of our souls if we are going to drive him away from our blessing and claim it as our own.

You may be going through some things right now, and you're saying, "Lord, what in the world am I going to do? My finances are under attack. My marriage is under attack. My reputation is under attack." This is what you're going to do: Be strong in the Lord and in the power of His might!

Unfortunately, this generation of believers has been taught that anything that comes against us can simply be removed, gotten around, or cast out. The strength of God is not proven in how much we cast away. *The strength of God is proven in how much we endure.* Jesus proved His strength when they nailed Him to the tree and He kept preaching. Stephen didn't stop their stoning him, but he forgave his persecutors, looked up, and worshiped Jesus. This is being strong in the Lord and in the power of His might!

This generation of the church in America has not endured much of anything. It's going to be embarrassing when many of us get to heaven and gather with the saints of the ages. They will talk about being beheaded, skinned alive, boiled to death, tortured, and seeing their whole family executed. In this country, we think suffering for the Lord is sitting through a service when the air-conditioning has gone out. Suffering for the Lord is not getting our usual parking spot and having to walk across the parking lot to get to church. In a testimony service in heaven, would we have anything significant to say? How dare we complain about these light afflictions! If we don't get busy, we're not going to have anything to say in heaven. We'll be in the back row, over in the corner, with our head down, saying, "Thank you, Lord, for letting me in. I'm just glad to hang out with these good brothers and sisters."

We are to take up our cross and go forward. But when we fight to possess the promises of God and fulfill His calling, the Scripture verse we are studying says that we are not to fight in our own strength: "Finally, my brethren, be strong in *the Lord,* and in the power of *his* might" (Ephesians 6:10, emphasis mine).

Any time people attempt to go into battle against spiritual forces in their own strength, they invite disaster into their lives, setting themselves up for heartache and failure. The Greek language in this verse gives us a key to receiving the strength of the Lord. The phrase "be strong" means being "empowered." Paul is saying, "Allow God to fill you with His power."

The image here is not of an athlete who has become strong because he has worked out. Believers who are strong become so because they receive the strength of God from God himself. They allow God to empower them.

The phrase "the power of his might" is full of meaning also. We could translate these words as "Finally, allow yourselves to be made strong by the power of His power." We must allow the Lord to empower us with the very essence and substance of His power.

## IT'S A BIG PUT-ON

It's one thing for Paul to tell us, "Just allow God to fill you with His power," and it's another thing to know how to allow God to do that. Do we just go into our prayer closet, close our eyes, and say, "Do it, God"? I don't know about you, but I need a little more explanation of this process. Thank God, the Holy Spirit gives it to us: "Put on the whole armour of God, that ye may be able to stand against the wiles of the devil" (Ephesians 6:11).

As an act of our will, we are to allow God to empower us by suiting up in His armor. Only then can we hold our ground when the Devil assaults us. We stand immovable and unshakable against the attacks of the Enemy and defeat him with God's power and might when we put on the armor of God.

The truth is, we don't have any idea what we look like in God's armor or what it can do until we put it on. Most of us have gone shopping for clothes, and we look through racks and racks of different things. We know, however, that until we take that new outfit back to the dressing room, remove everything that goes with the old outfit, and actually put on the new clothes, we are never going to get a true picture of what it will look like.

The same is true when it comes to spiritual clothes. We must put off the old man to fully see and appreciate the new man. We must take off every natural piece of armor to fully see and appreciate our spiritual armor. Paul describes this casting-off-and-putting-on process in a number of his letters:

The night is far spent, the day is at hand: let us therefore cast off the works of darkness, and let us put on the armour of light.
—Romans 13:12

For as many of you as have been baptized into Christ have put on Christ.
—Galatians 3:27

To put on the *whole* armor, we must strip off every warring device of the carnal man, every weapon and strategy of the flesh we have used to engage in natural fights, overcome natural obstacles, and endure natural phenomenon. We must put off our own ideas and strategies and put on God's armor and strategy for fighting in the spirit realm.

We must take off lies and put on truth.

We must put away sin and put on righteousness.

We must cast off guilt and death and put on salvation and eternal life.

We must get rid of strife and put on peace.

We must put off doubt and unbelief and put on faith.

We must put away ignorance and put on knowledge of the Word.

Every piece of spiritual armor is vital, and no piece of the old natural armor can be retained, because none of it is suitable for the spiritual fight ahead. The old weaponry and strategies are only going to weigh us down, slow us down, and cause us to stumble in the heat of battle.

It's almost difficult to fathom that this is the same Paul who, just a few verses before in chapter 5 of Ephesians, wrote about our intimacy with the Lord. We enjoy the gentle embrace of Jesus as He holds His bride tenderly in His arms, our head lying on His breast, covered by His love and protection. Now suddenly we are moved from the warmth of His touch to the battlefield of the soul! But friend, that's the way life is: One minute you are worshiping God with ecstasy and the next you are in the heat of spiritual battle. And it's all God! He's the God of the warm and intimate embrace, and He's the God of fierce and enduring battle—and you cannot win a spiritual battle without being intimate with the Lord.

Think again of our analogy of the dressing room, which is a private place in which we can put on new clothes. Our spiritual dressing room is lying in the arms of our Bridegroom, the place where we become strong in the Lord and in the power of His might. In the secret place of the Most High, under the shadow of Almighty God, is the private place where we put on His armor and receive our battle plan. *We must first be the bride of Christ to become a warring church!*

## STAND, STAND, STAND

The very thought of armor evokes a picture of war—battling, fighting, and life-and-death conflict. There's no need for armor unless we are in imminent danger of being injured or destroyed by an enemy. The armor Paul tells us to put on is armor aimed at diverting a disaster. We must wear this armor if we intend to stand against the onslaughts of the Devil: "Put on the whole armour of God, that ye may be able to stand against the wiles of the devil" (Ephesians 6:11).

I find these words of Paul extremely encouraging. For the Lord to tell me to put on armor so that I might stand indicates to me that I'm in the right spot. When the time comes for the Lord to tell me to suit up for a fight, the Lord has me precisely where He wants me to be. It's as if He walked me right up to my destiny and said, "We're here on the edge of your Promised Land. Don't let any of the things you see make you think that what lies ahead of you isn't for you. Don't look at how high the wall is or how many enemy chariots you see. Don't see how many problems are coming against you. Don't focus on your inner weaknesses and fears. I've brought you here. Now all you have to do is to suit up in my armor and stand until the land is yours!"

To stand is to both obtain and maintain what God has given us. We must never enter a spiritual battle thinking that we simply need to fight it and win it and never think about it again. Once we have obtained a promise of God, we must continue to stand strong in the power of His might in order to maintain our position and blessing.

Don't let the wind blow you this way and that or move you to the left or to the right. Don't let the cunning persuasion of men sway you from your spot. Once God has placed you in a position, stand there until He calls you to move forward. Celebrate your victory, but never let down your guard. You must continue to stand if you intend to keep what God has given you!

Paul had some interesting things to say about Satan's attempts to break him:

And now, behold, I go bound in the spirit unto Jerusalem, not knowing the things that shall befall me there: Save that the Holy Ghost witnesseth in every city, saying that bonds and afflictions abide me. *But none of these things move me,* neither count I my life dear unto myself, so that I might finish my course with joy, and the ministry, which I have received of the Lord Jesus, to testify the gospel of the grace of God.
**—Acts 20:22–24 (emphasis mine)**

Even though Paul knew great trials awaited him if he continued his call to preach the Gospel, he refused to be dislodged from his spot in the Lord. He was fully girded up in the armor of God, and he refused to be moved from the territory He had given him. He refused to give in and return to reliance upon fleshly desires and human caution. He refused to be constrained by a desire to take it easy and let others carry the banner of the Gospel.

God calls and equips us and empowers us to progress, but He also calls us to stand in our faith, fully clothed in His armor, so that we don't digress. It is up to us to stand in the land where He has placed us until He calls us to move forward and claim more land. The armor is God's, but the stand is ours. Armor doesn't stand up by itself! We stand in the armor.

Furthermore, there's no need to put armor on a person who is running away! God's armor is for those who are going to stand and defend those things that are truly important to them. Is there anything today that God has given you about which you feel strongly enough to stand with all your faith? That's the stuff you want the armor for! The armor God gives you is used to stand against the Enemy so that he cannot take back what God has already given to you in the spirit realm.

Are you willing to stand for your eternal salvation and the gift of the Holy Spirit within you?

Are you willing to stand for your peace?

Are you willing to stand for the salvation of your children?

Are you willing to stand for your marriage and your family?

Are you willing to stand for the opportunity to preach the Gospel?

Are you willing to stand for the ministry the Lord has given to you?

In case you are questioning the importance of standing, notice how many times Paul repeats the word *stand* in this passage about spiritual warfare:

**Put on the whole armour of God, that ye may be able to *stand* against the wiles of the devil. . . . Wherefore take unto you the whole armour of God, that ye may be able to *withstand* in the evil day, and having done all, to *stand*. *Stand* therefore.**
**—Ephesians 6:11, 13–14 (emphasis mine)**

As for me and my house, we will choose to be strong in the Lord, then stand and keep on standing!

# 4

# KNOW YOUR FOE

M ost of us in the body of Christ know who we are fighting in the spirit realm. Whether we call him the Devil, Satan, or the Evil One, he is the Enemy of the Lord Jesus Christ and of our own souls. What many of us do not know is where and how he strikes. We don't know his tactics. We don't understand the spirit realm in which he operates. But if we are going to defeat him, we need to know where and how he works.

## WHERE IS THE ENEMY?

When Joshua began his campaign to conquer the Promised Land and faced the formidable wall of Jericho, Jesus appeared to him:

And it came to pass, when Joshua was by Jericho, that he lifted up his eyes and looked, and, behold, there stood a man over against him with his sword drawn in his hand: and Joshua went unto him, and said unto him, Art thou for us, or for our adversaries? And he said, Nay; but as captain of the host of the Lord am I now come. And Joshua fell on his face to the earth, and did worship, and said unto him, What saith my lord unto his servant? And the captain of the Lord's host said unto Joshua, Loose thy shoe from off thy foot; for the place whereon thou standest is holy. And Joshua did so. Now Jericho was straitly shut up because of the children of Israel: none went out, and none came in.

—Joshua 5:13–6:1

Then Jesus gave him explicit instructions about how to take the city, which was heavily fortified:

And the Lord said unto Joshua, See, I have given into thine hand Jericho, and the king thereof, and the mighty men of valour. And ye shall compass the city, all ye men of war, and go round about the city once. Thus shalt thou do six days. And seven priests shall bear before the ark seven trumpets of rams' horns: and the seventh day ye shall compass the city seven times, and the priests shall blow with the trumpets. And it shall come to pass, that when they make a long blast with the ram's horn, and when ye hear the sound of the trumpet, all the people shall shout with a great shout; and the wall of the city shall fall down flat, and the people shall ascend up every man straight before him.

—Joshua 6:2–5

The Bible records that when Joshua did exactly as Jesus commanded, the wall of Jericho fell down flat and the city was Israel's. Thank God, Jesus is our Captain too! He knows how to gain the victory over all the demons because He crushed them at the resurrection. Earlier in the book of Ephesians, Paul declared that Jesus overcame death and was raised and seated "far above all principality and power and might and dominion and every name that is named." He is the Warrior who defeated all enemies and "put all things under his feet." (See Ephesians 1:19–22.)

Jesus revealed to Joshua that Jericho would be his when the wall came down, and Joshua understood that the wall was merely the key that unlocked the city. Let me tell you two things about your problems and the challenges that stand between you and the promises of God that are yours. *First, your promise is locked up behind a problem.* A problem is nothing but a door to a promise. Don't allow the problem to intimidate you from getting the promise! The promise is yours to possess. It's simply trapped behind a wall like Jericho, and Jesus is your wall-toppling Captain!

*Second, you must fight* when Jesus tells you how to unlock the promise. He knows it and you need to recognize it. You need to know there will be a struggle, and you cannot be paralyzed or discouraged by that fact. You need to know that the fight will take place and you have no need to fear. How can you know you are about to engage in a struggle and not be afraid? Because your faith is in Jesus Christ, the Living Word of God!

"Through faith we understand that the worlds were framed by the word of God, so that things which are seen were not made of things which do appear" (Hebrews 11:3). God is saying to us that everything we call physical was manifested from something spiritual. We also understand that the spiritual reality becomes physical reality as the Word of God is spoken in faith. The promises of God are ours the moment we believe them in our hearts and then confess them in faith. Jesus declared this principle of the kingdom of God:

And Jesus answering saith unto them, Have faith in God. For verily I say unto you, That whosoever shall say unto this mountain, Be thou removed, and be thou cast into the sea; and shall not doubt in his heart, but shall believe that those things which he saith shall come to pass; he shall have whatsoever he saith. Therefore I say unto you, What things soever ye desire, when ye pray, believe that ye receive them, and ye shall have them.
—**Mark 11:22–24**

Right now we must recognize that we live simultaneously in two spheres of existence—the spiritual realm and the natural realm—and our enemy is in the spiritual realm. The spiritual realm is the "parent" realm from which everything natural is given birth. The natural realm is an outworking of the spiritual realm. Therefore, if we are to be successful in defeating the Enemy, we must defeat him in the spiritual realm. Then the natural realm will fall in line with what has been accomplished in the Spirit.

At every moment and in every situation, Jesus knows where the Enemy is and what he is doing to try to wreak havoc in the body of Christ. Our challenge is to follow Jesus in the Spirit and stop the Devil before he even gets started!

## WHO IS THE ENEMY?

Put on the whole armour of God, that ye may be able to stand against the wiles of the devil. For we wrestle not against flesh and blood, but against principalities, against powers, against the rulers of the darkness of this world, against spiritual wickedness in high places.

**—Ephesians 6:11–12**

Our Bridegroom is issuing a battle cry to His warrior bride, and that cry is not against people, but against spiritual evil. One thing we must always remember about spiritual warfare is that our battle is against the Enemy of our souls, Satan and his demonic forces. We are never against people, particularly our brothers and sisters in Christ. Although the Enemy may manifest himself through human beings, our warfare is against the principalities, the powers, and the rulers of darkness that are causing evil behavior.

Believers are in a deadly wrestling match. *Principalities* refers to rulers and authorities, in this context speaking of the demonic realm. This term points to the existence of a political organization in the demonic realm, a hierarchy of ranking demons who have authority over territories.

*Powers* is used in Scripture for ability. It most often implies authority. Paul is telling us that within the political hierarchy of demonic beings, some have authority over others. Then we have the "rulers," who are literally world rulers of this darkness. The text here is not referring to government officials, kings, or dictators. This passage peers into the spiritual realm, where these rulers preside over the "darkness of this world," or Satan's kingdom. You might call these evil territorial spirits.

This evil hierarchy makes life miserable on planet earth. No matter what people do to us, we must be mindful that they are not our enemy, and we are never to seek revenge or restitution. We are to forgive our offenders, turn them over to God, and look to Him for justice and mercy. Throughout the Scriptures we find admonitions that our battle belongs to God and that He alone exacts vengeance: "Dearly beloved, avenge not yourselves, but rather give place unto wrath: for it is written, Vengeance is mine; I will repay, saith the Lord" (Romans 12:19).

"For we know him that hath said, Vengeance belongeth unto me, I will recompense, saith the Lord. And again, the Lord shall judge his people. It is a fearful thing to fall into the hands of the living God" (Hebrews 10:30–31).

So how do we battle when people hurt and wound us, defraud

us, and seek to destroy us in some way? The wiles of the Devil are mental attacks. He assaults our minds with evil, deceptive thoughts, and he counts on the fact that we will believe these to be our thoughts and will accept them as truth. Primarily, our battle is fought in the mind.

The Greek word for *wiles* means "trickery." This word covers evil thinking, evil strategies, and evil motivations. Because Satan was utterly defeated and rendered powerless at the cross and resurrection of Jesus Christ, he must persuade us that he has power and deceive us into seeing and doing things his way. Therefore, in order to control our wills, he and his demons direct their trickery toward our minds.

The Devil seeks to turn us against people while he hides in the shadows of deception. You've probably experienced this many times, usually without knowing it. You're troubled about something, and you don't even know what it is. You drive around and around, but you don't know where you're going. The Devil introduces an entire thought process that will convince you that your problem is your boss: *He's working you too hard. He doesn't understand you. Your work is valueless and unappreciated.* And you become obsessed with this horrible situation.

In reality, you're not fighting with flesh and blood—your boss—but with demons of restlessness and fear who are making you believe lies to get you to abort God's will for your life. If you don't stop those thoughts dead in their tracks and cast down the vain imaginations, you will do something completely contrary to God's will and plan for your life. You will hurt yourself and others.

What will keep you straight and focused in spiritual warfare is to remember at all times that people are not your enemy. Your battle is with Satan and his demonic forces.

## HOW DOES THE ENEMY OPERATE?

Put on the whole armour of God, that ye may be able to stand against the wiles of the devil. For we wrestle not against flesh and blood, but against principalities, against powers, against the rulers of the darkness of this world, against spiritual wickedness in high places.

**—Ephesians 6:11–12**

In the sport of wrestling, when you wrestle someone, your body is pressed against his. All your strength and knowledge of the sport is concentrated on pinning your opponent so that he cannot move and is rendered powerless. When the apostle Paul spoke of wrestling to the Ephesians, however, he described a hand-to-hand, face-to-face combat that proved to be a brutal end for the loser. In the Roman Empire, the loser had his eyes gouged out! Paul is clearly saying, "You've got to know what you're doing because you cannot lose this battle!" We are in a wrestling match with an enemy whose sole intent is to steal, kill, and destroy us. (See John 10:10.)

We need to know that the Devil is not impulsive in his attacks against us. He develops strategies, plans, and schemes. He calculates his moves, anticipates our counter moves, and waits patiently, like the snake he is, to strike us at our weakest moment. That is why it seems he always attacks us when we're down. He attacks when he feels it will have the maximum impact. He wants to stop us dead in our tracks. He wants our vehicles to run out of fuel, our soldiers to run out of resolve, our weapons to run out of ammunition, and our faith to fizzle out.

Yes, we have been given authority over Satan and his evil de-monic cohorts through the name and the blood of Jesus Christ, but we must never underestimate their cunning craftiness and trickery. They've been around a lot longer than we have and are a lot smarter than we are! Our natural understanding, therefore, is worthless against their knowledge and ability. That is why we must put on the armor *of God* and stand in the strength *of the Lord*. We cannot fight and win a spiritual war in our own strength or understanding. We must have the mind and might of Christ.

So many in the body of Christ live in a terrible state of confu-sion and difficulty simply because they do not take every thought captive and line up their thinking with the Word of God. Paul strongly admonishes us in his second letter to the Corinthians:

**For though we walk in the flesh, we do not war after the flesh: (For the weapons of our warfare are not carnal, but mighty through God to the pulling down of strong holds;) casting down imaginations, and every high thing that exalteth itself against the knowledge of God, and bringing into captivity every thought to the obedience of Christ.**

**—2 Corinthians 10:3–5**

Christians are having nervous breakdowns, having stress attacks, and losing their minds because Satan sends demons to attack them in their thought life and they do not cast down those imaginations that are against God and His Word. Husbands are leaving their wives, and they don't know why. They just say, "I have to go. It's not that I don't love you. I'll send you money. No, it's not another woman."

In another home, a woman has fallen in love with somebody else's husband and she's out of control. She doesn't even know why she loves him. He's not somebody she would be attracted to. But she thinks about him so much she's dreaming about him.

Evil spirits are planting thoughts in our minds that are not our thoughts, and we must cast them down. For example, today with the shootings in schools and in churches, many parents are frightened for their children. This is what the Devil wants! He wants us to be tormented and fearful, because then our faith is completely ineffective. We are the ones who are hiding in corners trying to survive when we should be out jeopardizing every tactic of the Enemy.

When we send our children off to school and suddenly our heart jumps into our throat because a picture of them being gunned down races through our mind—that is demonic and we must immediately submit our minds to God's Word and drive that mental image out. Say, "My children are taught of the Lord, and great is the peace of my children. I plead the blood of Jesus over my children. Satan, you have no right to harm them in any way. I take authority over you through the name and by the blood of Jesus Christ. I declare any strategies or attacks you have planned for my children to be null and void, this day and forever!" We do battle in the spirit until the Holy Spirit floods our hearts again with the peace that passes all understanding.

If we think any thought that is contrary to what God says in His Word—no matter how pleasant it is—we must put it down also. In most cases, the Devil will introduce a thought pattern that is not terrifying but very comfortable and pleasing, something that strokes our flesh and makes our ego tingle with excitement. But we must fight as hard as we fought for our children! We must submit ourselves immediately to God and His Word, resist the Devil, and cause him to flee! (See James 4:7.) It's a fight to hold our homes together and resist the warm fantasy of an affair. It's a fight to finish our assignments and not go to the movies instead. It's a fight to walk in love toward people and make war against evil spirits instead of satisfying our flesh by seeking revenge. And sometimes it's a fight just to get out of bed in the morning!

Our fight is in the supernatural realm, but the church has become so worldly that the minute someone has a problem, we automatically respond, "She needs counseling." We want to sit down and use our human understanding to solve problems that are spiritual. Oftentimes we judge the person who is oppressed. We think we are so smart! The fact is, we are totally ignorant of the reality of spiritual matters and walk in the futility of our intellect. Many of those with problems need *deliverance from* them, not *counseling about* them. Others need to learn how to fight spiritual battles and win them. Still others need to be encouraged in their spiritual battle to stand strong until the victory comes.

Just a generation ago, there were those in the church who didn't "counsel" anybody. They put a person on the altar! They would plead the blood of Jesus over that person and begin calling on His name. They didn't know much Greek or Hebrew, and they hadn't studied theology or church history, but they would call on His name and plead the blood. And when they did, the power of God would break through in that person's life and freedom would burst forth! They knew who their real enemy was, so oppressive evil was set to flight and lives were changed. Our fathers and mothers of the faith knew how to wrestle the Enemy to the ground *in the spiritual realm.*

The revelation the Holy Spirit wants to give us in these verses of Scripture is that we are fighting a very organized and intelligent horde of evil beings. They have studied humans for thousands of years. They worked on our fathers and mothers, our grandfathers and grandmothers, all the way back to Adam and Eve. They know every weakness and every strength, and how to turn them all against us. But God has given us a powerful and mighty redemption from this evil! Our hope and assurance of victory is to walk this earth in Christ, stay suited up in the armor of God, and refuse to back down from what God has promised in His Word.

# DON'T QUIT!

**Wherefore take unto you the whole armour of God, that ye may be able to withstand in the evil day, and having done all, to stand.**

**—Ephesians 6:13**

Paul says, "Wherefore," or because you are fighting spiritual wickedness, you are to "take unto you the whole armour of God." The Greek language used for "take unto you" gives us great insight into the seriousness of Paul's admonition. "Take unto you" is like a military command that is to be obeyed immediately and for all time. You are to put on God's armor right now and never even consider taking it off. You are to maintain discipline over your flesh and keep your spirit alert so that the Holy Spirit can keep you apprised of the Enemy's movements at all times.

When we persevere in the Spirit and keep the armor of God on, we will "be able to withstand in the evil day." I have underlined that word *day* in my Bible because that says to me that the Devil's attack is only for a day! He has a limit. He won't last if we'll put on our armor and fight. If we'll stand, his attack will soon be over and he'll have to flee.

Two of the greatest wiles of the Devil are *discouragement* and *exhaustion*. If all else fails, he will simply come at us again and again and again to wear us down and get us to quit. When Jesus was in the wilderness and Satan tempted Him, He stood against the Devil with the Word of God until the Devil simply couldn't stay any longer. The Bible says, "Then the devil leaveth him" (Matthew 4:11). His time was up. Jesus outlasted him, and he had to go.

Today, we don't see Joshua and the children of Israel still circling the wall of Jericho! No! They had a certain number of times to march and then their shout of victory brought the wall to the ground. So be encouraged! The evil coming against you only has a "day"! If you keep standing, his day will soon be over. Whatever is coming against you in the spirit realm isn't permanent. It isn't going to last that long—not if you'll keep God's armor on and stand. Maybe the sun is already setting, the day is nearly over, and evil is about to flee into the night. Paul wrote to the Galatians, "And let us not be weary in well doing: for in due season we shall reap, if we faint not" (Galatians 6:9).

How many believers have not possessed the promises and blessings of God purely because they got tired of the struggle and quit just moments before all was theirs? How many were inches away from conquering their land and they dropped their sword or their shield to the ground? That thought makes my entire being shudder! What would have happened if Joshua had quit before the seventh time around the walls of Jericho? What would have happened if he gave up before the shout?

*O God, help us to stop running in our own strength and be endued with yours, to listen to the voice of our Captain and follow His battle plan, to keep your armor on at all times, and when we've done all, to continue resisting the discouraging wiles of the Devil until the victory is manifested.*

When we know our enemy, understand his tactics, stay suited in the whole armor of God, and refuse to budge from His perfect will for our lives, we can defeat the Enemy and keep him defeated. We can love people, hate evil, and stay focused on the prize until it is ours.

# 5

# THE ARMOR OF GOD PART ONE: TRUTH, RIGHTEOUSNESS, AND PEACE

---

The main thing to remember about the armor of God is that it's *God's* armor. You can't go out to the department store and put on this armor. You cannot think about His armor or imagine yourself in His armor. You have to move from the outer court of praise into the Holy of Holies of worship and completely surrender to God in order to put on His armor. This is holy armor!

**Stand therefore, having your loins girt about with truth, and having on the breastplate of righteousness; and your feet shod with the preparation of the gospel of peace; above all, taking the shield of faith, wherewith ye shall be able to quench all the fiery darts of the wicked. And take the helmet of salvation, and the sword of the Spirit, which is the word of God.**
**—Ephesians 6:14–17**

Every piece of the armor of God pertains to our identity in Christ Jesus. The illustration of external armor reflects the internal reality of being *in Him*. Each piece is a mirror image of a spiritual truth concerning who we are in Christ.

Who is our truth? Jesus Christ!

Who is our righteousness? Jesus Christ!

Who is the one who establishes us in the Gospel of peace? Jesus Christ!

Who is the author and finisher of our faith? Jesus Christ!

Who is our Savior? Jesus Christ!

Who is the living, incarnate Word of God? Jesus Christ!

All of the armor we wear for spiritual battle is found in Christ Jesus!

No doubt the apostle Paul was thinking of the armor of the Roman soldier when he received the revelation of our spiritual armor from the Holy Spirit. From the many times he was imprisoned and heavily guarded by them, Paul spent hours in the company of the Roman guard. He was well familiar with their armor!

This analogy only applies to a certain point, however. The natural armor *covered* a Roman soldier from head to foot, but our spiritual armor permeates and purifies our entire being. The armor of God fully equips us for the spiritual war we wage in spirit, soul, and body. No matter how big we are on the outside, we are ten feet tall and filled with the glory and power of God on the inside when we suit up in God's armor. Putting on the armor of God makes us holy as He is holy, and it all begins with facing the truth and getting rid of all the lies.

## LOINS GIRT ABOUT WITH TRUTH

Paul begins with a belt or girdle, which the Roman soldier wore around his loins. This piece held some of the other pieces of armor in place, including the breastplate, which was attached to it, and the sword, which hung from it. The support and tension around the middle of the soldier's body also served as an attitude check, saying to the soldier, "You're here to fight. You've got a job to do. Keep focused."

The obvious application is that we cannot accomplish anything for the kingdom of God if our lives are not based on truth. In the Greek, this word *truth* does not only refer to God's written Word but to an honesty of heart and purity of motive. We cannot win a spiritual battle if we are lying to ourselves, deceiving others, and running from the conviction of the Holy Spirit. Our foundation is shifting sand, and we will be tossed to and fro by the wiles of the Devil if we do not stand in truth.

Being brutally honest with ourselves is often difficult and many times painful. Ask any woman who wears a girdle or any soldier who has cinched up that belt around his loins—it isn't very comfortable! The belt of truth squeezes us! It causes us to come clean with God and get real about our lives.

Our "loins" also represent our reproductive organs, the most private area of our bodies. When we allow the Holy Spirit to deal with deception and lies in our lives, all our secret places that perhaps no one but our spouses know about are laid bare before Him. These are areas where we are so deceived we don't even know we're deceived. These are areas where we are so ashamed, we are embarrassed that God knows about them. The trouble is, the Enemy knows about these secret places too! That's why I believe the Holy Spirit begins with truth. *Truth is the foundation for the entire armor.* If we do not get healed and delivered in these weak areas of our lives, the Devil will use them to divert us from God's plan and eventually destroy us.

Since the loins are our reproductive organs, Paul is also saying to the Ephesians, "Don't reproduce anything that is not rooted in truth. Don't reproduce anything that is based upon a lie. Reproduce God's truth." This is a powerful principle of the kingdom of God! Our loins contain the potential of our God-given creativity to reproduce spiritual things that will extend into eternity, things that will have everlasting value and significance! Unfortunately, our loins also have the capability to reproduce a lie.

Many Christians today are reproducing things based on anything but the truth of God's Word. They are reproducing their past. They are acting on the basis of something the Lord declared null and void long ago. Some are reproducing things based upon what others have said about them. Others are acting on the basis of insufficient information, and in many cases, false information. Still others are reproducing things based upon what they see and know in the temporal, natural realm. They are acting on the basis of information that is not eternal.

We should never engage in the production of anything that rests upon a false premise, but deal only in honesty and truth as we engage in any form of ministry or battle with the Enemy. We must speak only God's truth about ourselves, and we must engage only in those activities that are in line with the truth of God, those things that God declares to be holy, pure, and righteous. We must act only as we know Jesus would act because He is literally walking in our shoes by the power of the Holy Spirit in us. *When our loins are girded with truth, we are completely identified in our innermost being with Christ Jesus.*

The Enemy will always try to sidetrack us by enticing us to lie and operate according to that lie. Jesus called our enemy the father of all liars and said that no truth was to be found in him. (See John 8:44.) He will try to get us into frustration and restlessness and worry on the basis of lies. He may present the thought that we aren't worthy of God's promises, that we are not good enough, that our past negates our future, that we can't truly minister in the Lord's name, and he'll say, "What you see is what you're always going to get." Our response to these lies is to declare what *God* says about us—now and forever!

The Devil may also use another, more deadly tactic on us. He will reinforce our comfort with sin. He will say things like, "The grace of God is so great, go ahead and sin for a little while. He'll forgive you later. Look at that magazine. Take a drink. Smoke that joint. Fantasize about another man's wife. Have an affair. The IRS won't miss that amount. Just take the dress. God knows you need it and you don't have the money." The moment the snake introduces these evil thoughts and desires, we must jerk ourselves up on our most holy faith and declare the truth! "Devil, my trust and comfort are in God and God alone, so get out of my life!"

Any involvement in *lying* also endangers us. Speaking a lie destroys trust, a vital component in our relationships. When we lie about someone else, we disrupt our relationship with that person, other people's relationships with that person, and our relationship with God. When lying occurs frequently in a body of believers, eventually no one trusts anyone else, and some will not even trust God.

Believing and acting upon a lie of the Devil is a terrible experience, but it doesn't necessarily mean we don't trust God. We may be honestly deceived. However, deliberately lying about something or someone is simply not trusting God to work all things for our good. We step in to cover our tracks and clean up the mess ourselves, but in the end we make a bigger mess than we started with. So it always pays to tell the truth and to be totally honest with God, with ourselves, and with others.

When you are girded with truth, you are planted squarely on the rock of Jesus Christ, and every other piece of armor can be securely fastened onto you. But don't even think about putting on the breastplate of righteousness or the sword of the Spirit if you aren't girded with truth!

## THE BREASTPLATE OF RIGHTEOUSNESS

The Roman soldier's breastplate covered everything from his shoulders to his loins, and its main purpose was to protect him from a life-threatening wound to the heart. In God's armor, righteousness deals with the essence of our spiritual condition in Christ, keeping our hearts pure and open to God. Although we hear and use the term *righteousness* frequently in the church, do we really know what it means?

Righteousness originates in God alone. It is His standard of motive, behavior, and character. God embodies righteousness because everything He says and does is absolutely, eternally *right*. When the Word of God declares that we are righteous through the blood of Jesus, we are absolutely, eternally right with God. Moreover, we are like God in our spirit. The Bible tells us that through Adam we were made sinners, but through Jesus Christ we are *made* righteous: "For as by one man's disobedience many were made sinners, so by the obedience of one shall many be made righteous" (Romans 5:19).

Notice that we were *made* righteous, not *covered* with righteousness. In the Old Testament, the blood sacrifices covered believers. God demonstrated this first when He killed animals and used their skins to cover Adam and Eve's nakedness after they had sinned. But in the New Testament, Jesus Christ made the absolute, eternal blood sacrifice so that believers could *be* righteous. The Greek word used for *made* indicates a permanent condition of *being*.

The Word of God says that we become the righteousness of God the moment we believe in Jesus Christ and are saved. Afterward, when we put on the breastplate of righteousness as believers, we are literally allowing the righteousness of God to manifest in our lives. We are coming to grips with our identity as children of God, made in His image. We are not to take His righteousness and cover our sinful nature because we now have God's nature in our hearts. We are simply choosing to live from God's nature and righteousness instead of our own.

We must never count on our own righteousness! The Bible declares that our righteousness is as filthy rags before the Father: "But we are all as an unclean thing, and all our righteousnesses are as filthy rags; and we all do fade as a leaf; and our iniquities, like the wind, have taken us away" (Isaiah 64:6).

This verse means we are never justified in saying, "I am righteous because I have lived a good life. My grandfather was a Christian and my father was a Christian and I'm a Christian. I'm a good person. I go to church and sing in the choir. I give to the poor!"

No! Our righteousness must rest only in the shed blood of Jesus Christ, which transforms our lives from the inside out and wraps us up in His identity. Then our only legitimate declaration to the Enemy is not what we have made of ourselves but what Jesus has made us to be in Him. The truth is, we have no power over the Enemy and even place ourselves in his hands when we stand in our own goodness.

When we start declaring our self-righteousness to the Devil, we place ourselves in great jeopardy because it is impossible to withstand the attacks of the Enemy in our own goodness. We open up ourselves to the Devil's scorn, and he's going to laugh in our faces. He's going to say, "And who are you?"

Remember the seven sons of a man named Sceva? They didn't possess the righteousness of Jesus Christ, and they attempted to cast out an evil spirit in Jesus' name. The evil spirit responded, "Jesus I know, and Paul I know; but who are ye?" (Acts 19:15). As a result, the "man in whom the evil spirit was leaped on them, and overcame them, and prevailed against them, so that they fled out of that house naked and wounded" (Acts 19:16). It's not a good idea to stand in your own righteousness!

Our righteousness does not stand in anything we have done, are doing, or will ever do. No person can earn righteousness or attain it on their own merits. Our righteousness exists solely because we are in relationship with the only Righteous One who ever walked this earth. Paul wrote to the Philippians, "And be found in him, not having mine own righteousness, which is of the law, but that which is through the faith of Christ, the righteousness which is of God by faith" (Philippians 3:9).

When we put on the breastplate of righteousness and identify fully with Jesus Christ, we purge ourselves of sin, make our flesh come in line, and put off the old man. We allow God's righteousness to come forth in our motives, our thoughts, and our deeds. Then we are in a position to bear spiritual fruit, to discern and display all things that are excellent, and we are called "sincere and without offense till the day of Christ" (Philippians 1:10). Paul wrote to the Philippians: "Being filled with the fruits of righteousness, which are by Jesus Christ, unto the glory and praise of God" (Philippians 1:11).

The righteousness of Jesus Christ puts us in the spiritual position to choose the right things, do the right things, say the right things, and stand holy and spotless before the Enemy. Confronted with the righteousness of God, the Devil must flee from us! He cannot wound our hearts, because God's breastplate of righteousness is in place. All he sees is the bride of Christ, and the Bible tells us how we are clothed:

**Let us be glad and rejoice, and give honour to him: for the marriage of the Lamb is come, and his wife hath made herself ready. And to her was granted that she should be arrayed in fine linen, clean and white: for the fine linen is the righteousness of saints.**
**—Revelation 19:7–8**

Putting on the breastplate of righteousness purifies and protects our hearts and centers our lives on God. When we meditate on and wonder at the awesome reality that we are righteous through Jesus' blood, that the Father looks at us and sees a pure, shining-bright saint and not the terrible sinner we have been, all we want to do is that which is right in God's eyes! None of the Devil's temptations hold any allure for us. None of his lies entice us because all we want is God. A purified heart is a protected heart and a strong heart. None of the tactics of the Devil will prevail when our hearts beat with the righteousness of God through Jesus Christ our Lord!

## THE GOSPEL OF PEACE

Paul tells us to put on the armor of God so we can stand against evil, but how can we stand if our feet are injured or not working properly? Remember Mephibosheth, Jonathan's son and King Saul's grandson? He was dropped on his feet as a small child. As a result, he was lame in both feet and had to be carried everywhere he went. (See 2 Samuel 4:4.) This is not a picture of standing strong!

Physically, our feet provide balance to our entire body and are a major component of our ability to move from one place to another. When our feet are injured our whole body is affected. Although our feet are precious parts of our body, they are often neglected and overlooked until something happens to them.

It is so important to protect our feet from harm, which is why wearing the proper shoes is vital. Though shoes are now seen as fashion statements, they really function to protect our feet from injuries that would impair our walking or even prohibit us from walking altogether. For the soldier, however, having the proper shoes can mean the difference between life and death, victory and defeat.

The Roman soldier wore a very distinctive shoe in battle. It was a strong sandal-type shoe and had a sole studded with nails, which pierced the ground and provided tremendous stability. To add to this illustration, Paul uses the word that the King James Version translates *preparation,* but would best be translated *established* or *a firm foundation.* As the shoe provided a firm foundation for the Roman soldier, we are established and have a firm foundation in the gospel of peace.

Next, we need to distinguish the phrase "gospel of peace" from the phrase "the Gospel." Paul is not talking specifically about spreading the Gospel, but rather he is pointing out one of the benefits of the Gospel: the peace of God. The Gospel settles, strengthens, and stabilizes believers.

Then we have the word *shod,* which is one of those antiquated words simply meaning to cover our feet. However, the word used in the context of this verse has a greater meaning, "to put under or bind under." The thought is that our feet should never touch the ground in their bare form. We should walk on the protective, peaceful cushion of the Gospel. Ephesians 6:15 is saying that *the firm foundation of the Gospel is that we walk in peace.*

- We have peace with God through our Lord Jesus Christ. (See Romans 5:1.)
- We have peace between Jew and Gentile (see Ephesians 2:14) as well as among races, social and economic classes, and genders. (See Galatians 3:28.)
- We have peace in believing, which causes us to abound in hope. (See Romans 15:13.)
- We have peace in the Holy Spirit. (See Galatians 5:22.)
- We are unified as a body through the bond of peace. (See Ephesians 4:3.)
- We have peace from God at all times. (See 2 Thessalonians 3:16.)

The Bible also says that we are not to go anywhere or do anything, think any thought or make any statement that does not maintain the peace of God in our lives. Only the peace of God will keep us standing firm when the violent attacks of the Enemy come against us.

For ye shall go out with joy, and be led forth with peace.
        **—Isaiah 55:12**

And let the peace of God rule in your hearts.
        **—Colossians 3:15**

And make straight paths for your feet. . . . Follow peace with all men.
        **—Hebrews 12:13–14**

And the peace of God, which passeth all understanding, shall keep your hearts and minds through Christ Jesus.
        **—Philippians 4:7**

Not only do feet support the entire body, but they take us wherever we go. Thus the feet represent our will. When our feet are shod with the gospel of peace, we will go only where God gives us peace to go. We will not obey any other voice but His because only His voice gives us peace. The peace of God brings balance to our lives, keeps our priorities in godly order, and shows us His perfect will. *God's peace is our compass in life.*

When the Devil does his utmost to get us to walk down this wrong path to lead us astray, the peace of God will keep us on the right road. The Enemy will introduce false teachings and false doctrines to capture our minds. He will present alluring and seductive temptations, trying to get us to take idols into our hearts. But when we wear our gospel shoes of peace, we will believe only God's Word, walk only where the Holy Spirit gives us peace to walk, and worship only Jesus! Any lack of peace will alert us that we are off the path and headed for the Devil's quicksand, and God's peace will lead us back to the safety of His will.

Spiritually, then, having our feet fitted with or bound with the gospel of peace keeps our will firmly established in God's will and our walk with Jesus unhindered. Our hearts and minds are led by peace and we have no need to fear the Enemy. Therefore, we should put on the firm foundation of the gospel of peace at all times.

Stay in alignment with God's commandments to you. Walk out the prophecy He has spoken over your life. Direct your path toward those things that the Holy Spirit says belong to you.

We read in Habakkuk, "Write the vision, and make it plain upon tables, that he may run that readeth it" (Habakkuk 2:2). I love to teach, "Write it, read it, and run it." Whatever God has told you He will do in your life, write it down. Refer to it often, and live as if you are already receiving it. Don't go into places or situations where the name of Jesus isn't lifted up. Don't get your feet tangled up in relationships that conflict with God's will for your life. Don't get bogged down in projects and ideas that fail to bring glory to God. Go only where the Gospel is welcome and the peace of the Lord prevails.

You begin to put on the armor of God by first baring your soul to Him in complete honesty and truth, making certain that your mind and heart are totally in line with His Word. When this belt of truth is firmly in place around the most private areas of your life, then you can attach the breastplate of righteousness, which declares that you stand absolutely and eternally right before God through the blood of Jesus Christ. Next, you put on your gospel shoes of God's peace and line up your will and your way with God's will.

At this point you have purified your heart, embraced the reality of who you are in Christ, and faced the right direction. You are ready to put on the rest of God's armor.

# 6

# THE ARMOR OF GOD
# PART TWO:
# FAITH, SALVATION,
# AND GOD'S WORD

## THE SHIELD OF FAITH

**Above all, taking the shield of faith, wherewith ye shall be able to quench all the fiery darts of the wicked.**
**—Ephesians 6:16**

We must first address the phrase "Above all" because it adds a lot of depth to our understanding of faith as spiritual armor. The Greek language could be translated, "In addition to," in which case Paul would be saying, "Not only do you need the belt of truth, the breastplate of righteousness, and the gospel shoes of peace, but you also need the shield of faith." But this phrase could also be translated, "Over all," in which case Paul is saying, "Covering and protecting all the pieces of God's armor is the shield of faith." Either way you look at it, Paul is emphasizing the importance of faith in spiritual warfare.

The writer of Hebrews says it is impossible to please God without faith.

**But without faith it is impossible to please him: for he that cometh to God must believe that he is, and that he is a rewarder of them that diligently seek him.**
**—Hebrews 11:6**

Furthermore, if we ever doubt the vital significance of faith, all we need to do is research how often Jesus talked about it. He commended people for their faith and even marveled at the centurion's faith: "When Jesus heard it, he marvelled, and said to them that followed, Verily I say unto you, I have not found so great faith, no, not in Israel" (Matthew 8:10).

Jesus also marveled at unbelief, however. He appeared disappointed and even exasperated when people had no faith, such as when His disciples had no faith during a storm: "And he arose, and rebuked the wind, and said unto the sea, Peace, be still. And the wind ceased, and there was a great calm. And he said unto them, Why are ye so fearful? how is it that ye have no faith?" (Mark 4:39–40).

Jesus told many who were healed that they were healed because of their faith: "And he said unto her, Daughter, be of good comfort: thy faith hath made thee whole; go in peace" (Luke 8:48).

The Bible even says that Jesus himself could not do many miracles in His hometown because the people lacked faith: "And he did not many mighty works there because of their unbelief" (Matthew 13:58).

The shield of faith, therefore, is a part of God's armor that we need to study well! The Greek word translated *shield* tells us a lot because there were two kinds of shields in Paul's time. This word refers to the Roman soldier's larger shield, which was the size of a door. It was not only large but well constructed, and it fully protected the warrior in battle. This shield was the first piece of armor that came in contact with the Enemy, so it had to be strong and formidable.

*When the Enemy attacks, our faith will meet him and defeat him!*

In Paul's day, soldiers often dipped their arrows into combustible fluids and lit them so that their arrows would burn whatever they hit. No doubt these "fire arrows" were what Paul was referring to when he mentioned the "fiery darts of the wicked." When soldiers saw that the enemy was using fiery darts, they immediately prepared their shields, which were made of an iron frame covered with layers of leather. They would soak their shields in water so that when a fiery dart hit, it would fizzle out in a puff of smoke.

With what are we to soak our shields? Throughout Scripture, water is a symbol for the Word of God: "That he might sanctify and cleanse it with the washing of water by the word" (Ephesians 5:26).

Paul says that our faith grows, matures, and gains strength by reading, studying, meditating upon, and living by the Word of God:

"So then faith cometh by hearing, and hearing by the word of God" (Romans 10:17).

To win the victory in spiritual warfare, you must soak your mind with the Word of God. Your faith in God's Word and *knowing* God's Word, that unshakable confidence and trust in the reliability of what God says, will quench every fiery dart of the Enemy. The more you read the Word of God, the more you will think the Word, feel the Word, and respond with the Word. The more your faith grows, the more your life will reflect the Word, be grounded in the Word, and be in complete alignment with the Word.

Whatever the Enemy shoots your way isn't going to sting if you know the Word, because your faith and trust will be entirely in Jesus, the Living Word. You will have no fear of what the Devil and his demons will do to you because you will be walking hand-in-hand and arm-in-arm with the King of Kings and Lord of Lords.

The fiery dart will hit your shield with "Your children are never going to serve God!" Your shield will quench it with "Isaiah 54:13 says that my children are taught of the Lord and great is their peace in Him."

The fiery dart will hit your shield with "You're going crazy! The stress of all your problems is too much for you. You'll never make it!" Your shield will quench it with "Philippians 4:13 says that I can do all things through Christ who strengthens me!"

The fiery dart will hit your shield with "Flu season is coming! Get ready to be sick!" Your shield will quench it with "2 Peter 2:24 and Isaiah 53:5 declare that by the stripes of Jesus Christ, I am healed!"

The fiery dart will hit your shield with "Look around you. This world is out of control with earthquakes, hurricanes, tornadoes, and volcanic eruptions! Planes are crashing and trains are derailing and gangs are shooting people in the streets!" Your shield will quench it with "Read Psalm 91, Devil! Read 2 Timothy 1:7! I dwell in the secret place of the Most High and fear nothing because I have the love of God, the power of the Holy Spirit, and the mind of Christ!"

Paul did not say that knowing the Word would keep the Devil from shooting fiery darts at you! What he said was that *when* the Devil shoots his arrows, the Word of God that is in you will protect you. The fiery darts won't break your heart or penetrate your soul. They won't cause a firestorm of worry, frustration, depression, or anxiety in your life.

**No weapon that is formed against thee shall prosper; and every tongue that shall rise against thee in judgment thou shalt condemn. This is the heritage of the servants of the Lord, and their righteousness is of me, saith the Lord.**
**—Isaiah 54:17**

Rumors, innuendoes, and false reports may be fired against you, but they won't hurt your heart if you have your faith saturated with God's Word. The Devil may come at you with all kinds of threats, accusations, and lies, but they won't lodge in your spirit and burn there if you have your faith saturated with God's Word. Satan may tempt you with worldly riches and honor and power, but the Word of God in you will give you the strength to resist and the Devil will flee!

The shield of faith meets the attack of the Enemy with God's Word, and our unswerving trust in our God makes it impossible for the Devil to prevail.

## THE HELMET OF SALVATION

Some parts of the Roman soldier's armor were elaborate and expensive because they were designed to make a statement of indomitable strength and authority. Other than the large shield, the helmet made the biggest impression. It covered the head entirely, including cheek pieces, and it was made of bronze, with ornate carvings and etchings. To help the soldier bear the weight of the helmet, it was lined with a soft, spongy material.

The helmet was extremely heavy, and only the sharpest ax or heaviest hammer could pierce it. Without this kind of protection, the soldier would quickly lose his head! But the helmet also had the most flamboyant feature in the entire armor of God: a tall plume on the top made of feathers or horsehair. This plume was extremely striking and made the soldier look as much as two feet taller than he actually was.

By calling this piece of spiritual armor "the helmet of salvation," Paul could not have made a more powerful statement about our redemption. When we truly understand and appreciate that we are eternally, perfectly, and absolutely saved, that we are forgiven and cleansed through the blood of Jesus Christ, and that we are completely reconciled to God, we stand ten feet tall!

When we know we are God's child and walk in His presence, people notice our confidence and strength. They sense a courage and strength about us. Furthermore, when everyone around us are losing their heads because of the stresses and strains of life, we keep ours because of the joy of our salvation!

Because the helmet of salvation covers the head, Paul is saying that our minds must be stayed at all times upon the most basic of all spiritual truths: We are saved! We must keep this reality at the forefront of our thinking always. So many Christians today spend the bulk of their praise time rejoicing over the fact that the Lord has given them power and authority. They are thanking God for this gift, that healing, and another person's deliverance. This is good, but Jesus told us specifically that there was only one reason to praise God and rejoice: "Notwithstanding in this rejoice not, that the spirits are subject unto you; but rather rejoice, because your names are written in heaven" (Luke 10:20).

The disciples had just returned from casting out demons and healing the sick all over the countryside, and they were rejoicing at their newfound authority. Jesus pulled them back to center by reminding them that none of this was possible without salvation. *None of the blessings of this life compare to the eternal life we have in Christ Jesus.*

Rejoice that you are saved! You have eternal life! Your sins have been cast as far from you as the east is from the west and the slate of your soul has been wiped clean! You have no reason for guilt, no reason for shame, and you can remind the Devil of that fact whenever he tries to bring up the past. No matter what he says to you, say right back, "Satan, I'm saved and you cannot touch me, deceive me, or defeat me. Jesus Christ died on the cross for me. He shed His blood for me, and when I gave my life to Him my sins were forgiven and I became heaven-bound. Nothing can ever change the fact that I am a child of God. I'm saved and I'm going to live forever with Him."

If things look bad today, remember you are saved!

If things are not turning out as you had thought they would, you are saved!

If you don't yet have all the things you have been promised by God, you are saved!

No matter what others may think about you, say about you, or do to you, you are saved!

Your salvation is the greatest blessing you can ever know and the greatest gift you can ever receive.

Putting on the helmet of salvation means dwelling on your salvation. Meditate on it. Remind yourself of it. The Devil cannot upset or distract a mind that is focused on the blessed salvation of Jesus Christ, and the reality of knowing your salvation will make you stand ten feet tall in the Spirit!

## THE SWORD OF THE SPIRIT

Our belt of truth, our breastplate of righteousness, our helmet of salvation, our gospel shoes of peace, and our shield of faith are all defensive armor. But now we must put on the one piece of offensive armor we are given: "the sword of the Spirit, which is the word of God."

When we hear the word *sword,* we immediately imagine pirates, Robin Hood, and Zorro wielding long swords that have fancy handles. But the Greek word Paul chose for *sword* in this verse refers to a dagger. He chose a large knifelike weapon over the heavy broadsword (the one Robin Hood used) and the lighter foil-like version (the one Zorro used). By using this word, Paul indicates that we fight spiritual battles at close range.

**For the word of God is quick, and powerful, and sharper than any two-edged sword, piercing even to the dividing asunder of soul and spirit, and of the joints and marrow, and is a discerner of the thoughts and intents of the heart.**
**—Hebrews 4:12**

This verse in Hebrews provides even more information about the type of sword used. The word *quick* here is the Greek word for *life.* The Word of God is alive, powerful, and sharp. It has pinpoint accuracy to determine exactly what is going on in our lives. When we enter into spiritual warfare, we come nose to nose with the Devil and every wickedness of this world's system. So it is imperative that we have a weapon that is capable of rendering the Enemy powerless. Because Jesus is our Captain, let's see how He dealt with Satan.

Then was Jesus led up of the Spirit into the wilderness to be tempted of the devil. And when he had fasted forty days and forty nights, he was afterward an hungred. And when the tempter came to him, he said, If thou be the Son of God, command that these stones be made bread. But he answered and said, It is written, Man shall not live by bread alone, but by every word that proceedeth out of the mouth of God.

Then the devil taketh him up into the holy city, and setteth him on a pinnacle of the temple, and saith unto him, If thou be the Son of God, cast thyself down: for it is written, He shall give his angels charge concerning thee: and in their hands they shall bear thee up, lest at any time thou dash thy foot against a stone. Jesus said unto him, It is written again, Thou shalt not tempt the Lord thy God.

Again, the devil taketh him up into an exceeding high mountain, and sheweth him all the kingdoms of the world, and the glory of them; and saith unto him, All these things will I give thee, if thou wilt fall down and worship me. Then saith Jesus unto him, Get thee hence, Satan: for it is written, Thou shalt worship the Lord thy God, and him only shalt thou serve. Then the devil leaveth him, and, behold, angels came and ministered unto him.

**—Matthew 4:1–11**

Three times the Devil came to Jesus with powerful temptations, and three times the only weapon Jesus used to fight him was the Word of God. Again and again, He said, "It is written," and Satan finally had to give up and leave Him alone.

To wield the Word of God in battle, however, we have to *know* the Word of God. We cannot merely memorize it and give it mental assent. We have to have it hidden deep in our hearts. The only way for that to happen is to read it, study it, hear it—and keep reading, studying, and hearing it until we *know* it—for example, until we know that we are the righteousness of God through Christ Jesus as well as we know our name.

The Word of God must be "quick" or alive in your mind and heart, and then it will be "powerful" when you speak it in a time of crisis or battle. God's Word should be your automatic response to every challenge of life.

If the situation incites praise and thanksgiving, then a word of thanksgiving and praise should come alive in your mind and heart and then flow in power from your lips.

If the situation demands confrontation in the spirit, then a word of rebuke or deliverance should come alive in your mind and heart and then flow in power from your lips.

If the situation is rooted in falsehood or guilt or shame or lies, then a word of truth should come alive in your mind and heart and then flow in power from your lips.

If you really want to do damage to the Enemy in the spirit realm, declare the Word of God to him from your heart! He may hang around for a while to see if you really mean it, if the Word really is alive in you; but if it is, eventually this dead, corrupt evil spirit won't be able to endure being continually stabbed and cut with the very life of God, and he will flee!

Now you are completely fitted in God's magnificent armor. You have washed yourself in truth, identified with Christ in righteousness, established your will in God's peace, placed your faith and trust only in Him, raised your spiritual stature by focusing on your awesome salvation, and gripped the Word of God in your heart and mind. The time has come for you to take the Promised Land!

# 7

# THE BATTLEGROUND
# OF THE BELIEVER

A s we put on the whole armor of God and after we are fully prepared and equipped for battle, the apostle Paul says, "Pray!"

**Praying always with all prayer and supplication in the Spirit . . .**
**—Ephesians 6:18**

Prayer is the battleground of the believer.

A powerless, gutless, ineffective church is a prayerless church.

When the church doesn't pray, we are not even on the battleground. We take nothing back from the Enemy, we have no effect for the kingdom of God, and most likely we are being trampled by sin and the oppression of wicked spirits. When the church doesn't pray, we are giving the Enemy an open door to steal, kill, and destroy us. On the other hand, if we pray, we become Jesus' warrior bride!

What do you think Joshua and the children of Israel were doing when they marched seven times around the great wall of Jericho? They weren't talking politics. They weren't reminiscing about the past. They weren't discussing the latest blockbuster movie. They weren't even conferring about church doctrine. No! I believe they were praying, silently communing with the God of their fathers.

*The great wall of Jericho fell down flat by the power of God that was released through the prayer and obedience of Joshua and the children of Israel.*

The Lord commands us to pray and then obey so that He can

do great exploits! We spent the first few chapters of this book discussing the absolute necessity for obedience when it comes to waging a successful war. But now the apostle Paul reveals the other side to this coin: *We have nothing to obey if we do not pray!*

God commands us to pray and authorizes us to pray, and He says that He cannot act in many situations unless we pray. Yet believers will do anything to avoid praying. We would rather jump up and down in wild praises to the Lord than stay in our prayer closet and pray. In fact, I believe the church must accomplish in prayer what we have accomplished in praise and worship. We have praise singers and praise dancers and praise banners and praise trumpets. We have all kinds of praise, everything from country to classical in style. We know all the Hebrew words for praise. There has been tremendous teaching on praise and worship. But how many of us are prayer warriors?

How many of us spend time on our faces before God and petition Him daily?

How many of us consider the highlight of our existence to be those times spent in powerful prayer, basking in the warmth of God's presence and receiving revelation?

How many of us travail before the Lord in the Spirit until deliverance breaks forth and people are set free from the grip of the Enemy?

How many of us refuse to take the Devil's bondage and persist in prayer until the Devil desists?

*It was because Joshua tarried in the tabernacle that he took the Promised Land!*

## ALWAYS MEANS *ALWAYS!*

The Greek word for *praying* indicates that this is not only bringing our requests and petitions but it also means worship. We are not only to speak but we are also to listen. And the word *always* tells us not only to have an attitude of prayer at all times, but to take every opportunity to pray—for ourselves, for our loved ones, and for anyone else who crosses our path.

Johnny comes in crying because he skinned his knee. Let's pray!

The rent is due tomorrow and the money is not in the bank. Let's pray!

A crisis happens at work and important decisions need to be made. Let's pray!

The next-door neighbor's child has run away from home. Let's pray!

Paul repeats the command to pray in 1 Thessalonians 5:17: "Pray without ceasing." Prayer is something the Lord expects us to engage in constantly, which means prayer must be something we *can* do at all times and in all situations. This is possible because there are different types of prayer, even silent prayer, which is communing in our hearts with God. If we are in a place where we cannot speak, we can still commune in our hearts with God. When we stay in an attitude of prayer, nothing can separate us from Him and we can remain in communication with Him always.

Prayer is vital to spiritual warfare because we must commune with God to put on His armor. We must communicate with Him to receive His battle plan, and sometimes He tells us of battles to come. Then we can allow Him to prepare us. As a result of maintaining an attitude of prayer, whenever and however the Enemy strikes, we are suited up for warfare and ready to fight and win. Although we do not live in a constant state of warfare, we do live in a constant attitude of prayer because the Enemy is roaming the earth, seeking whom he may devour: "Be sober, be vigilant; because your adversary the devil, as a roaring lion, walketh about, seeking whom he may devour" (1 Peter 5:8).

I cannot emphasize this enough: Prayer connects us to God, and God knows the strategies and battle plans that will defeat the Enemy. David said of the Lord, "He teacheth my hands to war" (Psalm 18:34). In other words, "The Lord has taught me how to fight the battles I face. He gives me the victory." We must rely fully on the Lord as David relied upon Him:

It is God that girdeth me with strength, and maketh my way perfect. He maketh my feet like hinds' feet, and setteth me upon my high places. He teacheth my hands to war, so that a bow of steel is broken by mine arms. Thou hast also given me the shield of thy salvation: and thy right hand hath holden me up, and thy gentleness hath made me great. Thou hast enlarged my steps under me, that my feet did not slip. I have pursued mine enemies, and overtaken them: neither did I turn again till they were consumed. I have wounded them that they were not able to rise:

they are fallen under my feet. For thou hast girded me with strength unto the battle: thou hast subdued under me those that rose up against me. Thou hast also given me the necks of mine enemies; that I might destroy them that hate me.
**—Psalm 18:32–40**

David was a man after God's own heart and one of the most unusual believers of the Old Testament. He was a man of war who recognized that the only way to defeat the Enemy in the natural was to defeat the Enemy in the spirit realm first. He knew that prayer was the real battleground for all the issues of life. Throughout his lifetime, whether he was a shepherd, a hero, a fugitive, or a king, David trusted the Lord for his safety and his provision from day to day, week to week, month to month, and year to year—communing continually with the Lord in prayer.

## ALL PRAYER AND SUPPLICATION

Praying always with all prayer and supplication in the Spirit, and watching thereunto with all perseverance and supplication for all saints; and for me, that utterance may be given unto me, that I may open my mouth boldly, to make known the mystery of the gospel, for which I am an ambassador in bonds: that therein I may speak boldly, as I ought to speak.
**—Ephesians 6:18–20**

Paul initially calls upon the Ephesians to pray for him that he will be even more bold in making known the mystery of the Gospel. Paul, perhaps the boldest preacher in the history of the church, asks for prayer that he can be even more bold! This statement always puts me to shame! Am I praying such a prayer today? Am I asking that believers everywhere, especially myself, might be even more bold in declaring the Gospel to an unbelieving world?

It's time to pray until we tear down the strongholds of the Enemy that are being built against our personal lives, our families, our churches, and the body of Christ in this generation—so we can preach the Gospel boldly. It's time we pray until those who are being persecuted for the Gospel's sake around the world are set free to continue preaching boldly. It's time we pray for missionaries who are getting souls saved in those remote, easy-to-forget areas of the world, that they may be even more bold.

Paul also exhorts us to pray "with all prayer and supplication for all saints." He says, "Be specific and be thorough. Cover all the bases. Don't leave any stone unturned. Pray about every area of your life and everything that concerns you. Pray about your level of commitment and purity of heart toward the Lord. Pray about your family, your church, your job, and your ministry. Pray about everything the Holy Spirit brings to mind. Oh, and pray for *all the saints* in this way too."

When Paul addresses the Ephesians, he illustrates how thorough we are to be in prayer with his own situation. He doesn't ask the Ephesians to pray for him in only one area. He also makes provision for them to know all his needs so that they might pray more effectively and specifically for his entire life. He writes,

**But that ye also may know my affairs, and how I do, Tychicus, a beloved brother and faithful minister in the Lord, shall make known to you all things: Whom I have sent unto you for the same purpose, that ye might know our affairs, and that he might comfort your hearts.**
**—Ephesians 6:21–22**

When we pray for one another, we are to pray with the most accurate information we can obtain. When was the last time you prayed about something until you knew in your heart and mind that you had prayed about every facet of that problem or situation? So often we pray, "Oh, Lord, you know the need. Please meet the need." But the Bible says that we are to pray with wisdom and understanding. We are to pray about everything we know to pray. We are to pray about a problem inside and out, upside and down, through and through.

Pray thoroughly. Pray all the way through a problem. Pray every aspect and every detail and every consequence of a situation. And pray for the entire body of Christ to prosper in all areas of life. This sounds like a lot to do! However, Paul also gives us the key to doing it.

## WATCHING, PERSEVERING PRAYER

We are to pray "watching thereunto with all perseverance." The Greek word translated *watching* means to be sleepless, to be always awake and alert. And *perseverance* is the word that means to give constant care and attention. Not only are we to pray for ourselves, for all the saints, and for all the ministers of the Gospel, but we are to be alert at all times, day or night, and be ready to pray for anyone who needs it. The message Paul is trying to impart here is a message of compassion and care among the saints. We are to love and care for one another at all times and in all situations. What concerns you concerns me. My problem is your problem. And our neighbor's crisis is our crisis.

This is an impossible standard to achieve until we add the phrase "in the Spirit." Watching, persevering prayer is praying in the Spirit. There is no way we can come into oneness and unity apart from the Holy Spirit. And apart from the Holy Spirit, our prayers are lifeless and powerless, and so are we! To continue to pray fervently and passionately until we get the victory we must allow the Holy Spirit to be our inspiration, strength, and guide.

Paul wrote to the Romans that there will be times when we have no idea what to pray, but the Holy Spirit will take care of the matter:

**Likewise the Spirit also helpeth our infirmities: for we know not what we should pray for as we ought: but the Spirit itself maketh intercession for us with groanings which cannot be uttered. And he that searcheth the hearts knoweth what is the mind of the Spirit, because he maketh intercession for the saints according to the will of God.**
**—Romans 8:26–27**

At times we may feel vulnerable, confused, and inept as we face certain situations in our lives. We may even look vulnerable to others. But if we will pray in the Holy Ghost and be filled with the Holy Ghost, we will not stay vulnerable! The more we pray in the Spirit, the stronger we experience the anointing, or the tangible presence and life-changing power of the Spirit. It is the anointing that breaks every yoke of bondage and sets us and others free. It is the Holy Spirit who empowers our prayers and brings them to the effective, devil-crushing level of fervency, and we know from James 5:16 that the "effectual fervent prayer" is the prayer that availeth much!

## TOGETHER WE STAND

Notice that Paul does not say, "Now all you *intercessors,* pray," nor did Jesus tell Joshua, "Now just take the ones who can pray to march around the wall." No! The whole nation of Israel marched around Jericho—men, women, and children. God commands *all* believers to pray! I believe the call of God to the church today is a call to prayer, both to the individual believer and to the corporate body.

It's a known fact that war is one of life's great equalizers. We often see the dismissal of prejudice and bigotry in the middle of a war. No soldier in a foxhole cares what color a fellow soldier's skin is—he only cares whether that soldier is on his side. Blacks who have never cared for whites and whites who have never cared for blacks have left foxholes as friends. A prejudiced person might say after the war is over, "Oh, I can't stand people of that color or that race," but then he usually adds, "But Fred isn't like the rest of them. Fred is a good brother." And the reason Fred isn't like "the rest of them" is solely because Fred was on his side in the foxhole!

In chapter 2 of Ephesians, we saw how God brought Jew and Gentile together in Christ Jesus. In Christ, believers of all shapes, colors, sizes, ethnic groups, and cultures have a common enemy, and it's God's desire that we come together. Moreover, it is a necessity that we come together in order to win the war against Satan and his demonic forces of evil.

When Paul wrote to the Ephesians, the large shields used by the Roman soldiers at that time could be locked together in such a way that an entire row of soldiers could move forward as a single unit, fully protected. It probably looked like a moving wall. The protection over each soldier multiplied because of this union, but so did their power and ability to move forward and conquer.

What an awesome picture of corporate prayer in the church! We do not stand alone. We do not fight alone. We are to fight as a united front taking on the Enemy and standing strong against him both for each one of us individually and for the body as a whole. As we join our faith with one another in prayer, the power of God to save, heal, deliver, and set free is multiplied hundreds of thousands—even millions—of times over!

We need to be unified and organized as a fighting force because the Enemy is unified and organized. When Jesus encountered a demon-possessed man in the country of the Gadarenes, He asked him, "What is your name?" And the man replied, "Legion." (See Luke 8:26–36.) *Legion* not only refers to the fact that there were many demons in this man, but it is a military term that also means those demons were an organized stronghold in him. Those demons were fulfilling their assignment and working with the other demons to hold this man in bondage.

The Bible tells us that one believer may send a few demons to flight, but two in prayerful agreement send many demons to flight. As we read in Leviticus 26:8, "Five of you shall chase an hundred, and an hundred of you shall put ten thousand to flight." Being locked together in prayer, praying in faith as a body, releases the multiplied power of God against the Enemy.

There are times when we are alone in the lions' den and God delivers us. Then there are times when we are with our buddies in the fiery furnace and our collective faith brings us through. In most situations, however, we need one another because God planned it that way. We need Him and we need one another to succeed. We are not a loose group of lone rangers, each one doing his own thing. We are the family of God.

The family that prays together stays together. And the family that stays together conquers the land!

# 8

# THE POINT OF IT ALL

Obey your parents in the Lord.
    Do not provoke your children to wrath.
Servants, obey your masters.
Masters, treat your servants with respect and kindness.
Do all things as unto the Lord and look to Him for your reward.
Be strong in the Lord and in the power of His might.
Know your enemy: Hate the Devil and love the people.
Put on truth: Get honest with God and purify your life.
Put on righteousness: Know who you are in Christ.
Put on peace: Line your will up with God's will.
Put on faith: Trust God in all things at all times.
Put on salvation: Rejoice in your redemption and rise to the stature of Jesus Christ.
Put on the Word of God: Believe and speak only the living, life-transforming Word of God.
Have an attitude of prayer at all times for all the saints.
Pray individually and corporately until God's will is accomplished.

After the war has been won, then what? Here are Paul's closing words to the Ephesians:

**Peace be to the brethren, and love with faith, from God the Father and the Lord Jesus Christ. Grace be with all them that love our Lord Jesus Christ in sincerity. Amen.**
**—Ephesians 6:23–24**

There is the peace that leads us through the battle, but then there is another *peace* afterward. When victorious, conquering peace fills our hearts, stays our minds, and encompasses our being, we know the battle has been won. This is not a fleeting peace, but an abiding peace, a peace that is beyond rational explanation. It's real and it's pervasive. It floods our being and spills out onto everyone we touch.

There is the love that binds us together as a warrior bride in the heat of battle, but there is another *love* afterward. Love bursts forth from our innermost being upon defeating the Enemy of our souls. We grin at one another, our eyes shining with the unspoken understanding that we fought as one, laid down our lives for our Lord and one another, and now live to shout the victory together.

There is the faith that moves us on when we can go no further, but there is another *faith* afterward. A deep, abiding faith comes from having witnessed the massive wall of Jericho tumble to the ground. Turning from the scene of our incredible, unimaginable miracle, we gaze into the eyes of our Captain, tears running down our faces. Before the wall fell, we chose not to doubt Him. After the wall falls, we wonder why we doubted in the first place.

This victory, this peace, this love, and this faith have come "from God the Father and the Lord Jesus Christ." After the battle is won, our hearts overflow with love and worship. Peter said in his second letter that grace and peace are multiplied through the knowledge of God, or to the degree to which we become intimate with Him. (See 2 Peter 1:2.) After all is said and done, when the war is won and the Enemy has been buried, we finally have the *grace* to "love our Lord Jesus Christ in sincerity."

*Sincerity* means without corruption. We are holy as He is holy and we love Him wholly. We love Him with our whole heart, soul, mind, and strength. And we realize that was His point all along as He brought us through all the facets of our life in Him.

We marvel at His wealth.

We are His workmanship.

We worship Him.

We walk in Him.

We are wed to Him.

We do warfare with Him.

And in the end, we are His people and He is our God!

# REFERENCES

*Adam Clarke Commentary*, 6 Vols. Adam Clarke. *PC Study Bible,* Version 2.1J. CD-ROM. Seattle, WA: Biblesoft, 1993–1998.

*Barnes' Notes on the OT and NT*, 14 Vols. Albert Barnes. *PC Study Bible,* Version 2.1J. CD-ROM. Seattle, WA: Biblesoft, 1993–1998.

*The Bible Knowledge Commentary: An Exposition of the Scriptures.* Dallas Seminary faculty. Editors, John F. Walvoord, Roy B. Zuck. Wheaton, IL: Victor Books. 1983–1985. Published in electronic form by Logos Research Systems Inc., 1996.

*Brown, Driver, and Briggs' Definitions.* Francis Brown, D.D., D. Litt., S.R. Driver, D.D., D. Litt., and Charles A. Briggs, D.D., D. Litt. *PC Study Bible,* Version 2.1J. CD-ROM. Seattle, WA: Biblesoft, 1993–1998.

*Dressed to Kill.* Rick Renner. Tulsa, OK: Albury Publishing, 1989.

*Expositor's Bible Commentary, New Testament.* Frank E. Gaebelein, General Editor. J.D. Douglas, associate editor. Grand Rapids, MI: Zondervan Publishing House, 1976–1992.

*A Greek-English Lexicon of the New Testament and Other Early Christian Literature.* Walter Bauer. Second edition, revised and augmented by F.W. Gingrich, Fredrick Danker from Walter Bauer's fifth edition. Chicago and London: The University of Chicago Press, 1958.

*The Greek New Testament.* Editor Kurt Aland, et al. CD-ROM of the 3rd edition, corrected. Federal Republic of Germany: United Bible Societies, 1983. Published in electronic form by Logos Research Systems, Inc. 1996.

*Greek (UBS) Text and Hebrew (BHS) Text. PC Study Bible,* Version 2.1J. CD-ROM. Seattle, WA: Biblesoft, 1993–1998.

*The Hebrew-Greek Key Study Bible.* Compiled and edited by Spiros Zodhiates, Th.D. World Bible Publishers, Inc., 1984, 1991.

*Interlinear Bible. PC Study Bible,* Version 2.1J. CD-ROM. Seattle, WA: Biblesoft, 1993–1998.

*Jamieson, Fausset, and Brown Commentary,* 6 Vols. Robert Jamieson, A.R. Fausset, and David Brown. *PC Study Bible,* Version 2.1J. CD-ROM. Seattle, WA: Biblesoft, 1993–1998.

*A Manual Grammar of the Greek New Testament.* H.E. Dana, Th.D., and Julius R. Mantey. Toronto, Canada: MacMillan Publishing Company, 1927.

*Matthew Henry's Commentary,* 6 Vols. Matthew Henry. *PC Study Bible,* Version 2.1J. CD-ROM. Seattle, WA: Biblesoft, 1993–1998.

*The New Linguistic and Exegetical Key to the Greek New Testament.* Fritz Reineker, revised version by Cleon Rogers and Cleon Rogers III. Grand Rapids, MI: Zondervan Publishing Company, 1998.

*Strong's Exhaustive Concordance of the Bible.* J.B. Strong. *PC Study Bible,* Version 2.1J. CD-ROM. Seattle, WA: Biblesoft, 1993–1998.

*Vincent's Word Studies in the NT,* 4 Vols. Marvin R. Vincent, D.D. *PC Study Bible,* Version 2.1J. CD-ROM. Seattle, WA: Biblesoft, 1993–1998.

*Wuest's Word Studies From the Greek New Testament for the English Reader.* Volume One, Ephesians. Kenneth S. Wuest. Grand Rapids, MI: Wm. B. Eerdmans Publishing Company, 1953.

# Books by T.D. Jakes

*Lay Aside the Weight* (with workbook & journal)
*Loose That Man & Let Him Go!*
*Loose That Man & Let Him Go!* (with workbook)
*So You Call Yourself a Man?*
*T.D. Jakes Speaks to Men!*
*T.D. Jakes Speaks to Women!*
*Woman, Thou Art Loosed!*

SIX PILLARS FOR THE BELIEVER
*Celebrating Marriage*
*Experiencing Jesus*
*Intimacy With God*
*Life Overflowing*
*Loved by God*
*Overcoming the Enemy*

## Devotionals

*Loose That Man & Let Him Go! Devotional*
*Woman, Thou Art Loosed! Devotional*

## To contact T.D. Jakes, write:

T.D. Jakes Ministries
P.O. Box 5390
Dallas, Texas 75208
*www.tdjakes.org*

T.D. JAKES, founder and senior pastor of The Potter's House Church in Dallas, Texas, is a celebrated speaker and author with many bestselling books to his credit. His weekly television broadcast is viewed in millions of homes nationwide. Featured on the cover of *Time* magazine, he is known around the world for his message of freedom to be found in Christ.